THE
2012
STORY

THE
2012
STORY

The Myths, Fallacies, and Truth
Behind the Most Intriguing
Date in History

John Major Jenkins

Jeremy P. Tarcher/Penguin
a member of Penguin Group (USA) Inc.
New York

JEREMY P. TARCHER / PENGUIN
Published by the Penguin Group
Penguin Group (USA) Inc., 375 Hudson Street, New York, New York 10014, USA ·
Penguin Group (Canada), 90 Eglinton Avenue East, Suite 700, Toronto, Ontario M4P 2Y3,
Canada (a division of Pearson Penguin Canada Inc.) · Penguin Books Ltd, 80 Strand, London WC2R 0RL,
England · Penguin Ireland, 25 St Stephen's Green, Dublin 2, Ireland (a division of Penguin Books Ltd) ·
Penguin Group (Australia), 250 Camberwell Road, Camberwell, Victoria 3124, Australia (a division of
Pearson Australia Group Pty Ltd) · Penguin Books India Pvt Ltd, 11 Community Centre, Panchsheel Park,
New Delhi–110 017, India · Penguin Group (NZ), 67 Apollo Drive, Rosedale, North Shore 0632,
New Zealand (a division of Pearson New Zealand Ltd) · Penguin Books (South Africa) (Pty) Ltd,
24 Sturdee Avenue, Rosebank, Johannesburg 2196, South Africa

Penguin Books Ltd, Registered Offices: 80 Strand, London WC2R 0RL, England

First trade paperback edition 2010

Photo of Joseph T. Goodman used with permission from Special Collections, University of Nevada-Reno Library; quotes
from Maya leaders in Chapter 11 courtesy of Robert Sitler; "Sheba's Throne" by Rumi, translated by Coleman Barks, is
reprinted courtesy of Maypop Books, Athens GA, 1995; figure 6, originally published as "Geographical distribution of early
script traditions, overlying distribution of ca. 1600 BC pottery traditions, Locona (stippled area) and red-on-buff to the west
(after Clark 1991: fig. 8; Flannery and Marcus 2000: fig. 3)" in *Maya Calendar Origins: Monuments, Mythistory, and the
Materialization of Time* by Prudence M. Rice, © 2007, is reprinted courtesy of University of Texas Press.

Most Tarcher/Penguin books are available at special quantity discounts for bulk purchase for sales
promotions, premiums, fund-raising, and educational needs. Special books or book excerpts also can be
created to fit specific needs. For details, write Penguin Group (USA) Inc. Special Markets,
375 Hudson Street, New York, NY 10014.

The Library of Congress catalogued the hardcover edition as follows:

Jenkins, John Major.
The 2012 story: the myths, fallacies, and truth behind the most intriguing date in history /
John Major Jenkins.
p.   cm.
Includes bibliographical references and index.
ISBN 978-1-58542-766-6
1. Maya calendar.   2. Maya astronomy.   3. Two thousand twelve, A.D.   I. Title.
F1435.3.C14J398   2009   2009031572
001.9—dc22

ISBN 978-1-58542-823-6 (paperback edition)

Printed in the United States of America
1   3   5   7   9   10   8   6   4   2

Book design by Claire Vaccaro

Frontispiece photo of Yaxchilán by the author, 2007

Into the Blue

Dreaming of clouds in Waxactun
   angels grab my eyes
Peaceful stones transcend my reason
   a shadowless noon
    in the midsummer season
    Defines this location as wise

Tropical moss enshrouds old stone
   forgotten town decays
Soul sparks, long in tireless flight
    arrive alone
    on a moonless night
    Upon the back of stellar rays

Time and fate will wait for you
   to find eternal rest
When the world dissolves away
    into the blue
    of a dimming day
    Just watch it all unmanifest[1]

—JOHN MAJOR JENKINS
Waxactun, Guatemala
August 2008

Contents

LIST OF FIGURES

2012:
An Unstoppable Idea

This was the peopling of the face of the earth:

They came into being, they multiplied, they

had daughters, they had sons, these manikins,

woodcarvings. But there was nothing in their hearts

and nothing in their minds, no memory of their

mason and builder. They just went and walked

wherever they wanted . . . they did not remember

the Heart of Sky.[1]

—*The Popol Vuh*

Writing this book was an immense undertaking that had to accommodate new developments in the ever-shifting features of a quickly evolving field. Because of its curious crescendo in our immediate future, and therefore unlike any other topic, 2012ology ("twentytwelvology") has been growing exponentially with a unique set of issues and attractions. This accelerating growth of interest in the public arena is driven primarily by urgent doomsday scenarios spun out by the mainstream media and opportunistic writers. And yet the date is not simply a newfangled gadget invented by the marketplace. It is, in fact, a true artifact of the authentic Maya calendar, which has suffered the cut-and-paste cosmologizing of wannabe wizards, pocket-protector prophets, and celebrity showmen. This heady stew is all stirred up in the Google cauldron, making a dangerous potion for the unsuspecting newcomer. As you step into this

ever-shifting discussion, it will be helpful to have some historical background and a guiding survey of who has been saying what. This is part of
what this book offers.

I've been investigating Maya culture since 1985, and I have written many
research-oriented books and articles on Maya calendars and cosmology. My
first two books were self-published travelogues peppered with historical facts
and comments on the Mesoamerican worldview. I quickly became fascinated
with various unresolved enigmas, including the 2012 cycle-ending date. My
1992 book, *Tzolkin: Visionary Perspectives and Calendar Studies*, presented my
work on the Venus calendar found in the Dresden Codex, one of the few
surviving Maya books. My 1998 book *Maya Cosmogenesis 2012* broke new
ground on identifying why 2012 was important to the ancient Maya, offering
a new reconstruction of ancient Maya thought. Key questions were posed:
When and where did the early Maya devise the calendar that gives us the cycle
ending in 2012? Why did they place this cycle ending on December 21, 2012,
and how did they think about it? These questions led me to discoveries and
conclusions that integrated the domains of astronomy, mythology, prophecy,
and spiritual teachings.

I found that a rare astronomical alignment culminates in the years leading up to 2012, when the position of the solstice sun will be aligned with the
Milky Way galaxy. This solstice-galaxy alignment is a rare occurrence, happening only once every 26,000 years. It can be called a "galactic alignment"
and was perceived by ancient astronomers as a shifting of the position of the
sun, on the solstice, in relation to background features such as stars, constellations, and the Milky Way. Based on evidence in Maya traditions and key
archaeological sites, it became overwhelmingly apparent to me that the future
convergence of sun and galaxy was calculated, with good accuracy, by the
ancient Maya and the cycle-ending date in 2012 was chosen to target it. Without going into any further questions and complexities, this situation means
that the ancient Maya had astronomical abilities at least on par with their
contemporaries in other parts of the world, including Greece, India, Babylo-
nia, and Egypt.

Importantly, I noticed that the astronomical features involved in the galactic alignment were key players in Maya cosmology and Creation Mythology. These connections were not free-floating opinions based on imagined associations that had no real relevance for the ancient Maya. In fact, the evidence was there in the academic literature itself. I was merely stitching all the pieces together. The solstice sun, the Milky Way, and a curious feature that lies along the Milky Way called the dark rift were utilized in the sacred ballgame, king-making rites, the calendar systems, and the Hero Twin Creation Myth. These real connections anchored the galactic alignment firmly within known Maya concepts and traditions. In my studies I quickly focused my attention on the early Maya site called Izapa, which scholars suspected as being involved in the formulation of the Long Count calendar. By 1994 the results of this approach had revealed Izapa as a critically important place for understanding how the Maya thought about the galactic alignment in era-2012. Furthermore, the astronomy was woven together with spiritual teachings, conveyed as mythological dynamics in the Creation Myth on Izapa's many pictographic monuments.

Astronomy, the calendar, and the Creation Myth were facets of the same cosmology. Beliefs about cycle endings, especially the big one in 2012, were represented in these traditions and revealed how the creators of the Long Count thought about 2012. It was not perceived as some dramatic doomsday apocalypse, as our modern media repeatedly prefers to portray it. Instead, the creators of the 2012 calendar utilized sophisticated spiritual teachings intended to facilitate a process of spiritual transformation and renewal. This was clearly big news, given that, in the mid-1990s when I made these discoveries, scholars had said nothing about 2012 and the doomsday interpretation was on the rise in the popular media. For me, the years after my first trip south of the border in 1986 were filled with exciting discoveries, continuing travels, field investigations at Maya sites, living and working with the modern Maya, meeting remarkable people, writing and teaching.

Through the years I've been invited to contribute articles to anthologies, speak at conferences, attend irresistible events, and conduct radio and TV interviews. Naturally, some of these were well produced, but others were ill conceived, and I've learned a lot about working with conference organizers and documentary producers. Throughout the aforementioned wonderland of opportunities and farragoes my goal of finding a suitable publisher for a book telling the definitive 2012 story remained elusive. When the 2012 bug started to bite the mainstream press and many more books started to appear, I noticed that authors and the media were pulling the 2012 topic in predictably weird directions. For example, one prominent trend has involved slowly, and almost imperceptibly, divorcing the 2012 icon from its Maya roots. Another enlists 2012 into serving the dubious cause of fear-based doomsday scenarios populated by alien gene splicers, invisible planets, searing solar flares, and menacing asteroids. The vast majority of this unbridled superstorm of alarmist and hype-driven marketing ploys was problematic. I realized that I was in a unique position to offer clarity and discernment, so I got to work, building from scratch a new book that I envisioned to be the definitive 2012 story.

Chapter 1 presents the indispensable discoveries and academic work that over many centuries have led to an astonishing picture of ancient Maya civilization. How did explorers come to rediscover the lost cities of the Maya? How did scholars come to reconstruct the calendar systems? How did breakthroughs and biases help and hinder the process? And going further back in time, how and when did civilization in Mesoamerica develop? The material covered in Chapter 1 could easily have been expanded into a book of its own, telling the story of fascinating rogues and colorful characters who discovered and explored the jungle temples of ancient Maya civilization, reconstructing an entire worldview beginning with the barest of fragments. Since my goal was to write one book rather than a ten-volume series, I have summarized the most notable events and as a result many interesting episodes and characters have been left out.

Distilling the endless information down to its alchemical essence, I've highlighted certain themes that I believe define the remarkable ongoing process of recovering the lost knowledge of the Maya, America's most persistently mind-boggling civilization. One of these themes is the important place occupied, time and again, by the independent outsider. Quirky, eccentric, dealing genuine insights and controversial fancies, they have been the triggers and the mainstay of real progress. Visionary philosopher Terence McKenna said in one of his talks:

> What we need to celebrate is the individual. Have you not noticed (I certainly have), that every historical change you can think of—in fact any change you can think of, forget about human beings—any change in any system that you can think of is always ultimately traceable to one unit in the system undergoing a phase state change of some sort. There are no group decisions, those things come later. The genius of creativity and of initiation of activity always lies with the individual.[2]

The efforts made by these upstarts to transcend status quo biases inflicted by degreed gatekeepers wielding their own limiting brands of logic and decorum can be observed time and time again. Usually the truth eventually came through, even though it was often reviled and marginalized for decades and the trailblazers themselves died without due acknowledgment.

I count myself among the autodidacts, the self-taught perpetual students fueled by passion and a sense of mission. The early independent Maya researchers had little to work with. Things have sped up since the days of Förstemann, Goodman, and Bourbourg, and I expect the next decade will see many unexpected breakthroughs in how we understand Maya astronomy, the hieroglyphic inscriptions, and the much maligned and misunderstood 2012 date—including, as we will see, new evidence that supports my reconstruction of the original intentions behind the 2012 date. Even after the 2012 party is over, the work will continue.

Another theme is 2012's wide appeal. By this I mean it is of interest to scientists, New Age spiritualists, novelists, survivalists, evangelizing model makers, and the mass media—although, it must be said, its millenarian aspect finds particularly fertile soil in the United States. Whether manifesting in negative or positive aspects, 2012 nevertheless has *meaning* in virtually every domain where it appears. This situation calls into question critics who declare, with a surprisingly smug certainty, that 2012 is a hoax or completely meaningless. I've observed and directly experienced this treatment and have dialogued with those who inflict it, so I feel obligated to report the following: In academia as well as in the skeptical popular press, 2012 is rendered meaningless to the extent that it is misunderstood. This is an interesting equation. If a prejudice exists that 2012 is meaningless, then myriad creative ways to misunderstand it can and must be implemented. One overarching misunderstanding is endlessly repeated: that the Maya predicted the end of the world in 2012.[3] If you look at the Maya doctrine of World Ages, the hieroglyphic inscriptions that relate to 2012, and the Creation Mythology (*The Popol Vuh*), you find nothing of the sort. These misconceptions have currency because access to good information on 2012 has been either seriously limited or buried under the endless bric-a-brac of the spiritual marketplace. Discerning books and websites, including my own, are out there and have been for years, but they must compete with formulaic attention-grabbing marketplace products that are almost always sensationalized and riddled with errors.

I found it challenging to review, for this book, the many distortions and misapprehensions that have clogged the 2012 marketplace. I felt it would be important to clarify, for the record, the facts of the matter and have assessed materials from theories, models, so-called prophets, and visionaries. The real stories that underlie many of these authors and ideas are filled with ironies, debacles, and exposés, and I happen to have had the insider's view of all these telltale goings-on in the tortured topic of 2012. I offer my carefully considered overviews and assessments on the best-known theories connected to 2012, and I provide these candid critiques as a guide for unwary wayfarers on the road to 2012. Much of what is connected to 2012 is misleading and panders to fear and paranoia. Delving into this messy situation will, I hope, be made easier with some well-placed sardonic humor and wry wit. One thing I've learned from twenty years in the 2012 game is that humor is absolutely necessary if one hopes to survive the 2012 superstorm of surreal scenarios that are flooding the discussion. Surprisingly, we'll find that an unwillingness to investigate the 2012 topic *rationally*, which is diagnostic of many misconceptions in the popular literature, also infects academia. A critical survey of the "modern Maya calendar movement" and its relationship to academic treatments will be a frequent reference point.

Part I was conceived as a nuts-and-bolts chronological survey of the 2012 topic, bringing us up to speed on the facts of the matter. Summarizing the various theories inevitably invites a presentation of my reconstruction work and "galactic alignment theory." Chapter 4 frames this presentation within the larger issue of how breakthroughs occur, emphasizing that my work is built upon the previous breakthroughs of other scholars working in Maya studies. With new decipherments of hieroglyphic texts, the multifarious ways in which the ancient Maya utilized the concept of the alignment of the solstice sun and the Milky Way's dark rift (the "galactic alignment") in their traditions is becoming clearer. I found that the Maya ballgame, king-making rites, and the Maya Creation Mythology encoded the astronomy of the era-2012 alignment, which happens only once every 26,000 years. This galactic alignment is caused by a phenomenon called the precession of the equinoxes, the slow shifting of the positions of the equinoxes (and solstices) in the sky, resulting from the fact that the earth wobbles very slowly on its axis. My end-date alignment theory is now receiving new support from recent findings in academia, and after 2012 I'll continue the work that I've pursued since the mid-1980s.

This astronomical alignment has been generally and more compellingly referred to as an alignment to "the Galactic Center," a cause for confusion in terms of timing parameters, which I will explain and clarify. When the dust settles, I am confident that a paradigm justly identified as "galactic" in scope will become the consensus in academia and that college textbooks will include tutorials in hieroglyphic statements involving the dark rift in the Milky Way, precessional concepts and calculations in hieroglyphic inscriptions, and readings of the astrotheological iconography of pre-Classic Izapa.

Over the years I've traveled and talked with scholars and writers, and I will share their views in their own words. The academic Tulane conference on 2012 took place in February of 2009, just in time for inclusion in this book. It was a watershed event that consolidated closed-minded judgments in academia while paradoxically initiating a new era of scholarly openness (in some quarters) to considering 2012 as the valid artifact of Maya thought that it is. I attended and recorded the proceedings, and my exchanges with scholars reveal the current state of the 2012 discussion in mainstream academia. The first part of the book closes with a concise summary of new discoveries, in the inscriptions and elsewhere, that lend support to my galactic alignment theory while expanding our understanding of 2012 and Maya cosmovision in profound and compelling new ways.

My angle of approach to 2012 in Part I is guided by a straightforward, informed, and objective assessment. But something is missing. The deeper meaning that New Agers believe 2012 contains is, I venture, an important and valid part of the discussion. It has, in fact, been present for me from the early days of my research. What I've noticed is that Maya teachings, including those pertaining to cycle endings, belong to a Perennial Philosophy, or Primordial Tradition, a reservoir of knowledge and spiritual wisdom common in its essential form to all great religious traditions. The inner, symbolic message of 2012 can have meaning for all humanity. Approaching 2012 in this way is suspect to Maya specialists, even though it can be undertaken rationally. Comparative mythologist Joseph Campbell, for example, drew from the integrative perspectives of this Perennial Philosophy to show patterns of similarity between widely separated global mythologies. He pierced beyond the veil of surface appearances and culture-specific terminology to see the archetypal level of meaning. Ancient Hindu teachings and Buddhist insights, for Campbell, could thus have spiritual meaning for modern seekers. So, too, Maya teachings belong in their archetypal essence to this primordial wisdom, and can speak to us today, or to any human being in any era.

One might suspect that this approach to 2012 would have been colonized by New Agers and spiritual seekers, but it hasn't. The thirst for spiritual insight has not been quenched by the wells plumbed by spiritual writers on 2012, because instead of tapping into Maya traditional wisdom as an expression of the Perennial Philosophy, all manner of inventive models charted in the name of the Maya calendar have instead staked a claim in the spiritual marketplace. The vein of pure gnosis is there, right before our eyes, in the Maya Creation Mythology; we just need to read it with eyes attuned to the symbolic, archetypal, universal content.

Part II ventures into this deeper area of inquiry, and beyond it is the ultimate invitation—for the reader to lay down books and open up their own initiatory conduit into a direct inner experience of the universal gnosis that all spiritual teachings point to. This is no time to insulate ourselves from the profound universal teachings of ancient Maya philosophy. Chapter 12 is dedicated to discussing the importance of this big picture, how we can open to it, how it can be embodied, and how its implicit values can be put into practice. We are being called to engage the initiatory sacrifice that the Maya's 2012 teaching insists is indispensable. Ultimately, this is the only way that anyone will be able to understand for themselves what 2012 is all about. It's an understanding not limited to facts and figures—it is the gnosis of union with the whole consciousness that lies at the root of ego and world. These ideas are centrally important to the universal meaning of 2012 and must be taken seriously. For now we are coming down to the wire; the 2012 date is looming like an unwanted intruder in the dream of Western civilization, urgently screaming that something is very wrong with the way we've been running the planet.

These are the big questions, ones that any 2012ologist is required to address. But to my mind they aren't concerns that will last. Or, I should rather say, the concerns for sustainable worldview and spiritual wholeness will last but their connection to 2012 will expire. After 2012 no one will care anymore about relating the Maya calendar to events in the world or to the importance of spiritual awakening. For mainstream culture it will pass into oblivion while the next trendy topic is lined up for consideration. What will last, in my view, is twofold: the ongoing effort to reconstruct ancient Maya cosmology and the growing indigenous cultural movement that Maya scholar Victor Montejo has called "the Maya Renaissance." An upwelling of indigenous consciousness defines this renaissance, which I believe heralds a much larger, and much needed, global awakening and renewal. Our entire world needs to have a turnabout in its deepest seat of consciousness, flipping the values of a self-serving dominator ethic back around to the community-building partnership strategies that were the ideal of indigenous societies. In this regard, the very idea of era-2012 as a time of renewal is exactly what the world at large needs to hear.

This book is the culmination of a quarter century of committed and constant research into Maya culture, cosmology, and the 2012 question. It was not written on assignment by a hired novice, as so many recent 2012 books have been. I've invested much time to sort out the wheat from the chaff and offer here a carefully considered treatment of a controversial phenomenon that is as thorough as such a complex topic allows. For many readers it will probably be challenging and enervating. Every reader will find in here things to agree with and others to disagree with. In a book that deals with a subject of so many labyrinthine layers and perplexing possibilities, that is how it should be; it is, in fact, unavoidable. Be prepared to dive in and get your feet wet. This is what you're in for, and I hope you will find it useful, challenging, and informative.

John Major Jenkins
May 31, 2009
4 Ahau
Long Count 12.19.16.7.0

PART ONE

THE

2012 STORY

CHAPTER ONE

RECOVERING A LOST WORLD

*Unfortunately the modern priests were not so
conscious of the historical and artistic value of Mitla
as their predecessors; a room full of ancient frescoes
of invaluable archaeological importance was used
in 1904 as the priest's stable, and part of the frescoes
were knocked down to build a pigsty.*[1]

—MIGUEL COVARRUBIAS

The story of the human presence in Mesoamerica is an epic journey, stretching over at least 10,000 years with intermingling boundaries between the Olmec, Izapan, Maya, Toltec, and Nahuatl cultures. It flowered in the Classic Maya civilization (300 AD to 900 AD), whose most important cosmological artifact (the Long Count calendar) pointed beyond its own demise to a great cycle ending: December 21, 2012. The Maya's knowledge of that date was lost centuries ago, but was recovered from the barest fragments by explorers and iconoclasts, rogues and scholars, who all contributed in their own ways to the realization, achieved only recently, that the end date of a cycle of 13 Baktuns was an intentional forward calculation. This chapter unfolds the process by which this most intriguing date, and the profound paradigm connected to it, was rediscovered right on the cusp of the cycle's conclusion.

Something incredible occurred in the center of the Americas that has persistently intrigued and baffled European colonizers. The discoveries and achievements of American Indian civilizations reveal an unparalleled genius.

A demonstration of this genius is found in the early domestication of corn, which occurred in Central Mexico's Balsas River Valley roughly 8,700 years ago.[2] Decades, centuries, of persistent interbreeding was required to tease juicy corn kernels out of teosinte, a skinny wild grain. As their civilizations developed, the trailblazers of the Western Hemisphere attained profound achievements in mathematics, medicine, philosophy, and astronomy, and gave to the modern world essential staples such as corn, chocolate, tobacco, and potatoes. Without their discoveries, the modern world would be stripped of many of its best possessions.[3]

In Mesoamerica, the land stretching between central Mexico and Honduras, a native genius unfolded itself through the centuries, producing insights about the cosmos while building huge stone cities and creating unique calendars. A curiously advanced worldview is encoded into these calendars, one that saw the processes of earth and sky interwoven. Seasonal cycles of rain and heat, sowing and growing, blended with a creation mythos centered on maize. The life cycle of a human being and the astronomical cycles above were seen to be integrated as one majestic symphony. For the ancient Mesoamericans, life was essentially a mystery that could never be completely figured out in the definitive sense that Western science seeks to achieve. But for the ancient Maya, gazing into the night sky from their lofty temples, alive to the mingling rhythms of the sky and their own beating hearts, it was a mystery that could be experienced.

In the rise and fall of the human enterprise, the Maya achievement had already passed by the time Spanish conquistadors arrived in 1519. The Classic Maya civilization was long gone. What the invaders found instead was a new, upstart Aztec empire sprawling over the high plateau of Central Mexico, far to the west of Maya dominions. After long peregrinations searching for a new homeland, the Aztecs had stumbled upon the central Mexican plateau. There they saw an eagle land on a nopal cactus with a snake in its mouth. This was the fulfillment of the prophecy, a sign that they had found their new homeland. They built what would later become Mexico City, and by 1500 AD their capital, Tenochtitlán, was a bustling metropolis.

The Aztecs inherited fading echoes of long-gone kingdoms and cosmologies, including fragments of a pan-Mesoamerican calendar of 260 days
developed more than two millennia earlier by the Olmec civilization. Although the Aztecs appeared five centuries after the collapse of the Classic
Maya civilization (which developed in eastern Mexico and parts of modern-
day Central America), certain traditions, such as the idea of a succession of
World Ages experienced by humanity, were shared. The end of each World

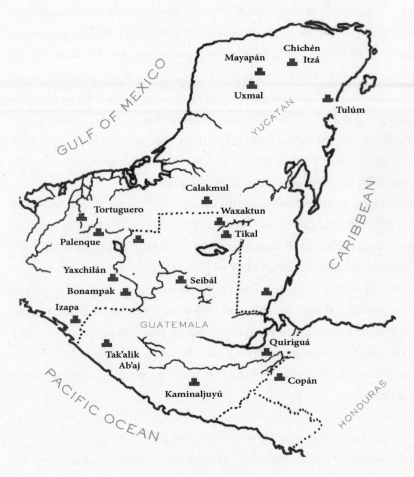

Maya country.

Age was thought to signal a transformation. And for the Aztecs their world would indeed soon come to an end. The dramatic events that transpired between Cortés's small but determined army and the people of Moctezuma in Central Mexico define what we consider to be the conquest of Mexico. But Mexico is a big place. It would be several more years before the Spanish invaders pushed their way far enough into the lands of the Maya to realize that another ancient civilization once flourished in the decaying jungle cities of the east.

Although the old stone cities of the Maya were crumbling and forgotten, the tribes found by the Spanish were engaged in a thriving new phase of cultural activity. From the hot lowlands of the Yucatán Peninsula to the highlands of Chiapas and Guatemala, the Maya were deeply involved with the business of civilization. Trade networks stretched for hundreds of miles from seacoast to high volcanic peaks. City-states expressing new architectural styles, including the Quiché Maya kingdom, arose in the Guatemalan highlands. As with the Aztecs far to the west, an upsurge in cultural growth had spiked in the early 1500s, but was cut short by the strange foreigners riding beasts like deer and wearing invincible coats of metal.

Pedro de Alvarado defeated the Quiché king Tecun Uman in 1524, Cortés defeated Moctezuma and subjugated the Aztecs, and the Yucatec Maya were tortured and their books were burned in Inquisitorial bonfires. Franciscan missionaries targeted Maya religion as a heresy that must be stamped out, and Maya leaders were often tortured and put to death for practicing their traditional ways. In a letter of 1563 sent to the king of Spain, a citizen of Mérida named Diego Rodríguez Bibanco, who had received a royal appointment as "Defender of the Indians of Yucatán," documented the "irregularities and punishments" inflicted on Maya people accused of practicing idolatry:

> And so, with the power they claimed as ecclesiastical judges, and that
> which your Justice gave them, they set about the business with great
> rigor and atrocity, putting the Indians to great tortures of ropes and

water, hanging them by pulleys with stones of 50 or 75 pounds tied to their feet, and so suspended gave them many lashes until the blood ran to the ground from their shoulders and legs. Besides this they tarred them with boiling fat as was the custom to do with Negro slaves, with the melted wax of lit candles dropped on their bare parts; all this without preceding information, or seeking first for the facts. This seemed to them the way to teach them.[4]

Millions of indigenous citizens of the New World also died of diseases brought by Europeans, and by 1600 the native population of Mesoamerica had been reduced to a fraction of its former number.

It was a clash of civilizations unlike anything the world had ever experienced, as strange for the Maya as an armada of spaceships from Antares landing on the White House lawn, bringing alien beings hungry for megatons of gold, or copper, or soil. Most cultures would have become dust in the wind, but the Maya, ever resilient, having the adaptable strength of the willow tree, received and allowed the invaders to wash over them so that now, five hundred years later, they still stand. In certain important respects, mainly in the preservation of spiritual beliefs and calendar ceremonies, the Maya have never been conquered.

STILL HERE AFTER ALL THESE YEARS

To emphatically clarify a common misconception, the Maya didn't simply vanish in some intergalactic recall of the ninth century. After the great cities of Copán, Palenque, Tikal, and Yaxchilán faltered and fell some eleven hundred years ago, succumbing to greed, plague, and drought, different Maya groups split and dispersed, embarking on long journeys looking for new homelands. They carried their cultural identities and accomplishments with them like burdens on their backs, eventually setting up house in new regions, such as the crenellated ravines and plateaus of the Guatemalan highlands.

But by 900 AD the end of the Maya Classic Period had come, signaling the end of a style of civilization that crumbled under the weight of its own hubris, much in the way that our own crumbles now. Cultures rise and fall as day follows night, and a plethora of Maya groups multiplied as new generations played ever-evolving variations on the theme of Mesoamerican civilization. The history of Mesoamerica is as complex as any other region of the world, perhaps more so due to the tumultuous landscape of earthquakes and eruptions in which the Maya have traditionally lived. But core beliefs and traditions, such as the old mythologies and ceremonies, have withstood the erosions of time.

In 1700, a Dominican friar named Francisco Ximénez took up his orders in the highland town of Santo Tomás Chichicastenango. The domain was still called New Spain, as Guatemala would not come into being as an independent republic until 1821. He discovered among the Maya people of his parish a strange book penned in an alphabetic script in the native Quiché language. It was closely guarded as a sacred text, handed down for generations from one elder to the next, and now it was placed into his hands. Sensitive to the plight of his Maya flock, and how people in his world harbored so many mistaken notions about them, he decided to translate it. In the foreword to his work he wrote:

> Because I have seen many historians who write about these peoples and their beliefs, say and touch upon some things contained in their histories which were only scattered fragments, and since the historians had not seen the actual histories themselves, as they were written, I decide to put here and transcribe all of their histories, according to the way they had written them.[5]

And so *The Popol Vuh (Book of Council, Book of the Dawn of Life)* was copied for posterity and translated into Spanish. Father Ximénez, an accomplished linguist and student of Mayan grammar, was well suited to the task. The original manuscript that he worked from was written in the 1550s. Some scholars believe that the Maya elders who did it were drawing from an older hieroglyphic book.[6] Certain mythological scenes and deities found in *The Popol Vuh* are also portrayed on ancient carved monuments at early Maya sites dating back more than 2,100 years, suggesting that an ideological gold mine of great antiquity was preserved in the ancient text.

But metaphorical gold is not real gold. As so often happened with the treatment of native wisdom, Ximénez's offering to the outside world slipped into the shadows and was not published until 1857. By then, intrepid explorers had already delved into the jungles of Central America and were finding evidence of a forgotten civilization—people who, a thousand years prior to Ximénez, were painting the stories of *The Popol Vuh* on vases and in their books. In those pages the gods and planets danced to the tune of the sacred 260-day calendar, a system of divination and timekeeping that survives today in the remote villages of Guatemala. But not all areas inhabited by the Maya have retained this continuity of the ancient calendar traditions.

During the conquest of the Maya in the Yucatán, the 260-day calendar was still being followed. Franciscan friars were streaming off the boats, arriving armed with the mandate of the Catholic auto-da-fé, the jihadlike Inquisition, their heads loaded with deep prejudices against pagans who were ignorant of the One Holy Faith. Bishop Diego de Landa was one of these early evangelicals, hell-bent on converting the heathens. His intent was to curtail idolatrous devil worship, and the result was the destruction of native genius.

De Landa's book burning in the Yucatec Maya village of Mani in 1562 largely succeeded in this endeavor of unbridled zealotry. Hundreds of Maya books were heaped in piles and destroyed. Today, only four known examples survive: the Dresden, Madrid, Paris, and Grolier codices. In time, the native calendars in Yucatán were likewise stamped out. This kind of act was nothing new for Christianity, whose champion Emperor Theodosius likewise ordered "pagan" temples destroyed in 391 AD, including the Alexandrian Museum and the Serapeum that housed major parts of the Alexandrian library. The dearth of direct evidence about what the ancient Maya knew and believed has caused prejudices and misconceptions to multiply. An embedded bias within Western assumptions, installed by both religious and scientific training, that the Maya were unscientific has continued to today and often prevents a clear assessment of Maya culture on its own terms.

The case of de Landa contains within it one redeeming component, for he was also responsible for recording and preserving information about the dates and glyphs of the Maya calendar. In an act of curiosity that, for once, outweighed his disgust, he compiled information from various Maya informants and attempted to interpret the day-signs of the calendar, believing they were phonetic letters of the Maya alphabet. Although de Landa was far off base, his *Relación de las Cosas de Yucatán* preserved important facets of Maya writing and language. His book, rediscovered and published three centuries later by French cleric Brasseur de Bourbourg, became the key with which early scholars of the Maya were able to begin reconstructing knowledge that had been lost, such as the workings of the Maya calendar and the enigmatic hieroglyphic writing system.

During the sixteenth century a theological debate was raging among the Franciscans—did the Maya have souls? Why even try to spread the Christian faith to soulless, irreversibly damned heathens? Can animals enter the kingdom of heaven? These debates were typical in the mid-1500s, revealing popular attitudes and the formulation of official church policy. Today, despite progress in allowing indigenous Americans to have souls, prejudices remain deeply rooted. One way out of the mire of prejudice that emerged in the 1800s was to see them as noble savages. Charles Darwin was both an evolutionist who saw naked savages as repugnant and a stalwart abolitionist, a paradoxical stance that explains contradictory attitudes toward natives in his famous book *The Descent of Man*. On one hand he saw them as gentle and kind, peace-loving tribes. On the other, they were naked, disgusting, and unintelligible. Nevertheless, a romanticized portrait of natives appealed to the European imagination. It countered negative attitudes, but the alienation between the "civilized" nations and the "uncivilized" heathens was sustained as the Maya remained objects of contemplation rather than fellow humans.

In the lowlands of the Lacandon rain forest, running west of the great Usumacinta River that divides Mexico from Guatemala, the last remnants of unconquered Maya have, technically, survived up into the twenty-first century. As recently as the 1960s anthropologists were studying the ancient beliefs, dreams, and ceremonies of the Lacandon.[7] They still visited the ancient altar shrines of their long-dead ancestors, burning incense in "god pots" (ritual ceramic vessels) in the overgrown ruins of Bonampak. But the Lacandon were in the twilight phase of their cycle of existence, their numbers dwindling to less than a hundred, and therefore they fell prey to problems caused by inbreeding. Though they have been known for refusing to join the ways of the Europeans, the recent generation of this dwindling group of holdouts has now finally made the leap. They wear their characteristic flowing white tunics only when making appearances at the site of Palenque, or at the Na Bolon study center and museum in San Cristobal de las Casas. But back in the 1870s they were ghosts in the jungle, strange forest dwellers who ate monkeys and moved here and there between ceiba-shrouded encampments.

In a bizarre meeting that signaled the end of their jungle idyll, explorer Alfred Maudslay sought out the Lacandon Maya, the archetypal "other," on his way to Yaxchilán in 1882. Punting down the Usumacinta River, his guides directed him to pull ashore. The path they took was marked in spots with jaguar skulls. Eventually they came to a clearing containing three huts, where a Lacandon woman came out to meet them. Maudslay wrote:

> She had not the slightest trace of fear; she smiled quite happily and received us most courteously, asked us to go into a small open house and said that all the men were away hunting cacao . . . the woman had features exactly like the faces at Palenque and Menché, receding forehead, hooked nose, and big lips. She was quite pleasant and talkative. . . .[8]

Stereotypes of the Lacandon as fierce jungle savages were not confirmed by Maudslay's experience.

The Lacandon were only one leaf on the tree of Mesoamerican civilization. In fact, after the Conquest most of what was known and studied about the New World Indians came out of the remnants of the Aztec empire. The situation there as it unfolded through the centuries is fairly unique in the development of European and native interactions in the New World. As Carlos Fuentes said, "Mexicans descend from the Aztecs, while Argentinians descend from ships."[9] Blood mixture and intermarrying have made the Aztecs an essential ingredient of what a modern Mexican is. Today, many Latinos and Chicanos proudly recognize their Aztec heritage. While "the other" was and still is rejected as a matter of course by many Americans (meaning denizens of all the Americas), the modern Mexicans *have become the other.*

AZTEC DOMAINS

In Central Mexico, far to the west of the Maya heartland, another friar, Bernardino de Sahagún, spoke with native informants and documented the beliefs of the children of Moctezuma. The sense of something profound in native traditions that should be preserved continued with other well-intentioned Spaniards. Diego Durán compiled and preserved many documents on the native calendar and histories, and in the late 1500s he wrote *The Book of the Gods and Rites of the Ancient Calendar.* As usual, however, his work was suppressed and filed away in the archives and remained unpublished for almost three hundred years.[10]

In the late 1600s, Don Carlos de Sigüenza y Góngora rescued many documents from the archives during a fire that consumed the city. He studied the traditions of the Aztecs and claimed that the pre-Conquest Indians possessed advanced knowledge of mathematics and astronomy. Upon examining the pictographic manuscripts left by the Aztecs, he observed that they had a calendar of 52 years, today known as the Calendar Round. It was a combination of two native time-counts, one being 260 days and the other being a 365-day approximation of the solar year.

Sigüenza's examination of the documents and pictographic manuscripts also enabled him to calculate a chronology of the pre-Conquest kings of Mexico. A primary supporting source for this work was the writings of Fernando de Alva Ixtlilxochitl, a descendant of Aztec royalty. During Sigüenza's day and for some time thereafter, the family of Ixtlilxochitl were still the titular lords to the grounds of Teotihuacán, the great Central Mexican city of the early Nahuatl people that had thrived between 150 and 750 AD. Who were those mysterious people who once lived there? When did they build the city? The answers to these kinds of questions were unclear at the time, but breakthroughs were soon to occur. The grandeur and allure of the Pyramids of the Sun and Moon and the Street of the Dead would soon come to the notice of the world.

A traveler from Italy named Gemelli Careri arrived in Acapulco by boat in 1697 and learned of Sigüenza's findings. Inspired and intrigued by Sigüenza's work, he journeyed on ancient trails into the central plateau to visit the ruins. Making his way north of Mexico City by mule, he noted the abject squalor of the natives. After arriving, he was shown the site by Pedro de Alva, grandson of the famous Juan de Alva Ixtlilxochitl, and he learned of huge stone statues located on the tops of the Pyramids of Sun and Moon. The dramatic pyramids and long Street of the Dead at Teotihuacán must have been an incredible sight for Careri. Even for this seasoned world traveler, the scale of the remains was impressive, rivaling what he had seen on the Giza Plateau.

Careri's six-volume opus *Voyage Around the World* was published (in Italian) in 1719. Quickly condensed and translated into other languages, it contained the first and best description of Mexico to reach the outside world. His book was a huge success, and his itinerant method of taking public transportation inspired Jules Verne to write *Around the World in Eighty Days*. However, many could not believe Careri's observations of the pre-Conquest cultures of the New World, and he was roundly criticized as a fraud. The eighteenth-century Scottish historian William Robertson refused to include Careri's findings in his highly inaccurate *History of America* (1777). Instead, he asserted that "America was not peopled by any nation of the ancient continent, which had made considerable progress in civilization." The Mexicans and the Peruvians were not "entitled to rank with those nations which merit the name civilized."[11]

Another well-known historian of the mid-1700s, Cornelius de Pauw, wrote in his book *Recherches Philosophiques sur les Américains* (1769) that the so-called palace of the Mexican kings was no more than a hut. He criticized both Careri and Sigüenza, calling into question their reports of a sophisticated calendar with intricate wheels that calculated astronomical cycles over many centuries. Such a scenario was completely unbelievable to him, and without further examination he asserted that astronomical observations of this sort were "incompatible with the prodigious ignorance of those people" who "did not have words enough to count to ten."[12] This kind of prejudice has become woven into popular views of the native peoples of Mesoamerica such that even today we see rather loud echoes of it in movies like Mel Gibson's *Apocalypto*. The History Channel's "2012: Decoding the Past, Mayan Doomsday Prophecy" of 2006 also insisted on emphasizing salacious scenarios of sacrifice and violence, and committed a completely false assertion that the ancient Maya predicted doomsday in 2012.

These attitudes are thought to be the expressions of common sense, raw honesty, or healthy skepticism. The sentiments of de Pauw are found repeated in various guises down through the centuries, putting the brakes on how deeply we might dare understand the genius of Native Americans. And the ingrained problem can be difficult to detect, because "it often omits critical facts about both American Indian and European history. The fact that it is frequently written by well-respected scholars and authorities makes it even more difficult to detect. Like a low-grade infection, it works below the level of awareness, affecting students from elementary school to graduate school."[13] Here are some things that American Indians were doing all on their own: metallurgy, brain surgery, plant breeding, medicinal healing, mathematics, astronomy, massive architecture, art, music, and poetry. The gist of the prejudice is to not allow the Maya and other Native Amercian groups the same level of intellectual ability and cultural sophistication as that attributed to Western cultures. The problem has been endemic in scholarship. In the evolving understanding of the 2012 topic over the last twenty-five years, I've often encountered echoes of this attitude, an underinformed prejudice masquerading as coolheaded rationalism.

Throughout the 1700s few explorers and writers commented on the wealth of culture buried under the political tumult that was Mexico. But then, in 1790, a potential breakthrough came, one that by its sheer size and magnificence just might make a difference. The Aztec Calendar Stone, also known as the Sunstone or Eagle Bowl, was found under Mexico City and hauled up into the light. Because of its immense size and central location, it was probably a primary icon in the Aztec capital of Tenochtitlán that was destroyed by Cortés two and a half centuries earlier. Mexico in the 1790s was still a colony of Spain, its independence not to be won until 1821. Mexican writer Antonio de León y Gama analyzed the symbolism of the Sunstone and with an impressive amount of careful research combined with insight he revealed it to be a depiction of the ancient Mexican calendar system. But more than that, it was the slam dunk that proved a level of genius previously considered ridiculous. The ancients clearly observed the cycles of the sun, moon, and planets, and had devised a sophisticated calendar system to track those movements.

Up through the revolution for independence that culminated in 1821, traveling to New Spain was quite rightly viewed as a dangerous undertaking. Revolutionary violence was everywhere in a chaotic environment of unrest, and foreigners were suspect. In 1822, just after the Mexican Independence, an Englishman named William Bullock traveled to Mexico, entering by the Gulf Coast port of Veracruz. It was a quick but effective trip. Returning to London, he published a popular book, *Six Months' Residence and Travels in Mexico*, in 1825. Bullock was part of a new phase of interest in Mexico. Romantic poets such as Shelley and Keats were capturing the imaginations of

Europeans in the 1810s and 1820s, and the romance of Mexican ruins was irresistible. The Mexican Independence promised a new era of stability for the region, which was appealing to foreign visitors, and to outsiders Mexico was starting to look more like a land of opportunity.

Interest in the mysteries of Mexico was building. William Prescott's monumental *History of the Conquest of Mexico* (1843) was a watershed work that made clear the scale of destruction exacted on the Aztec civilization by Cortés. A call to collect all the native documents of Mexico together in one place was expressed by von Humbolt, and a young Englishman named Edward King took up the challenge. Later known as Lord Kingsborough, he spent a fortune between 1831 and 1848 hiring lithographers and artists to copy and hand-color the original pictographic documents. When it was done, the massive nine-volume work was offered for a price equivalent to $3,500.

It was filled with commentaries in Latin, Hebrew, Greek, and Sanskrit supporting the idea, which Kingsborough had lifted from las Casas, that the Maya descended from the Lost Tribes of Israel. This idea became a point of theological doctrine for the Mormons, whose archaeologists have done impressive scientific work at early Maya sites in southern Mexico. Kingsborough's obsession got him into trouble, as his lavishly produced volumes put him in debt. The handmade paper he had chosen for his opus were more than he could afford. Sadly, he died of typhus in a debtors' prison in Ireland, a circumstance that caused the British Museum to purge his name from its catalog, listing Kingsborough's work instead under the name of Aglio, his hired artist.

EXPLORERS AND LOST CITIES

Mexico was often accessed by travelers landing in Veracruz or Acapulco. But the Maya heartland lay far to the east, and the remnants of the ancient civilization of the Maya, more distantly remote in time than the Aztecs, were off the beaten path and had largely escaped the attention of travelers. Nevertheless, rumors of what lay hidden in the thick jungles of the east began reaching the ears of adventurers, including a colorful character named Count Waldeck.

Antonio Del Rio visited Palenque when it was very difficult to reach. He managed to publish his account in 1822, and to illustrate his book his London publisher hired a man named Jean-Frédéric Maximilien de Waldeck. An artist, traveler, and womanizer, Waldeck was so intrigued with Del Rio's story of a lost city in the jungles of Mexico that, at age fifty-six, he crossed the ocean to see it for himself. While insinuating himself into society circles in Mexico City, doing portraits while seeking funds for his expedition to Palenque, Waldeck claimed to have been close friends with Lord Byron and Marie Antoinette. Eventually, the self-described count spent an entire year in the village of Santo Domingo near Palenque, plus four months in a hut he built in the shadows of Palenque's crumbling tower. Joining him during his tenure studying the ruins was a young mestizo woman who probably provided some incentive for staying in that sweltering, bug-infested place. In these inhospitable circumstances he produced some ninety drawings, striking in their artful execution but deceiving in their embellished details.

After Palenque he went to the sites of Yucatán and made more drawings, escaping to London when he found out that the local authorities thought he was a spy. His drawings narrowly avoided being seized. Discovering that government officials were suspicious of his activities, he quickly copied the entire lot of drawings and let them seize the copies, while the originals were safely hidden away. His ruse made further searches of his belongings unnecessary. With his pictographic booty in hand, he published a selection of twenty-one plates with a hundred pages of text, in which he elaborated his theory that Palenque was built by Chaldeans and Hindus. Considering that no one had any clue as to when the Maya cities were built and lived in, Waldeck's estimate for Palenque's demise (600 AD) was surprisingly accurate. His book was immensely pricey, some $1,500 apiece in today's dollars, apparently intended for nobles and counts like himself. Waldeck had accomplished what he set out to do, and he did it in his characteristic roguish style. For all we know, descendants of Waldeck are living in Palenque's environs today.

By the late 1830s, many explorers had crisscrossed Anahuac (Mexico), looking for and finding evidence of many layers of ancient civilizations and fragments of a lost calendar. But for most outsiders—Europeans as well as people in the quickly expanding United States—Mexico and Central America were still seen as hot, disease-ridden, and uncivilized places best avoided. Two explorers were to change everything, and the world was ready to receive what they had to share.

In 1838, John Lloyd Stephens flipped through Waldeck's book in Bartlett's bookstore in New York City. Already a seasoned traveler at age thirty-two, having just written the critically acclaimed *Travels in Egypt and Arabia Petraea* (1837), Stephens was inspired, despite Waldeck's reputation as an embellisher, to mount his own expedition to Central America. He invited a British acquaintance, artist Frederick Catherwood, to join him and document their findings. Their trip took place prior to photography becoming practical, but the detailed drawings Catherwood produced exceeded in quality anything produced by photography for another four decades.

Stephens had helped elect president Martin Van Buren, and through his office he secured an appointment: He would be U.S. Diplomatic Agent to the Republic of Central America. Despite the flimsy status of such a republic, his title and official-looking papers would help him navigate uncharted territories where governments rose and fell with the seasons. In October of 1839, they sailed from New York. Landing in Belize, they followed the reports of one Juan Galindo and ascended the Motagua River into Guatemala before turning south to cross a range of mountains, making a beeline for the rumored lost city that we now call Copán. Their trip was just beginning. Malaria, bandits, and civil wars were a constant threat, and would be over the next three months and 5,000 miles.

The sun barely pierced the heavy jungle canopy, but the oppressive heat of midday smothered everything. Three mules labored and slid on the muddy trail, burdened with packs, canvasses, and provisions. The two men patiently followed behind, swatting bugs while looking intently through the foliage, trying to spot the telltale signs of lost temples—an oddly placed stone, a cockeyed carving, rock walls hulking through the shadowy arboretum. On November 17, 1839, they entered Copán. Stephens later recalled, understating the surprise they really felt: "I am entering abruptly upon new ground."[14]

So began a new era in the exploration and recovery of the Maya civilization. After weeks of clearing away debris from temple stairways and platforms, Catherwood carefully making dozens of drawings, they realized they had barely scratched the surface. Stephens, realizing the importance of the site, purchased

Palenque in 1840. Drawing by Frederick Catherwood

it from the rightful owner for $50. Anxious to get to Palenque, they set out across the mountains of Guatemala, down the Usumacinta River valley, and through the Lacandon rain forest, a journey of more than three hundred miles.

Arriving at Palenque, Stephens and Catherwood saw with their own eyes that Waldeck and Del Rio had not been exaggerating. By happenstance, another expedition, led by Walker and Caddy, had just visited and left Palenque. These kinds of close calls would occur time and again in the "discovery" of lost cities. Palenque, however, was never lost to the locals, although for centuries the stones languished half forgotten—and were often pillaged as a resource for good building stone.

Stephens and Catherwood continued their journey by visiting the extensive sites of the Yucatán peninsula. Labna, Uxmal, and the awe-inspiring site of Chichén Itzá topped their list of sites they explored and documented. From a man in Mérida Stephens learned about the dot and bar numeration that could be clearly seen in the glyphs. He could thus get a rudimentary handle on numerology in the Long Count dates, for a bar represented 5 and a dot represented 1. He duly reported these things in his engaging though somewhat dry travelogue, stoking the curiosity of many readers for years to come. *Incidents of Travel in Central America and Yucatan*, published and priced affordably in 1841, was a huge success. It has remained in print to this day.

The realistic drawings by Catherwood were no doubt critical for helping outsiders understand the scope and scale of the lost civilization. Unfortunately, Catherwood's name was left off the cover. It's a sad and ironic fact that neither Stephens nor Catherwood lived long enough to see the era of scientific exploration they had spawned. Stephens died of liver disease at the age of forty-six in 1852. Catherwood drowned in a shipwreck in the Atlantic in 1854. By the 1860s, poor though compelling photographs were being made at the sites, providing undeniable proof that a lost civilization was buried in the jungles of Mexico. And other indications of an ancient high culture were emerging, in manuscripts discovered and published by an enterprising cleric who hid Atlantean theories under his ecclesiastical robe.

THE POPOL VUH APPEARS

Born in Holland in 1813, Charles Étienne Brasseur de Bourbourg spent his early years writing novels in Paris. He then went to Rome to study theology and was ordained for the priesthood. His eye, however, was always on Maya mysteries. Inspired by Stephens's and Del Rio's books, he set off for America in 1845. His ability to find forgotten manuscripts in moldy archives was uncanny. He located unpublished histories of New Spain penned by Las Casas and Durán, and an original history of the Aztecs written by Ixtlilxochitl. He spent several years in Mexico City and environs, learning the Nahuatl language, and thereafter traveled through Guatemala, El Salvador, as far as Nicaragua, looking for artifacts and manuscripts. In Guatemala he found *The Annals of the Cakchiquels* as well as Ximénez's translation of *The Popol Vuh* stashed away in church archives.

Returning to Paris in 1861, he published *The Popol Vuh* in a French translation. While there, he was given access to the Aubin collection of rare books and manuscripts from the Americas. Studying his own findings and the unparalleled Aubin collection, never before made available for perusal, de Bourbourg produced a four-volume study of Mesoamerican history and religion called *Histoire des Nations Civilisées du Mexique et de l'Amérique Centrale*. It so impressed Spanish historians that they opened their own museum collections for his study. In the Archives of the Academy of History he found de Landa's long-forgotten manuscript *Relación de las Cosas de Yucatán*. Brasseur quickly published it, recognizing it as a key to helping decipher the Maya script. He could now identify the glyphs for the 20 day-signs of the 260-day sacred calendar as well the month signs of the 365-day civil calendar, but as a Rosetta Stone de Landa's ideas and misleading presentations proved maddening.

As if these accomplishments in bringing to light lost books weren't enough, Brasseur befriended a descendant of Hernan Cortés in Madrid and in 1864 was shown what became known as the Madrid Codex—an original Maya book from Yucatán containing astronomical almanacs and bewildering arrays of glyphs, gods, and calendar dates. It was an inscrutable text in which Brasseur nevertheless claimed to see many things. Following Alexander von Humbolt's earlier belief that primitive contemporary cultures were fragments of an older high civilization destroyed by natural catastrophes, Brasseur came to believe that Egypt and Central America were rooted in the same cultural origin, and at other times migrations were caused by comets, meteors, and geological disruptions having celestial origins. The flood myths he encountered were seen to be evidence for cataclysms in ancient times, and he described them as an early rendition of the Atlantis myth, soon to be made popular by Ignatius Donnelly's *Atlantis: The Antediluvian World* (1882).

Brasseur de Bourbourg continued writing books, but his ideas on the origins of Mesoamerican cultures grew progressively less credible to his peers. By the time he wrote *Chronologie Historique des Mexicains* he firmly believed that the Aztec legend of Quetzalcoatl was connected with Plato's myth of Atlantis. He elaborated the theme freely and asserted that in 10,500 BC a sequence of four cataclysms occurred and that human civilizations originated not in the Middle East but in a continent that once extended from Yucatán into the Atlantic Ocean. Having sunk beneath the waves in cataclysmic upheavals perhaps triggered by meteors, the remnants were the Canary Islands. Here we find the seed point for much Atlantean speculation and writing that is a constantly resurfacing theme in the treatment of Maya history.

Perhaps a grain of truth is preserved in the persistence of this Atlantis mythos. The Maya were indeed advanced in ways bizarre and difficult to fathom. They held metaphysically elegant and spiritually profound doctrines that the modern scientific mind-set in particular is ill-disposed to grasp. Did they achieve a kind of consciousness fundamentally different from modern consciousness, and might that consciousness in some way be called, with good reason, "Atlantean"? Certainly the topic has been distorted, used, and abused through the years, but its very persistence suggests that it would benefit from a reappraisal.

Brasseur's critics, once his fans, observed his increasingly alienating interpretations with disappointment. His perspective grew more and more strange, such that serious scholars who had once deferred to him became less and less confident in his ideas. Brasseur, for his part, insinuated that his critics had not studied the traditions of the Americas enough and harbored

Old World biases. World history, he insisted, would be incomplete if the documents of the New World were left out. Despite his fall from grace in the eyes of his contemporaries, he is remembered as single-handedly bringing to light many hidden and forgotten texts of great importance, earning him a place of respect in the annals of independent sleuth-scholarship. Many of Brasseur de Bourbourg's insights have slipped into consensus with barely a mention of credit.

DR. LE PLONGEON RAISES THE CHAC MOOL

The curious career of Dr. Augustus Le Plongeon was passed over almost without comment by Michael Coe in his book *Breaking the Maya Code*. But of all the fascinating characters that have danced on the stage of Maya studies, he should receive top billing. Completely self-funded, the sheer commitment and effort of Le Plongeon to recover monstrous stone artifacts and explain their perplexing circumstances are amazing to consider.

Born in France in 1826, he came to idolize John Lloyd Stephens, whose accounts of traveling among Maya ruins must have stimulated his young mind. On his way to the Americas at age fourteen, he was one of two survivors of a disastrous shipwreck. He lived in South America for some years before arriving in California in time for the '49 Gold Rush. There he became a surveyor, practiced law in San Francisco, and acquired a degree in medicine (how he acquired it is not very clear). Traveling around the world, he eventually set up a private hospital in Peru in the 1860s, offering an experimental therapy of applying electrical current to medicinal baths. Always attentive to the mysteries that surrounded him, he studied Inca ruins, history, and culture. While in Peru he wrote religious books on Jesus and a practical manual on photography.

In 1873, Le Plongeon traveled to Yucatán with his new wife, twenty-two-year-old Alice Dixon. He was always quick to mention his wife as his collaborator in the field, and they spent twelve years exploring the Maya ruins in Yucatán. Together they lived near Chichén Itzá while taking more than five hundred photographs, making drawings, surveying buildings and site alignments, and unearthing a huge sculpture of a reclining Chac Mool, a Yucatec Maya deity whose belly contained a stone bowl in which new fire was ceremonially drilled. Those days in Yucatán, a distant backwater from the ruling center of Mexico City, were dangerous because revolutionary sentiments that had exploded in the Caste War, an indigenous uprising in the 1860s, were still simmering.

Le Plongeon mastered the Maya language while in Yucatán and befriended local Maya priests, including one wisdom keeper he believed to be 150 years old. Adding a Casteneda-like mysticism to his life among the temples, he sometimes experienced dislocations of time and space while working at the site, or a bright light that inexplicably bathed them in a mystic glow. He felt that among the Maya survived "a rich living current of occult wisdom and practice, with its sources in an extremely ancient past, far beyond the purview of ordinary historical research."[15] We can imagine Maya archaeologist J. Eric S. Thompson thinking something along the same lines, considering his long-term friendship with Jacinto Cunil, his Maya *compadre* (his spiritual "co-godparent"), whom Thompson greatly respected.

But Le Plongeon, unfettered by university propriety, went far beyond anything Thompson would have dared commit to print, and speculated that the pre-Columbian Maya practiced mesmerism, were clairvoyant, and used magic mirrors to predict the future. They did have "magic mirrors" of a sort—dark obsidian reflecting dishes and pyrite plates—as well as oracular scrying stones, one of which fell into the hands of Elizabethan astrologer John Dee. Through this magical object from across the western ocean Dee communicated, by his own frank reports, with angels.[16]

Le Plongeon's most impressive achievement, the recovery of a massive stone Chac Mool sculpture from a depth of twenty-two feet under Chichén Itzá's ground level, remains one of the truly bizarre events in Mesoamerican archaeology. For it must be said that, although his methods were odd and primitive by modern standards, Le Plongeon was in 1876 one of the first archaeologists digging in Mexico. His methods were, admittedly, unorthodox. On one of the buildings at Chichén Itzá, Le Plongeon claimed he had deciphered the glyph for "Chac Mool" and he could thereby pinpoint a place to dig where he would find an effigy of this deity. To all appearances the spot was located more by random selection than by a hieroglyphic map. His assistants labored for days, and everyone must have thought the endeavor was doomed, when at a depth of twenty-two feet they struck solid stone. As they dug around its contours a huge sculpture in-the-round took shape. Using only jungle vines, tree trunks, and bark, they managed to raise it to the surface. A picture survives of a bemused and tired-looking Le Plongeon sitting next to the monolith he dubbed Chac Mool, right outside the hole where it had been interred for centuries. His long Rasputin-like beard and wide forehead are somehow archetypal, a nineteenth-century Indiana Jones destined from birth to do what he just did.

His comments about the Maya culture being 12,000 years old are somewhat understandable given the depth at which this sculpture was found. In fact, its depth is hard to explain unless the Maya themselves

Le Plongeon raises the Chac Mool.
From Salisbury (1877)

buried it when they would have had to do so, a brief nine centuries earlier, which is currently the consensus opinion of archaeologists. After raising the monolith, Le Plongeon promptly wrote a letter to the president of the Republic of Mexico, advising him of his findings and intentions, while offering a lesson in the antiquity and genius of the Maya race:

> *The results of my investigations, although made in territories for-*
> *bidden to the whites, and even the pacific Indians obedient to Mexi-*
> *can authority; surrounded by constant dangers, amid forests, where,*
> *besides the wild beasts, the fierce Indians of Chan-Santa-Cruz lay*
> *in ambush for me; suffering the pangs of hunger, in company with*
> *my young wife Alice Dixon Le Plongeon, have surpassed my most*
> *flattering hopes. Today I can assert, without boasting, that the dis-*
> *coveries of my wife and myself place us in advance of the travelers*
> *and archaeologists who have occupied themselves with American*
> *antiquities.*[17]

From somewhere that magic figure of 12,000 years was invoked:

> *The atmospheric action, the inclemencies of the weather, and more*
> *than that, the exuberant vegetation, aided by the impious and de-*
> *structive hand of ignorant iconoclasts, have destroyed and destroy*
> *incessantly these opera magna of an enlightened and civilized gen-*
> *eration that passed from the theatre of the world some twelve thou-*
> *sand years ago, if the stones, in their eloquent muteness, do not*
> *deceive.*[18]

Always ambitious, Le Plongeon hoped to display the monolith in time for the 1876 United States centennial celebration in Philadelphia. He and his crew succeeded in dragging the two-ton sculpture by oxcart sixty-five miles to Mérida, where it was promptly seized by the local authorities (they simply waited until it was delivered into their hands). They, in turn, were one-upped by a warship from the central government, which took it and then trans-ported it to a rail line that brought it to Mexico City, where it resides today.

Although dejected at this loss, Le Plongeon renewed his effort to bring his findings before the community of intellectuals and scientists. He sent small artifacts and photographs to Philadelphia, which were conveyed to Stephen Salisbury, an active member of the American Antiquarian Society in Worcester, Massachusetts, who agreed to publish some of Le Plongeon's findings in the society's journal. The relationship eventually bogged down as Le Plongeon's radical views of human history were laid out in each subsequent article.

He spoke of ancient connections between the Western Hemisphere and Asia, Africa, and Europe. Based on his archaeological findings, he described previous cycles of humanity going back tens of thousands of years. Plato's Atlantis and the ancient Egyptians were all part of the picture. It was too much for the proper New England intellectuals associated with the Antiquarian Society; Le Plongeon's cosmic views offended their Christian sentiments. Civilization going back 12,000 years? Why, everyone knew that the earth was created in 4004 BC. Bishop Usher had demonstrated that—it's in the Bible. Atlantean fantasy was trumped by biblical fantasy, and Le Plongeon's writings were no longer welcome in that thinking man's journal.

Salisbury washed his hands of Le Plongeon and, with Charles Bowditch of the Peabody Museum of Anthropology in Cambridge, found another Yucatán liaison in a young man named Edward Thompson. For many years Ed Thompson worked hard at Chichén Itzá, dredging the cenote for gold and other objects, and stayed in Yucatán for three decades. Having arrived in Yucatán in 1885, the year Le Plongeon left, Thompson's more reasonable, levelheaded exploration and documentation could commence. His credentials? Thompson had aroused excitement in scholarly circles with an article he had published in *Popular Science Monthly*. The title of the article was "Atlantis Not a Myth."

Photography Leads to Decipherment

Stephens and Catherwood are considered to have triggered the scientific investigation of Maya archaeology, but it was a process of fits and starts. Eventually, explorers were making efforts to carefully document the carvings and measure the sites. But for many decades these careful investigators continued to rub shoulders with the Atlantis hunters. Sometimes, they were one and the same person.

The distinction between professional investigator and independent explorer was less clear-cut than it is today. Writers who harbored Atlantean fantasies also contributed legitimate breakthroughs. And even into the twentieth century, when the methodologies of archaeological and anthropological science were perfected and applied with great care, many of the most significant breakthroughs continued to be made by independent, outside-the-field thinkers. It's a situation that characterizes, and practically defines, the process of breakthroughs in Maya studies.

Meanwhile, respected scholars from the era of modern decipherment sometimes let their own quasiracist views escape into the open, betraying a bias that could hinder interpretation as much as any Atlantean fantasy. For example, Maya scholar and linguist Richard Long wrote in the 1930s that writing marked the difference between civilization and barbarism, and American Indians did not write grammatically correct sentences and therefore had not attained civilization.[19] Long used an academic opinion about grammatically correct writing being the defining hallmark of civilization as a foil for his racism. Michael Coe called this for what it was, saying that Long's intolerance was rooted in an "underlying agenda . . . his unwillingness to grant the brown-skinned Maya a culture as complex as that of Europe, China, or the Near East."[20]

The 1880s did see the arrival of more serious explorations at Maya sites. The transition is nicely symbolized in the encounter, at the remote jungle city of Yaxchilán, between English photographer and researcher Alfred Maudslay and French adventurer Désiré Charnay. Maudslay was as honorable and unprepossessing as Stephens. His work was patient and thorough. Born in 1850 and educated as a gentleman at Cambridge, he took to traveling and became British counsel in Samoa in 1878. He went to the Americas and oversaw the operations of a gold mine in Mexico and then a fruit orchard in California, where he met his future wife. Having read Stephens, Maudslay realized that a complete record of the hieroglyphic inscriptions at all the major sites had yet to be undertaken. So he did just this, funding his seven trips to Quiriguá, Copán, Palenque, Yaxchilán, Chichén Itzá, and lesser-known sites.

In March of 1882 Alfred Maudslay established camp at Yaxchilán, shortly after encountering a band of Lacandon Indians. As Charnay's boat approached the shore he could see the displeasure in Charnay's face. But Maudslay graciously defused the tension, saying, "It's all right, there is no reason why you should look so distressed. My having the start of you was a mere chance, as it would have been a mere chance had it been the other way around. You need have no fear on my account for I am only an amateur, traveling for pleasure . . . you can name the town, claim to have discovered it, do as you please."[21]

While in Guatemala Maudslay met an American doctor named Gustav Eisen who was intrigued with the carvings and strange hieroglyphs Maudslay was documenting. Men of learning were of course aware of the Egyptian hieroglyphs and efforts to decipher the lost languages of the Middle East. The Rosetta Stone became a catchphrase, and its ingenious decoder, Jean-François Champollion, was a much-noted celebrity. Could something similar be possible for the lost cultures of eastern Mexico and Guatemala, which were now being referred to as "the Maya" civilization?

Maudslay's photographs provided a rich corpus of material for Eisen to analyze, who had an advantage over other researchers because he had a hotline to Maudslay's work. A friendly correspondence and exchange of materials between the two over the next several years led Maudslay to attempt to visit Eisen when he passed through San Francisco in 1893. By that time, however, Eisen had relinquished the task of decipherment, believing it to be hopeless, to an acquaintance named Joseph Goodman. As fate would have it, influenza delayed Maudslay's departure to the Orient as he passed through San Francisco in 1893, so he called on Eisen. Finding him out of town, he was instead put in contact with Goodman, who impressed him with his knowledge of the ancient calendrical system and the glyphs. The pieces of the hieroglyphic puzzle were starting to fall into place.

Goodman was born in 1838 on the East Coast, and by age twenty-three became the editor and owner of the *Territorial Enterprise* newspaper in Virginia City, Nevada Territory. The essays and poetry he wrote earned him some notice. A patriotic homage to Abe Lincoln was widely quoted, and the "Sagebrush" literary genre born in the pages of his progressive and entertaining newspaper anticipated the Bohemian set that Ambrose Bierce, George Sterling, and Jack London defined, a fin de siècle San Francisco phenomenon that was echoed a half-century later by the Beat writers. Goodman had made a fortune on his Comstock Lode mining investments, and in 1862 he gave a young writer named Samuel Clemens—later Mark Twain—his first job. They remained friends for life. He bought a raisin farm, moved to San Francisco, and was leading a comfortable life when he took up his Maya studies in the early 1880s.

It was a chance meeting with Dr. Eisen in 1882 that led Goodman right to the best source material for studying the glyphs—Maudslay's high-quality photographs that Eisen had secured copies of. Maudslay did great fieldwork but made little effort to interpret and decipher the corpus of glyphs he was documenting. Maudslay recognized the pioneering nature of Goodman's work on deciphering the Maya script and invited him to contribute an appendix to the multivolume work he was preparing for the Peabody Museum. This was a boon for an independent researcher like Goodman, and it forced professional scholars to take seriously his analysis. His contribution, called *The Archaic Maya Inscriptions*, appeared in 1897 as Volume 5 of Maudslay's *Biologia Centrali-Americana*.

When I was researching my book on the Maya Venus Calendar, it was essential to have the correct correlation. I studied the literature on the topic, weighed and tested the issues involved, and read of Goodman. I became interested in his efforts, much like my own, as an independent investigator trying to push back the fringes of scholarly consensus.

I wanted to see for myself Goodman's appendix to Maudslay's opus. The only place that had it was the rare-book archive up at CSU in Fort Collins. I called ahead and made the appointment. It took about an hour to drive to Fort Collins, and soon the book was placed in front of me. Goodman's "appendix" was in truth a full-scale book, more than two hundred pages of text, charts, graphs, tables, and illustrations. I read it through and took notes. He graciously included Eisen as a companion in his ongoing study of the mysterious glyphs, developing his own conviction that the glyphs were strictly numerical and calendrical. He believed to the end of his life that they had little to do with mythology or astronomy, writing that "the Maya calendars, like all modern scientific creations, were godless affairs."[22] This limiting bias

Joseph T. Goodman,
independent Maya researcher.

perhaps prevented Goodman from seeing a larger field of operation for the glyphs, namely astronomy, that we now know is there to be seen. Maya writing is also deeply involved with mythology, religion, history, and mathematical computation.

The Long Count calendar is intimately involved in these disciplines, and was used on hundreds of carved monuments and ceramic vessels for almost a thousand years (from roughly 36 BC to 909 AD). Mathematically, it is a system of counting days that uses five place values: the Kin (1 day), the Uinal (20 days), the Tun (360 days), the Katun (7,200 days), and the Baktun (144,000 days). A Long Count date begins with the Baktuns on the left. For example, the date 9.16.4.1.1 indicates that 9 Baktuns, 16 Katuns, 4 Tuns, 1 Uinal, and 1 Kin (day) have elapsed since the "zero date," written 0.0.0.0.0. The following sequential list of dates helps to understand how the Long Count toggles forward as days are counted:

Example A:	Example B:
9.16.4.1.18	12.19.19.17.18
9.16.4.1.19	12.19.19.17.19
9.16.4.2.0	13.0.0.0.0
9.16.4.2.1	0.0.0.0.1

Almost every place value level in the Long Count uses a base-20 system (toggles to zero when reaching 20). Notice, however, that the Uinal level (second from the right) contains 360 days and therefore toggles to zero when it reaches 18. Likewise, the 13-Baktun cycle can be thought of as toggling back to zero when 13 Baktuns are completed.

When exactly the zero date occurred has been the subject of the correlation debate (how the Maya calendar is correlated with our own Gregorian system). Goodman's greatest contribution to Mesoamerican studies is that he solved this problem. Knowing the correlation, we can calculate exactly when the end of the 13-Baktun cycle occurs (13.0.0.0.0).

Goodman's preface admits his status as an independent scholar but asserts the merit of his work for one simple reason: his "years of servitude to the glyphs."[23] With a bit of discreet sarcasm, he advises scholars and scientists to not be surprised if they "find themselves pushed rudely from their stools by irreverent outsiders," because

> For quite half a century they have had this study almost exclusively to themselves. The material by which alone it could be prosecuted was practically in their keeping, sealed to the rest of the world as though it were a hieratic mystery. And what has been the result? A deal of learned and pompous kowtowing to each other, but not a single substantial gain toward bottoming [figuring out] the inscriptions . . . we look hopelessly to them for a solution of the momentous enigma.[24]

I was amazed to read such a modern-sounding critique of academia. Through the years I encountered confirmations of Goodman's prescient words, time and time again, as I confronted rejections and casual dismissals from scholars who were completely unwilling, or unable, to rationally investigate the 2012 topic.

In an effort to decipher the script, Goodman made some solid contributions that many years later were acknowledged by Mayanists. He identified the full-figure glyphs for the place values of the Long Count, decoded the "head variant" glyphs, and recognized the importance of the 13-Baktun cycle. In an obituary, Sylvanus Morley praised his breakthrough work and noted that his calendar tables continued to serve as a valuable reference for scholars.

Goodman apparently had learned of, but evaded crediting, Ernst Förstemann's insights that were being published in Germany in the 1880s. Förstemann, another great independent trailblazer, working single-handedly with the Dresden Codex, had decoded the eclipse tables, a Venus almanac, how the 260-day calendar operated within the codex, the 20-base system, and the Long Count's base date on 4 Ahau 8 Cumku.

Goodman may have discreetly drawn from Förstemann, or perhaps he had hit on the same insights independently but had no way to prove it. J. Eric S. Thompson, who idolized Förstemann, believed he found a smoking-gun indication in Goodman's own words to the effect that he had read Förstemann. Perhaps he did. But we just don't know whether or not Goodman had already figured out what he was reading.

In any case, as often happens when a new discipline is being pioneered, valuable insights were presented side by side with wrong convictions. For example, in his book Goodman notes many Long Count dates from Palenque that are dated in the late 12th Baktun, before the current era dawned at the close of the previous 13-Baktun cycle. He thus was convinced that Palenque must be a very ancient site. But we now know that these texts at Palenque were in fact written in the eighth century AD and they were theological and calendrical back calculations, speculations about the birth of their deities prior to the beginning of the current Creation Era. The texts at Palenque are unusual expressions and help us understand how Pakal, the great king of Palenque, cast himself into the story of the Creation Deities.

For Goodman, the numbers were inviolable and should be read at face value. Those numbers from Palenque must have been recorded before the current era began, he reasoned, many thousands of years ago. Strangely, he noted an era-base date at Quiriguá, the famous Stela C Creation Monument that is dated 13.0.0.0.0 in the Long Count—the end of the previous 13-Baktun cycle—but he didn't seem to apply the same logic to the site of Quiriguá. This era base is documented by Goodman in his book as the beginning of a great cycle, a period of 13 Baktuns. He knew how many days one of these Creation cycles would consist of, because he figured out the values the Maya ascribed to the five place values in the Long Count. A great cycle of 13 Baktuns would thus consist of 1,872,000 days, or 5125.36 years.

But the big question that remained unsolved in Goodman's 1897 book was the correlation. All of the Long Count periods in his charts were free floating—no one knew how the Long Count dates should be correlated to a time frame we, with our Gregorian calendar, could relate to. Goodman had noted that many of the dates occurred during the period of the 9th Baktun, but when was this? Before Christ? After Christ? Fifth century AD or fifteenth century BC? Archaeologists did not yet have carbon-14 dating at their disposal, so the challenge of figuring out the correlation had to begin by drawing from historical documents compiled during the Conquest.

Goodman, like other investigators of the correlation question, drew from the *Historia* of Diego de Landa, where Katun periods in the Long Count were recorded. Charles Bowditch, in a 1901 article, made use of another Yucatec document, the *Books of Chumayel*, translated by Daniel Brinton. Bowditch's attempt to fix the correlation was inconclusive, but suggested that the earliest date from Copán would probably correspond to 34 AD— hundreds of years earlier than what is now accepted.

Goodman determined that the important Great Cycle period must consist of 13 Baktuns, not 20, based on the 13.0.0.0.0 date recorded at Quiriguá. This assertion rankled scholars such as Cyrus Thomas, who wanted to preserve an elegant symmetry in the Long Count system, which operated on a base-20 principle. It was thus believed that the Baktun level should toggle to zero after 20 Baktuns were completed, rather than 13. Goodman, surely, must be fooling himself. In the end, archaeology has proven Goodman correct, for we have no Creation Texts dated with 20 Baktuns, but many dated with 13. This illustrates how scholars sometimes invoke the appearance of logic to oust the facts of the matter and dismiss the better-informed conclusions of an outsider.

By 1905 Goodman had published an innocuous paper called "Maya Dates" in *American Anthropologist.* The correlation he worked out placed the beginning of the current 13-Baktun cycle in August of 3114 BC, though this wasn't explicitly stated. In fact, his conclusions are strangely obscure and could be noticed only by those few scholars who were familiar with the language and issues of the correlation debate. This could very well be one reason why Goodman's contribution sank into obscurity and was easily upstaged by Sylvanus Morley's paper of 1910, which presented a correlation 260 years earlier than Goodman's. Maya archaeologist Herbert Spinden became a supporter of Morley's correlation, which added more fuel to that fire. The issue is, of course, essential to the 2012 topic because it determines the placement of the 13-Baktun cycle-ending date. December 21, 2012 (the 13-Baktun cycle-ending date), is a consequence of Goodman's work. In terms of the Long Count calendar and the Maya Creation Mythology, the date is important because it signifies the end of a World Age, a chapter or phase of humanity.

Other proposed correlations had the backing of consensus and Goodman, although correct, did not engage the debate to advance his insight. There is no defense by Goodman on record that I know of. In the Peabody Archive of his papers, an unpublished manuscript of 1908 called "Annual, perpetual, chronological calendar analyses" may provide charts for the Long Count anchored to his correlation. We might find there the very first conscious recognition that the 13-Baktun cycle would end around the solstice of 2012. Goodman died in 1917, harboring the mistaken notion that the glyphs were exclusively computational—a kind of pure mathematics that had no relation to astronomy or history. He also died not realizing that his contribution to the correlation question would soon find a champion. Attention to Goodman's work was revived by the Mexican anthropologist Juan Martínez Hernández in 1926, who wrote two important papers that verified and expanded Goodman's arguments. Then a young J. Eric S. Thompson joined the effort and in 1927 fine-tuned the correlation by a few days, resulting in what is now known as the original Goodman-Martínez-Thompson (GMT) correlation.

J. ERIC S. THOMPSON, THE GNOSTIC ANAGOGUE

The story of J. Eric S. Thompson is essential for understanding the vicissitudes of Maya glyph decipherment as well as a polarizing bias that sometimes hobbles Maya studies to this day. Thompson occupied an unusual position in academia. He was, in a sense, the ultimate independent researcher, the archetypal free agent—he never taught classes, never had students or held decision-making board positions at research institutions. His background involved fighting in World War I as a teenager, and perfecting Spanish while living on his family's ranch in Argentina. Returning to England, he studied anthropology at Oxford and graduated in 1925.

While a student he developed an interest in the Maya calendar glyphs and taught himself how to compute dates in that strange system. This was a major selling point when he wrote to Carnegie archaeologist Sylvanus Morley asking to be hired on for the excavations at Chichén Itzá. So it came to pass, but Thompson's mind was restless with sifting dirt and he soon took a job at Chicago's Field Museum. There, while still in his twenties, he began publishing insightful papers on the correlation and hieroglyphic writing.

For many years Thompson was a staunch supporter of a fairly romantic idea, that the ancient Maya were mystical dreamers, eyes on the stars, and their writing recorded the high-minded philosophies of intellects unburdened by worldly concerns. Thompson's vision of the ancient Maya was later amended when certain independent upstarts showed how the glyphs did indeed record mundane political events and local histories. But he tenaciously insisted on a loftier function of Maya writing for the great majority of his career. Where did Thompson get this idea, one that he held close and defended like an emotional conviction?

Thompson, during his fieldwork for Carnegie in the 1920s, befriended a Maya man named Jacinto Cunil. The two were close friends for decades, and Cunil became for Thompson the epitome of Maya brilliance—hardworking, smart, and a devout true friend. Michael Coe met Jacinto in 1949 and noted that, despite Thompson's lengthy homage to his friend in his *Rise and Fall of Maya Civilization*, he had suppressed some truly "weird" qualities. Cunil was, according to Coe, of the Dionysian temperament, brimming with mystical insights and spiritual observations. He must have symbolized for Thompson the true nature of the ancient Maya character: very smart in the expected way the term is used, but also of a genius operating on a level beyond the spare analyzing and deductions of archaeologists and anthropologists.[25] Curiously, Thompson was remiss in painting this fuller picture, perhaps because it was unscientific and yet informed his deepest convictions. Cunil was for Thompson what the 150-year-old shaman was for Le Plongeon; what Don Juan was for Casteneda.

As Thompson's academic star was rising in the early 1930s, the debate was raging between phonetic and ideographic approaches to deciphering Maya writing. Thompson vehemently opposed the phonetic approach. He held to a more expanded interpretation of the glyphs and resisted allowing them to be collapsed into one interpretation, one spoken decipherment (the goal of the phonetic approach). His viewpoint sometimes comes across in his writings as a belief that the glyphs were ambiguous or hopelessly complicated, that they could not be rendered into spoken language. At other times, an allowance for multiple meanings seems his position. He liked to refer to the glyphs not as phonetic components, or even ideograms, but as "metaphoragrams"—symbols that represented, via metaphor, other sets of information.

In his opus on Maya hieroglyphic writing from 1950, we hear some surprisingly mystical sentiments:

> *Without a full understanding of the text we can not, for instance, tell whether the presence of a dog refers to that animal's role as bringer of fire to mankind or to his duty of leading the dead to the underworld.* That such mystical meanings are embedded within the glyphs is beyond doubt, *but as yet we can only guess as to the association the Maya author had in mind.[Emphasis added.]*[26]

He further stated unequivocally that "the glyphs are anagogical," an incredible circumstance when you consider what "anagogical" means. The dictionary definition blandly defines the word as referring to a meaning that goes "beyond literal, allegorical, and moral" interpretations, to a sense that is "spiritual and mystical." In the use of the term by philosophers such as Henry Corbin, an anagogical symbol is "upward leading"—it leads one upward into an integrative understanding that transcends the literal domain of interpretation. Put simply, it points to a higher transcendent reality. The symbol, or glyph, is merely a device or doorway through which the "reader" can access a higher state to embrace multiple sets of references and interrelated meanings.

Let's get into this a little, as it is important for undertanding a key idea in this book—that of a higher, universal meaning implicit in Maya thought. Joseph Campbell said something very profound about the nature of myth, which counters the modern, tacitly agreed upon notion that "myth is a lie." Campbell wrote "myth is the secret opening through which the inexhaustible energies of the cosmos pour into human cultural manifestations."[27] Mythologies and the symbols they contain are not merely signposts for moral decrees, but embody collective and universal themes. The symbol, which is what hieroglyphic writing most closely represents (much more so than alphabetic script), is thus a doorway that leads the open mind into a higher, more integrative space. Religious art and iconography was originally intended to be anagogical in precisely this way, to lead the viewer, the initiate, upward into the mystery of the symbol's ineffable root.

Here we glimpse what is rightly called the Perennial Philosophy, a subject we'll explore in more detail in Chapter 8. For now, suffice it to say that symbols are the language of this Perennial Philosophy and should be correctly interpreted as being much more than signs. As Joseph Campbell said, signs denote exactly what they say: A yield sign means yield. Symbols, on the other hand, connote something beyond their surface appearance.

We seem to have hidden in Thompson a profound multidimensional (or, as he himself said, anagogical) approach to the glyphs, true to what hieroglyphic writing requires in order to do it justice. Thompson has apparently been largely misunderstood on his insistence that the glyphs be seen as anagogical metaphoragrams. Why? Simply because science and academicians don't allow for a "higher" perspective, or indigenous writing containing "gnosis" (even when it does). Furthermore, if scientists tend to deny the transcendent on the grounds that it is subjective and therefore less real than the objective order, one wonders to what extent this conviction colors their interpretations of Maya metaphysics and spirituality. If a metaphysics of transcendence is an essential key to Maya cosmology, how can scholars who are biased against such a notion be reliable interpreters of that worldview?

Although sensitive to a larger concept, Thompson defended his notions to the detriment of progress that could only occur if the phonetic elements were acknowledged. For the glyphs, if indeed they had multiple meanings, should also contain within them a range of components, including phonetic elements, rebus-style signs, astronomy, and references to mundane events. Notwithstanding his bias against phoneticism, the more nuanced implications of Thompson's "anagogical" approach to the glyphs have been lost and we remember only his romanticized vision of the ancient Maya as stargazing philosophers. And Thompson's myth of the dreamy stargazer was eventually trounced, but I think way too much of the baby was thrown out with the bathwater. Thompson was apparently a closet Gnostic, even if he himself disliked the term. He believed that the glyphs were tools for directly accessing a higher perspective. In addition to being a stubborn pedagogue, he was also a secret anagogue, one who believed in the anagogical nature of Maya writing, much as a devout Christian can gaze upon the icon of suffering Jesus and be led upward into the mystical unity of eternal love. The paradox of Thompson is probably best understood in this light, for behind every pedagogue stands an anagogue telling him he is wrong.

My reading of Thompson and Maya cosmovision is much closer to statements made by modern epigraphers (those who decipher the glyphs) than one might suspect. Stephen Houston, for example, wrote about the relationship between the built environment and Maya beliefs, observing that the two define and reinforce each other like a mutually arising chicken and egg. He asked: "Is the cosmos ordered like a house or is the house ordered like the cosmos?" (This polarity can also be stated "does the microcosm reflect the macrocosm, or vice versa?" and effectively works with any pairs of opposites.) He answered: "The concept of reciprocal metaphor allows us to resolve such questions by acknowledging the indissoluble, almost playful association between semantic domains."[28] In other words, both domains are mutually arising. What Houston said here, cloaked a bit in abstract terminology, is that the Maya held to a nondual philosophy. Their worldview was informed by the mystical vision of the transcendence of opposites. This is both Gnostic and anagogical. Of course, when I say it bluntly it sounds offensive to academic ears; better to cloak it in sufficiently labyrinthine grammatical constructs so, like Thompson but unlike Le Plongeon, you won't be accused of cavorting with Maya mystics.

Even today, discussion on the more ethereal achievements of the ancient Maya is likely to be scoffed at as a tiresome echo of Thompson's dreamy stargazer sentiment. The tides shift over the decades in academia. There has been, on one hand, a tendency to see the ancient Maya as high-minded philosophers advancing human knowledge in ways comparable to those of the Greeks, Egyptians, and Hindus. Then, on the other hand, scholars dispense with such views of the ancient Maya (even if they are true) and instead focus on warfare, sacrifice, resource management, kingly power trips, and all the tangible nuts and bolts of running a civilization.

There's a problem in how scholars emphasize certain facets of an ancient culture. A tendency to make them relatable to modern minds will emphasize characteristics that are recognizable in our own culture—a reflex called reification. This ethnocentric tendency often wafts through fields of investigation unconsciously, and the impulse to identify the aspects of ancient Maya culture that we can relate to seems natural, a given. Scholars consequently do not try to shift their consciousness in order to perceive the unique traits of an ancient culture and are instead content to interpret it through the unmoving filters of their own paradigm's values and assumptions.

Thus, a common idea in pop consciousness has been that the ancient Maya were barbaric, bloodlusting warmongers. This can be argued with specific examples from Maya history but shouldn't be generalized and applied to Maya civilization as a whole. It is partly true in the same way that unpro-voked wars launched by the United States, motivated by self-interest, have killed millions of civilians. But that doesn't tell the whole story, as any high civilization will engage in an entire spectrum of activities, achievements, and motivations. Those who see the ancient Maya as warmongers are more likely than not engaging in a psychological shadow projection, denying their own ignorance and savagery and projecting it onto a handy "other." The same kind of projection happens with 2012, which is turned into an apocalypse when the Maya, having a cyclic time philosophy, would never have thought about cycle endings in such a way. Many have projected the concept of the apoca-lypse onto 2012 when it was never there in the first place.

Thompson was willing to advance and defend the notion that the glyphs were more than just sounds, phonemes, or even signs that could be easily deciphered. He preferred the concept of metaphoragrams and believed, much like Goodman, that the hieroglyphs didn't contain histories. The picture he painted of the ancient Maya was one of idealized stargazers philosophizing in towered observatories like the ancient Greeks. These views were eventually overturned, but at an early stage of his career he made his mark by decoding the correlation question, with the help of Goodman and Martínez. The cor-relation thus became known as the original GMT (Goodman, Martínez, and Thompson). By 1927 it was clear that the fabled zero date of the Long Count calendar could be located in mid-August, 3114 BC.

With this now in place and on the billboard for scholars to ponder over, we should expect that they would immediately calculate the Long Count periods using the free-floating tables Goodman published in 1897. A very significant Long Count period, documented on the Quiriguá monument Maudslay had found and Goodman commented on, is the 13-Baktun "Cre-ation" cycle. And so we find, in Thompson's article of 1927, a table that calculates the various Katun and Baktun endings, utilizing the unprecedented, slightly revised, Goodman correlation.[29] The chart, unfortunately, ends with Katun 12.16.0.0.0, correlated to February 15, 1934 (original GMT). However, an astute reader could easily isolate the Baktun endings given on pages 19–21 of the chart and extrapolate the date of the great 13-Baktun ending:

7.0.0.0.0	10 Ahau	June 5, 353 BC
8.0.0.0.0	9 Ahau	September 6, 41 AD
9.0.0.0.0	8 Ahau	December 10, 435
10.0.0.0.0	7 Ahau	March 16, 830
11.0.0.0.0	6 Ahau	June 17, 1224
12.0.0.0.0	5 Ahau	September 20, 1618

Based on a simple visual assessment, the next date in the sequence, for 13.0.0.0.0, looks like it should fall on or about December 23, 2012 AD. And that it did, according to the original GMT correlation that Thompson was arguing for (later corrected to December 21). It's hard to imagine that this projection was never performed, and how Thompson or other scholars might have speculated on what it might mean for the 13-Baktun cycle to end near a solstice. There are no essays or articles that I am aware of that reveal any brainstorming along these lines. The reason why, I believe, is twofold. First, the original GMT correlation still needed to be revised two days, which occurred by 1950, only then effectively bringing the end-date into exact congruence with the solstice on December 21. Without this, scholars may have calculated the 13-Baktun cycle end-date but, seeing it fell on December 23, dismissed it as irrelevant. In addition, it wasn't until 1930 and then 1934 that Thompson contributed more-detailed arguments to the correlation question. By then the depression was in full swing; everyone's minds were on other things, perhaps.

The second reason is, I believe, the real culprit, and it involves a conceptual bias in how scholars tended to treat the Maya calendar. The bias would have had all the support of the conventional attitudes of Western science and the Judeo-Christian worldview. Science says that time flows from past to future, that all events are the effects of previous causes. This model of causality rejects the idea that future states might define the events that are being drawn toward that future state. This is called teleology, anathema to scientific causality. It's more welcome in the discourses of philosophy, and philosopher Alfred North Whitehead is the best-known proponent of the idea, which was adopted by Terence McKenna.

Judeo-Christian time philosophy is linear; Creation happened a long time ago. An inherently different time concept, which is evident in Mesoamerican calendars and cosmology, has been largely overlooked by scholars: the cyclic time philosophy that sees past and future Creation events being analogically united during cycle endings. The idea that ancient Maya calendar makers were projecting into the future, to target a future event, is also supported by two observations: In Maya thought the important event, such as birth, happens at the end of a time process—in this example, the end of a 260-day interval during which embryogenesis occurs. Second, end naming is used in the Long Count such that a given period is named by its last day. For example, we are currently in the 4 Ahau Katun because its last day falls on 4 Ahau.

These considerations apparently mattered little to scholars of the 1930s and '40s, for other challenges were demanding their attention. Ethnographic opportunities, for example, were opening up in Mexico and Central America. Anthropologists such as Oliver La Farge, J. Lincoln, and Maud Oakes were spending lots of time in remote Maya villages documenting survivals of calendar rites thought to have been long forgotten. And, of course, the decipherment of the ever-enigmatic Maya hieroglyphic script came to be of primary importance. But Thompson resisted what promised to crack the whole thing wide open.

When the brilliant independent linguist Benjamin Whorf decoded, in the early 1930s, phonetic elements in the glyphs, Thompson pounced. He craftily critiqued the weak details of the arguments yet evaded the overall importance of the new perspective. After Whorf died at the young age of forty-four, Thompson flayed Whorf's work. It was a difficult and revealing chapter for both Thompson's and Whorf's legacy. In retrospect, Thompson was very right about the errors in Whorf's work. However, Whorf's overall hunch was correct—the glyphs did contain phonetic elements. Unfortunately for Thompson, two more pioneer figures were soon to appear, and they hailed from a country that he had a personal problem with: Russia. Like many people, Thompson adopted a hatred of Communism after World War I and harbored bad feelings toward Russians throughout his life.

Russian artist Tatiana Proskouriakoff belonged to a sector of humanity that is often overlooked but has made some of the most important breakthroughs in Maya studies. That category is: woman. When she worked on the Maya site of Piedras Negras as an artist, she naturally became intrigued with Maya writing. Copying the glyphs over and over again, she became familiar with repeating patterns. Soon she identified what she believed to be historical events and glyph names for rulers. This, from Thompson's ahistorical viewpoint, was not acceptable. And yet, as he himself had to eventually admit, almost on his deathbed, she was right.

Yuri Knorosov, the second Russian of note, experienced the epitome of what happens when an outsider advances a new insight. The insight was shocking to the establishment because it came about not by amassing more and more data until the correct interpretation appeared; no, the data had been lying around for decades, waiting for the right person to come along and reframe the material in such a way that the right interpretation clicked into place. This was especially true for the breakthroughs in hieroglyphic decipherment advanced by Knorosov in the 1960s. There was a key, long present, that had gone unrecognized for many years. That key, as Benjamin Whorf had proposed decades earlier, was that the glyphs were both phonetic and logographic (representing a spoken word). Thompson resisted Knorosov's work as if it heralded a Communist invasion, and the avalanche of epigraphic progress really got under way only after Thompson's death in 1975.

WHO SAID IT'S THE CYCLE ENDING?

All these players in the evolution of Maya studies contributed in their own ways to the key issue for the 2012 discussion: the correlation question. Despite Thompson's confirmation of Goodman's neglected work, the correlation question continued to tug at scholars. When ethnographic information was gathered in the 1930s and '40s, it became apparent that the surviving 260-day count did not jibe with the proposed original GMT correlation. It was two days out of joint. Thompson took another look at the historical documents and realized that two leap days had been overlooked in the de Landa material. Thus, as of 1950 the modified GMT-2 became the final correction, which brought all the criteria into congruence.

In 1946, elder archaeologist Sylvanus Morley published his magnum opus, *The Ancient Maya*. It offered a curious table as Appendix 1, in which Katun and half-Katun endings were correlated with their Gregorian equivalents. But the table ended with 12.5.0.0.0, 8 Ahau 3 Pax, April 4, 1717 AD. As with Thompson's chart of 1927, however, the sharp reader could track the Baktun endings given and easily extrapolate that the 13th Baktun would end just about on December 23, 2012. But the entire table was calculated with the original GMT correlation. The third edition of *The Ancient Maya* (1956) corrected the table two days, to the new value of the GMT-2 correlation, but the table, as in the first edition, remained incomplete. Nevertheless, the table provided a convenient resource that could have been easily extended out to the cycle ending in 2012. In fact, Maya epigrapher Barbara MacLeod told me that, as a Peace Corp worker in Belize in 1973, she did just that. It wasn't until the fourth edition of *The Ancient Maya* (1983) that the tables were extended out to the end of the 13-Baktun cycle: 13.0.0.0.0, 4 Ahau 3 Kankin = December 21, 2012.

By that time, Michael Coe's 1966 book, *The Maya*, had already offered what was to be the first documented mention of the 13-Baktun cycle ending. But there was a problem. Although Coe knew and followed the correct GMT correlation, the date reported (December 24, 2011) was in error. It's not exactly clear how Coe arrived at this date, especially when the reference table in Morley's book was so easily available. Coe's error was corrected in a later edition, but the damage was done. By 1971 other developments in the popular appreciation of the ancient calendar were astir. Tony Shearer published his poetic treatise that year, *Quetzalcoatl: Lord of Dawn*, in which he suggested that 1987 would be a great cycle ending prophesied by the ancient Aztecs. Soon afterward Frank Waters came out with his book on the Maya cycle ending, *Mexico Mystique*, using Michael Coe's date. A watershed moment occurs here in the transmission of obscure academic machinations out into the public arena. The first wave in a growing tsunami of popular books on 2012 was about to begin.

CHAPTER TWO

THE LONG CAREER OF THE LONG COUNT

We can, therefore, with all good conscience hail our
"New World Hipparchus" as a creative genius in his
own right, not beholden to the ideas or ideology of
any other people or region of the world . . .
Soconusco may well have served as a bridgehead
into Mesoamerica for a variety of South American
cultural traits, but there seems little doubt that it
constituted the very "hearth," or cradle, of the
intellectual life of indigenous North America. The
unique 260-day sacred almanac is the product of a
convergence of time and space that may be directly
traced to Izapa.[1]

—VINCENT MÄLMSTROM

Time doesn't have an end, but it does have a middle—so say the modern Quiché Maya.[2] And that middle, always, is located right dead center in the Now. A calendar, however, is not time, in the same way that a map is not the territory. As philosopher Ken Wilber said, "It's fatal to confuse the two."[3]

The 13-Baktun cycle of the Long Count calendar has a beginning, a middle, and an end. Its beginning or "zero date" (August 11, 3114 BC) does not indicate when the system was invented. That date was a back calculation made thousands of years later by the creators of the Long Count. Similarly, the end date in 2012 was a forward calculation. Together, the alpha and omega of Maya time philosophy delineate a World Age lasting 5,125.36 years. That's 1,872,000 days, to be exact.

The Maya doctrine of World Ages is found in *The Popol Vuh*, a document recorded in the 1550s by Quiché Maya elders. In it, we read that humanity has passed through a sequence of World Ages, and each time one of these World Age cycles comes to completion, a transformation and renewal of humanity occurs. Right away, it's clear that the 13-Baktun cycle of the Long Count and the World Age doctrine in *The Popol Vuh* are linked. They are both expressions of an underlying World Age doctrine.

At San Bartolo, Izapa, and Calakmul archaeologists have found murals, sculptures, and carvings depicting very early scenes from *The Popol Vuh* that are more than 2,100 years old—right around the time that Long Count dates began to be carved on monuments. Why did the ancient people of Mesoamerica create the Long Count? Who were they, where was it done, and when? These are important questions to explore if we really want to understand the 2012 story.

When my investigation of the Maya calendars began some twenty-five years ago, there was no context in academia for studying 2012, and the scant references in the literature were completely unconcerned with trying to reconstruct the original intentions of the Maya. (Waters's book *Mexico Mystique* is the exception, which I'll discuss in Chapter 3.) In an effort to pierce the many layers of disinformation that accrete around the 2012 topic, we should consider these four guiding questions to be paramount to understanding 2012, indispensable if we care at all about the authentic perspective on the meaning of the cycle-ending date in 2012: What is the Long Count calendar, how does it work, where was it developed, and when?

It's a bizarre fact that the vast majority of current commentaries on 2012 (including popular books, academic appraisal, and mass media documentaries) do not concern themselves with these questions. It's as if approaching 2012 through the tradition that created it is anathema, is irrelevant, is a distraction from the juicier hype that is supposedly "what the public wants to hear." Why this incredible disregard for the most obvious, and clearest, approach to 2012? The best I can surmise is that 2012 has gained the status of an icon, a cultural symbol, to be used and often abused for purposes that have nothing to do with its origins and the intentions of its creators.

It's important to hold up a mirror to what is happening in the 2012 discussion, which I've observed gaining steam for two decades, and identify this one overarching circumstance. Doing so will help us understand why the 2012 discussion is such a mess and difficult for newcomers to navigate. And yes, gaining a good working knowledge of the Maya calendar system takes some commitment and study. But by sweeping the Maya source of the 2012 topic under the carpet, the way has been cleared for a smorgasbord of under-informed writers and market-driven hypesters to pillage 2012 on their way through to the next trendy topic. The solution? Well, it's simple: Ask the four questions and go right to the heart of the 2012 calendar. We'll undertake this first, and later we'll look at the wider implications of the 2012 cultural meme (a meme is an idea complex that takes on great meaning and spreads).

Approaching the thing in itself, it must be said, is not necessarily easy. Not as easy as spinning out clever designer interpretations, recycled dooms-day prophecies, or relabeled ascension techniques. What is really at stake, and what will be meaningful after 2012, is the accurate recovery of a lost para-digm, a forgotten cosmology. The problem is that the answers to the four questions are, on one level, not that clear cut. The precise "when and where" of the origins of the Long Count are not laid out in some hieroglyphic text. On the other hand, investigators of 2012 ("2012ologists," as I've called them) should be willing to work harder than that. After we've made some informed deductions about the Long Count's purpose and origins, we will be able to identify some very clear answers.

LONG COUNT ORIGINS

Several reconstructions of the origin point of the Long Count have been of-fered by scholars. Despite the complex relationships between the Long Count, the 260-day tzolkin (pronounced zol-KEEN), and the 365-day haab, scholars have attempted to track the calendars backward to when all the various cycles met at a seasonal quarter, such as the summer solstice. With this methodology, Munro Edmonson proposed that the Long Count was inaugurated on the June solstice of 355 BC, when all the cycles came together.[4] Other scholars suggested other dates, and it's hard to really know for sure which criteria defined the procedure for the ancient calendar makers. There's no direct evidence.

It's certain, however, that by 36 BC the Long Count was being carved in stone, because on Stela 2 from Chiapa de Corzo in Mexico we find the date 7.16.3.2.13, corresponding to December 6, 36 BC. Five years later, the famous Stela C from Tres Zapotes was carved with the date 7.16.6.16.18 (corresponding to September 1, 32 BC). On both these monuments, the full Long Count date could be reconstructed. An incomplete Baktun 7 date is recorded on Stela 2 from Tak'alik Ab'aj, meaning it must have been carved before the commencement of Baktun 8 in 41 AD. The Baktun number is clearly 7, but the Katun could be 6, 11, or 16, meaning possibly as old as 236 BC, 137 BC, or 39 BC. If it represents the last possible date in the 16th Katun of the 7th Baktun, it would correspond to July of 19 BC. There's a fair chance it is the oldest Long Count monument known.

Continuing farther down the Pacific coast from Tak'alik Ab'aj, a well preserved late Cycle 7 monument at El Baúl clearly reads 7.19.15.7.12 (March 2, 37 AD). Stela 5 from Tak'alik Ab'aj contains two Long Count dates; one is clearly 126 AD and the other is either 83 AD or 103 AD. Farther to the north but within the region known as the Isthmus of Tehuantepec, the site of Cerro de las Mesas contains two early Cycle 8 dates.[5] La Mojarra Stela 1, inscribed in "the Isthmian script," contains Long Count dates corresponding to 143 AD and 156 AD.[6] Linda Schele was able to date the Hauberg Stela with astronomical references in its inscription to March of 197 AD (Long Count 8.7.17.14.4).[7]

However far back the Long Count's origins may go, something definite happened in the middle of the first century BC—it was carved in stone. As

"Cycle 7" (355 BC to 41 AD). Drawing by Barbara MacLeod

scholar Prudence Rice said, "time became materialized."[8] The willingness to commit the calendar to stone could be considered analogous to images of the Buddha, which only began to appear hundreds of years after he lived. Before that, it was forbidden. However, we can't even be sure that there wasn't a previous legacy of uncarved Long Count records written on perishable bark paper. But the material evidence, assessed at face value, suggests an appearance of the tradition in the first century BC.

As for where this occurred, the locations of the earliest Long Count dates embrace a rather large region of southern Mexico, stretching through the Isthmus of Tehuantepec south along the Pacific coast (a region called Soconusco) and into the steep coastal piedmont of Guatemala. The southern part of this Isthmian region was home to a pre-Maya culture called by Michael Coe "the Izapan civilization."[9]

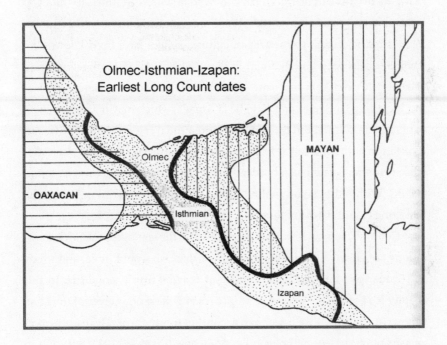

The Isthmian region, origin of the Long Count. After Rice (2007)

Vincent Malmström emphasized that Izapa is situated at an important latitude, 15° North. Within the tropics, the sun can pass through the zenith, the exact center of the sky overhead. It does so at high noon on two days every year, but the exact days depend on your latitude. It just so happens that at Izapa, the solar zenith transit dates are May 1 and August 12. These dates divide the year into 105- and 260-day sections. Furthermore, August 12 is within a day of the zero date of the 13-Baktun cycle of the Long Count. Izapa's latitude thus highlights the 260-day period and the zero date (or "base" date) of the Long Count. For these reasons, Malmström and other scholars believe that Izapa was the origin place of the 260-day tzolkin as well as the Long Count calendar.[10]

The Izapan civilization was transitional, between the Olmec and the Maya. Its origins can be traced back to overlap with the Olmec, around 600 BC, and its end came around 100 AD as it transitioned into early Maya forms. Many sites belonging to the Izapan cultural sphere have been known and studied for decades, among them El Baúl, Tak'alik Ab'aj, Kaminaljuyu, and Chiapa de Corzo. Very early sites are now being uncovered, dating to 1000 BC, including La Blanca and Paso de la Amada, which may have given birth to the Izapan culture. But the ritual and ceremonial centerpiece of the Izapan civilization is the site called Izapa, located in southern Chiapas a short distance from the Guatemalan border. Its first monuments were carved around 400 BC. Within the Izapan civilization's considerable sphere of influence, the first Long Count dates are found.

Cultural changes, historical processes, and the genesis of calendrical traditions are always a lot more complicated than we would hope, and to say that Izapa gave birth to the Long Count may be overly simplistic. In this chapter it's not all that critical, as we are tracing the entire career of the Long Count. In Chapter 4 we'll see that, according to my theory, Izapa preserves an astronomy-based mythology that points us directly to 2012. Suffice it to say that the earliest Long Count dates appear in the first century BC and it is likely that the Isthmian region and the Izapan civilization gave rise to the calendars. As Michael Coe said, "The priority of Izapa in the very important adoption of the Long Count is quite clear cut."[11] It's interesting to note that the development of hieroglyphic writing accelerated as the adoption of the Long Count spread.

On the fascinating Stela 5 from Tak'alik Ab'aj, Izapan figures are engaged in a ritual with other figures that are clothed differently. Archaeologists believe it represents a transfer of power from Izapa to Tak'alik Ab'aj, complete by the monument's final Long Count date, 126 AD.[12] The dawn of Maya civilization was beginning. Today, Maya day-keepers (those who track the 260-day tzolkin calendar) do rituals and burn incense in front of this monument. By 126 AD, Izapa was basically frozen in time. Instead of its monuments being ritually destroyed, as often happened, the site was preserved and was likely a pilgrimage destination over the centuries.[13] Many of its sixty carved monuments depict various episodes from the Maya Creation Myth. For two reasons, the site apparently was intended to provide initiations into cosmological knowledge and shamanic mysteries. Initiatory teaching stories about the three cosmic centers were elaborated in the three main monument groups and traditional tools of initiatory rites, powerful hallucinogens found in toads and mushrooms, were used by the shamans at Izapa. This is clear from the Bufo marines toad depicted on Stela 6, which secretes a fluid containing the powerful hallucinogen 5-MEO-DMT, as well as the many ritual mushroom stones found in the region.

Stela 29 from Tikal contains a completely fleshed-out Long Count date, corresponding to 292 AD. It is written with the full Calendar Round and Long Count positions according to the Tikal haab system. It has often been called "the first Maya Long Count date" and was, in fact, used to define the onset of the Maya Classic Period (300 AD). But thereby calling it the first Maya date is circular and misleading (like saying "the car is mine because it belongs to me"). It gives the unsuspecting reader the impression that there were no real Long Count dates prior to this. This perspective is obsolete considering all the previous Long Count dates just overviewed.

At Tikal, the Long Count was used for a very long time, up into the ninth century AD. As other sites adopted the Long Count, its functions embraced more than just timekeeping. It was inextricably interwoven with kingship, astronomy, building dedications, sacrifice and renewal rites, warfare, mythology, huge distance-number calculations, and ritually timed ceremony. Given the Long Count's multifarious applications, this would be a good time to get a handle on the basics of how the Maya calendar system works.

The three main components of the system are the 260-day tzolkin, the 365-day haab, and the 20-base Long Count system. A study of these various calendars and day-counts, with their attendant deities and ceremonies, could keep us busy for many years. The tzolkin, the haab, the Calendar Round, and the Venus Round comprise one coherently integrated system of timekeeping, astronomy, and theological beliefs and was used by both the Maya and the Central Mexican cultures, including the Aztecs. None of these calendars, however, are responsible for the famed 2012 cycle-ending date. The cycle ending in 2012 is an artifact of a uniquely Maya calendar called the Long Count. This is fact numero uno of the 2012 topic, in light of which the many designer systems that modern authors are inventing should be taken with a rather large grain of salt.

CALENDAR SYSTEM BASICS

The keystone of the Mesoamerican calendar system is the 260-day tzolkin (a term derived from the Quiché Maya term *chol-qih*, "count of days"). The tzolkin consists of 13 numbers and 20 day-signs. Each day-sign has an oracular meaning, with many layers of linguistic puns and cultural references that provide a rich database for Maya calendar priests to weave their interpretations. The special role of the calendar priest in Maya culture was, and is, to track and interpret the days of the sacred tzolkin calendar, to do ceremony at shrines, offer prayers to the ancestors, and consult with clients on personal and community matters.

The 260-day tzolkin calendar first appears in the archaeological record around 600 BC, and it is still being followed today in the remote villages of highland Guatemala. The thirteen numbers provide three levels of qualities that affect the intensity of the day-sign. Numbers 1–4 are mild, 5–9 are neutral, and numbers 10–13 are intense. The twenty day-signs in the surviving Quiché Maya calendar have the following meanings:

Quiché Maya:	English:	Yucatec Maya:
Imox	Left-handed	Imix
Iq	*Wind*	Ik
Aq'ab'al	Foredawn	Akbal
K'at	Net	Kan
Kan	Snake	Chicchan
Kame	Death	Cimi
Kej	*Deer*	Manik
Q'anil	Yellow	Lamat
Toj	Thunder	Muluc
Tz'i	Dog	Oc
B'atz	Monkey	Chuen
E	*Tooth*	Eb
Aj	Cane	Ben
Ix	Jaguar	Ix
Tz'ikin	Bird	Men
Ajmak	Sinner	Cib
N'oj	*Thought*	Caban
Tijax	Blade	Eznab
Kawuq	Rain	Cauac
Junajpu	Marksman[14]	Ahau

The Yucatec Maya day-sign words are given in the third column, since those are often used as a standard reference. Notice that the Quiché and Yucatec words are often different. This does not mean that the calendars followed were essentially different, as some have presumed. The day-signs use different words in different languages, just as our calendar's weekday names are different in different languages. For example, Lunes (Spanish) equals Monday (English). The important thing to be aware of is that the same placement of the tzolkin was followed throughout Mesoamerica prior to the Conquest. Calendar priests in Central Mexico, Yucatán, and Guatemala were following the same day-sign placement. The tradition stemmed from the same root and spread in an unbroken fashion throughout Mesoamerica. At the time of the Conquest, day-keepers in widely separate regions were essentially following the same tzolkin placement.

Also notice in the table above that four of the day-signs are italicized. These are the four Year Bearers, the four day-signs that can inaugurate a New Year. The Year Bearers arise when the tzolkin interfaces with the 365-day year. The 365-day vague year, or haab, scheduled mundane agricultural events and festivals. Together with the tzolkin, it is an essential component of the calendar system known as the Calendar Round. Notice here that the smaller cycles combine to generate larger metacycles—an indication that the Maya thought of time as taking the form of harmonically nested cycles.

A Calendar Round is completed when the tzolkin and haab come back to their starting points together, which takes 18,980 days (13 days less than 52 solar years). All of the combinations of tzolkin and haab are then exhausted, and ritual observances in the New Fire ceremony occurred to facilitate the renewal of time. The 365-day haab is a vague approximation of the solar year, which is about one-quarter of a day longer. For this reason, New Year's Day falls back one day every four years. It is clear, however, that the Maya allowed this to happen for calculational purposes, while at the same time they were aware of the precise length of the solar year by way of their "year drift formula" (in which 1,507 solar years = 1,508 haab).

There are four Year Bearers because the five-day "extra" month in the haab makes each successive New Year's Day toggle forward five days in the tzolkin. Since there are twenty day-signs, it takes four of these five-day leaps to return to the first Year Bearer; thus, four Year Bearers. The Year Bearers symbolize the four directions, the four quarters of the year (two equinoxes and two solstices), and the four sacred mountains. Of the four Year Bearers one is chief, and in the earliest calendar system the chief Year Bearer was symbolically associated with the December solstice, because that is the most important turnabout day in the year, when the light returns and the sun is reborn. For the modern Quiché Maya the chief Year Bearer is Kej (Deer). A Calendar Round (roughly 52 years) is completed when the chief Year Bearer cycles through the 13 numbers until it once again has a 1 coefficient. The next Quiché Calendar Round begins on 1 Deer, February 18, 2026. This means that the present Calendar Round began on 1 Deer on March 3, 1974.

The cycles of Venus were brought into this calendar scheme by a fortunate relationship with the double Calendar Round. Venus goes through periods as evening star and morning star, and will rise in the east as morning star every 584 days. The Mesoamerican astronomers noticed that five of these Venus periods equal eight years. In other words, Venus will rise as morning star five times every eight years, returning to the same place in the zodiac. In effect, Venus traces a five-pointed star around the zodiac during this time, explaining the ancient Babylonian association of Venus with pentagrams. All of the cycles of sun, tzolkin, and Venus are completed in two Calendar Rounds, just under 104 years. This period is called the Venus Round.

The 52-haab Calendar Round is a complete system of timekeeping and was used throughout Mesoamerica in ancient times. In fact, the Aztecs used it in their New Fire ceremony, in which the Pleiades were observed passing through the zenith at midnight at the end of a Calendar Round period. In my 1998 book *Maya Cosmogenesis 2012* I reconstructed how this tradition was designed to track the celestial shifting called the precession of the equinoxes. The New Fire ceremony and Calendar Round periods were essential to the Central Mexican understanding of World Ages.

The Maya used this system but also developed their own unique timekeeping system, the Long Count. This is the calendar that targets 2012 as the end of a vast cycle of time, a key concept in the Maya doctrine of World Ages. The Long Count basically utilizes five place values. It is often said that it is a base-20 system, which is generally true, but in fact two of the five levels do not follow the base-20 math:

1 day = 1 Kin (day)

20 days = 1 Uinal (vague month)

360 days = 1 Tun (vague year)

7,200 days = 1 Katun (19.7 years)

144,000 days = 1 Baktun (394.26 years)

13.0.0.0.0 Creation Text from
Quiriguá, August 11, 3114 BC.
Drawing by the author

Thirteen Baktuns equal 1,872,000 days, which is one "era" or World Age cycle (5,125.36 years). Notice that the Baktun is multiplied by 13 rather than 20 to reach to World Age cycle, and the Uinal is multiplied by 18 rather than 20 to reach the Tun. We know that the 13-Baktun period ends on December 21, 2012, because, as we saw in Chapter 1, scholars have verified Goodman's work that accurately correlated our Gregorian calendar with the Maya Long Count.

A date in the Long Count utilizes "dot and bar" notation, in which a dot equals one and a bar equals five. A typical date on a carved monument is pictured to the left.

You can see two bars and three dots in the upper left, next to a Baktun glyph. There are no dots or bars in the following glyphs for Katun, Tun, Uinal, and Kin, because those values are zero in this example. Next follows the tzolkin date, 4 Ahau (four dots next to the Ahau day-sign). And finally, in the lower left, 8 Cumku in the haab calendar. The final glyph block contains the event: "the image was made to appear."[15]

Scholars have simplified the notation so that a Long Count date written 9.16.4.4.1 means that 9 Baktuns, 16 Katuns, 4 Tuns, 4 Uinals, and 1 day have elapsed since the zero day of the Long Count, which the correct correlation fixes at August 11, 3114 BC. The "zero" date is written 0.0.0.0.0 but can also be written 13.0.0.0.0 (as the completion day of the previous cycle). The "end-date" of a 13-Baktun cycle is thus written 13.0.0.0.0. The use of the term "end-date" gives rise to the mistaken notion that the Maya calendar ends in 2012. But Maya time is cyclic, and it should go without saying that time continues into the next cycle. We use similar conventions in our language when we speak of "the end of the day," but we don't expect the world to end at midnight.

After decades of testing, the correlation question was finally settled by 1950. The result was that the 13th Baktun would end on December 21, 2012, on the tzolkin day 4 Ahau. This date in the tzolkin confirmed the surviving day-count in highland Guatemala, and also validated the carvings in the archaeological record called Creation monuments, which always correlate 13.0.0.0.0 with 4 Ahau.

The correlation issue is settled, and in my experience confusion arises only among those who have not studied or understood the topic. Thus, many popular books dismiss or neglect the correct correlation and instead proceed to invent new correlations, including completely fabricated day-counts as well as alternate end-dates. A great deal of unity could be achieved if researchers and writers would understand and heed the fundamentals of the Maya calendar. A primary fact that needs to be appreciated is what I call "the equation of Maya time," which is this: 13.0.0.0.0 = December 21, 2012 = 4 Ahau.[16]

In addition to these systems, the Maya also tracked the 9-day cycle of the Lords of the Night, as well as an 819-day cycle that involves Jupiter. Even a basic introduction to the Maya calendar can get quite complex. For the purpose of understanding 2012, one first needs to know that December 21, 2012, is the end of the 13-Baktun cycle in the Long Count calendar, and in Maya philosophy the 13-Baktun cycle equals one "World Age." Furthermore, it is important to clarify that December 21, 2012, is not the invention of imaginative modern writers but is a true and established artifact of the Maya philosophy of time.

THE CLASSIC PERIOD:
THE LONG COUNT IN ITS PRIME

The way in which the Long Count appears in hieroglyphic texts reveals its multifarious uses. It provided a sequential day-count from the zero date baseline. It provided interval calculations between two dates, sometimes tens of thousands of years apart. It was a framework for astronomical calculations. Solstice and equinox dates fall within the framework of the Long Count in a predictable pattern, suggesting that it incorporated an accurate tropical year calculation, which modern science places at 365.2422 days.[17] Three Katuns in the Long Count equal 37 Venus cycles of 584 days. Thus, if a Venus event, such as a first appearance as morning star, happened on 9.11.0.0.0 in the Long Count, Maya astronomers were on the alert for the same event three Katuns later, on 9.14.0.0.0.

Let's look at an early Classic Period inscription, from Tikal Stela 31. In this case it's a retrospective date, made by a ruler named Stormy Sky (Siyaj Chan K'awil II) recalling his grandfather's accession to kingship on 8.18.15.11.0 (November 25, 411 AD). Maya scholars Linda Schele and David Freidel noted that Jupiter and Saturn were in conjunction on this date, precisely when Venus had reached its evening star "station" (stationary between forward and retrograde motions).[18] Maya scholar Michael Grofe pointed out to me that the date was also within a few days of a visible solar eclipse.[19] The Maya would have expected this Venus station to happen again three Katuns later, on 9.1.15.11.0. Apparently, Stormy Sky's grandfather selected the date of his coronation to correspond to these celestial events, as it would confer upon him a special relationship with the sky deities.

This Long Count example didn't occur on a period ending, such as a Tun ending or a Katun ending. If celestial events occurred perfectly on one of these period endings, future events would more easily fit into the Long Count's predictive framework. For this, we can look at the Long Count date 9.14.0.0.0—the completion of the 14th Katun of the 9th Baktun. Corresponding to December 3, 711 AD, this particular Long Count period ending is found at Copán, Tortuguero, Tikal, Calakmul, and other sites, suggesting it had a meaning with universal appeal. We should immediately suspect that some unusual astronomy was happening on that date, and indeed it was. First, we have the first appearance of Venus as evening star. On Copán Stela C, which contains this Long Count date, the ruler 18 Rabbit has the Venus emblem in his headgear. Also on this date, the sun was aligned with the dark rift. The popularity of this date may be rooted in this astronomical occurrence, since it evokes the alignment that falls on the cycle ending in 2012 (sun in the dark rift, *on the solstice*).

Long Count dates often seem intended to highlight Jupiter and Saturn events, either conjunction, stations, or alignments with sidereal features such as Antares, the Pleiades, or the dark rift in the Milky Way. Research by Maya scholar Susan Milbrath showed that the Katuns of the Long Count were used to track Saturn and Jupiter events, such as stations and maximum elongations.[20] Following the work of Floyd Lounsbury, who showed that the deity named Kawil was related to the planet Jupiter, Milbrath tracked the astronomy connected with Kawil-related Long Count dates in the inscriptions, and found definite patterns involving not only Jupiter but Saturn. Both planets can take on the role of Kawil, the serpent-footed lightning deity, often at Katun endings or midpoints. This is because the Jupiter-Saturn conjunction cycle is just under 20 years, and the Katun period is 19.71 years. Classic Period sites such as Tikal, Yaxchilán, and Copán were particularly interested in how the Long Count provided a framework for planetary astronomy.

In the far north at Chichén Itzá, a renaissance occurred in the early ninth century when Central Mexicans flooded into Yucatán. They brought with them traditions such as the New Fire ceremony and a unique blending of Maya and Central Mexican culture occurred. The Long Count already had a long history of use in Yucatán, at sites such as Uxmal, Ek Balam, and Coba, and there was an effort to integrate the Calendar Round system and the Long Count. The Baktun ending of 830 AD may have signaled a new era at Chichén Itzá, triggering the construction of its most enduring monuments, the Great Ballcourt and the Pyramid of Kukulcan.

The famous Long Count date at Coba is interesting because it takes the Long Count far beyond the level of the Baktun. Most dates in the Long Count use only the first five place value levels, but it theoretically can be extended indefinitely. The Coba date is basically the same date as that in the Creation Texts found elsewhere, which identify the end of the last era of 13 Baktuns on August 11, 3114 BC. This is usually written 13.0.0.0.0, but at Coba the previous cyclic periods are also given, such that we have a total of nineteen levels above the Baktun, thousands of times larger than modern science's estimate for the age of the universe: 13.13.13.13.13.13.13.13.13.13.13.13.13. 13.13.13.13.13.13.13.0.0.0.0. As Anthony Aveni said, it seems that a Baktunomaniac was set loose on this stone. Much has been made of this representation of the Long Count. Some have suggested that it renders the 13-Baktun cycle meaningless. But this is like saying that century periods in our own calendar render the decade periods meaningless.

A distinction must be made between practical calendrics, in which the 13-Baktun period was a standardized doctrine, and theoretical mathematics. The Maya were apparently fond of generating huge numbers, which may have been attempts to find the grand number that would unify all the astronomical cycles. Greek mathematicians attempted the same thing as they grappled with the duration of the Great Year—it was supposed to be a harmonious 36,000 years, according to Plato, but the discovery of the great cycle of the precession of the equinoxes suggests a figure thousands of years less. Perhaps the Maya intended these huge numbers to represent, in a very general sense, the awesome immensity of the universe.

Coba doesn't disqualify the importance of the 13-Baktun period. In fact, it can be added to the many other examples that point to 13.0.0.0.0, 4 Ahau 8 Cumku, August 11, 3114 BC. There are many examples of this era inauguration being alluded to with only the Calendar Round position. For example, on the famous Vase of the Seven Lords, we see Creation imagery and the date 4 Ahau 8 Cumku. This tzolkin-haab combination corresponds to a period ending in the Long Count very rarely, and that's how scholars determine it to be a reliable shorthand for the full 13.0.0.0.0 date. Suffice it to say that the Creation Mythology's "three-stone" symbolism itself was used as a shorthand for the 3114 BC date.[21] This practice has important ramifications for understanding how the Maya referenced the 2012 date in their hieroglyphic texts.

Critics have often stated that there are no dates recorded in the inscriptions that point directly to the cycle ending in 2012. This is not true, as we have an important date from Tortuguero, a kingdom near Palenque, that has far-reaching implications. In addition, as we'll see in Chapter 7, secondary references to the astronomical alignment of era-2012 are found in the inscriptions, just as secondary references to 3114 BC are common. It is this new perspective on textual evidence for 2012 being an intentional and important concept in ancient Maya cosmology that constitutes a very promising new tool for identfying 2012 references in the inscriptions.

The Long Count served as a framework for building dedications, anniversaries of important events in a king's life, and aided both astronomical calculations and shamanic prophecies. Period endings were treated as important junctures and involved sacrifice and renewal. Maya scholar Dennis Puleston suggested that the Baktun ending of 830 AD may have instigated a breakdown for some Maya cities, a fatalistic expectation that a phase of their existence as a civilization was coming to an end.[22] The old Janus-face of cycle endings may have been just as perplexing for the Maya as it is for us today, as the dissolution of one era blends with the birth of a new one. Something drastic definitely occurred around the end of Baktun 10 in 830 AD, which signaled the beginning of the end for the Classic Maya civilization.

The causes of the Classic Maya collapse were many, including changing weather patterns and erosion caused by deforestation and the burning of trees to make lime (used for plaster), as well as increasing greed throughout a proliferation of kingdoms and princedoms. Within the complex network of dozens of Maya cities of the Petén (northern Guatemala), a series of inter-related cascades, including environmental degradation, warfare, drought, and greed, began to take their toll. Populated by over two million people at its height around 750 AD, the Petén's population dropped by two-thirds in the mid–eighth century. By 900 AD the Classic Maya civilization had ground to a halt. The last Long Count date was carved on the western periphery, at Toniná, in 909 AD.

But the Long Count tracking system did not end there; it just stopped being carved in stone. Just as time had "materialized" with the first stone carvings of the Long Count in the first century BC, it now dematerialized, relegated to the heads of day-keepers and perishable bark paper books. The collapse of civilization was much more severe in the Petén than it was in Yucatán, where Chichén Itzá, Mayapán, and other cities continued to thrive, although beset as usual by warfare and strife. Those cities, too, eventually were abandoned as a different style of culture arose.

It's nevertheless clear that a healthy manuscript tradition developed in Yucatán. The fact is tragically apparent in the historical accounts of hun-dreds, if not thousands, of Maya books being destroyed during the Conquest in book burnings like the one at Mani in 1562. It is a sad and astounding fact that, given their prolific literacy we today have only four surviving Maya books. Fortunately, these remnants have provided intrepid researchers with enough information to reconstruct a great deal about Maya astronomy, reli-gion, calendrics, and mythology. The bark paper books continued the Long Count tradition in Yucatán. But at some point after the collapse, the larger cycle of 13 Baktuns slipped into the background as a Short Count system was favored, emphasizing prophecy cycles of 13 Katuns. The new system was still congruent with the authentic, ancient calendar—there was no explicit break in the Katuns.

The Dresden Codex (one of the four surviving Maya books), believed to date to the eleventh or twelfth century but containing astronomical data going further back in time, contains an almanac called the Serpent Series. Research by Maya scholar Michael Grofe published in his PhD dissertation presents compelling new insights into how the distance numbers in the Serpent Series track very large astronomical periods.[23] Grofe has determined that these distance numbers provide very accurate calculations for the sidereal year and the precession of the equinoxes. Subsequent research by Grofe and Maya epigrapher Barbara MacLeod has uncovered other precessional calculations connected to kingship rites in the inscriptions.

THE ITZA SHORT COUNT

By the early 1500s a rich and elaborate tradition had tied the 13-Katun prophecy cycle (the Short Count) into rotating political duties, shifting power from one town to another over successive Katuns. This practice was not unlike the cofradia system employed by the highland Tzutujil Maya, in which different groups successively take their turns in charge of the religious customs.[24] The 13-Katun prophecy system was fueled by the prognostications offered by the jaguar priests, the Chilam Balam (this name doesn't refer to one specific person, but served as a title; there were many Chilam Balam from different towns). Many of these post-Conquest oracle books have survived and provide important information about the Short Count's usage and survival through the centuries after the Conquest. They list years and Katun prophecies, and astute scholars have noted that they retain a continuity with the ancient Long Count.

For example, the Long Count date we previously discussed, 9.14.0.0.0, was the end of a "6 Ahau" Katun that ran from 692 to 711 AD. In the *Chilam Balam Book of Tizimin* we find a retrospective account that begins with this Katun, and sequences through the following Katuns with historical recollections of wars and rulers celebrated in the memories of the Itza people. It brings the accounting all the way up to the 6 Ahau Katun that began in 1717.

The one right after this in the list is the 4 Ahau Katun, which began in 1737 and ended in 1756—exactly one 13-Katun prophecy cycle before the 2012 cycle-ending date.[25]

A festive ceremonial for the 12.0.0.0.0 Baktun ending in 1618 AD is recorded in the *Book of Chilam Balam of Chumayel*. The Baktun 11 ending of 1224 AD was also recognized by the Yucatec Maya jaguar priests, so a knowledge of larger Baktun cycles was at least a footnote in the tradition, which nevertheless now preferred 13-Katun cycles over 13-Baktun cycles.[26] One wonders if jaguar priests present for the 1618 Baktun ceremonial had the ability, or desire, to project forward one more Baktun to 2012.

0.0.0.0.0	3114 BC
1.0.0.0.0	2715 BC
2.0.0.0.0	2325 BC
3.0.0.0.0	1932 BC
4.0.0.0.0	1537 BC
5.0.0.0.0	1143 BC
6.0.0.0.0	748 BC
7.0.0.0.0	354 BC
8.0.0.0.0	41 AD
9.0.0.0.0	435 AD
10.0.0.0.0	830 AD
11.0.0.0.0	1224 AD
12.0.0.0.0	1618 AD
13.0.0.0.0	2012 AD

I always found it interesting that the middle of the 13-Baktun cycle (6.19.5.0.0 = 550 BC) corresponds to the appearance of two pivotal historical figures, key avatars of Western and Eastern religion and philosophy—the Buddha and Pythagoras.

At any rate, it's clear that all the Baktun endings during the 13-Baktun cycle were recognized in one way or another by the Maya. This includes retrospective calculations of Baktun endings in the distant past as well as projections to future ones, including the one in 2012. That the Yucatec Maya may have been aware of the overarching important of the one in 2012 is suggested by the language used in the various Chilam Balam books. British researcher and author Geoff Stray has carefully investigated this material and points out that Maud Makemson's translation of the *Chilam Balam Book of Tizimin* infers a reference to a 13-Baktun ending, indirectly. It's a passage often glossed as 13-Katun, but the original Yucatec phrasing cannot be translated that way. And the context is for a larger temporal period. Stray relates that "Four Ahau is the Katun for remembering knowledge and compressing it within annals" and explains:

> In Makemson's translation of the Chilam Balam of Tizimin, evidence is presented in Makemson's commentary, that many of the prophecies probably did refer to the end of the 13-baktun cycle, but due to loss of knowledge of the Long Count, and the changing of naming katuns after their last day instead of their first, plus the introduction of 24-year katuns, the resulting confusion detached the prophecies from their original predicted time.[27]

Adding to this confusion, the continuity of the Short Count system was disrupted by a calendar reform in 1752. The pressures of acculturation, historical distancing from the origins of the calendar tradition, modernization—all these factors made this dislocation inevitable. Perhaps agents of cultural assimilation had infiltrated the ranks of the Maya calendar priests.[28] For whatever reason, a new standard was implemented in which the 13-Katun prophecy cycle was altered. Now a 24-year period would be used. Why this was preferable is not clear. The impending completion of the 4 Ahau Katun in 1756 offered a perfect 13-Katun time resonance with the great 13-Baktun cycle ending in 2012, but divisiveness and confusion must have ruled the day. Whatever the motivations of the innovators, the result was clear: one more notch of dislocation for the ancient tradition.

Maya tradition in Yucatán during this time was experiencing other death blows. In 1761 a well-respected Maya leader and Christian theologian named Jacinto Canek led a short-lived uprising against Spanish landowners. He traveled the countryside and visited towns, observing the conditions of his people and their relationships with the Spanish overlords. He did not like what he saw. After a religious ceremony he spoke to the people:

> *My beloved children, I do not know what you await to shake off the heavy yoke and laborious servitude in which the subjugation of the Spanish has placed you. I have traveled through all of the province and have inspected all of the villages and, considering carefully the usefulness the Spanish subjugation has brought to us, I have not found a single thing but painful and inexorable servitude. . . . The demand for tribute is not appeased by the poverty that locks up our comrades as in a jail, nor is the thirst for our blood satisfied by the continuous whippings that bite and tear our bodies to pieces.[29]*

Within days of this speech Canek was involved in a clash in which a Spanish merchant was killed. The Maya people rallied around Canek the same day and crowned him their king. Within a week an armed Spanish militia arrived and the Maya were overpowered, five hundred being killed in a fire set by the Spanish. Canek and some guards escaped but were soon apprehended. They were immediately condemned to death. Eight of his closest followers were hanged and dismembered, and their body parts were sent for display in outlying villages as a reminder of the price to pay for disobeying the overlords. Jacinto Canek was himself publicly tortured in the plaza at Mérida, his flesh ripped from his bones by hot pincers and his bones broken one by one with heavy metal bars. At some point during this torture, he died. His body was then burned. If anything symbolized the dislocation of Maya tradition in Yucatán, it had to be this event.

Continuity of the calendar after this period of time is dubious, possibly explaining why calendrical counting got more confused and why the 260-day tzolkin was eventually lost in the Yucatán. "Katun prophecies" in Yucatán (the *Books of Chilam Balam*) expressed a lingering legacy that has served as a germinal catalyst for modern prophets and visionaries, since it contains classic elements of prognostication and prophecy, much like the Nostradamus prophecies that Westerners know so well.

Only the barest fragments of the Long Count can be found today. Michael Coe wrote that the Yucatec Maya believe the current World Age is to end in the year "2000 plus a little,"[30] but it's unclear whether this information comes from modern sources or ancestral lore. In highland Guatemala, a Jacaltek Maya legend called "Man of Lightning" mentions the dire events of the Oxlan ben (Oxlan = 13; be = road), which Victor Montejo believes might be a reference to the end of 13 Baktuns in 2012.[31] But exactly *when* the 13th Baktun is to conclude was not preserved; the Long Count had slipped away.

The complete loss of the Long Count following its latter-day echoes in Yucatán brings us to the cusp of the rediscovery of the ancient Maya civilization. By 1800, just when the final glimmer of the accurately timed Long Count–Short Count faded out, an interest in the Maya grew among Europeans and Americans fueled by rumors that the jungles of Mexico hid a lost civilization. In 1839, Catherwood and Stephens mounted their expedition. Perhaps there was still time for the Long Count to be pulled back from the brink of oblivion and brought back to life. As it turned out, that's exactly what happened.

CHAPTER THREE

SEDUCTIVE SPELLS

O son, no one can ascertain how this mysterious
illusion came into being. As to why it arose it is
because of the person's lack of discerning inquiry.[1]

—THE KAIVALYA NAVANITAM

I've always been interested in how the 2012 meme first entered public awareness. We saw in Chapter 1 how it was floating around as something that could have been extrapolated from Goodman's charts as early as 1905, when his correlation was published. It could have been easily extrapolated with Thompson's incomplete table of 1927, and again with Morley's 1946 appendix (in his book *The Ancient Maya*), but it wasn't until Coe's book *The Maya*, in 1966, that the end-date of the 13-Baktun cycle was actually computed and discussed, albeit briefly. Unfortunately, although Coe subscribed to the correct correlation, the date he reported was off by one year and three days. December 24, 2011, became the date adopted by other authors. The sad fact of the situation is that the popular treatment of the Maya's 2012 calendar, misinformed at the very get-go, has been confused ever since.

In 1967 Tony Shearer, the great-granddaddy of the Mesoamerican calendar movement, self-published a pamphlet called *The Sacred Calendar*. Part Native American, Shearer abandoned a lucrative career in Denver's news media and nurtured his deepening relationship with Mexico and its mysteries. In 1971, Sun Books published his *Lord of the Dawn, Quetzalcoatl: The Plumed Serpent of Mexico*. It explored the spiritual content, as he saw it, of the Aztec and Toltec Sacred Calendar of 260 days, the *tonalpohualli*. Shearer's travels in the 1960s led him from Denver to Central Mexico and the state of Oaxaca, where he wandered the ancient Zapotec capital of Monte Alban and visited contemporary Mazatec Indians living in remote villages. He fell in love with a new life and nurtured an inspired poetic vision of the ancient calendar's power to spiritually awaken and transform those who learned to follow it.

In his introduction to Shearer's book, author Vinson Brown wrote:

This is an adventure that you can follow too and find the meanings behind the rainbow and the morning star, and follow the ghost path of the Milky Way, and the carvings of an ancient and vanished civilization whose prophetic dreams and warnings may come to us just in time to save our world from a destruction and degradation too horrible to imagine.[2]

By the early 1970s the consciousness-raising cultural and human rights events of the 1960s had morphed into other concerns. The youth culture was speaking out against the dangers of industrial pollution. Brown's words express a sentiment for the growing concern over gas shortages and impending environmental catastrophe, something that Shearer illustrated in his book with dramatic effect. We also catch a clue about "prophetic dreams" that may come "just in time." The book was an inspired poetic treatise, and on page 184 we read that, according to Shearer's reconstruction of the ancient calendar prophecy, the modern nightmare of hellish materialism will end on August 16, 1987. No other details are presented in the book on how this date was derived.

The modern world's insane materialism has been a recurring theme in the 2012 discussion. It is perhaps the one common thread woven through the works of many authors who otherwise hold wildly different views. A useful framework for understanding this particular thread is the Perennial Philosophy, which subscribes to the idea that all cycles in nature go through periods of increase and decrease. Thus, the materialism and corruption that maximize at the end of a historical cycle are to be expected, and signal an impending shift or turnabout in which the neglected opposite half of human nature, spirituality and integrity, becomes increasingly emphasized.

In 1975 Shearer published *Beneath the Moon and Under the Sun*, which contained both poetic elements and explanations of his research. On his acknowledgments page, dated September 13, 1974, he graciously thanked many people, including "José and Miriam Argüelles for their interest in my thesis of 13 Heavens and 9 Hells." This is a clear indication of how José Argüelles, an art teacher, author, and visionary, later became the leader of the Harmonic Convergence of August 16–17, 1987.

The "thesis" that Shearer refers to is a reconstruction he advanced as to how the Aztec World Ages are timed. He noted that the Aztec worldview was divided into 13 Heaven realms above and 9 Hell realms below, making 22 distinct levels of the cosmos. Shearer believed the model worked for time as well as space, a valid insight considering the interwoven nature of time and space in Aztec cosmovision. So he connected the 22 realms with levels of time, each one representing a 52-year Calendar Round period, making a total Great Age of $22 \times 52 = 1,144$ years.

He proposed that the 9 Hell periods commenced when Cortés landed on the Gulf Coast at Veracruz on April 21, 1519. Thus, it would take $9 \times 52 = 468$ years for the Hells to play themselves out. Similar to the Hindu concept of the Yugas, Shearer saw each Hell as being worse than the last, a deepening darkness of spiritual bankruptcy. In this way he arrived at the year 1987 as the end of the process, when the calendar's cycles all came together and humanity could experience a return to the Heaven periods. This is, in a nutshell, the idea adopted later by Argüelles, which he applied to the Baktun periods of the Maya Long Count.

Shearer's first book focused exclusively on the Central Mexican Calendar Round tradition, far outside the Maya realm, but in his 1975 sequel he mentions Palenque, *The Popol Vuh*, and other uniquely Maya material, revealing how the Aztec and Maya traditions started to be blended together.

We still have this problem in the popular press today, where the famous Aztec Sunstone is used as a Maya calendar symbol. But Shearer did not, at this stage, specifically discuss the Long Count or 2012—that was taken up later by Argüelles.

Shearer must be recognized for three things: (1) the origin of the Harmonic Convergence date (August 16–17, 1987); (2) advocating that modern seekers could follow the 260-day sacred calendar as a spiritual system; (3) furthering the idea of a dire turning point looming in the near future, based on mysterious calendar systems perfected long ago in Mexico. But it's important to realize that Shearer worked solely with ideas connected to the 52-year Calendar Round, and his 1987 cycle-ending date is not based on the Long Count.

As we will see, his friend José Argüelles took the baton from Shearer and morphed the entire movement in several ways. He blended the Harmonic Convergence with the Maya 2012 date, suggesting a 25- or 26-year countdown from 1987 to 2012 or 2013 (the exact idea is unclear in his various interviews and writings). He also sparked grassroots gatherings at sacred sites with his Planet Art Network and tied his call for these events to the Harmonic Convergence date. The "be-in" concept, wherein people up for anything gather together to celebrate their being-ness, has been an unquestioned meme in 2012 party planning; it appeals to children of the 1960s. I'll address in Chapter 13 the effectiveness of these types of gatherings and whether it is worth trying to craft "Partay 2012" in their image.

Finally, Argüelles adopted and advanced Shearer's notion that following the 260-day calendar could be a spiritual path for modern non-Maya seekers, the only solution to the world's corrupt materialism. This approach became particularly central to his Dreamspell kit, a teaching tool or game that included a dial for calculating your "galactic signature" (your birthday) and a gameboard, intended to be played with other people who wanted to learn how to be in touch with "natural time." The kit was printed in China, packaged in a box, and was initially intended to be bought by the case by self-selected Dreamspell evangelists and distributed to potential new members. It came with a book but was lacking in clear instructions.

In 1992, Argüelles announced that the artist formerly known as Argüelles was dead and that he was now the voice of the seventh-century Maya King of Palenque, Pakal. Argüelles's revealed identity as a wizard-channeler who renamed himself Valum Votan, Pakal's living channel, is not at all foreshadowed in his brilliant early book from 1975 called *The Transformative Vision.* In an endnote in that book we read of his awareness of Shearer's work and a glimpse of how he would link it to 2012:

> . . . *attention should also be drawn to the fact that a larger 5,125-year cycle which began in 3113 B.C.* [sic] *will draw to an end in A.D. 2012. What this may mean in relation to the information given by Shearer has yet to be worked out. Obviously, time will tell!*[3]

Before we venture more deeply into the controversial work of Argüelles, we need to discuss two other important early books that invoked 2012. They too appeared in that pivotal year, 1975. One used 2012 as an anchor point for a novel theory of time but didn't mention the Maya. The other was all about the Maya and their Long Count calendar but failed, on a technicality, to actually mention the year 2012.

EARLY 2012 BOOKS:
MCKENNA AND WATERS

Terence McKenna was a brilliant speaker and a pop icon, having boldly taken center stage as an advocate for psychedelic drugs. Born in Colorado, McKenna came of age in Berkeley, California, in the 1960s and graduated in 1969 with a bachelor of science degree in ecology and conservation from the Tussman Experimental College, a short-lived outgrowth of UC Berkeley. Thereafter he traveled widely in India, Southeast Asia, and South America in pursuit of shamans and hallucinogenic plants. The term "psychedelic drugs" is misleading. Terence encouraged greater sophistication in how drugs are categorized and talked about. He played a formative role in a new field of study called ethnomycology—the study of the interplay between psychoactive mushrooms, culture, and human consciousness.

Terence's far-reaching and comprehensive mind allowed him to operate on many levels. He was at once a visionary philosopher, a pioneer ethnomycologist, a botanical preservationist, an extemporaneous speaker, a writer, a logos bard, a world explorer, and a shaman of inner realms. His work deserves a comprehensive treatment, which I can't undertake here, but by focusing on his Time Wave Zero theory we'll be able to understand his work with 2012 and how several ideas have become tenaciously attached to 2012. In *The Invisible Landscape*, a book Terence cowrote and published with his brother Dennis in 1975, we learn of the unusual experiment they undertook in Colombia in 1971. That experiment triggered the formulation of the Time Wave Zero theory. The McKenna brothers had traveled with several friends to Colombia in search of an exotic hallucinogenic mixture called *oo-hoo-hé*. What they found instead were fields of psilocybin mushrooms.

After several weeks of tripping and gathering samples, Dennis formulated an experimental plan: On a certain night they would ingest the mushrooms and Dennis would induce a visionary breakthrough by forcefully humming in a high pitch. The vibratory catalyst of the humming would, theoretically, open him up to collective memories and universal truths believed to reside in DNA. That was the plan. Terence recounts the experiment at La Chorrera in his 1993 book *True Hallucinations*:

> As I watched my mind and listened to my brother rave, I began to realize that the experiment had unleashed some sort of bizarre effect. I ask myself now why it was so easy for me to make the leap from assuming we were having a peculiar localized experience to the idea that we were key parts of a planet-wide phenomenon? . . . The psilocybin-induced cognitive hallucination made the impossible and

unlikely seem probable and reasonable. I became flooded with ec-
stasy as the realization passed over me that we had passed the omega
point, that we were now operating in the first few moments of the
millennium.[4]

The inner perceptions of explorers stumbling through uncharted domains of Mind may be hard for the uninitiated to digest. But the fact is that *something* did happen. And although Dennis eventually came down from his trip, Terence was launched into an ongoing dance with the I Ching (an ancient Chinese oracle), elaborating its secret contents through mathematical operations that were inspired by intuitions he was being given by the mushrooms. The I Ching seemed to him to contain ancient insights about the nature of time. Terence found corresponding insights in the work of philosopher Alfred North Whitehead, whose term "concrescence" perfectly fit what Terence was seeing—something in the very nature of time that caused unconnected events through history to speed up and converge on a precise moment in the not-too-distant future. That totalized convergence would immanentize, or reveal in the now, the eschaton, the "transcendental object at the end of time." The term *eschaton* comes from Middle Eastern studies in reference to eschatology, the study of the final ends of all things.

Terence advanced the notion that time is not a constant but has different qualities tending toward either "habit" or "novelty." This idea counters a fundamental premise of Western science—that the quality of time is constant. An experiment conducted on Tuesday should give the same results as the exact same experiment conducted on Friday, all other conditions being equal. The fluidity of time and the advance of new or novel occurrences is what interested Terence, and his perception that novelty was increasing over time implied something profound: time and history were speeding up and approaching a culmination point. Change might be, according to the ancient Chinese Taoists, the only constant in nature, but that change was accelerating.

Over a period of inspired investigation in the early 1970s, Terence worked out a mathematical wave form based on the 384 lines of change that make up the 64 hexagrams of the I Ching. Each of the 64 hexagrams contains six lines, each being either solid or broken. When you consult the I Ching as a traditional oracle, you build these binary lines sequentially from bottom to top. When you are finished, you can look up your hexagram in the *I Ching: Book of Changes* and consult the reading. The sequence in which the 64 hexagrams are ordered, known as the King Wen sequence, appears to be random, but Terence did an analysis of the "degree of difference" between each successive hexagram and found a statistical anomaly suggesting that, for some reason, the Ken Wen sequence was an intentional construct. With the degrees of difference codified into numerical values, Terence was able to graph a wave, and this became the Novelty Time Wave. His friend Peter Meyer worked out the formula and computer software enabling them to graph it and explore its dynamics.

Terence noticed that the time wave exhibited a quality of "self-same similarity." It unfolded like a fractal pattern in which a given small section of the wave was found to be identical in form to a larger section of the wave. Because the wave displayed the ebb and flow of novelty within time, Terence called this fractal modeling of time Temporal Resonance.[5] It implied that larger intervals, occurring long ago, contained the same amount of information as shorter, more recent, intervals. History was being compressed, moving quicker. And the process had to have an end.

Terence's tetherball analogy describes the quickening process nicely: A ball tied by a long rope to a pole will swing around and around very slowly, but as the rope wraps around the pole and the ball draws closer it revolves more and more quickly. The closer the ball gets to the center, the more quickly it is drawn toward it. The center point is when the ball theoretically reaches infinite velocity. In truth, the mathematical wave form doesn't really describe a *constant* acceleration; the staccato up-and-down pattern of the wave implies an ongoing vacillation between habit and novelty. The wave trends, however, with each successive iteration, toward infinite novelty. The mean average trend is one of increasing novelty, experienced as accelerating change. A requirement of the Time Wave Zero theory is thus that infinite novelty will be reached on a specific date.

Terence suspected that notable events in history could be identified that would help him locate the time wave's end date. He took the atomic explosion of 1945 as an extremely novel event in human history and the signal that a final phase had begun, a 67-year fractal subpattern of the entire wave. Thus, add 67 to 1945 and 2012 was a possible target year. Population growth, peak oil, and pollution statistics also pointed him to the early twenty-first century. In *The Invisible Landscape* he mentions the year 2012 but goes no further in precision. He later admits that his original calculation was to November 17, 2012, but after he learned of the Maya calendar end date on December 21, he recalibrated the wave form and found that December 21 fit even better. Thus, Terence's model was forever after correlated with the end date of the 13-Baktun cycle of the Maya Long Count.

Although Terence would sometimes mention the Maya in various contexts, usually for their psychoactive shamanism, the fact that his Time Wave also pointed to the cycle ending of the Maya Long Count was merely an ancillary confirmation of his theory. In one rumination on the topic, Terence noted that both he and the Maya were aficionados of psilocybin mushrooms and wondered if somehow this could explain why both his system and the Maya calendar pointed to 2012.

In all the hundreds of interviews and recorded talks that Terence did, many of which are freely available on the Internet, one finds scant details about the Maya calendar. In fact, the length of the 13-Baktun cycle is mistakenly reported as being either 5,128 or 5,200 years. The reasons why the Maya calendar points to 2012 were not things he pursued. Yet the precessional alignment of sun and galaxy (the galactic alignment) was there in *The Invisible Landscape*, mentioned briefly and obliquely. In his introduction to my book *Maya Cosmogenesis 2012* Terence took the opportunity to elaborate a recommendation he had for further investigation of the galactic alignment:

[I]s there some scientific basis for the idea that when the winter solstice sunrise "stands" on the galactic center that any unusual physical effects might be expected? Today science answers in the negative. But science, unlike religion, is ever growing and revisiting and revising its own past simplifications. . . . Is human fate and the larger drama of the galaxy somehow linked? Coupling mechanisms may be difficult to prove, but elucidation of subtle coupling mechanisms is what the new science of dynamics is designed to do.[6]

As so often happens in the process by which ideas develop into breakthroughs, the key to understanding 2012 was noted early on as an oddity but passed by. After all, one might note both the alignment and the end date but not believe they were close enough to each other in time. This would be a *prima facie* conclusion that, upon some consideration, could be disposed of—primarily because the alignment must be conceived as a range extending over at least thirty-six years.

Furthermore, how would one go about proving that the Maya intended their end date to target the alignment? It simply wasn't something that Terence was drawn to elaborate—it requires a long-term commitment to carefully researching many different areas of Maya thought and tradition. My own interests and studies were to converge with this alignment concept, however, and by 1992 I was on it. And to his credit Terence encouraged my work, even though it would call into question his requirement that something drastic and sudden should occur on December 22, 2012. (Terence often used December 22, perhaps because the twenty-second would be the "first" day of the new era.)

Another idea I proposed to Terence in our conversations—and he was always willing to entertain ideas—is based on the idea that the flow of time is subjective. One's experience of time, fast or slow, is a function of the state of mind one is in. This can be noted in the reports of elderly people, for whom time seems to go very quickly. How many times has Grandma said, "Why, it seems like I just woke up and now it's time to go to bed," or "Last Christmas seems like it was here just yesterday!"

There are real neurological reasons for this experience of the elderly, based in the brain's synaptic processing of information, which slows down with age. The bandwidth, you might say, has narrowed and therefore events (time) must pass through a smaller conduit. Consciousness thus restricted experiences time moving more quickly. Visionaries experiencing ecstasy, however, undergo a heightened and intensified cerebral processing, an enlarging of the synaptic bandwidth, resulting in time slowing down. When it slows down so much that the experience of the flow of time has ceased, the door to eternity is opened. Eternity isn't a long period of time; eternity is the cessation of time.

Being deeply in love provides another example. When two people are having a peak experience of intimacy, the heart and mind (even the eyes) will dilate. It can be a profound experience in which both feel they have, together, entered a timeless inner sanctum and eternity has been glimpsed. Eternity is the experience of the cessation of the passage of time, time slowed down because the mind and heart have been completely opened in love. The consciousness expansion that frequently occurs after ingesting psychoactive plants can also provide an experience of glimpsing infinity or eternity, as explorers have reported. In ancient mystery religions, the experience was an initiation into the eternal Mysteries.

The thought experiment I shared with Terence is as follows. Imagine that a garden hose is your consciousness. A bigger hose diameter means a larger consciousness. The water flowing through the hose represents events occurring in time. The volume of water that wants to pass through the hose represents the number of events that are passing through the mind. Even if this amount remains constant, the speed at which the water travels through the hose (the mind) depends on how dilated or constricted the hose is. (Pinch the end of the hose and the water flows faster and more forcefully.) This model suggests that our minds determine whether or not time speeds up.

Time acceleration may not be an inherent property of history, the necessary consequence of the passage of time, but could also be the result of an increasing constriction of consciousness. This idea gains meaning in consideration of the ancient Hindu doctrine of World Ages, the Yugas, in which each successive Yuga is characterized by a diminishment of spirituality, an ongoing restriction of consciousness.[7] Time speeds up because consciousness closes down. If the speed of time's passage is indeed a function of the dilation of consciousness, then the acceleration of time is a direct result of the collective constriction of consciousness (the disconnect from a larger spiritual context and the rise of materialism) that the end of a historical cycle brings.

Terence was a fan of the writings of Teilhard de Chardin, whose Omega Point and noosphere concepts also influenced José Argüelles (his "technosphere" concept is a type of technologized noosphere). Chardin's work basically applies Darwinian evolution to spiritual unfolding. It was an attempt to marry science with a spiritual theology. Chardin was a Jesuit scientist-priest. His concept of the Omega Point suggested that humankind was approaching a new unification of consciousness on a higher level—a breakthrough into a new level of organizational complexity, in the same way that cells create an organ and organs work together in an organism.

The Omega Point is much like McKenna's Singularity, his "trans-dimensional object" that is supposed to be born from the concrescence to occur on December 21, 2012. This new state of being touches and reflects more intimately the infinite and eternal ground state from which it originally came. Beings thereby evolve to progressively and more fully reflect their infinite Creator. An objection to Chardin's model, which would equally apply to McKenna's, is that infinity can't possibly "evolve." It's already there, latent, and nothing in the material of historical process can "build" it. It is more accurate to think of it as being progressively revealed. How else can we explain the inner visions of mystics who have glimpsed eternity? Darwin's idea is a bottoms-up model of new forms and species evolving over time. Chardin adds a wrinkle by suggesting that discrete levels preexist in the very architecture of the universe, just as electrons tend to group into distinct orbits around a proton, giving us law-defined predictable elements. But it's still basically a spiritualized Darwinism, in which mutations result in a being fully conscious of its eternal ground and origin. But here's the key difference:

For Chardin, as for Terence, the process was teleological—meaning it is pulled forward by the end state, not pushed from behind by historical evolution through time.

This tops-down concept is a key idea in the Perennial Philosophy, a view of the cosmos inspired by direct experience of universal truth. Such a perspective on spirituality is found, for example, in the metaphysical wisdom taught by the twelfth-century Persian sage Suhrawardi. It is an echo of Plato's preexisting Ideas, which are a bit closer to the concept that all change descends from above, from the immaterial spiritual realm that pours itself into lower realms of physical manifestation. The idea is alien to all but the most esoteric forms of Christianity and is central to Islamic and Oriental metaphysics. Indeed, teleology threatens causality, the cause-and-effect principle at the heart of Western science, which is why it is anathema.

In order to avoid irking the priests of scientism too much, both McKenna and Chardin attempted to discreetly incorporate into the deficient models of Western science certain ancient perennial insights regarding how time and consciousness really work. But importing Oriental insights into containers built by Occidental minds is like trying to squeeze the ocean into a bottle. The implications of the Omega Point, the Singularity, and 2012ology require a radical revisioning of Western philosophy's approach to reality. In a nutshell, consciousness doesn't evolve, it remembers, or awakens, to its full potential. From this top-down perspective, physical brains evolve in order to accommodate awakened minds.

My friend Curt Joy noted that Terence mentioned, at one point or another, virtually *everything* about 2012 so it is not really possible to nail him down to one official position, especially when he's no longer around to engage in a dialogue. His theory, however, is most known for two things: Time speeds up and something definite is going to happen on December 21, 2012. We've already addressed the unacknowledged subjective source of the experience of time speeding up. On the other point, the future may be predetermined but our subjective experience of it is not. So the idea of a predictable definite "something" happening for all of us specifically on December 21, 2012, seems incredibly unrealistic.

It's possible that, for Terence, the idea made sense as a projection of the sudden "rupture of plane" experienced in the psychedelic breakthrough. Projected onto historical process, a global rupture of plane should occur at the precise moment that the molecules of time-events avalanched en masse into the central pineal gland of our collective consciousness. In other words, the subjective visionary breakthrough experienced by the shaman perhaps became a model, for Terence, for a collective breakthrough of higher consciousness. There may be some truth to this, but the main issue with this scenario is, I think, the role of individual free will.

The warning to newcomers that I would offer here is that the idea of something suddenly occurring on December 21, 2012, is highly unlikely. I don't personally believe that it is built into the architecture of external events in quite the way that Terence laid out in his Time Wave Zero theory. Similarly, the experience of time speeding up probably has more to do with the state of our consciousness than with the boiling over of external events in history.

Finally, I'd like to offer a topsy-turvy twist on Terence's Time Wave Zero theory. To use one of Terence's favorite terms, it's quite the conundrum. His Time Wave Zero theory, or Novelty Theory, describes an intensification of novel or new events as we approach 2012. In his examination of historical events, Terence saw novelty increasing when unusual or unexpected events occurred. The Berlin Wall coming down, for example. So the ultimate novel event, the most bizarre and unexpected occurrence, should occur on December 21, 2012—and that would be *for the theory itself to fail,* with a grand business-as-usual occurring. But with the fateful day transpiring in this way, the theory then instantly vindicates itself. The grand Nothing-In-Particular at the end of time would be *the most unexpected and novel thing* that could possibly occur, according to the Novelty Theory itself. Its own failure would prove its efficacy. Now, that's a conundrum. I hope that somewhere Terence is smiling at that one.

FRANK WATERS AND THE MEXICO MYSTIQUE

Frank Waters was a brilliant thinker and an engaging writer. His classic book on the Hopi was published in 1963 and opened the discerning reading public to the vast and mysterious psyche of a misunderstood Native American group. His novel *The Man Who Killed the Deer* was a compassionate and profound account of the inner world of the Pueblo Indians. Waters, himself part Cheyenne, was born outside of Colorado Springs in 1902. He lived among the Hopi in the Four Corners area for many years and retired to the mountains near Taos, New Mexico. His observations in his book *Mexico Mystique* are those of a mature, elder philosopher, presented in sure-handed tones. We see in his explanation of his book's title the belief that ancient worldviews can have great meaning for modern people:

> Since Jung's discovery of the collective unconscious, we are no longer obliged to regard ancient Nahuatl and Mayan gods as idolatrous pagan images concocted by a primitive people merely to bring rain and ward off evil spirits. They are primordial images of soul significance rising from the unconscious into consciousness where they are given form and meaning. A universal meaning as pertinent now as it was two thousand years ago. So today, despite the flood of archaeological and anthropological reports, documented histories, and popular writings of all kinds, there is still a Mexican mystique.[8]

In writing his book on the Mexican calendar, Waters practiced something that has been, in recent years, winnowed out of books on 2012 as a kind of irrelevant annoyance. He actually researched and studied the Maya tradition. Based on his general knowledge of indigenous cultures, tempered with specific details on the Maya gathered from his studies, Waters drew some insightful conclusions about the Long Count and its cycle ending. For example, it was patently clear to him that the 13-Baktun cycle was part of a

World Age doctrine. This is a clear conclusion to draw, and Maya scholars such as Gordon Brotherston and Eva Hunt supported and explored the idea, but in more reactive and defensive quarters my emphasis on the idea has drawn an incredible amount of scholarly backlash.

Waters also concluded that the importance of the 13-Baktun cycle must involve astronomy. He thus presents an astrological interpretation of the cycle-ending date, based on a planetary horoscope for the date and an astrologer's assessment of it. Unfortunately, Waters's academic source for the end date (Coe's book *The Maya*) contained a flaw, resulting in a mistaken calculation for the end date that he used. Strangely, in *Mexico Mystique* Waters cited the book *Hamlet's Mill* but didn't seem to catch the oblique reference to a precessional alignment model. Waters's book was the first one dedicated to the end-date question, and he can be considered the man who launched the 2012 phenomenon. It planted a seed but did not spawn a great legacy of followers, as Shearer's book drew attention away from the Long Count to the 1987 date while the 2012 meme morphed in other directions in the hands of McKenna and Argüelles. A later edition of Coe's book provided a corrected end date, which for all intents and purposes must have rendered Waters's theory irrelevant, although as late as 1990 I attended a talk by an astrologer in Boulder, Colorado, who utilized Waters's horoscope charts.

Efforts to track early references to 2012 reveal a lack of coherence and agreement. Peter Tompkins's 1976 book *Mysteries of the Mexican Pyramids* makes a wry reference to "2011" in the final pages, reporting that "sensitives say the Serpent People are due to return to earth in 2011 to help create a world government."[9] Peter Balin, an artist and traveler, published a book in 1978 called *Flight of the Feathered Serpent* and put another astronomical observation for 2012 on the table, setting the stage for seeing the Maya calendar as a teaching game and oracle. Balin's book is a well-illustrated poetic treatise, somewhat after the fashion of Shearer's books, that presents a tarot-like game/oracle that spiritual seekers could engage and learn from. The artistic presentation of the system anticipates and resembles the Dreamspell game created by Argüelles in the early 1990s.

Balin also mentioned, briefly, the Venus transits of the sun that were to occur in 2004 and 2012—an idea taken up later by Swedish author Carl Calleman. Good diagrams of the Venus transit are provided, along with a brief discussion of the facts that such a transit occurs roughly once every 130 years and one will happen in June of 2012. It's interesting that Balin points out this fact, but the next step would be to demonstrate how the Maya were aware of Venus transits and how Venus transits evoke a known theme in Mexican cosmology. For example, the myth of Quetzalcoatl involves the morning star rebirth of Venus from the sun, which takes place after the inferior conjunction of the sun and Venus. This event occurs once every 584 days. The Venus *transit* is a much more precise, and therefore rare, version of inferior conjunction, such that the planet Venus actually transits across the disk of the sun. Balin listed Waters's *Mexico Mystique* in his bibliography, and he states that the end date falls on December 21, 2011—a partial correction of Waters's erroneous sourcing from Coe. With these examples, by 1980 there were clearly several books in print that mentioned or explored more fully the cycle ending.

In my own process of encountering and studying all things 2012, I can't help notice that my life has been interwoven with these authors and the 2012 meme from an early age. I have a vivid memory from 1976 of my friend Joe's dad reading *Mexico Mystique*. It was described as a book about the Indians in Mexico who invented a calendar that will end in 2011. That encounter stuck with me, and I recognized Waters's book years later when I began my studies. I spent the summer of '76 at my uncle's campground in Colorado, helping out and camping under the shooting stars of the Rocky Mountains. We would sometimes congregate around an old hippie storyteller's campfire at night and listen to legends and ghost stories. One day as I was emptying garbage cans for my uncle, the old hippie called me over and gave me a copy of Shearer's *Quetzalcoatl, Lord of the Dawn*. After moving to Colorado in 1985, I read *The Invisible Landscape* by the McKenna brothers (both of whom were born and raised in Colorado). I encountered Argüelles's *Earth Ascending* book in 1986 and then the more informative and fulfilling *Time and the Highland Maya* by Barbara Tedlock.

All along, the books of Frank Waters were with me: *Masked Gods, The Book of the Hopi, Pumpkin Seed Point, Mountain Dialogues.* I loved the guy and wanted to meet him. In getaways from Boulder every summer I used to hike and camp in Bandelier National Monument, near Taos, New Mexico. The Mesa Verde cliff dwellings and Chaco Canyon were close by, and so was Frank Waters's home in Arroyo Seco above Taos. On a whim I tried to visit Waters at his home near Taos in August 1988. I spoke with his wife, Barbara, and hung out in the courtyard for a while, but he was out of town. His *Mexico Mystique* book, despite the one glaring mistake that renders it obsolete, remains an important early exploration of what we now call the 2012 phenomenon.

SPIRITUAL MATERIALISM IN THE 1980S AND BEYOND

By 1980, lots of changes were happening in the cultural landscape of America. The 1960s breakthrough into liberal exploration of sex and drugs was accompanied by explorations of esoteric teachings and Oriental mysticism. The 1970s brought the shock of a gas shortage, the end of the Vietnam War, and a presidential debacle. As the '70s closed, disco set the tone while more conservative life strategies emerged as the hippies prepared to turn into yuppies. It was the beginning of the twelve-year Reagan-Bush era, which would see an assassination attempt and a recession (in 1982) and end with the Gulf War.

The landscape of the spiritual marketplace would be changing too. Deep yet popular studies of profound ideas that were all the rage in the 1960s, such as Alan Watts's *Way of Zen*, gave way to dumbed-down self-help books and trendy (and expensive) encounter groups. Good books come out in every decade, but the general trend throughout the 1980s was clear—market ancient wisdom teachings by figuring out how to make it palatable to people on the go; the intellectual equivalent of fast food at a drive-thru. One way to do this was signaled by Shirley MacLaine's spiritual biography *Out On a Limb* in 1981. Spiritually themed personal-growth books could sell very well if driven by a famous and popular personality. Eventually, it was realized that the popularity could come from scandal or outrageous claims—it didn't matter, it just had to draw attention.

The era of Argüelles coincided with this rise of New Age spiritual materialism, a trendy self-help approach to ancient perennial wisdom that appealed to the boomer generation and typified books of this genre written in the 1980s. Admittedly, Argüelles is very much a unique breed of visionary writer and his legacy combines the qualities of a Carlos Casteneda, the channeled Seth material, the mystic art of Robert Fludd, and the incomprehensibility of a Buckminster Fuller on LSD, with a dash of Merlin playing the pipes of Pan for good effect.[10] José Argüelles, one-half of a dyad with his twin brother Ivan (a poet), started his career with a fascinating PhD thesis from the University of Chicago, which became the book *Charles Henry and the Formation of a Psychospiritual Aesthetic.* That was followed by an artistic compilation called *Mandala,* which did so well he was able to buy a house in Oakland with the royalties.[11] The evolution of this artist-mythmaker can be traced in his books, and his recent autobiography provides many more details. His ideation changed rapidly after 1979, when "he was at the peak of his alcoholism, and his marriage of 13 years was about to collapse, along with his entire life as he knew it."[12] His well-documented and intriguing book *The Transformative Vision* (1975), which he considered his seminal text, was a far cry from the cosmic diagrams and inventive speculations of *Earth Ascending* (1984).

Along the lines of Buckminster Fuller's integrative vision, *Earth Ascending* wove connections between DNA, the I Ching, and the Maya sacred calendar. While Argüelles was teaching at the University of Colorado in Boulder in 1985, he invited a Maya day-keeper from Mexico named Hunbatz Men to come and speak. That friendship set the stage for later developments, including the spread of Argüelles's ideas to Mexico. Something opened up in the mid-1980s as Shearer's old Harmonic Convergence date approached. The stage was prepared, the curtain rose, and Argüelles walked on. Shearer himself did his own thing with the Harmonic Convergence date, involving a presentation he gave near Denver.[13]

The up-and-coming New Age publisher Bear & Company got strategic with the Maya material and collaborated with Argüelles for his 1987 book *The Mayan Factor*. Bear & Company was cofounded by radical Christian theologian Matthew Fox. When Barbara Hand Clow stepped up to run Bear in the mid-1980s, it became a conduit for popular Native American teachings as well as books on Pleiadian channeling—Clow's own métier, as we can see in her various books, an exception being her less overtly channeled *Pleiadian Agenda* (1995), which presented a smorgasbord of 2012 ideas. The *Native American Medicine Cards* oracle was a huge hit for Bear & Company, as was Barbara Marciniak's *Bringers of the Dawn*.

An idea called the Photon Belt appeared in Marciniak's book, which was a vaguely defined mystical concept that visualized the earth passing through a photon beam, or belt of energy, that supposedly emanates from the Galactic Center. As earth travels through space it would enter this zone of increased energy, connecting us to the Pleiadian interdimensional superhighway, and all kinds of speculations were offered as to what it would mean. (The beam was also sometimes described as sweeping through space.) The topic merged nicely with UFOs and crop circles. Communications or visits with extraterrestrials, enlightenment of the race, lizard alien takeovers—the Photon Belt's extended family of scenarios was large and creative.

A variation of this Photon Belt idea became a major component in Argüelles's *The Mayan Factor* book, which he connected with 2012 and called "galactic synchronization." In Brian Swimme's introduction to *The Mayan Factor*, we find an explanation of what the galactic beams are, astronomically speaking:

Current astrophysics describes these beams as density waves that sweep through the galaxy and that influence galactic evolution. For instance, our Sun's birth was a result of this wave . . . the density wave passed through and ignited a giant star, which exploded and evoked our own Sun's existence.[14]

Galactic synchronization, "synchronization with the beyond," is, according to Argüelles, "to surpass all fantasy and all of our wildest dreams."[15]

This idea eventually morphed into a concept involving the orbit of our solar system around the Galactic Center, in an up-and-down motion above and below the galactic plane over some 240 million years. Our solar system is in this way thought to enter different "density sectors" in its passage through space (see the figure on page 234). Argüelles believed that our passage through the "synchronization beam" was linked to the 5,125-year Great Cycle of 13 Baktuns. It was an evolutionary beam, which he philosophized with artistic finesse in his book, and 2012 represented the critical emergence point, our last chance for "getting on the beam" before we left its transformative presence.

The only thing I need to emphasize here, which I'll clarify later, is that these concepts have nothing to do with the "galactic alignment" astronomy that is demonstrably embedded in the Maya Creation Mythology and other traditions. The galactic alignment and galactic synchronization are not at all the same thing. I was adamant about the distinction from the get-go, and for more than a decade have clarified the issue in my books, on my website, and in interviews.[16] Unfortunately, today the concepts are still frequently confused, to the detriment of understanding a key concept of ancient Maya cosmology that demonstrably relates to 2012. In addition, the galactic alignment concept as I have defined it has been retroactively adopted by or applied to Argüelles and others, even though there is no mention of it in their previous books.[17]

In a 1991 article I wrote (reprinted in my 1992 book *Tzolkin: Visionary Perspectives and Calendar Studies*), I took an open-minded position on the larger visionary work that Argüelles was doing and defended the role of the mythmaker in our society, especially at critical ideological junctures like the one we find ourselves in:

> *The role of the myth-makers is hard to understand. They seem to break with tradition and flaunt a speculative certainty; they seem just one step up from a raving maniac or doomsayer ... The myth-maker recognizes the end as a new beginning and starts to formulate the new values and myths to serve the changing needs of humanity. A myth-maker is a living oracle for the vaguely sensed needs of a people undergoing transformation. It is a time to create the future, not arbitrarily or according to one person's agenda, but based on collective need; the "new world order" in a sense "congeals" or crystallizes from the field of human unfolding. A myth-maker facilitates this birth by naming what's happening.[18]*

And Argüelles is without doubt a mythmaker. But I also knew that a free-form kind of mythmaking can be dangerous—especially if it develops into a self-referential system divorced from traditional principles (in this instance, the facts of the Maya calendar), dislocating rather than illuminating the core ideas. It then makes a gamble for being a "new dispensation" or falls off as an irrelevant sideshow. It can grow as a new dispensation only if it has a clear channel into universal wisdom, or Truth (with a capital *T* in the theological sense of that which is rooted in the higher spiritual wisdom).

By 1991 Argüelles's nascent Dreamspell group promoted July 26, 1992, as the next Harmonic Convergence, a date that would supposedly signal the beginning of the final Katun (20-year period) of the Great Cycle of 13 Baktuns. July 26 was presented as New Year's Day, to be celebrated right after the "day out of time," July 25, which was a necessary fudge factor in order to incorporate the 364-day 13-moon calendar (another component of the Dreamspell system). If this all sounds complicated and contrived, as well as not recognizable as having much to do with the real Maya calendar, it is and it doesn't. And it's just the tip of a very messy iceberg.

My book *Tzolkin* primarily offered a reconstruction of the Venus calendar in the Dresden Codex, but also exposed the factual errors in the calendar system Argüelles had just presented in his new Dreamspell game/oracle. The seeds of that system had been planted, and were evident, in *The Mayan Factor*. The following offers a quick rundown on the factual problems.

The correlation used in the Dreamspell system is not aligned with the traditional, surviving day-count in the highlands of Guatemala, which has a direct unbroken lineage going back to the Classic Period Maya and beyond—to the very dawn of the 260-day calendar at least 2,500 years ago. On page 211 of *The Mayan Factor*, we find a list of tzolkin dates that tells us that, according to Argüelles, July 26, 1992, corresponds to 12 Ix. The count promoted by Argüelles was thus, at that time, 53 days out of synchronization with the day-count actually used today by the Maya. The discrepancy was repeated in the birthday calculator included in the Dreamspell game released in late 1991. In my early writings I referred to the surviving traditional day-count as "the True Count," and I proposed that, in order to be clear, Argüelles's day-count could charitably be referred to as a "Newly Created Count."[19]

The Dreamspell system skips counting leap day, February 29, which comes around every four years. This is the biggest no-no one could imagine, as it throws out of whack the internal consistency of the sacred 260-day rhythm. Every 260 days the same day-sign and number combination should come around and synchronize. By skipping a day, the "time resonance" factor of 260 days is compromised. For example, if you were born on June 15, 1966, your birthday according to the traditional tzolkin is 4 Muluc. Every 20 days Muluc recurs and every 260 days, 4 Muluc recurs, defining resonances with others whose birthdays fall on Muluc or another day-sign that has a resonant relationship with Muluc—for example, Cauac (opposite Muluc on the 20-day wheel of the day-signs). You might find that your grandfather was born on April 7, 1903, which was a 12 Muluc day. You would, according to the oracular use of the 260-day tzolkin calendar, have a special resonance with your grandfather. The traditional, surviving calendar utilizes these kinds of concepts and operations. Not so for Dreamspell. Because it skips counting February 29, there will be an accumulated error of 16 uncounted days between your grandfather's birthday and your own. Looking up your birthdays in the Dreamspell calculator will not accurately reflect the real passage of days. It's obvious that there is a problem here.

The reason why this feature was implemented in the Dreamspell system involves the fixing of the New Year's Day to July 26. This date was indeed used by the Yucatec Maya as New Year's Day. They did so because at the latitude of northern Yucatán the sun passes through the zenith at high noon on that day (as well as May 23). However, Argüelles states that July 26 was chosen in his system because it correlates with the ancient Egyptian heliacal rise of Sirius.

Nevertheless, the New Year's Day wasn't fixed for the Maya; it was intended to fall back one day every four years, probably in order to track a larger cycle known as the "year drift formula" (in which 1,507 tropical years = 1,508 haab of 365 days each). The modern Quiché Maya, for example, allow their New Year's Day to cycle backward through the months of the year. Though somewhat counterintuitive to the modern mind, the ancient Maya didn't need their mundane solar calendar to stay fixed to one New Year's Day; instead, the sacred rhythm of 260 days had precedence.

It's very possible that the Yucatec Maya intentionally tracked their New Year's Day falling backward from July 26 to May 23, from one zenith passage to another, which took 256 years. This period corresponds to the all-important 13-Katun prophecy cycle, or May cycle, which scholar Prudence Rice has recently argued was an important key to Yucatec Maya cosmology and politics.

The point is that Argüelles's policy of fixing New Year's Day doesn't reflect how the ancient Maya themselves actually used their calendars. The *a priori* assumption that this must be done led Argüelles to implement the highly dubious February 29 day skipping. But, again, no day-keeper would ever consider not counting a day. As a result, the day-count discrepancy of Dreamspell changes by one day every four years. While it was 53 days out of accord with the True Count between 1988 and 1993, it became 52 days out of whack between 1992 and 1996. And so on.

The so-called "day out of time," July 25, is something entirely different. It was intended by Argüelles to keep the 364-day 13-moon calendar in sync with the New Year's Day, July 26. The 13-moon calendar is, according to the Dreamspell view, supposed to be the "natural rhythm" that we should follow in order to synchronize ourselves with the natural earth-moon rhythm of life, reflected in women's fertility cycles. A 28-day lunar cycle, however, is only an abstract average, useful only for an approximate reckoning of a numerologi- cally handy 13 × 28 = 364 days. It quickly will shift out of step with real lunar cycles and thus doesn't accurately track lunar rhythms. It can't really do what its designer says it is supposed to do.[20]

Another issue of dislocation, or misrepresentation, in Argüelles's thought occurred in regard to the commencement of the last Katun of the Long Count. A Katun contains 7,200 days. The end date is December 21, 2012. Thus, the final Katun commences on April 5, 1993. In the early 1990s I circulated an article I wrote called "The Importance of April 5, 1993" and published it in my book *Tzolkin*. I noted the strange synchronicity that the final Katun commenced on a day on which Venus rose as morning star, and it was a full moon. This suggested a patterning between Venus and Katun cycles, which I plotted out, discovering that 3 Katuns equal 37 Venus cycles. In a 1991 interview with Antero Alli in the magazine *Welcome to Planet Earth*, Argüelles stated that the final Katun begins on July 26, 1992—the date then being promoted as the next Harmonic Convergence. Clearly, this was a very generalized mathematical operation, and it detracted from the very striking fact that the correct beginning date of the last Katun coordinated with a first appearance of Venus as morning star. Consequently, the morning star Venus rise that fell on the commencement of the final Katun of the 13-Baktun cycle was lost upon Dreamspell followers. However, an original thinker named Marko Bartholomew, who had acquired the original self-published version of my book *Tzolkin* in 1992, led a group of seekers up a volcano in Hawaii to observe Venus, Quetzalcoatl reborn, and the dawn of the final Katun.

I'm not meaning to be difficult, but all of these errors are of a fundamental nature and to any discerning mind would render the Dreamspell system problematic, at best. It's not a matter of debatable opinions; my critique is addressed to the level of stated facts and functional operation. After I published my critique of Dreamspell-think in my book *Tzolkin*, I immediately came under fire by members of the Dreamspell group, who frequently accused me of impugning the wisdom of their teacher. For example, Steven Starsparks sent me a postcard filled with four-letter words after reading my book, aghast at my audacious questioning of the wisdom of the Dreamspell revelation. For four years I exchanged more than three hundred letters with various disillusioned Dreamspellers (this was before e-mail) in which I patiently tried to educate them about the existence of an authentic surviving day-count—and that the Argüellian system simply was not it. "Disillusioned" is an apt word for what they were going through. I hoped that Argüelles himself might offer some clarification, which was not forthcoming for many years. My 1993 book *7 Wind: A Quiché Calendar for 1993* was intended as a simple introductory guidebook to how the Maya day-keepers use their tzolkin calendar.

It should be emphasized here that in much of the early Dreamspell literature, the terminology labeled it "the Maya calendar." The primary result of my efforts has been to initiate a careful distinction in the group's literature, an acknowledgment that there is indeed an authentic day-count still followed by the Maya. In Argüelles's recent biography, the discussion of Dreamspell very carefully avoids calling it "the Maya calendar," whereas in earlier literature a conceptual conflation between the two existed. I count this a victory for accuracy and clarity, in retrospect, but it came only after a drastic step was taken, because for many years this truth was resisted.

In late 1995 I was encouraged by my friend Mark Valladares to write a piece in a different voice, one that might get through to the followers of Dreamspell. Instead of trying to engage Socratic dialogue based on facts, as

I'd been doing for years, I took on a high-toned science-fiction voice and laid out the dire energetic consequences of having a new system conflict with the ancient, traditional one. It's ironic that truth must sometimes be wrapped in allegorical satire. But it seemed to work. In late 1995 I posted "The Key to the Dreamspell Agenda" piece on my website, and although it ruffled some feathers it became the seed through which the Dreamspell camp began acknowledging that a True Count existed and the Dreamspell system was a different kind of bird.

The spin doctors stepped in pretty quickly, of course, and the Dreamspell count was soon identified as the preferable "Wizard Count" or "Galactic Count." So another creative level of apologetics has allowed the system to continue with only a minor deference to the facts of the matter. Although its acknowledgment of the True Count was progress, the Dreamspell movement tended to see its own perspective as a higher "galactic" calendar or a "new dispensation" that could replace the older traditional day-count. The idea of new things replacing old things is a common theme in the trendy marketplace of New Age capitalism, where "traditional" ideas are old and must be disposed of. Since all this went down, I've observed my work to clarify the fundamental problems with the Dreamspell system slip into public consensus. At the time, few others had noticed the issues, or dared or cared to make the corrections, but now my observations are adopted by a new generation of writers, without much awareness of how long it took to crack open the web of misconceptions.

In 1999, I shared a conference venue with José called the Fourth International Mayan Dreamtime Festival, set in the beautiful town of Glastonbury, England. After the conference we had a chance to talk. Glastonbury is part of a sacred landscape. Visionaries and mystics have long perceived a zodiac that runs around Glastonbury for miles, and the twelve constellations are represented by tors (hills), waterways, wells, and other features. A dinner for the speakers was organized by our hosts, Mikhail and Alloa, and it happened to take place at a country home in Baltonsborough. As our group of speakers drove through the countryside, sharing Maya chocolate, the mood was light, and we laughed when someone mentioned that Baltonsborough was right between Sagittarius and Scorpio on the Glastonbury zodiac—right in the Galactic Center.

After dinner José spoke at length about a wide range of unrelated things, including his readings of the Koran, and it was a bit difficult for anyone to interject comments or questions. José was well aware of my criticisms of his Dreamspell system because we had exchanged e-mails, once, in 1996. I finally managed to bring up the issue of the day-count discrepancy, and his response was that it didn't really matter, both the Quiché calendar and his calendar worked in the same way. This was, of course, simply not true, as the day skipping on February 29 was a major stumbling block to continuity between the counts, and was just one of the many problems that set it apart from the authentic day-count. There was nowhere for a cordial conversation to go. Nervous laughter rippled among the guests, more chocolate was passed around, and I realized that my work on that front was done.

The writing was on the wall for the Argüellian Mothership: Dreamspell was a grab bag of contradictory mystifications, and the calendar Argüelles promoted was at odds with the surviving, traditional, authentic day-count in the highlands of Guatemala. Nevertheless, the system still has currency and is followed by many, which is the prerogative of free will. Some Dreamspell enthusiasts in England have adopted a rather complex two-part system in which the Dreamspell count and the traditional count are both factored into readings and birthday tabulations. My primary goal was to defend and emphasize the existence of the True Count so that people would at least know they had a choice. And that is, in the end, what has occurred, more or less.

An unfortunate side effect of Argüelles's decision to create his own day-count system manifested in his relationship with Hunbatz Men. In 1990 Bear & Company published Hunbatz Men's book *Secrets of Mayan Science and Religion*. Men's book was interesting in some respects, although his claim that a tribe in India, the Naga Mayas, were cousins to the Maya was a bit hard to swallow. Hunbatz came to the attention of Bear through Argüelles, who hosted a visit by Hunbatz to Boulder, Colorado, in 1985.

A collaboration between Hunbatz and Argüelles is apparent, especially in one important respect—the correlation they used. Both acknowledged 2012 as a significant reference point, but the question of what day it was in the Maya calendar defaulted to Argüelles, as the tzolkin calendar had stopped being followed in the Yucatán. Hunbatz had no tzolkin tradition to draw from. This kind of thing would be a bit of a sticky problem for any Maya shaman. The tradition had been lost in his homeland, so he had to rely on the authority of an outsider, a teacher at an American university believed to be accurately informed on the matter. Unfortunately, the information transmitted from Argüelles to Hunbatz was tainted by the questionable model that Argüelles himself had devised.

Hunbatz didn't mention a correlation in his 1990 book, but by 1992 a Maya enthusiast, writer, and tour leader named Aluna Joy Yaxkin started publishing Maya calendars in the magazine *Sedona*. This was a monthly feature that continued up through 1995, when Hunbatz led many thousands of people in solar initiations at Chichén Itzá and the cenote at nearby Dzibilchaltún—sacred ceremonies and initiations that were similar in nature to the Harmonic Convergence events. I had noticed that Aluna Joy's calendar charts followed the Argüelles day-count, yet she stated the system was taught to her by Hunbatz (she partnered with Hunbatz for tours in the early 1990s). The day-count she used thus seemed to have the stamp of approval from a real Maya elder. I immediately suspected what had happened, and I was able to confirm the underlying hidden story with the help of my friend Jim Reed.

Jim Reed, the charismatic "Mayaman" who leads tours to Maya temples and caves, served as president of the Institute of Maya Studies in Miami, and he continues to edit their informative newsletter. He hosted Hunbatz Men at events in Florida in the mid-1990s, and told me of Hunbatz's collaboration with Argüelles in Boulder in 1985. I came to understand the difficult work that Hunbatz has been engaged with in Mexico, where the Maya people are forbidden from doing rituals within the archaeological sites. Treading a thin legal line and often hassled by government officials, Hunbatz has performed rituals at places like Dzibilchaltún, where the rising equinox sun shines through the windows in the Temple of the Seven Dolls to illuminate the sacred walkway and visitors can swim in a sacred cenote. Hunbatz has performed annual initiations in the sacred waters of the cenote, and on the March equinox in 1995 hundreds of people were initiated by Hunbatz into the ancient solar religion.[21]

Aluna Joy Yaxkin was instrumental in Hunbatz's well-attended solar initiations of 1995. By 1998 the day-count discrepancy had become a question that Hunbatz wanted to resolve, and he invited me to speak at a Maya Calendar congress he organized in Mérida. Jim Reed led a group that I joined in Champotón, and together we visited Aké, Edzna, and other sites before joining Hunbatz in Mérida. Our groups planned to journey together, after the conference, to Dzibilchaltún and Chichén Itzá. On the conference day in Mérida, Jim encouraged me to emphasize the correct day-count and make no mistake about it. But there were a few other speakers, and I was on last.

The loquacious speaker before me, part of Hunbatz's group, ended up talking far beyond his allotted time, and I had to quickly adapt my slides for a quick forty-five-minute presentation. This presenter didn't seem to care or be aware of the duration of his time slot, and he finally had to be interrupted as he had gone on for more than two hours. I then was able to briefly share my reconstruction of the Maya's awareness of the sun's alignment with the Pleiades over the Pyramid of Kukulcan. I also emphasized that, historically, the tzolkin was lost in Yucatán but survived in the Guatemalan highlands. March 19, 1998 (the day of the conference), was equal to the day 8 Muluc. (I'll always remember this because an amazing artist, Furie, gifted me with a glass pendant that day, engraved with the Muluc day-sign.)

The situation of the correct day-count continued, nevertheless, to be unclear among Maya day-keepers, and Hunbatz had been following the Argüelles count. Some writers liked to say that 8 Batz (8 Monkey, the initiation day for day-keepers) was the Maya New Year, which was confusing because New Year's Day wasn't technically connected to 8 Batz. Also, the Long

Count calendar and 2012 were a lost tradition, and information on it in the literature was unclear. Some terminology and definitions needed to be worked out. Consequently, Hunbatz, as a representative of the Yucatec Maya, invited a contingency of Guatemalan calendar priests to attend the Calendar Congress in Mérida in 1999. The results were mixed, as the Guatemalan day-keepers did not seem to get any stage time at the conference. Hunbatz concluded by stating that they were all in agreement, which was clearly not the case. Hunbatz continues to lead a renewed calendar tradition in the Yucatán, driven by solar initiations at the Maya sites.

In the 1970s Argüelles lived in Boulder, Colorado, and he was involved in the founding of Naropa College in 1974. He was a devoted student of Trungpa Rinpoche, who was known for a spiritual teaching style called Crazy Wisdom. This school of thought, and its leader, became famous for techniques that disrupted the rational mind. The methods were unorthodox and, in retrospect, highly questionable. Some of its "graduates" have claimed that it left them in states of severe confusion. Author Sam Keen had this to say about the proliferation of Wisdom teachers:

> One of the things I frankly don't like about your magazine [What Is Enlightenment?] is the holding up of these people who are supposedly "in the absolute" and totally liberated. I don't know whether you remember, but for many years I was the person at Psychology Today who interviewed all these gurus. And so I've had a good bit of experience with a fair number of them—Chögyam Trungpa, Oscar Ichazo, Muktananda and others. And if these are all examples of people who are totally liberated, I say give me slavery because they were people with enormous illusions and who were cultivating enormous illusions in their followers. By and large almost all of them were totally unclear about three important things: sex, money and power. And they could

*play like they were liberated as long as they had a whole cult of dis-
ciples who did everything for them except wipe their asses—and probably that, too. And most of them were on enormous power trips. So I
think the idea of total liberation is sort of like the idea of perfection.
It's an idea that is more crippling than helpful.[22]*

Students of Trungpa Rinpoche in the early days of Naropa had to contend
with contradictory statements and behavior offered by their teacher, dealing
with jealousy issues by partner swapping, and similar practices characterized
as "crazy." Unfortunately, the progenitor of Crazy Wisdom teachings in the
West succumbed, at the age of forty-seven, to alcoholism and heart failure
after moving from Boulder to Nova Scotia. Those are the facts of the matter,
and I'm not intending to pass judgment on what may have been important
spiritual teachings for Westerners of the boomer generation to experience.

Argüelles, in his biography, discussed the extreme yet often endearing
nature of Trungpa's character, and remembers that he benefited from learning presence of mind by practicing dharma art projects, with Trungpa's guidance, in the late 1970s.[23] In my opinion, a devaluing of facts and rational
assessment might have been instilled in Argüelles at this time, and Argüelles's
own predilection for creative process and model-making took precedence.
The irrational teaching methods of the Crazy Wisdom school may in some
way underlie the unorthodox presentation of Dreamspell, which is, as I discussed, irrational and internally inconsistent. In this light I offer my own
conclusion that Dreamspell is best understood as a test for seekers who need
to strengthen the muscle of discernment and "discriminating wisdom." It's a
Way Station on the spiritual path, designed to snare seekers who need to
develop discernment and rational discrimination before moving on to transrational processing. Here we encounter the idea of a progression of spiritual
and cognitive development, from prerational to rational to transrational,
which is an important framework for understanding the larger implications
of 2012.

INTREPID INVESTIGATORS: HANCOCK, COTTERELL, AND GILBERT

In 1995, while I was finding evidence to support my thesis on the 2012 galactic alignment, two popular books on the Maya calendar appeared in the marketplace. One might suspect that this was triggered by breakthroughs occurring in academia with Linda Schele's book *Maya Cosmos* (1993, coauthored with David Freidel and Joy Parker), but neither book mentioned Schele's work.

Fingerprints of the Gods, by Graham Hancock, dealt tangentially with the Maya calendar while taking a global approach to reviving the old Atlantis hypothesis. To be sure, Hancock had new findings and theories to report, and that he paid special attention to the precession of the equinoxes is important. *The Mayan Prophecies*, on the other hand, was written largely by a hired co-author who had very little research into the Maya traditions under his belt. We should treat both books separately, as they are very different.

Graham Hancock had achieved some fame with his well-researched book on the Ark of the Covenant *The Sign and the Seal* (1992). He pretty much defined the genre of globe-trotting sleuth scholarship. His provocatively titled book *Fingerprints of the Gods* explored the premise that an unrecognized earlier civilization had existed before the widely accepted date for the advent of civilization—around 4000 BC. It's the old Atlantis idea that preoccupied Charnay and Le Plongeon, but today we can draw on the work of, for example, Marija Gimbutas, which shows conclusively that prior to the advent of patriarchal monotheism a cultural phenomenon bearing all the marks of civilization existed in Neolithic Europe. This Magdalenian phase began roughly 17,000 years ago. Likewise, compelling structures that seem to be megalithic sites recently found off the coasts of Japan and India imply high culture around 15,000 BC. Hancock rallied his own insights while summarizing the progressive research of others to present a compelling case that something wasn't being acknowledged by conventional historians and other status quo gatekeepers.

His chapter on the Maya presented a standard summary and didn't delve into the recent breakthroughs of Schele and others. Also, the galactic alignment concept remained unrecognized. He did discuss the 13-Baktun cycle end date, but following Coe's preference reported it as occurring on December 23, 2012. One of Hancock's beliefs is that the Maya's calendar wisdom must have been handed down from a previous high civilization, and this was a reiteration of his main thesis, that of an earlier source-civilization that existed before the currently accepted dawn of human civilization some 6,000 years ago in the Middle East. This view doesn't jibe too well with what we know about the independent development of civilization in Mesoamerica.

The situation that Hancock presupposes, however, of transoceanic contact between the Maya and Asia, Europe, and the Middle East, is complicated and needs to be examined carefully. In my view, the native genius of the ancient Maya was more than enough to create the Long Count and formulate profound astronomical insights. It's extremely unlikely that the specific details of these traditions were passed down from an ancient ur-culture. The Long Count and the 260-day tzolkin are unique cultural and scientific achievements that have no parallel in other parts of the world, past or present. However, more generally we may observe that the nondual orientation of Maya cosmovision, perceiving all domains of nature as being inextricably interwoven, belongs to an archaic kind of consciousness that has been increasingly eclipsed by modernity and scientific rationalism. So in this light certain elements of Maya civilization may resemble those found in Egypt not because of physical contact and transmission but because both cultures drew from the same type of philosophical and cosmological outlook. More to the point, both looked to the heavens for a celestial prototype, and this idea was explored in Hancock's subsequent volume, *Heaven's Mirror* (1997), a beautiful book containing many photographs by his wife, Santhfaiia.

Hancock went on to explore sunken ruins off the coasts of India, Japan, and elsewhere, finding more evidence to help identify a prehistoric civilization, and published *Underworld* in 2004. His next book, *Supernatural*, was an unexpected turn for those who were followers of Hancock's work. In it, he explored the visions induced by the South American jungle vine, *ayahuasca*, relating observations garnered from his own experiences taking the hallucinogenic brew. This latest offering exemplifies his continuing effort to challenge establishment limits and push back the fringes of knowledge.

The Mayan Prophecies also came out in 1995. As it promised to "decode the secret of the 2012 end date," I was faced with the possibility that the authors, Cotterell and Gilbert, had also discovered the galactic alignment as the key to 2012. Gilbert was coauthor, with Robert Bauval, of *The Orion Mystery*, a book hailed as a breakthrough in decoding the astronomical alignment embedded in the Great Pyramids of Egypt. I'd read that book with great interest. The alignments involved the precession of the equinoxes, as did my discoveries among the Maya, but there was no mention of the galactic alignment in the Egyptian material. It was a simple step to notice the possibility of the alignment, but it was a very new idea. At that time (1994), it was an obscure and relatively unknown fact of precession.[24]

The Mayan Prophecies proved to be a very problematic book that was riddled with basic errors and contradictions. Obsolete sources for Maya scholarship were used, and recent breakthroughs in Maya scholarship were neglected. The thesis didn't involve precession. Instead, it turned out that Gilbert largely served as a presenter of Cotterell's research on sunspot cycles. Using three statistical variables in solar phenomena, Cotterell claimed to be able to accurately model long-term sunspot cycle extremes, ranging between 3,300 and 3,700 years. The book presented one extreme as having occurred in 627 AD, with another one following in 2012. Clearly, there was a fundamental problem with the theory, as the interval between those two dates was nowhere near 3,300 or 3,700 years.[25]

The book did not attempt to show how sunspots and solar flare cycles may have been conceived by the Maya or were encoded into their books or traditions or inscriptions. The question of how the ancient Maya who created the Long Count might have discovered the sunspot cycle extremes and calculated one far off into the future also remained unposed. A fallacy of numerical coincidence permeates the book's premise. The laws of physics dictate that astronomical cycles often exhibit harmonic relations with one another. The Maya number 260 is a kind of key number—a common denominator, if you will—that the Maya used as a framework in their astronomical almanacs for predicting planetary cycles as well as eclipses. The sun's dark spots orbit in a twenty-six-day period. This does not mean the Maya were aware of the sun's dark spot periodicity.

It turned out that Gilbert, for his part, had his own ideas on 2012 to present. This confusing subplot involved the cycles of Venus. Utilizing nineteenth-century ideas proposed by Ernst Förstemann that postulated the beginning of the Long Count as "the birth of Venus," Gilbert looked at astronomy software and noted that, in 3114 BC, Venus was west of the sun, technically in the morning star position. However, in checking the facts I noticed that Venus was not in its first appearance as morning star, which would have been the critical event, nor was it even waxing to its morning star maximum. It was, in fact, in a retrograde fall toward superior conjunction, a phase of its cycle that was meaningless as a base for the Long Count.

Later in the book, Gilbert reiterated "the birth of Venus" to explain the end date, noting that "Venus sinks below the western horizon as the Pleiades rise over the eastern horizon . . . as the sun sets, Orion rises, perhaps signifying the start of a new precessional cycle."[26] This summary was supposed to reveal the revolutionary breakthrough promised by the book, but it came across as a contrived attempt to link the end date with Orion, the subject of Bauval's research. Oddly, the Orion connection to the Long Count was readily available in Schele's research, which was not, however, mentioned in the book.

I interviewed Gilbert by phone in late 1995 and learned that his investigation of Maya traditions had begun about eight months prior to the writing deadline. He had embarked on a fact-finding trip to Mexico and had made some interesting contacts among the people of Mexico—notably José Díaz Bolio. His summary of British explorers in Mexico and Central

America was interesting, if a bit ethnocentric. My observation here is not as flippant as it might sound, as Gilbert championed the old idea that Quetzalcoatl, who according to one apocryphal tale brought civilization to the heathens in Mexico long ago, was a bearded white guy from across the sea. Gilbert argued he might have been Saint Patrick, a fifth-century monk from Ireland.

During the book's writing Cotterell had managed to pull off a promo stunt with newspaper coverage that claimed he had "decoded the Maya hieroglyphs." This claim related not to his sunspot theory but to his fun and games with Maya art. He realized you could take drawings of pictographs from, say, Pakal's lid at Palenque, cut them in half, edge them up to their mirror image, and generate faces and alien-looking heads. Surely, these were the faces of the secret aliens behind the Maya culture, the "supergods," as he called them in one of his subsequent books. This is what I call a "cool stoner idea"—it appeals to a vast network of conspiracy-minded and gullible consumers. *The Mayan Prophecies* had all the bells and whistles in place and it sold well. Cotterell went on to produce a series of books capitalizing on his funny and entertaining art manipulations, which, however, he presented in complete seriousness.

I've realized through the years that some authors are adept at manipulating the showbiz side of publishing, that they maximize the appearance of having new breakthroughs while actually offering nothing new. This is a kind of magic trick, an illusion of appearances. Such authors are very often misleading and distort or ignore the facts in order to further a clever idea that serves as a compelling hook. If you shine a light on basic factual mistakes, you are either ignored or personally attacked, but rarely are your critiques rationally addressed. It's an unfortunate state of affairs, and 2012 is an easy target for exploitation in today's marketplace.

I was surprised that other researchers had not made the same breakthrough that I had, because the astronomy of the galactic alignment was clearly of central importance in the Maya Creation Myth and the symbolism of the ballgame. Although Linda Schele's work was heading in the right direction, there was a strong reaction in academia to some of her ideas, effectively curtailing forward progress. For this reason it was unlikely that Schele herself, nor her coauthor David Freidel, would go to the next level and acknowledge the role of the dark rift in the rare galactic alignment of era-2012.

In 1999, I met Geoff Stray in England. Here, finally, was a welcome development in the realm of independent research and investigation of 2012. In 2000, Geoff launched a website called Diagnosis 2012, in which he intended to review virtually everything that was published on 2012. Back in the early 1980s, Geoff had read the McKenna brothers' *The Invisible Landscape*, was inspired to investigate the Novelty Theory, and became more involved in Maya calendar studies. He, too, had noticed discrepancies in the system presented by Argüelles, and he had read my book *Tzolkin*. His website was to become an invaluable resource for anyone wanting to learn more about the various writings on 2012. In 1999, the list was small. Today, the list is immense. Geoff's site maintains thousands of pages of material in which he critiques and assesses new books and videos on 2012. These include not only nonfiction research but novels, prophecies, visions, dreams—virtually everything is included under the purview of Diagnosis 2012. Having immersed himself in the depths of 2012ology, he's offered his own integrative insights on "the 2012 phenomenon" with his book *Beyond 2012* (2005), illustrating how 2012 could be treated comprehensively and rationally.

As Year 2000 approached, I struggled to balance my meager-paying job with doing interviews and conference events at Esalen Institute and Naropa University, in Santa Fe, England, Copenhagen, Colorado Springs, and California. My book had been out for more than a year and, sadly, my friend Terence McKenna had just received a terminal brain cancer diagnosis. In April 1999, just weeks after I'd seen him at the Whole Life Expo in Denver, Terence had a seizure and he was flown to a hospital. He was diagnosed with a rare fast-moving form of brain cancer and was given four months to live. Terence opted for an experimental gene-replacement procedure, but he died within a year at his home in Hawaii, on April 3, 2000. The Logos Bard mused on death in a final interview, recorded by Erik Davis in November of 1999:

> *I always thought death would come on the freeway in a few horrifying moments, so you'd have no time to sort it out. Having months and months to look at it and think about it and talk to people and hear what they have to say, it's a kind of blessing. It's certainly an opportunity to grow up and get a grip and sort it all out. Just being told by an unsmiling guy in a white coat that you're going to be dead in four months definitely turns on the lights. . . . It makes life rich and poignant. When it first happened, and I got these diagnoses, I could see the light of eternity, a la William Blake, shining through every leaf. I mean, a bug walking across the ground moved me to tears.[27]*

In one of the last phone messages I received from Terence, he said: "Your book will mean a lot to all of us" and "Congratulations on not only a new book, but a book that actually moves the discourse on human transformation forward." Terence wanted to see 2012. One can only wonder what the 2012 discussion would look like today if he were still around.

Closure, of a sort, on the first twenty-five years of 2012ology came on the eve of the millennium. I was invited to give a talk at an event in Denver as part of a New Year's Eve Millennium Celebration, together with Tony Shearer's closest student, Amaurante Montez, and Neo-Precolumbian artist Stevon Lucero. There was even a Dreamspeller on hand selling 13-moon calendars. It was in celebration of the wisdom of the ancient Americans, particularly Tony Shearer, who although ancient was still alive, but could not make the journey from his home near Mesa Verde. I was among friends, waiting for the clock to strike Y2K, a moment indisputably analogous to how people would soon be thinking about 2012.

In my presentation I stated, in complete agreement with what so many others were insisting, that the world was not about to end in Y2K computer malfunctions. And at midnight, it didn't. In fact, no computer digits were harmed during the Y2K fiasco. And in my talk I reminded people that the ancient Maya didn't even believe "the world would end" in 2012. That's a statement I've had to continue making, over and over. Even today, as 2009 waxes to fullness, for that one idea to get through to the mass media and collective consciousness would be a major breakthrough. Breakthroughs, however, require a shift of consciousness.

CHAPTER FOUR

BREAKTHROUGHS OR BREAKDOWN?

It appears that Maya peoples have, and had in their Precolumbian past, differing systems of timekeeping that they used in the separate provinces of their biological, astronomical, psychological, religious, and social realities, and that these various systems underwent a process of totalization within the overlapping, intermeshing cycles of their calendars. Given the complexity of this cosmology, which is ritually reenacted, shared, and thus maintained by the contemporary Maya, their knowledge ought not be dismissed as the degenerate remains of classic Maya glory.[1]

—BARBARA TEDLOCK

What does it mean to say that a breakthrough has occurred? In the history of science, we are familiar with several important junctures that spawned a radical shift affecting all areas of civilization. The harnessing of electrical power, the splitting of the atom, and development of computers and information technology are recent examples. The development of agriculture at the very dawn of civilization, based on an understanding of seeds and seasons, is a breakthrough that changed everything. Notice that this breakthrough was driven by a new appreciation of how nature works. The seasons were always happening, seeds and plant growth were known and observed, but something else had to happen before the pieces were put together properly. Here we see an inkling of an idea I'll explore more thoroughly—that breakthroughs require an expansion of perspective, of consciousness.

The Copernican Revolution in the early sixteenth century, based on a fundamental rethinking of the structure of the universe, triggered the rise of rational science and, subsequently, the industrial revolution, which has completely transfigured the face of the earth. Let's take a closer look at this one. It's unlikely that Copernicus intended or could anticipate the effects of his work. In fact, he was dead seventy years before his theory received its biggest boost, from Galileo. Peering through his new telescope, he observed moons revolving around Jupiter, confirming a fundamental implication of Copernicus's theory—that not all things revolve around the earth.

Another implication was difficult for the rational people of the day to swallow. According to the theory, the twenty-four-hour day had to be caused by the earth spinning on its axis. But, the levelheaded scientists of the day contended that if that were true, we would all go flying off into space. One can only imagine the response of Copernicus or Galileo. What could they say to appease the skeptics? Galileo could only shrug his shoulders and confess he had no explanation for that, but that moons were indeed revolving around Jupiter. "Look for yourselves," he might have said, "peer through my telescope and confirm the evidence for yourselves." The rational critics of his day, however, refused, deeply suspicious of the newfangled device, afraid they would be infected by demons.[2] Such are the difficulties that radical new breakthroughs must contend with. It took Sir Isaac Newton, fifty years after Galileo's death, to provide the concept of gravity so that the problem could be resolved.

The solution to problems is often not reached by rationally processing the data. German chemist Friedrich August Kekulé discovered the symmetrical ring shape of the benzene molecule in a daydream, thereby solving the baffling problem of how to account for all its molecular constituents. He told his colleagues in a lecture that he envisioned a snake biting its tail (the esoteric image of the Ouroboros serpent) and realized that was the solution to the problematic structure of the benzene molecule—the atoms were linked together in a circle. The key was a shift in consciousness, a shift in how the problem was dealt with.

Now let's consider breakthroughs in understanding ancient cultures. Archaeologists, linguists, anthropologists, all chime in on this one. One thing stands out: The accumulation of more and more data is meaningless if the investigator's consciousness does not frame the problem correctly. The structure of revolutionary ideas and how they are received and incorporated by the consensus gatekeepers have been explored by Thomas Kuhn.[3] First of all, he observes that very often breakthroughs are made by outsiders. The reason why is that consensus perspectives tend to be self-reinforcing. The consensus perspective works its way into a corner made by its own self-defined limitations and it thus takes an outsider, someone not constrained by deep-seated prejudices, to push the whole thing forward. No additional evidence is necessary.

Problems that are intractable but won't go away usually indicate that a reframing of the issues is necessary. The problem is often solved when biases in the Western scientific mind are set aside and the evidence is examined at face value, with a sensitivity to the values and beliefs of the culture under consideration. It's as if the operating system, the source code, needs to be rewritten to incorporate data that don't fit into the previously maintained conceptual boxes. The data may be labeled superficially and filed away, nobody knowing what to do with them. Consciousness needs to shift, to expand, in order to embrace what the thing under investigation really is. Typically, ancient cultures and their cosmologies are fitted into small expectations and are enlarged grudgingly, only when demanded. And in-house scholars will never demand it, because their careers are at stake. Independent scholars have the benefit of being able to say progressive things without the fear of being fired. However, such impudent outsiders, storming the ivory tower, must deal with the NIH syndrome—Not Invented Here. If the new idea didn't emerge from the scholars' own factories of production, appearing in their own in-house "peer-reviewed" journals, then the new idea doesn't officially exist.

Kuhn noted that when a compelling breakthrough surfaces, it goes through three stages of integration into consensus. First, it is completely ignored. Second, it is violently resisted and maligned, the messenger often being subjected to *ad hominem* attacks. Third, it is accepted as if they knew it all along. In fields of study in which conceptual progress is expected and is constantly occurring, such as Maya studies, we can observe textbook examples of this process. Perhaps this is just the way things will always be. In Maya studies, a succession of independent outsiders have contributed key breakthroughs, including Joseph T. Goodman, Yuri Knorosov, and Tatiana Proskouriakoff, so we shouldn't be surprised when subsequent breakthroughs are offered by outsiders.

We can discern something else about breakthroughs in understanding 2012. This "understanding" has a threefold aspect. First, there is the nuts-and-bolts reconstruction of the Long Count calendar developed by the ancient Maya, along with any associated beliefs and traditions, which is what concerns us right now. Second, there is a more universal perennial wisdom that the Maya philosophy of time is an expression of. Doctrines of sacrifice, which the Maya are known for, are found practiced all over world history, and a study of their inner meaning reveals profound parallels.[4] Similarly, Amazonian shamanic rites of healing can be interpreted as psycho-spiritual methodologies analogous to the swooning initiatory rites in the mystery cult at Delphi in ancient Greece. Having identified these core archetypes of the belief system, we could then explore the implicit metaphysics of transformation with a more universal approach, drawing valid and illuminating cross-comparisons with other traditions. Third, we can understand that 2012 basically represents the shift from one World Age to the next World Age. In other words, it addresses the challenge of spiritual awakening or the transformation of consciousness (something that is a concern for many people).

We can then acknowledge, and practice, a type of understanding best called "gnosis"—direct inner experience of wisdom—which is achieved by applying perennial methods such as meditation.

These three levels of understanding proceed from a most tangible and exoteric level (the nuts and bolts of reconstructing a lost cosmology) to the most intangible, spiritual, and esoteric level (experiencing direct gnosis, or illumination). As such, the three domains are progressively more difficult to convey adequately in words. In fact, minds stuck in the first, most tangible level doubt that the third level even exists. But there is really no reason for a typical human being to not acquire a working, experiential, knowledge of all three levels. It's simply part of the entire package of being human.

Before these concepts are dismissed as going a bit too far left of center, consider that this framework is no different from the multileveled approach to knowledge that the first colleges of the Middle Ages took as a basic tenet. The Seven Liberal Arts were divided into two parts, the Quadrivium and the Trivium. Rooted in the structure of Pythagorean number theory, which emphasized qualitative characteristics of reality over quantifiable parts, the seven domains of knowledge are ranked sequentially from lowest to highest (although the order sometimes varies in different sources): The Trivium (grammar, rhetoric, logic) and the Quadrivium (arithmetic, geometry, music, astronomy).

A student's progress toward the highest, most subtle level of understanding was conferred by "degrees." That collegiate system was, in turn, modeled after the cosmic allegory of a Christian Neoplatonist named Dionysus the Areopagite, whose visionary insight into the many-leveled structure of reality informed Church theology and doctrine. The Seven Liberal Arts and the cosmic model of Dionysus the Areopagite are, in turn, based on the seven planetary planes and are thus an echo of the ancient Mystery School initiations found in, for example, Mithraism. The system was codified by later writers such as Varro and Martianus Capella. Perhaps it's best-known use was in Dante's *Divine Comedy*, which utilized this multidimensional structure as an allegory for the spiritual journey through purgatory and redemption.

Today, four levels are preserved in the four high school years, and beyond

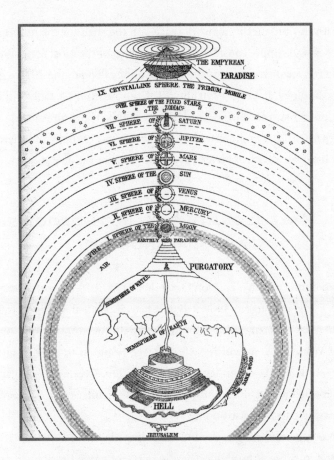

THE EMPYREAN
PARADISE
IX. CRYSTALLINE SPHERE. THE PRIMUM MOBILE
VIII. SPHERE OF THE FIXED STARS.
THE ZODIAC
VII. SPHERE OF SATURN
VI. SPHERE OF JUPITER
V. SPHERE OF MARS
IV. SPHERE OF THE SUN
III. SPHERE OF VENUS
II. SPHERE OF MERCURY
I. SPHERE OF THE MOON
EARTHLY PARADISE
FIRE
AIR
PURGATORY
HEMISPHERE OF WATER
HEMISPHERE OF EARTH
THE DARK WOOD
HELL
JERUSALEM

Dante's multidimensional cosmos based on the
Neoplatonic cosmology of seven planetary domains

that three levels are preserved in the bachelor's, master's, and doctoral degrees. The master of knowledge is bested only by a doctor, who unlike the master can confer knowledge and degrees on others.

Notice that the Trivium, in modern times, has been switched with the location of the Quadrivium, a circumstance that is revealing in that an inversion of perspective on what is real has occurred in modern times; spirit and spirituality is ambiguous, suspiciously subjective, and unreal, while matter (the physical) is the part of reality that everybody agrees exists.

With this broader framework placed on the shelf for the moment, let's slow down and simply consider the implications of the most accessible level, the tangible reconstruction of the Long Count calendar, the 2012 date, and Maya cosmology. If progress at this level can be even partially initiated, a revolution in Maya studies is in order, since at this stage professional scholars don't regard 2012 as an intentional artifact of Maya thought and therefore it doesn't have, for them, any merit as a valid topic of rational inquiry.

MAYA COSMOLOGY, MYTHOLOGY, AND CALENDRICS

The 13-Baktun cycle that ends on December 21, 2012, represents a large cycle of time. Dated carvings and hieroglyphic texts indicate that this cycle, lasting 5,125.36 years, was conceived as an Era or Age. It therefore belongs to a doctrine of World Ages in which each new Age begins with a Creation event. Scholars studying Maya iconography related to these Creation Myth narratives have identified deep connections between this calendar cycle, Maya mythology, kingship rites, and astronomy.

Recent breakthroughs in understanding the 2012 calendar are built upon previous breakthroughs. The discovery of carved monuments at archaeological sites in the 1800s, the decipherment of calendar glyphs, figuring out the correlation of the Long Count calendar with our own—all of these things had to happen before one could notice that a 13-Baktun cycle ends on the December solstice of 2012. I underscored how this fact was theoretically available to scholars as early as 1905, then 1927, more likely by 1946, and was finally noted in print (if one applied an important corrective caveat) with Michael Coe's 1966 book *The Maya*.

The precise solstice placement of the cycle ending in 2012 was challenged by linguist Floyd Lounsbury, who in 1983 argued for a reinstatement of the original GMT correlation of 1927, which makes the end date fall on December 23, 2012—two days after the solstice. Lounsbury's argument, published in two papers, has not stood up to a centrally important issue—the survival of the 260-day count in highland Guatemala.[5] Lounsbury made some highly regarded breakthroughs in epigraphy and was deeply involved in the exciting hubbub that surrounded the Palenque conferences in the 1970s.

Thompson, the old gatekeeper, died in 1975 and the floodgates were opened for a more interdisciplinary approach to deciphering the script. And progress happened quickly. But there was also a backlash against Thompson and the vindictive darts, long repressed, were thrown. It's quite possible that Lounsbury's attack on Thompson's revised 1950 correlation, which makes the end date fall precisely on December 21, 2012, was motivated by a desire to knock him down a few pegs, posthumously, as Thompson himself had done to linguist Benjamin Whorf.

At the Palenque conferences in the 1970s, Lounsbury was Linda Schele's epigraphic mentor. She dedicated her 1990 book *Forest of Kings* to him. Not being completely immersed in the correlation debates, Schele adopted and propagated Lounsbury's December 23 date, and Michael Coe followed suit in his fascinating 1992 book *Breaking the Maya Code.* Consensus prevailed, and for all appearances scholars agreed that the cycle ending fell not exactly on the solstice but on December 23. But despite this uncritical support from Schele and Coe, Lounsbury had to confront several better-informed detractors.

There are two points of Lounsbury's work that are central to his thesis and reveal the flaws. His argument is based on the Venus almanac in the Dresden Codex, which provides predictive dates for the first appearance of Venus as morning star. These occur on average every 583.92 days. Lounsbury tested the two correlations and found that the December 23 correlation was more accurate for a selected portion of the predictive almanac. However, Maya scholar Dennis Tedlock and Maya scholar-astronomer John B. Carlson pointed out that the morning star risings of Venus vary between 580 and 588 days—sometimes even from cycle to cycle.[6] Lounsbury had worked from the theoretical average of the cycle, rather than how the cycle actually happens in the sky. His two-day variance was not supported by the inherent vagaries of the Venus cycle itself.

The second problem with Lounsbury's theory is even more definitive. The ancient Creation monuments contain both Long Count and tzolkin dates combined. We can thus read on Quiriguá Stela C that the last 13-Baktun cycle ended on 13.0.0.0.0 in the Long Count, coordinated with 4 Ahau in the 260-day tzolkin. The current 13-Baktun cycle will of necessity also occur on the same coordination of dates, because 260 divides evenly into the full 13-Baktun cycle. The Long Count dating method was lost centuries ago, as previously explained, but the 260-day calendar has survived in Guatemala. Ethnographers such as Barbara Tedlock have shown that this surviving day-count represents an unbroken tradition going back to the Classic Period Maya, and beyond to the very dawn of the calendars. She wrote in her important book *Time and the Highland Maya*:

> Among the Lowland Maya of Yucatan, the ancient ways of reckoning and interpreting time are known from inscriptions on thousands of stone monuments, from the few ancient books that survived the fires of Spanish missionaries, and from early colonial documents. But the contemporary indigenous people of that region have long since forgotten how to keep time in the manner of their ancestors. With the Highland Maya, and especially those of the western highlands of Guatemala, the situation is reversed. Here, the archaeological monuments are bare of inscriptions, and not one of the ancient books escaped the flames, though the content of a few such books was transcribed into alphabetic writing and preserved in colonial documents. But it is among the Highland Maya rather than among their Lowland cousins that time continues to this day to be calculated and given meaning according to ancient methods. Scores of indigenous communities, principally those speaking the Maya languages known as Ixil, Mam, Pokomchi, and Quiché, keep the 260-day cycle and (in many cases) the ancient solar cycle as well.[7]

The 20 day-signs and the 13 numbers have been tracked sequentially without break. The surviving day-count thus provides a test for any proposed correlation because it locates the authentic placement of the tzolkin and, therefore, the Long Count. If we ask a Quiché Maya day-keeper what day it is today, January 9, 2009, they will respond it is "5 Tijax." Then, if we start with this day-count placement and count forward . . . January 9 = 5 Tijax, January 10 = 6 Kawuq, January 11 = 7 Junajpu . . . to December of 2012, we find that 4 Junajpu (4 Ahau) falls on December 21, not December 23. In this way, the surviving unbroken day-count confirms the revised GMT correlation of 1950. Lounsbury understood this issue, which was brought to his attention by Dennis Tedlock and other scholars, and tried to salvage his theory by proposing that a two-day shift in the day-count must have occurred prior to the Conquest. It had to happen before the Conquest because we have three historical date correlations from the Conquest period, from three widely separated regions—Central Mexico, Yucatán, and Guatemala. They all confirm the December 21, 2012, correlation.[8]

The practical coordination of Lounsbury's proposal is virtually inconceivable, requiring a coordinated effort between regions separated by thousands of miles. Also, it would be highly uncharacteristic of the pre-Conquest day-keepers to allow such a dislocation of their sacred count, which was treated as an inviolable sacred rhythm. Such proscriptions against sacred day-sign fiddling can be observed in other calendar traditions. The Gregorian reform of 1582, for example, skipped ten days but preserved the sequence of the seven weekdays, which were named after planetary deities. Thursday, October 4, 1582, was followed by Friday, October 15, 1582, in the new Gregorian calendar.

And here's the biggest snafu of all. If we accept Lounsbury's defense of his theory (his wildly improbable suggestion that a pre-Conquest two-day shift was achieved), then all post-Conquest dates must, in practice, conform to the December 21, 2012, correlation! According to his own revised theory, Lounsbury places the cycle ending on December 21, 2012, not December 23 as reported by Coe, Schele, and others. The problem here is a lack of attentiveness to the factual details of the correlation question. If a proposed correlation does not allow 13.0.0.0.0 to equate with 4 Ahau according to the surviving, authentic, tzolkin day-count, that proposal has some serious explaining to do. Scholars, not wanting to rock the boat and jeopardize their standing, often align themselves with the consensus opinion, nodding to authority, and ignore logic and facts.[9] In a nutshell, the unassailable final word on the correlation issue can be summed up very concisely, with what I call "the equation of Maya time": 13.0.0.0.0 = 4 Ahau = December 21, 2012.

This, again, is where independent scholars play a vital role, because they can point out that "the king is wearing no clothes" without fear of getting fired. My early research delved into the correlation issues deeply and formed a major portion of my 1992 book *Tzolkin*. I also critiqued Lounsbury's second article of 1992 and found it to engage in a curious bit of mathematical circular logic.[10] For anyone who was willing to study and understand the details of the correlation debate, this faux pas could easily be exposed—not to mention the even more egregious misconceptions of the correlation that have occurred in New Age books.

Luckily, scholars who understand these issues quietly support the correct correlation, rarely wanting to be vociferous enough to bruise egos or otherwise make waves. The Tedlocks, the Brickers, John Carlson, Prudence Rice, and Susan Milbrath all use the correct correlation. Lounsbury was a brilliant linguist and epigrapher who pioneered many important decipherments, insightfully connecting certain glyphs with planetary motions. His work to support December 23, however, doesn't withstand critical analysis.

The devil is in the details, and if you're willing to dance with the devil the truth can be teased out. The use of the surviving day-count as a litmus test for any proposed correlation should be considered a breakthrough, and my "Equation of Maya Time" is the formal expression of that underappreciated test, allowing us to be perfectly precise in understanding when the 13-Baktun cycle ending happens—the solstice of 2012. This precision therefore highlights the importance of asking the question: *Doesn't the solstice placement of the end date strongly suggest that it was intentionally calculated?*

At least one Maya scholar took this question seriously, albeit briefly. Insightful work on the calendar systems of Mesoamerica appeared with Munro Edmonson's *Book of the Year* in 1988. In it he wrote that every date in his book confirmed the GMT-2 correlation, placing the 13-Baktun cycle ending on December 21, 2012. He also noted the solstice placement of the cycle ending in 2012, and concluded it was unlikely to be a coincidence. When I began asking this question of other scholars in 1990, the response was always "coincidence" and, in my rather thorough experience with this item of contention, remained so until Susan Milbrath's statement in an Institute of Maya Studies newsletter in 2008.[11]

Because the cycle ending falls on a solstice, Edmonson believes the creators of the Long Count must have been employing a method for accurately calculating the tropical year (365.2422 days). He suggested that somehow they must have known that 1,508 haab (of 365 days) equal 1,507 tropical years (of 365.2422 days). This is known as the "year-drift formula," and it, or something like it, must have been used to accurately calculate future solstice dates. And it must have occurred at the very inception of the Long Count, which was 355 BC according to Edmonson, but certainly by 36 BC at the latest. The tropical year is not very easy to get a handle on; our own calendrical methods to adjust for the extra partial day have resulted in a fairly convoluted "leap year" method for keeping the seasons on track with our calendar. In our Gregorian calendar, a year that is divisible by 4 is a leap year unless it is also divisible by 100, but not by 400.

The simple implication of the solstice 2012 placement is that the people who invented the Long Count possessed scientific abilities and knowledge on par with what was achieved at the pinnacle of ancient Egyptian, Babylonian, and Greek astronomy.

LINDA SCHELE:
MYTHOLOGY AND ASTRONOMY

General shifts of approach have been breaking through in Maya studies since the beginning, but especially since the 1970s. An important new approach to ancient Maya cosmology gained acclaim with the work of University of Texas art history professor Linda Schele. Her work can be stated simply: There is a deep connection between Maya mythology and astronomy. Beyond this general principle, Schele and other scholars pieced together the astronomical basis of inscriptions that tie Maya Creation Mythology to the zero date of the 13-Baktun cycle, in 3114 BC. The whole picture came together at the Maya Meetings in March 1992, and was published in the 1993 book Schele wrote with David Freidel and Joy Parker called *Maya Cosmos: Three Thousand Years on the Shaman's Path.*

One of the key ideas in the book was based on the discoveries of Barbara MacLeod, whose 1991 essay "Maya Genesis" noted that the three hearthstones that were raised into the sky at the Creation event in 3114 BC were connected with the three stones that form a triangle under Orion's belt. The Ak turtle constellation is located just north of Orion, in parts of Gemini, which is significant because one of the crossing points formed by where the Milky Way crosses over the ecliptic is located there. The ecliptic is the path of the sun, moon, and planets, perceived as a "road" in the sky. It crosses over the bright band of the Milky Way in two places, Gemini and Sagittarius. Schele found this relevant because crosses designate cosmic centers and creation places in Maya astro-mythology. The Maize God is often depicted in Maya art as being reborn from the cracked back of the earth-turtle (when the sun passes through the Ak turtle constellation in summer). Thus, the summertime growth of corn was reflected in sky mythology.

In the center of the hearthstone triangle of stars, the Orion nebula can be seen, diffuse and glowing much like the fire in a hearth. Maya women placed three stones in the hearth as a base for the cooking plate. Schele checked the astronomy of mid-August, 3114 BC, and found a compelling night-sky picture of the Milky Way standing upright, just as the texts described the World Tree being raised into the sky.

Maya scholar Matthew Looper defined the astronomical image-complex connected to the August 11, 3114 BC, Creation date in this way: "the critical event was the appearance of a turtle constellation (in Orion and/or Gemini) at zenith at dawn."[12] The passage of Orion or Gemini through the "zenith at dawn" on that date defines a precession-specific era, which will be worth recalling when it becomes clear that my 2012 alignment theory is tied to a precession-specific era of alignment to the Milky Way. Scholars have come to see the three hearthstones as an archetypal structure that is suspected to refer to the 3114 BC Creation date anywhere it appears—in architectural arrangements of buildings, in non-date-containing inscriptions, or in sculptural assemblages.[13] For example, Looper sees the three-hearthstone Creation paradigm of 3114 BC replicated at the site of Naranjo, in three groups of sculptures associated with three triangulated temples.[14]

The cosmic Crossroads of the Milky Way and the ecliptic is clearly a reference point for Maya Creation events. Scholars such as Karl Taube have noted that the cross symbol is used on thrones to designate the idea of "center," and it has an additional connection with birth places.[15] The connection of the cross symbol with the Milky Way–ecliptic cross in the sky is demonstrated among the modern Quiché, Yucatec, and Chortí Maya. It has been traced back to the Olmec, is present at Izapa, manifests in Sacred Tree symbolism in the Classic Period, and occurs in the *Popol Vuh* Creation Myth as the Crossroads. All of this demonstrates the deep interconnectedness of Maya astronomy and mythology. Some of Schele's work has come under scrutiny and has undergone revision, but this one insight can be considered unassailable. It doesn't in fact originate with her. It has a long history in Maya studies and is still accepted by many scholars, but she was its most recent and most compelling champion.

Other researchers took for granted connections between mythology and astronomy. In 1977, Eva Hunt examined a Maya myth from Zinacantán called

"The Hummingbird" and traced its iconography back to the ancient doctrine of the four Tezcatlipocas, deities of World Ages who dance around the northern Pole Star. Since Tezcatlipoca was connected with the Big Dipper constellation, which revolves around the Pole Star, the myth thus preserved an ancient understanding of shifting seasonal positions of the Big Dipper caused by the precession of the equinoxes.[16] In books and articles from the 1980s, Maya scholar Gordon Brotherston summarized his belief in a deep connection between the precession of the equinoxes and Creation mythologies, writing: "The great year of equinoctial precession emerges as the missing link between the local and political chronology of our era and the vast evolutionary philosophy so vividly testified to in the Popol Vuh."[17]

In his intriguing book *The Inner Reaches of Outer Space*, mythologist Joseph Campbell explored number systems used in many World Age traditions, including Hindu chronology, Old Testament patriarch lists, and Norse mythology, and repeatedly found key precessional numbers. The comparative mythologist in him couldn't help but draw a connection, and after extensive research he took it as a basic truism that whenever you found a World Age doctrine in an ancient tradition you could bet that precession was lurking in the shadows.

These ideas are, in fact, found at a very early stage in Mesoamerican studies. In 1901, anthropologist Zelia Nuttall published a massive opus called "Fundamental Principles of Old and New World Civilizations" in the prestigious Peabody Museum Papers. She writes that she found "one, totally undreamed-of conclusion, concerning the law governing the evolution of religion and civilization. This leads me to think that, as I groped in the darkness, searching for the light, I unwittingly struck the key-note of that great universal theme which humanity, with a growing perception of existing, universal harmony, has ever been striving to seize and incorporate into their lives."[18] She was alluding to none other than the precession of the equinoxes, as the "key theme" that illuminated Mesoamerican civilization. She believed that the Pole Star was a key reference point for Mesoamerican cosmology, and its shifting position through the seasons, caused by precession, was recognized by Mesoamerican astronomers and defined, for them, the World Ages. Her insights inspired and informed Eva Hunt's work much later.

Astro-mythology, astro-theology, archaeo-astronomy, mytho-astronomical ideation—however you phrase it, the connection between celestial cycles and cultural ideas on earth defines the highest insight of Mesoamerican religion, which can best be described with the Hermetic principle "as above, so below." Sky and earth, subjective and objective realities, are interrelated, two sides of the same coin. We see this very tangibly in astronomically timed rites of Maya kingship. We also see it in city names and city planning, in which cities were oriented to astronomically significant horizons and reflected the structure of the cosmos.

The precessional basis of these profound philosophical ideas has, unfortunately, been misconstrued as a latter-day echo of Panbabylonianism, an interpretation of ancient mythology that arose among German historians of science in the early twentieth century. Alfred Jeremias was the best-known proponent of this school of thought, which believed that ancient civilizations knew about the precession of the equinoxes and all mythologies and religions are rooted in that knowledge. The claims of the most vociferous exponents of this doctrine met with the criticisms of a scientific community that couldn't accept such sophistication in ancient cultures.

The Panbabylonians overstated their case and were duly chastised by consensus academia, but the core idea has proven resilient. In the 1940s it reemerged in Hertha von Dechend's work with Polynesians who navigated by the stars. She found many pieces of evidence from many cultures that indicated an awareness of the shifting skies, and later teamed up with science historian Giorgio de Santillana to explore this neglected area. Together they wrote the book *Hamlet's Mill: An Essay on Myth and the Frame of Time*, published in 1969. Even before the book was released, Santillana, who was terminally ill as the book was being completed, wrote: "Whatever fate awaits this last enterprise of my latter years, and be it that of Odysseus's last voyage, I feel comforted by the awareness that it shall be the right conclusion of a life dedicated to the search for truth."[19]

And what was the "search for truth" fathomed in *Hamlet's Mill*? Apart from the general idea that many later researchers have taken to heart, that ancient mythology and astronomy go together, there is a more specific thesis. It was clear to these respected authors that many ancient mythological traditions were describing the slow shifting of the heavens, the precession of the equinoxes, and certain alignments that occur within this cycle involving the bright band of the Milky Way and the shifting positions of the equinoxes and solstices. The "framework of the seasonal quarters" shifts slowly with precession and periodically aligns with the Milky Way. Readers familiar with *Hamlet's Mill* may, at this point, be a bit baffled, as this idea is obliquely buried in the labyrinthine structure of the book. It must be inferred from seeds planted in several places. Yet it is, in fact, a first inkling of the galactic alignment concept.[20]

This isn't really the place to lay out the detailed assessment that *Hamlet's Mill* deserves. Its disorganized presentation is an easy target for critics who dislike the implications of the evidence. Suffice it to say that its central idea is compelling: Many ancient cultures encoded an awareness of precession into their mythologies and religions. Research not connected with or inspired by *Hamlet's Mill* has uncovered evidence in Egypt, Vedic India, and elsewhere. Vedic historian and astrologer David Frawley, for example, decoded precessional positions of the sun and full moon in the Vedic scriptures, allowing an early dating of those sacred texts.[21] Without utilizing any data from *Hamlet's Mill*, my own theory on the 2012 cycle ending argues that the ancient Maya hung their philosophy of time on a rare "galactic alignment" that occurs during the precession of the equinoxes, and this is the key to understanding 2012.

THE GALACTIC ALIGNMENT OF ERA-2012

The 2012 topic relates to many areas of Maya studies, embracing iconography, calendars, mythology, astronomy, archaeology, and epigraphy. Any attempt to understand 2012 must strive for an interdisciplinary synthesis, otherwise the whole picture will never be grasped. The lack of coherence resulting from an incomplete approach of a specialist will likely render potential insights unclear, anomalous, dismissible. An informed nonspecialist who values interdisciplinary synthesis has a better chance of making important breakthroughs. The steps that led to the galactic alignment theory are as follows.

Inspired by the work of Linda Schele and others, I pushed the investigation of Maya astro-mythology further and looked at the other cosmic Crossroads (the one in Sagittarius), noting previously unrecognized connections between astronomy and Maya Creation Mythology. The key came for me when I read, in a 1993 interview with Barbara and Dennis Tedlock, that "Maya Creation happens at a celestial crossroads."[22] This echoed Schele's work, but it made me revisit Dennis Tedlock's translation of the Maya Creation Myth, *The Popol Vuh*. In his notes I found compelling identifications of astronomical features in the myth, including the crossroads formed by the Milky Way and the ecliptic, and the role of the dark rift. The part of the Milky Way that contains the dark rift is on the other side of the sky from Orion. Schele focused on one crossroads, but in fact there are two, and both yield meaningful and interesting insights.

Since the position of the December solstice sun was shifting into alignment with the center of the Crossroads in Sagittarius, and the southern terminus of the dark rift touched that crossing point, I was drawn to look more deeply at the role of these features in the Maya Creation Myth. The dark rift appears frequently as the *Xibalba be*, the "road to the underworld." The Hero Twins and their father pass through it several times to do battle with the Lords of the Underworld. In one scene, the dark rift speaks to the Hero Twins; it therefore either has, or is, a mouth. The dark rift was also the crook in the calabash tree where One Hunahpu's skull was hung. From that spot he magically conceived the Hero Twins, who later avenge his death and facilitate his resurrection. It was thus a place of death and magical rebirth, or conception.

In the underworld the Twins embarked upon the shamanic underworld journey, seeking to avenge their father's beheading and to facilitate his triumphant resurrection. Although it's not explicitly stated in the myth, that same portal would have to serve as the place of return, or rebirth, after the symbolic death of the underworld initiation.

In other areas of Mesoamerican symbolism and mythology, I recognized additional uses that the dark rift was put to. It was the mouth of a cosmic monster, portrayed variously as a frog, snake, or caiman. It was seen as a temple doorway or the mouth of a cave, called *ch'en* in the highland Tzotzil Maya language, which also means vagina. Here, again, the birthplace metaphor is encountered. The dark rift connects with a wide complex of Mesoamerican concepts that also includes ballcourts, cenotes, thrones, and the sweat bath. In the Classic Period inscriptions, it is referenced as the "impinged bone" glyph meaning "the Black Hole place," the upturned frog-mouth glyph that designates a place of birth, and in the skeletal maw iconography. It is clearly also the reference point for "sky-cave" glyphs at Copán and elsewhere, although epigraphers neglect to look at the sky for these "supernatural" locations.[23]

The alignment of planets, the moon, or the sun with the dark rift at various times throughout the Classic Period was repeatedly noted and utilized in rites of Maya kingship, including those involving births, accessions, anniversaries, and ritual decapitations. The dark rift in the Milky Way is a previously unrecognized key to my end-date alignment theory because the December solstice sun will align with it in the years around 2012. This is in fact a good definition of the galactic alignment, a simple and easy way to think about it that eliminates extraneous and misleading ideas: *The galactic alignment is the alignment of the December solstice sun with the dark rift in the Milky Way.*

A slight variation of this definition replaces "dark rift in the Milky Way" with the more abstract astronomical term "galactic equator." The galactic equator is the precise midline of the Milky Way, a line that we could draw in our mind's eye as we looked at the bright road of the Milky Way in the sky.

Like the earth's equator, which divides the earth into two lobes, the Milky Way divides the sky into two hemispheres. I prefer the first definition because it connects the galactic alignment directly into the astronomical feature (the dark rift) that would have been of interest to naked-eye sky-watchers. Early on, I realized that ancient sky-watchers needed to utilize astronomical features that were compelling to the naked eye. The Milky Way itself is compelling but quite wide. The dark rift itself is more narrow, and with its various mythological connotations it would serve well in a developing mytho-cosmic scheme.

A related issue is the generalized understanding of the galactic alignment as an alignment to the Galactic Center. Astronomers take the term "Galactic Center" to mean a precise point they can identify with absolute certainty (itself a highly problematic proposition), and thus a calculation of the solstice point's closest approach to this abstract point has been offered.[24] Since the closest approach of the solstice point to the Galactic Center point occurs some two hundred years after 2012, critics believe the galactic alignment theory is invalid. The critics, however, unconscionably evade the fact that the visually perceivable nuclear bulge of the Galactic Center is quite wide. It would have served as a generalized idea for the ancient Maya rather than a precise scientific reference point for calculations. Within this nuclear bulge, you find the Crossroads formed by the Milky Way and the ecliptic as well as the southern terminus of the dark rift. These are the features that would have provided conceptual references for ancient precessional calculations. I don't take issue with referring to the galactic alignment as an alignment to the Galactic Center. Often, in interview situations, it is necessary to get the point across in a simple way, as long as the proper definitions, the naked-eye appearance of astronomical features, and the timing issues are understood.

In any case, the galactic alignment concept is based in the facts of astronomy. However, the phenomenon is often confused with other ideas that have nothing to do with the precession of the equinoxes, including the Photon Belt, Argüelles's galactic synchronization, and our solar system's orbital motion above and below the galactic midplane. These misconceptions reared their heads early on in my work, and it became clear to me that I had to define the specifics of the galactic alignment and address confusing issues in the timing of it. I performed this task and published the book *Galactic Alignment* in 2002, but oddly that book is very often overlooked as a resource.

In 1994 very few sources had ever mentioned the galactic alignment, and even then it was poorly defined. In writing up my early research on the alignment, I used the ACS ephemeris to estimate the precise alignment of the solstice point (the precise middle point of the sun) with the galactic equator (the precise midline of the Milky Way) as occurring sometime between 1997 and 1999. That's about the best that could be done. I felt it was important to

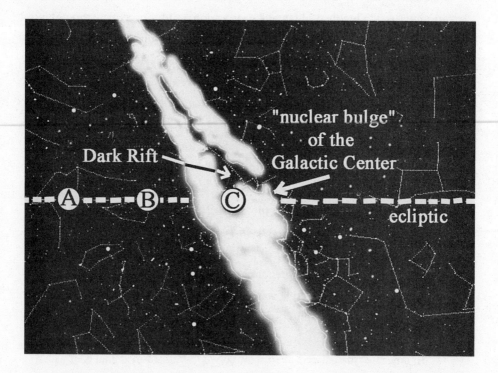

The galactic alignment of era-2012. A = position of the December solstice sun 6,000 years ago. B = position of the December solstice sun 3,000 years ago. C = position of the December solstice sun in our era.

have a good scientific calculation and definition of the alignment. That this estimate was some fourteen years away from 2012 initially might seem like a deal breaker for the theory, but it isn't. To assume that the ancient Maya astronomers had to make an absolutely perfect forward calculation of precession, more than 2,000 years into the future, is completely unrealistic.

The assumption that the end date must target the precise day of something that will happen forms the basis of many contentious attempts to discredit the fact of the December 21, 2012, correlation. But this is putting the cart before the horse, an inversion of the facts. This misleading assumption gives rise to the following problem. Someone might have a prophetic dream that "the end" or "the shift" or "whatever" will happen on, say, May 12, 2014. Someone else might make charts on climate change that point to 2019 as the year of an irreversible Omega Point. These theorists thus claim that December 21, 2012, is not correct.

This kind of critique is called a *fallacia consequentis*—a fallacy having (unfortunate) consequences. If you embrace the fallacious assumption that the Maya end date is supposed to pinpoint an event that is hardwired into the structure of the universe, or in the fractal math of time, misleading conclusions are likely to follow.

In identifying the galactic alignment as the key to why the Maya placed their cycle-ending date on December 21, 2012, I am not implying that the galactic alignment is a scientifically provable causative agent of change. That is an interesting topic for further exploration, and the first conclusion is that, if that is indeed true, it can't possibly be nailed down to a specific year, let alone a specific day. Even if we accepted a precise scientific calculation for the galactic alignment and believed that it affects life on earth, the slow nature of the process and the unknown interdynamics of the causative forces involved demands we accept a range of influence. Like the full moon, there is in fact a precise theoretical point of maximum fullness, but any alleged astrological effect falls within an "orb" of influence.

Nick Kollerstrom, an astrologer in England, published a brief note on the alignment in 1993; he said it would occur around 1999. After the publication of my article in December 1994, the writings of astrologer Raymond Mardyks came to my attention. In articles published in 1987, 1991, and 1994 he mentioned the galactic alignment and interpreted it through the filters of Western astrology. Over the years I've had many exchanges with Ray, who believes he is the spokesman for a secret school of galactic initiates and takes offense at my findings and the way I have pursued my research. I've now read the articles he's written, and they contain interesting ideas from a Western astrological viewpoint, but he did not attempt to reconstruct the galactic alignment's presence in Maya cosmology. Our approaches are fundamentally different. His comment that astrologer Charles Jayne mentioned the galactic alignment back in the 1950s is intriguing, and it should be verified and added to the ever-growing list of early references to the galactic alignment, which include Terence McKenna and the authors of the 1969 book *Hamlet's Mill*.

Many other early observers of the galactic alignment came to my attention, including Franklin Lavoie, who contacted me in 2007 and told me of the articles he contributed to Dan Winters's *Planet Heartworks* book of 1989. His observations include the following comments: "The Mayans were galactic astronomers . . . their calendar is a masterpiece even by modern standards . . . the ancient astronomers recognized a connection between the precession of the equinox and the galaxy . . . it's as if they intuited some sort of field existing along the plane of the Milky Way, upon which to steady the heavens as the Ages precessed. The axis of precession lies at ninety degrees to galactic center . . . I believe this is a clue to the (orientation of) yet undiscovered lines of force generated by the galactic dynamo."[25]

Moira Timms, James Roylance, Daniel Giamario, Patrizia Norelli-Bachelet, and Nick Fiorenza were other astrologers and futurists who all mentioned, in one form or another, the galactic alignment. I recounted the process by which I came to understand the galactic alignment, and did my best to document the history of this idea, in an appendix to my book *Maya Cosmogenesis 2012*. It's probably one of the most important ideas of modern times, one that is greatly distorted and misunderstood. Joscelyn Godwin observed that there is now a whole new genre of research by "Galactic Center theorists."[26] I certainly have offered my own theories and speculations as to the empirical nature of the galactic alignment, but for me that has been only a sideline. The most important work, and what I believe will outlast the craze that will pass when the date passes, has been the effort to uncover, document, and reconstruct how the Maya used and thought about this galactic alignment. After all, the 2012 date comes to us from the Maya calendar tradition.

How the galactic alignment emerged into common discourse remains, however, an intriguing topic. Shamanic astrologer Daniel Giamario played an important role in his communications with European astronomer Jean Meeus, inviting him to calculate the alignment as accurately as possible.[27] Meeus did, and published the results in his 1997 book *Mathematical Astronomy Morsels*, and that was the first mathematically precise calculation of the galactic alignment published. His calculation arrived at May of 1998, but no error range was offered. The apparent precision here is somewhat misleading. To place the precise calculation in May assumes an abstract interpretation of astronomical features that has no meaning for ancient naked-eye sky-watchers. Why? Since the alignment involves the solstice position, any proposed calculation for an alignment should occur on a solstice date. Science strives for precision when, in fact, the apparent achievement of precision has no real meaning for naked-eye sky-watchers. It's like supplying a carpet layer with room dimensions down to 1/100,000th of an inch, and making sure he knows where the ceiling lights are.

Given the potential vagaries in the location of abstract features utilized in the calculation offered by Meeus, such as the galactic equator, and the very slow movement of precession, one would expect at least a ± three-year error range. This range admits the possibility of 1/24th of a degree of error in precessional motion—2½ minutes of arc, which is less than one-tenth of the diameter of the full moon in the sky, a mere sliver. It's likely that a greater error range can be expected for the 1998 calculation.

In order to emphasize the fact that no precise year can really be identified, and that an alignment zone is the best way to think about the galactic alignment, I took the width of the sun (½ degree), noted that this equaled 36 years of precessional motion, and suggested a 36-year alignment window between 1980 and 2016 (1998 ± 18 years). This is thus the amount of time it takes the actual body of the sun to precess through the galactic equator.[28] This zone was never meant to imply that "the big event" or "the changes" would therefore happen within this window of time. It merely suggests: (1) a minimal target zone that the ancient Maya astronomers might have shot for; and (2) a logically reasonable way that modern commentators, investigators, and critics can talk about it.

My efforts were built upon a reasonable definition for the alignment that I had suggested in 1995: *The galactic alignment is the alignment of the December solstice sun with the galactic equator (in Sagittarius).* And since the sun is ½ degree wide, it is true to say that "the solstice sun" touches the galactic equator for all 36 of those years. This widening of the arc of the alignment carried with it an important acknowledgment that the sun has width—it's a real body that ancient sky-watchers observed, not just an abstract center point that modern astronomers use to make calculations.

That some astronomers have taken Meeus's 1998 calculation and conclude that the Maya's 2012 date could not have been a target for the alignment (because of the fourteen-year difference) reveals either a willful intellectual dishonesty or a disregard for addressing the context of what ancient sky-watchers would have been tracking with the naked eye. There is no way to turn back the clock on the sequence of how this galactic alignment concept emerged as a key item of rational discourse. To a large extent it is still confused with other ideas, which are either mystically vague, factually inaccurate, or not related to precession. A clear understanding of the astronomy behind the galactic alignment happened for me very early on, and I've tried to lend some sanity to the discussion by providing careful definitions, caveats, and explanations. Maya scholar Anthony Aveni offered, at the Tulane 2012 conference, what many scholars consider to be the best critiques of the galactic alignment theory. They deserve a considered response, which I'll offer in Chapter 6.

A s I studied the source material it became clear that something profound was lurking, unrecognized by scholars, connecting the astronomy of the end-date alignment with core symbols and concepts in Maya mythology. To make a long story short, and to summarize the nub of what I've found as concisely as possible before elaborating on the details, I'd say this:

> On the end date of the 13-Baktun cycle of the Mayan Long Count (December 21, 2012 AD), the winter solstice sun will be in conjunction with the "Dark Rift" in the Milky Way. This is actually a rare event, slowly culminating over a period of centuries and millennia, and is a function of the precession of the equinoxes. Beginning with another fact, that this Dark Rift in the Milky Way was known to the ancient Maya as the xibalba be (the Road to the Underworld), additional connections between astronomy and Mayan mythology present themselves. In looking seriously at what these simple facts might imply, questions arise. . . . Now, I take the unavoidable view that a profound and unsung dimension of ancient Mesoamerican cosmology is patiently awaiting recognition and further elucidation.[29]

That was taken from the introduction to my book The Center of Mayan Time, written in 1995. Fourteen years have now elapsed. Soon after writing that, I found more evidence in many Maya traditions for what I suspected to be true. I worked out the details of this reconstruction over several years of intense research that culminated in my 1998 book Maya Cosmogenesis 2012. Recently, more evidence from hieroglyphic inscriptions has been identified, and it revolves, as I suspected, around the "Black Hole" glyph in Maya

Creation Texts representing the dark rift in the Milky Way. The dark-rift hieroglyph was frequently found in relation to king-making rites, cosmological Creation events, and the sacred ballgame.

RECONSTRUCTING THE LOST
2012 COSMOLOGY

The galactic alignment is caused by the precession of the equinoxes and occurs in era-2012. This congruence of astronomy and the calendar is striking, but it cannot alone stand as evidence that the ancient Maya intended their end date to target the galactic alignment. For that, we need to recognize the key astronomical features involved in the galactic alignment, and they must have been viewable to the ancient naked-eye sky-watchers. These include the dark rift, the Milky Way–ecliptic cross, and the solstice sun, all of which the ancient sky-watchers could have noted. It is a strong support for the thesis that these astronomical features are central to the Maya Creation Myth, king-making rites, and ballgame symbolism.

My theory offers an answer to the question: Why does the Maya calendar end on December 21, 2012? Since it falls on an accurate solstice date, we should suspect that its location is not a random occurrence but was intentional. With this as a working hypothesis, we observe that the date is the end of a 13-Baktun cycle, a calendrical concept that appears occasionally in the inscriptions and dated carvings of the Classic Period, always in the context of cosmological Creation Mythology. The end of a 13-Baktun cycle, as recorded at Quiriguá and elsewhere, is the end of an Era, otherwise known as a Sun or Age. These Ages, or World Ages, belonged to a World Age doctrine that, as a mythological construct, is described in the Maya Creation Myth (*The Popol Vuh*). In this way we can see that the Long Count's 13-Baktun cycle and the Maya Creation Myth are both expressions of an underlying World Age paradigm. One is calendrical and the other is mythological, and as we will see they both encode astronomy.

Where were these two traditions formulated? By whom, and when? As we explored in Chapter 2, the pre-Classic Izapan civilization, centered on the astronomically oriented site called Izapa, was involved in the establishment of these two traditions. The site contains sixty carved monuments, many depicting episodes from the Creation Myth (also called "the Hero Twin Myth"), some of the earliest such portrayals that are known. As for the Long Count, its earliest dated carvings appear within the sphere of the Izapan civilization, toward the tail end of Izapa's florescence. Although no Long Count dates have yet been found within the exact boundaries of the site of Izapa, we'll see that Izapa encodes the astronomical alignment that culminates in era-2012, and thus was the observational laboratory that led to the inauguration of the Long Count system, taken up in earnest at nearby sites. The appearance of early Long Count monuments trend southward from Izapa, showing up at Tak'alik Ab'aj and El Baúl, sister cities to Izapa.

My work presents evidence that Izapan astronomers formulated a cosmology of World Age transformation connected to a rare alignment that would culminate, for them, in the distant future. They knew it would eventually happen, but couldn't know the precise timing until they inaugurated the Long Count, whose 13-Baktun cycle ending was designed to target the alignment. In other words, the mythological paradigm came first, was depicted on Izapa's monuments as an early version of the Hero Twin Creation Myth, while the calendrical and astronomical system (the Long Count) that would calibrate the future alignment was still being perfected. This happened by the late first century BC, and thereafter Izapa was frozen in time and preserved, perhaps as a pilgrimage site, but certainly as an honored place that couldn't be destroyed.

According to my theory, the key to understanding why the early Maya chose the solstice of the year our calendar calls 2012, to end a large World Age cycle, is found in a rare astronomical alignment called "the solstice-galaxy alignment" or "the galactic alignment," and we've already explored the various issues and definitions connected with it. By the time I began examining and studying Izapa in 1994 I already suspected that the galactic alignment was the reason behind the 2012 end date. As such, I was alert to evidence at Izapa that would indicate a conscious awareness of the future galactic alignment. The first thing I noticed was the dark-rift symbolism of the frog's mouth on Stela 11 out of which emerges a sun deity, facing the December solstice sunrise horizon. The second thing I noticed was that the ballcourt in Group F points to the December solstice sunrise horizon. Since the ballgame is going to be central to what follows, we need to take a brief detour here to concisely summarize the symbolism of Maya ballgame.

It's really quite simple. The ballcourt symbolizes the Milky Way, the goal ring is the dark rift, and the game is about the rebirth of the sun. The ball represents the sun, and some ballcourts are aligned with the solstice, proving that, at least for those ballcourts, the solar rebirth occurred on the solstice. That's it. This symbolism was integrated with the Creation Myth, in which One Hunahpu's head represents the gameball. Generally speaking, the ball represents the sun and the game is about the rebirth of the sun. The game was not so much about athletic prowess; it was performed as part of the Creation Myth. It was an eschatological mystery play depicting the transformation and renewal that happens at cycle endings. In this play, the goal ring was the place of victory and rebirth. Thus, the ball's passage through the goal ring symbolized the sun's rebirth, its emergence from the underworld and the victory of light over darkness. It is easy to see that the goal ring represents the meanings given to the dark rift in the Milky Way. A more general interpretation loosely connects ballcourts with the underworld. According to Linda Schele, Creation myths played out in the ballgame "happened at the black hole."[30] She clearly spelled out the connection to the dark rift, but didn't pursue the implications. She wrote that the black hole toponym found in Creation Texts points to "the Black Road, through the Cleft in the Milky Way . . . from the ballcourts of the Maya to the Court of Creation in the Land of Death."[31] Her information for this assessment came from Dennis Tedlock's observations on the role of the dark rift in *The Popol Vuh*.

Scholars haven't paid a lot of attention to the specific significance of the goal ring and have been content to simply see ballcourts as underworld places. This is generally true, but the specific role of the goal ring in the game ball's rebirth is unavoidable. It is the place where the game ball, symbol of the sun, is reborn, thus ending the game that ends a cycle of time and begins a new one. Here we see the relevance of the December solstice in this narrative, and how the game ball likely symbolizes not just the sun but the December solstice sun, because it is the December solstice sun that ends a cycle and begins a new one. For the purpose of our 2012 theme, it would be best to try to identify the site and the ballcourt that was most closely associated with the origins of the Long Count calendar. As we will see, the situation is rich and complex, but as I pursued my studies in the early 1990s it became clear that Izapa is this place.

Returning to the Izapa monuments, I read in the archaeological reports that the monuments were found *in situ*—as they were left some 1,900 years ago. On the west end of the ballcourt at Izapa, there is a throne with a head in the middle of the front edge, emerging from between two legs that indicate how a person would have sat on the throne. They would have sat facing down the lengthwise axis of the ballcourt, toward the December solstice sunrise. Behind the throne are six flat seating stones on a raised mound. People sitting on these seats would face the December solstice sunrise and would also be able to view the ballcourt over the throne. The sun reaches its farthest southern rise point on the December solstice, the day of greatest night, prior to the sun and the year being reborn to begin the return journey northward along the horizon. The Maya ballgame was about the rebirth of the sun.[32] The head emerging from between the legs on the throne is a symbol of the sun, as well as the game ball. The game ball moving through the goal ring is a metaphor for the rebirth of the sun. Also, at one point in the Creation Myth, the head of the father of the Hero Twins, One Hunahpu, is used as the game ball. The ballgame and the Hero Twin Myth is a mystery play, enacted on the ball field, and is all about facilitating the resurrection of One Hunahpu.

These things are well known in Maya studies and we are firmly inside the boundaries of status quo consensus here. But what do they tell us about the astronomical symbolism of the ballgame as it was played at Izapa? First

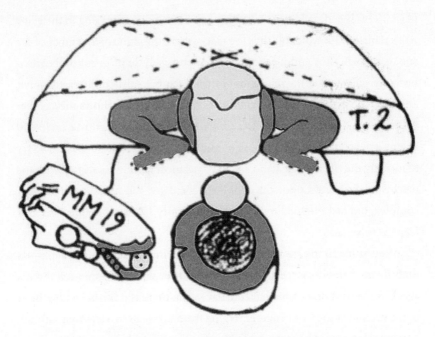

Throne monuments from the Izapan ballcourt. Transformation and renewal.
Drawing by the author

of all, the solar rebirth that the ballgame symbolizes was apparently, for the Izapans, referential to the sun's rebirth at the December solstice. This is not at all surprising, as most ancient culture saw the December solstice as the time of the sun's rebirth, for obvious reasons. That's pretty neat, and tells us something about how the Izapans thought about their monuments, symbolism, and astronomy. This is a "reading" of the iconography and structural orientations at Izapa that gives meaning to the otherwise mute stones. Scholars similarly "read" or interpret hieroglyphic writing, which is an abstract form of miniature iconography. Interpreting iconographic symbolism is no less rigorous an enterprise than epigraphic interpretation; in fact, it is perhaps more rigorous because, especially at Izapa, *astronomical orientation* is an additional interpretive aid that is usually not relevant in hieroglyphic decipherment.

So we can say that the ballcourt at Izapa is telling a story about the sun's rebirth on the December solstice. But something else is going on here. As I studied the many carved monuments found in the Izapan ballcourt, a cohesive story with more profound implications unfolded. On the eastern end of the ballcourt, opposite the throne, is a monument that shows the demise of the vain and false ruler Seven Macaw. A ballplayer, probably one of the Hero Twins, is standing over him as he has crashed on the ground (see figure below). This scene represents a key episode from the Hero Twin Myth—the Hero Twins must do away with Seven Macaw, make him fall from his prideful perch, before they can resurrect their father. This event happens at the culmination of the World Age, at the end of the cycle. The death of the false god must precede the rebirth of the true one. Importantly, we have a solar cycle at work here, *but it is much larger than an annual cycle of some 365 days.* Yes, this is a *World Age context.* The sun gets reborn every morning and every December solstice, but this rebirth happens on the level of the World Age.

Earlier, we saw that the Long Count's 13-Baktun cycle is a World Age, so we can expect that the Creation Mythology depicted in the ballcourt would

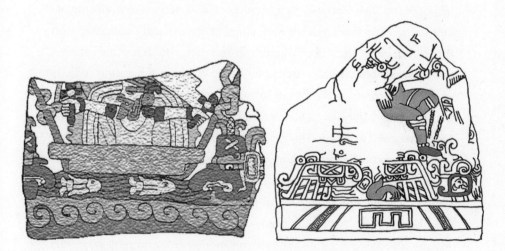

Stela 67 and Stela 60 from Izapa. The demise of Seven Macaw and the resurrection of One Hunahpu in the Izapan ballcourt. Drawing by the author

have been conceptually connected to the Long Count's cycle ending. As if to reinforce this deduction, yet another carved monument is found in the middle of the north wall of the ballcourt, halfway between the other two monuments. This is labeled Stela 67, and it contributes a key to understanding an important astronomical reference in this mytho-cosmic schema.

We see an Ahau Lord with his arms outstretched, holding what appear to be scepters of rulership or perhaps sighting devices. He doesn't represent a historical figure, but rather a mythological archetype—the First Father deity who partitions and measures the cosmos at the dawn of a World Age. The arms-outstretched gesture, according to Maya scholars who have studied Izapa's symbolism, is a "period-ending" gesture and testifies to this interpretation. He is seated or standing in the middle of a canoe. Maya scholars have noted that canoes in which Creation deities ride represent the Milky Way. Stela 67 is located in *the middle* of the ballcourt, and ballcourts were also symbols of the Milky Way. Here we have several different and accepted interlocking readings of the canoe symbol, connecting it meaningfully to the ballcourt and the Milky Way. Ballcourts were also evocative of earth depressions, entrances into the underworld where the Creation Mythology was to be played out. The "entrance to the underworld" concept is centrally important in the *Popol Vuh* Creation Mythology, and is explicitly associated with the feature along the Milky Way called "the dark rift." Since the canoe is analogous to both the ballcourt and the Milky Way, then the seating declivity of the canoe in which the reborn solar lord stands or sits is most likely the dark rift in the Milky Way. There is no other feature along the Milky Way that fits the required function. This makes sense because the solar lord isn't simply sitting or standing, he is being born, at the dawn of a new World Age.

I've been referring to this character anonymously, but we can identify him as One Hunahpu, the father of the Hero Twins. His head also emerges from between the legs on the nearby throne, and he is reborn after Seven Macaw falls, as depicted on the east-end monument. And remember, that reborn solar head on the throne points toward the December solstice rebirth. My argument for the astronomical identity of the Hero Twins' father as the

December solstice sun is especially relevant and evident right here in the Izapan ballcourt. We don't know what might have occurred to this original, primordial identification later on in Maya history, as the original concepts evolved and were perhaps forgotten. Sometimes, the solar rebirth of the ball-game was elsewhere connected to the spring equinox sun. The point is that here, at Izapa, at the very origins of this astro-theological paradigm, the solar rebirth of the ballgame and the rebirth of the solar father of the Hero Twins is without doubt connected to the December solstice. The rebirth takes place through many symbols in these monuments—the goal ring, the throne legs, the canoe seat, but they are all referential to one celestial location, the dark rift in the Milky Way. The emphasis on World Age rebirth at the December

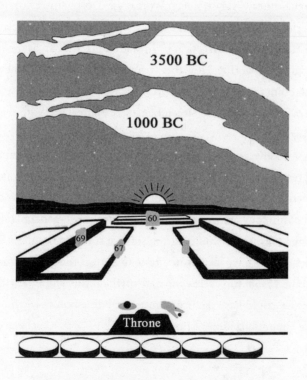

The Izapan ballcourt, oriented to the December solstice
sunrise and the future galactic alignment

solstice is, of course, meaningful and compelling in reference to the 13-Bak-tun cycle's December solstice placement, when the December solstice sun will be positioned in the dark rift in the Milky Way.

This deduction gains support when we actually look at what was hap-pening over the solstice horizon some 2,100 years ago, when the ballgame's mystery play was being enacted on this "ballcourt of creation."

We should expect that the ballgame was played on the December sol-stice, as that is the day indicated by the ballcourt's orientation and is thus the locus of the ceremonial act of solar rebirth. In the predawn skies of a typical December solstice at Izapa some 2,100 years ago, the Milky Way could be seen arching some 30° above the dawning sun. Right there, in the middle of the Milky Way canoe, could be seen the dark rift in the Milky Way, the celestial "portal to the otherworld," the next World Age. Deeply interwoven symbol-ism connects the "portal, doorway, maw" opening to the birthplace arche-type. One Hunahpu's resurrection is through this dark rift, as the game ball goes through the goal ring. How this symbolism can be read in the sky is the connection point to 2012: The future resurrection of One Hunahpu, the birth of a new era, occurs when the December solstice sun aligns with the dark rift in the Milky Way.

Their awareness of this future alignment requires that the Izapans knew about the precessional shifting. We know that the earlier Olmec at La Venta and the people at nearby Tak'alik Ab'aj were aware of precession.[33] Izapa encodes a cosmology associated with this future convergence. They knew it would happen, as the positions of the solstice sun and the dark rift slowly drew closer. It may have taken some time to perfect the Long Count system and target the 13-Baktun cycle's end date on the future alignment accurately, but they easily could have deduced the general direction of the motion long before that "materialization of time."[34]

The section above presents the bare bones of my reconstruction work. A slightly expanded consideration of additional evidence at Izapa follows.

Izapa, Stela 11

The author with Stela 11, Izapa. December 2006

I mentioned earlier that my first indication that the carved monuments of Izapa were going to provide evidence for an awareness of the galactic alignment came from Stela 11. There are two main symbols on this monument: the frog's mouth and the human figure that is emerging from it. Here we can benefit from definitions that come to us from epigraphers, where the up-turned frog-mouth glyph means "to be born." It is likely that hieroglyphic writing, developed after Izapa's monuments were carved, evolved into more abstract shorthand forms from the earlier pictorial presentations, such as the one on Stela 11. The figure in the frog's mouth on this carving is much like the one on Stela 67, displaying the "arms outstretched" gesture that scholars identify as a "period-ending" sign. He is the primordial first solar lord, the First Father deity who measures the cosmos at the dawn of an Age. He represents the Sun or Era that is newly born, emerging from the "to be born" place that is the frog's mouth. Maya birthing concepts envision the newborn coming into the earth realm from the underworld. The frog's mouth is thus the portal to the underworld.

Other carvings at Izapa testify to frogs, caimans, and alligators' being

symbols of the Milky Way, and their mouths are the dark rift. This belongs
to a near-universal symbology in Mesoamerican religion, where even among
the latter-day Aztecs the cloud serpent, Mixcoatl, symbolized the Milky Way
and its mouth was the dark rift.[35] We can thus deduce with good confidence
that the frog's mouth on Stela 11 represents the dark rift in the Milky Way.
The carving, by the way, faces the December solstice sunrise horizon, over
which the dark rift could be viewed some 2,100 years ago. This circumstance
also helps us interpret the astronomical identity of the first solar lord that is
born from the mouth. In the same way that the solar head on the throne in
the ballcourt represents the December solstice sun because it faces down the
lengthwise axis of the ballcourt toward the December solstice sunrise, so too
the Stela 11 solar lord represents the December solstice sun. This is elementary yet striking in its implications: Stela 11 depicts the December solstice sun
being reborn from the dark rift in the Milky Way. It doesn't state the date in
hieroglyphic terms or with a Long Count date, but it points to era-2012 via
an astronomical image-complex. We will see that this isn't the only time that
a strategy of referring to a precession-specific era solely with iconography
was employed by the ancient Maya.

Two Centers of Consciousness

The astronomy connected with One Hunahpu's future rebirth at the end of
the current 13-Baktun cycle is matched with the astronomy of Seven Macaw's
downfall. I haven't emphasized this until now, but it is very important for
understanding the overall cosmology pioneered at Izapa. In Group A at Izapa,
a row of five monuments with altars is located on the north end of the plaza.
A priest making offerings on the altars would face the five carvings, over
which Tacaná volcano looms to the north. In fact, the 23° azimuth of Izapa's
northward orientation seems intentionally cited on Tacaná. The perpendicular angle to this provides the approximate 113° azimuth of the December
solstice sunrise position, which as we have seen is a significant aid in inter-

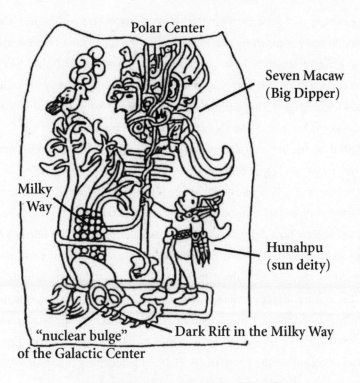

Polar Center

Seven Macaw
(Big Dipper)

Milky
Way

Hunahpu
(sun deity)

"nuclear bulge" — Dark Rift in the Milky Way
of the Galactic Center

Stela 25 from Izapa. Drawing by the author

preting the astronomical symbolism in the ballcourt. I've pointed out that the Big Dipper rises over Tacaná's eastern flank and then falls down around the Pole Star to the west. In *The Popol Vuh* and in other contexts documented by translator Dennis Tedlock, the primary bird deity, Seven Macaw, was associated with the Big Dipper, a constellation of the northern polar region that circles closely around the Pole Star. The five carved monuments in Group A depict this bird deity rising and falling at the hands of the Hero Twins.

Seven Macaw's fall is the event that must precede the resurrection of One Hunahpu. Again, the Creation Myth is being played out in the sky, but notice that in the astronomical dynamic between these two competing deities, two "cosmic centers" were utilized by the Izapan sky-watchers: the Polar Center (Seven Macaw) and the Galactic Center (One Hunahpu). I can't emphasize enough that the dark rift in the Milky Way is located within the rather large and visually compelling nuclear bulge of the Milky Way's center, which may have been referred to as "the cloud center" in the Classic Period hieroglyphic writing. This region is also targeted by the cross formed by the Milky Way and the ecliptic and, significantly, in Maya iconography crosses designate the location of "cosmic centers" (and underworld passages).

This dynamic between the Polar Center and the Galactic Center is beautifully portrayed on Izapa's Stela 25.

This carving is an indispensable key for understanding the true scope of the astronomical and cosmological thinking of the ancient Izapans. We see the Seven Macaw bird deity at the top, in his polar perch in the north. The caiman arching around the left side of the carving sprouts leaves and thus belongs to the complex of caiman-tree images that is well known. Its bulging head (the nuclear bulge of the Galactic Center) is at the bottom, near the earth plane in the south. This caiman figure symbolizes the Milky Way, and the entire Stela 25 carving can be seen as a picture of the sky. The figure on the right is one of the Hero Twins. His foot is touching the snout of the caiman, surely not accidental and suggestive of a special connection between the two in a cyclic process. The mouth of this Milky Way caiman, like that of frogs or snakes, represents the dark rift. Notice that this Hero Twin's arm is torn off, the stump is bleeding, and the arm is held in the talons of the bird deity above. This depicts a specific episode preserved in the much later sixteenth-century *Popol Vuh* document, but Stela 25 was carved sometime between 400 BC and 50 BC.

What we have in Stela 25 is a cosmological diagram showing a dialectic between the Polar Center and the Galactic Center, and two deities that represent two different eras. On one level, I've argued that a cosmological shift is documented in this carving, from an older Olmec-era polar cosmology to the new Galactic-Centered cosmology of the early Maya. As we'll explore in Part II, the two deities associated with those two cosmic centers also represent two different types of consciousness, one centered in the ego and one centered in the unity consciousness of the original mind. This is how we can understand a deeper level of philosophical and spiritual teachings embedded in Izapa's monumental message.

Several monuments at Izapa are iconographic depictions of the era-2012 alignment. The ballcourt throne, Stela 67, and Stela 11 are the best examples. One scholar criticized this as being a dateless interpretation of iconography. A double standard is evident in this critique, however. Over in Group B, there are three pillar-and-ball monuments. Scholars, including Linda Schele, Prudence Rice, Karl Taube, and Matthew Looper, recognize these as the three hearthstones of Creation. Anywhere they are found, even if no dates are associated with them, they are recognized as symbols of the astronomical Creation event that transpired in 3114 BC—the setting in place of the three hearthstones of Creation in the constellation of Orion. The nearby cross of the Milky Way and the ecliptic, above Orion in Gemini, is recognized as a player in this mytho-cosmic construct, since crosses symbolize the idea of source and center. (The Gemini Ak-turtle glyph is an essential feature of the scheme, from which the Maize God is born; the Maize God and the Sun God are related.)

The way that the Creation event astronomy is defined reveals that a precession-specific era is implied, since it is observed as significant that the turtle constellation and Orion passed through the zenith at sunrise on August 11, 3114 BC. Now let's look at the other side of the sky, where the other cross formed by the Milky Way and the ecliptic is located. This cross, symbolizing (like the other one) a cosmic source and center, is very near the dark rift in the Milky Way. This important eschatological feature is portrayed as a frog/caiman mouth at Izapa, most notably on Stela 11. By analogy it is the seating cleft in the canoe on the iconographically similar Stela 67.

What we have, then, in the ballcourt at Izapa is a dateless reference to an astronomical scenario that points to era-2012, the end of the 13-Baktun cycle. Similarly, in Group B we have, as described above, a dateless reference to era-3114 BC, the beginning of the Long Count's 13-Baktun cycle. In a startling display of intellectual contretemps and selective application of logic, scholars happily accept the latter scenario but quickly reject the former. One argument is that no demonstration of precession knowledge is evident. However, precession is present as an identifying characteristic of both scenarios. So, again, scholars make it a problem for one scenario but not the other.

With the inclusion of the zenith center monuments in Group B, it becomes apparent that Izapa integrated the ideas connected with three different cosmic center regions: zenith, polar, and galactic. This fascinating situation suggests that Izapa truly was an origin place of much greater importance than it has been previously accorded. The tripartite framework evident in the three main monument groups also has a corresponding meaning in terms of the three deities associated with those centers, whose roles and functions often overlap in that they are all regents of their respective cosmic centers. I believe that confusing cross-identifications between deities could probably be sorted out if we acknowledge this foundational template.

IMPLICATIONS OF THE GALACTIC ALIGNMENT THEORY

There are several things about my work that need to be emphasized. It is an interdisciplinary synthesis of the best scholarship. It makes informed deductions based on evidence that is largely accepted by mainstream scholars. I like to think of my work as placing all the accepted evidence on the table, for all to see, and then simply enunciating what is there. I noted the ballcourt's alignment to the solstice, which then become a factual crux for my unexpected conclusions. In addition, the entire site of Izapa provides a coherent picture of a tripartite cosmology that implicates the 13-Baktun cycle-ending date (in 2012) as well as its beginning date (in 3114 BC).

Second, my work gives voice to spiritual teachings that are in the Creation Myth. I honor them as expressions of a Perennial Philosophy that is part of the collective human heritage and has inherent worth. This is an engaged type of scholarship, much like that undertaken by Joseph Campbell, whose clear appreciation for and defense of the profound wisdom he could read in the ancient texts placed him at odds with colleagues who believed a scholar must be objective and dispassionate, a floating eye dissecting the object of examination like a surgeon picks apart a carcass. Noninvolvement with the object of one's interest is basically impossible, however, and scholars like Barbara Tedlock have normalized the fact of anthropologists' unavoidable subjective involvement with their studies by identifying it as "human intersubjectivity."[36] Using her apprenticeship to a calendar priest (a daykeeper) in Guatemala as an example, she argued that there is no reason why a scientist cannot be personally involved in a subject while retaining objectivity. The criticism of such a practice follows from a naïve fallacy of exclusion in which the subjective and the objective positions cannot overlap. But they do overlap, all the time; such an overlap of inner and outer realities, mutually reflecting each other, is in fact the way reality is. This is why it is impossible for a scientist to be completely objective, as their ideal would insist that they must be. Instead, objectivity can be practiced best if one acknowledges and owns one's involvement instead of denying it. This is what Joseph Campbell did.

My own tendency is to gladly accept the possibility that the Maya were truly onto something unique and fascinating, a profound cosmovision that for some reason has been invisible to Western science. But I've learned that when addressing scientists the domains of physics and metaphysics must be carefully kept apart—at least semantically and conceptually—for those who are committed to physics cannot accept a larger perspective that embraces all that they hold dear while transcending it to allow for a larger *meta*-physical understanding of reality. That's right, metaphysics includes physics. It "can do" physics, but sees physics as only one slice of a larger model of the universe in which all faculties of the human being are used.

These clarifications are important if we are to approach the 2012 reconstruction honestly with interference noise minimized. By this I mean we need to separate the 2012 topic into two domains. First, there is the reconstruction of a lost or forgotten paradigm. We should assess that as a model that the Maya once established and believed in. It was a paradigm that apparently involved our changing relationship to the galaxy, alignments to the Galactic Center, and spiritual teachings and prophecies connected to that alignment. We don't have to prove that the model is true, or believe in it ourselves, for it to have once existed. Contrary to how my "theory" is often taken, my theory doesn't state that "the world will be transformed when the galactic alignment happens." My theory states that, according to my reconstruction of ancient Maya cosmology, *the Maya believed that galactic alignments are involved in a potential awakening experienced by human consciousness.* That's an important distinction, as it helps us avoid denying the existence of a once-grand galactic cosmovision because it currently cannot be proven true. My theory argues that it once existed, whether or not we can prove that its central tenets are true. I'm very insistent on making this distinction, because without it many silly notions follow.

Let's say my reconstruction is accurate. Ancient people living in southern Mexico about 2,100 years ago achieved an impressive understanding of the precession of the equinoxes. This in itself isn't as far-fetched as one might think, as Greek and Babylonian astronomers were onto the same discovery at the same time—also without the help of high-tech instruments like telescopes. One implication of noticing precession is that the equinoxes and solstices cycle around the zodiac path, backward, and periodically come into alignment with background features such as stars, asterisms, and the bright band of the Milky Way. An idea, a future occurrence, in this process could very well have been extrapolated by those early astronomers who tracked precession. Since the sun's position on the solstice was moving westward, sometime in the distant future it would converge with the Milky Way. Or perhaps the Milky Way was thought to be falling toward the solstice horizon—it doesn't matter. In either case, it's a profound idea; it implies seasons of change timed by alignments between the solstices, equinoxes, and the Milky Way. How would we go about investigating whether the ancient Maya were aware of this alignment? We would study the relevant World Age traditions—namely, the Long Count and the Creation Myth, and the site where the earliest Creation Myth scenes are found, carved in stone: Izapa. My work documents what is found when these traditions are rationally investigated.

The alignment of the solstice sun and the dark rift had a profound meaning for the ancient Maya calendar makers. A veritable symphony of similar astronomical alignments with the dark rift, involving Jupiter, eclipses, the moon, Mars, and probably Uranus, were tracked through the Classic Period. Their meanings are abundantly clear, supported by specific Long Count date references, and contribute to our own understanding of how the ancient Maya thought about the cycle ending in 2012. King-making rites, the sacred ball-game, time cycles, and a Creation Mythos form different facets of a lost cosmology, ancient beliefs that center around one idea: transformation. There is nothing in this material that suggests the kinds of cataclysmic prophecies currently being peddled in the 2012 marketplace, cheap cardboard cutouts that mock the profound cosmovision of the ancient Maya. This is the galactic cosmology in a nutshell. I don't want to complicate the presentation with myriad sideline arguments and discussions of other monuments at Izapa and related sites, such as Tak'alik Ab'aj, of which there is much to discuss.[37] Enough can be found in this brief survey to help you understand the compelling and reasonable basis of my end-date alignment theory.

With the nuts and bolts of the astronomy identified, we can consider the deeper spiritual ideas and beliefs connected with 2012. Transformation and renewal were facilitated by sacrifice, but what does this mean? And do these teachings have meaning for us, for all humanity? Are they simply quaint, culturally relative beliefs of a forgotten people, or are they perennial wisdom teachings that speak to the crisis we in the modern world are experiencing? These questions are important, perhaps much more important than the reconstruction of the 2012 paradigm that I've just offered. And they'll be taken up in Part II. Before we do that, we need to get up to date on how the 2012 topic has been faring in the first decade of the third millennium. It's not that surprising to find that in the pop culture it has become a hot topic, but in academic circles it's been subject to cold dismissals.

CHAPTER FIVE

THE 2012 EXPLOSION

The theories concern solar cycles, asteroids and
comets, rogue planets, plasma bands, the exploding
galactic core and other ideas, and the results are
predicted to be anything from burnt-out power
stations to total wipeout. One thing is for sure—they
can't all be right![1]

—GEOFF STRAY

The third millennium opened inauspiciously, with Y2K fizzling. If 2012 was at all on anyone's radar at the time, it probably became entangled with Y2K as just another hoax that would need to be dealt with when its time came. As the first decade of the new millennium unfolded, 2012 was often dismissed as a hoax. To even frame one's approach to 2012 in this way is patently absurd and reveals a superficial understanding of the topic. For 2012, whatever you think about it, is a true artifact of the ancient Maya calendar system. It is simply a fact of that system, as much as the century marker 1900 is a true artifact of the Gregorian calendar. To presume to prove that 2012 is a hoax is much like trying to prove that sex is a hoax. Sex is a fact of biology, so how can one prove it is a hoax? It baffles common sense. Unfortunately, much of the 2012 discussion as it unfolded between 2000 and 2010 has been littered with similarly ridiculous approaches and assumptions.

"That's the end of the world, right?" The grinning young man looked to me hopefully for confirmation. It was late January of 2000 in downtown

Denver, and I was sitting at a card table in a corner of the Barnes & Noble bookstore. Stacks of my book *Maya Cosmogenesis 2012* were piled next to me. People occasionally glanced over, on their way to a movie or dinner, killing time at the bookstore. "No, in fact the Maya material doesn't indicate that 2012 is about the end of the world." He looked at me quizzically, as if I was raining on his parade.

As a 2012 author, I'm often thought to be a sci-fi wordsmith spinning out fantastic scenarios, and plenty of readers are happy to play along. Horror fictioneers like Whitley Strieber have strategically placed 2012 in their book titles. Sci-fi writers like Steve Alten have adapted my end-date alignment theory to frame fast-paced narratives with doomsday overtones. My bookstore appearance was not strategically arranged, blessed by neither the stars nor the weather. It was Super Bowl Sunday, a freezing snow blew outside, and Y2K had just made fools of many prophets of doom. Never mind that I've never taken that position on 2012; people sneered and rolled their eyes as they walked by. I could tell it was going to be a long decade.

Things were astir in distant corners of the 2012 meme. In the first five years of the new millennium, a bevy of books appeared. They indicated, if nothing else, that the 2012 meme was gaining ground as a hot topic. In 2000, a documentary called *The Fifth Gate* was released in Europe and the United Kingdom. It focused on American Indian prophecies for the new millennium and included coverage of the Maya, the Hopi, and the Native American Church's efforts to legalize their sacraments, such as peyote. I was impressed with the producer, Bente Milton, and her serious and detailed treatment of the subject matter.

Another documentary opportunity occurred that summer. The Discovery Channel contacted me, and after some long discussions with the producer I was able to convey the key ideas of my work on 2012. Although they had contacted me as a go-to guy for some standard clichés on the Maya (such as "why did they disappear?"), the script was adapted to present my reconstruction work on the Maya's awareness of the galactic alignment in era-2012. I'd been on national radio shows, but this would be the first place in which my work received prime-time mainstream media coverage. I was hoping for some dynamic digital workups of the galactic alignment astronomy that could be easily conveyed visually, but instead they used a primitively animated portrayal of a diagram from my book. (An earlier documentary I was in, called *Earth Under Fire*, used me saying something about the Galactic Center, but the galactic alignment itself went unreported.)

Nevertheless, the two Discovery Channel "Places of Mystery" programs— one on Copán and one on Chichén Itzá—aired in October of 2000 and depicted my galactic alignment work more or less accurately. Any author should expect such treatment, but over the next eight years my work was consistently distorted and abused in the nefarious doomsday agendas of the History Channel and other production houses. Likewise, my interviews for many indie film producers were selectively edited to bolster perspectives that I don't agree with. It's a trick of the trade, and I was tricked many times. In a supreme catch-22, Maya scholars note these distortions and conclude I'm a willing architect of the mass media's stupefactions. There have been a few exceptions, which I'll mention as we move through a decade that has seen an explosion of 2012-related manifestations, far more intense and busy than the period 1970–2000.

In January of 2000, I learned of a prophecy for 2012 offered by Don Alejandro Cirilo Perez Oxlaj, a Quiché Maya leader and day-keeper from the highlands of Guatemala. It was reported in a piece by journalists Patrisia Gonzales and Roberto Rodriguez called "The Mayan Worldview of the Universe":

> *Based on thousands of years of astronomical observation, a cataclysm is indeed predicted by indigenous elders, as opposed to "prophesized." No one is predicting that at the strike of midnight, Dec. 20, 2012, the world will end. Instead, Mayan elders predict that the cataclysm can occur within a year or 100 years—and the cause would be something astronomical as opposed to metaphysical.*[2]

I've always agreed with the idea that, if any causal effects are to be credited to the astronomical basis of the Maya calendar, we should think of the 2012 end date as being a "zone" stretching over a period of decades. I don't, how-ever, agree with the above view that the end date is simply about an astro-nomical event. The interview continues:

> We don't know what will happen in the next few days or in the next
> 12 years. What we do know is that it wouldn't hurt to listen to the
> words of Don Alejandro who said that on Dec. 20, 2012 Mother Earth
> will pass inside the center of a magnetic axis and that it may be dark-
> ened with a great cloud for 60 or 70 hours and that because of envi-
> ronmental degradation, she may not be strong enough to survive the
> effects. It will enter another age, but when it does, there will be great
> and serious events. Earthquakes, marimotos (tsunamis), floods, vol-
> canic eruptions, and great illness on the planet Earth. Few survivors
> will be left.[3]

Thus, beginning on December 20, as stated, the events stretch over almost three full days ("60 or 70 hours") through to December 22. The earth's pas-sage "inside the center of a magnetic axis" is a striking description that sounds much like the way I described the alignment in the last chapter of *Maya Cosmogenesis 2012*:

> On the Galactic level, the Milky Way's equator, like the earth's equa-
> tor, is a field-effect dividing line. As with a spinning magnetic top, the
> field effects on one side are different from those on the other, and
> Maya insights offer us the notion that a field effect reversal occurs
> when the solstice meridian crosses over this line.[4]

"Darkened with a great cloud" sounds very similar to how one might imagine the sun passing through the dark rift in the Milky Way. Notice, however, the difference between the prophetic conception of the earth being cast into darkness and my alignment description—where I describe it as *the sun* pass-ing through the dark rift, as viewed from earth. I suppose Don Alejandro's wording works fine; it's just an interpretation that emphasizes where the "effect" is believed to be felt (on earth, ultimately).

This all sounded eerily familiar, like a folksy retelling of my galactic alignment theory, complete with references to a dark cloud (the dark rift), the sun's passage through this dark cloud, and a magnetic axis (the Milky Way's equator). I remembered that Don Alejandro had been interviewed by Morton and Thomas for their 1997 book *The Mystery of the Crystal Skulls*, but didn't recall his saying anything like this. My friend in England, Geoff Stray, had been tracking the 2012 phenomenon for a number of years, and I asked him for his comments. He had already assessed the *Crystal Skulls* book and noted that Don Alejandro's comments were an echo of the ideas Argüelles had published in *The Mayan Factor* and in his Dreamspell system.

I then recalled that an acquaintance of mine, Ian Lungold, had traveled to Guatemala to meet with Don Alejandro in the fall of 1998. We had spoken on the phone several times at odd intervals since 1997, and Ian would occasionally send me e-mail updates on his travels and plans to market a day-sign place mat for restaurants. A skilled jeweler, he was producing fine miniature pendants of Maya art. In early 1999 he related to me how he had met with Don Alejandro and showed him a copy of my book, *Maya Cosmogenesis 2012*, which had been released the previous year. He had had certain passages read to Don Alejandro by a translator.

Ian was inquiring about whether any of my work jibed with anything Don Alejandro knew about 2012, an inherently difficult approach for two reasons. First, as previously discussed, the Long Count system has been lost to the modern Maya. Second, Maya leaders are often threatened that foreigners are interpreting their lost tradition. A consequence of this is the uncomfortable position they are forced into when they are asked about 2012, not wanting to cite others on what should be a knowledge transmitted through ancestral lineage, but not having any real information at hand. A tendency to adopt and reimagine pieces of what comes before their consideration is a tactic of syncretism that the Maya have been engaged in for their entire history. It's not just a response to the Conquest, or modern writers, but is a characteristic of flexible adaptation to new ideas and needs. It's actually a sign of strength and fosters longevity, much as the willow tree flexes and survives the storm.

Ian told me that Don Alejandro received the information from my book with interest. Ian was also there to confirm, for himself, the correlation of the 260-day tzolkin count that I had presented and defended. He, like Swedish author Carl Calleman, had come out of the Argüelles camp, which supported a day-count placement that was at odds with the authentic surviving day-count in the highlands. The day-count Ian found in the highlands, verified by Don Alejandro, was indeed the traditional day-count I'd been advocating since my early books, especially in my 1992 book *Tzolkin: Visionary Perspectives and Calendar Studies.*

After Ian's visit with Don Alejandro, an international gathering of indigenous elders happened in Arizona. It was a meeting of elders from many indigenous nations, and Don Alejandro was present. That's when the reporters from Albuquerque interviewed him and received the oddly familiar prophecy for 2012.

If one suspects that Don Alejandro's words represent an ancient lineage teaching, then we must account for his earlier interview with Morton and Thomas, which clearly echoed Argüelles's work. These are complicated and sensitive issues, but I believe that truth and accountability are necessary if we are to stay as clear as possible with 2012 and its multifarious tentacles. We've already seen a tendency, in the connections between José Argüelles, Hunbatz Men, and Aluna Joy Yaxkin, for a reinforcing interplay to develop between writers and Maya elders, especially when a popular movement driven by temple tours and New Age gatherings is at work. But the truth does often surface, if given a chance. In fact, there eventually came a time in the late 1990s when, after many e-mail exchanges with Aluna Joy Yaxkin, she switched to the authentic day-count (the "True Count") and began organizing tours to the Guatemalan highlands with Don Alejandro.

I was bemused as I reconstructed the sequence of events and reread my e-mails with Ian. It was clear that something of my alignment work had been adapted by Don Alejandro. I felt conflicted, because on one hand I imagined that if my work were indeed an accurate reconstruction of the ancient Maya's understanding of 2012, then it should somehow be reintegrated into contemporary Maya consciousness. But for an outsider to offer this was difficult for the modern Maya to accept, having been betrayed by relations with outsiders in the past. If I played up Don Alejandro's statement as independent confirmation of my work by an elder, my handlers at Marketing Central would be pleased but it would also be a deception. Nevertheless, the marketing world preferred that the galactic alignment prophecy for 2012 should be delivered by the Maya, as subsequent events made very clear.

As a result of Don Alejandro's statements, I began thinking hard about the fact that the Maya lost their connection to the details of the ancient 2012 calendar system. I recalled my travels in the highlands, hanging out at the altar shrines of Momostenengo, reading of the Year Bearer ceremonies at year's end, and I realized that the Maya still retained core beliefs about cycle endings, generally speaking, and these were very important. The fire ceremony and the sweat bath were both beautiful traditions that the Maya still retained, and they both involved the themes of sacrifice, transformation, and renewal central to ancient spiritual teachings for cycle endings.

I felt I should collaborate with Maya teachers who were creating ceremonial spaces of renewal. I remembered conversations I had had with Erick Gonzalez back in 1996. Ironically, he had introduced Ian Lungold to my book *Tzolkin*, which led Ian to adopting the True Count and deriving the day-sign conversion tables he used in his place mats (which were a simplified method based on the charts in my book). And through a mutual friend I learned that Erick was actively traveling the country facilitating renewal rites with Maya fire ceremonies. Reconnecting with Erick, we discussed the importance of having a collaboration between the intellectual and spiritual approaches to 2012. My reconstruction could proceed as an academic presentation. Although I also enjoyed speaking about the spiritual teachings in the Maya Creation Myth, I was glad to have Erick give participatory fire ceremonies so that people could experience transformation and renewal directly. Most people considered this the more important part of the weekend gathering. Fire is, indeed, the great transformer, and I could frame that ceremony as the logical expression of what the 2012 alignment to the Galactic Center was inviting—humanity reconnecting with the renewing fire of the central heart and source. We gave two well-attended events in Boulder, one in October of 2000 and another in April of 2001. It was good. After April I was deeply involved in writing my book *Galactic Alignment*; Erick and I were content to move on and did not set up any more events.

Naropa University is located in Boulder, Colorado. I had taught a series of classes there in late 1999. In early 2002 I came across a write-up on Erick's work in a journal published by Naropa. I was surprised to read of the "Maya prophecy" of the galactic alignment and Erick's fire ceremonies, but no mention of my work. These kinds of things happen. Remembering the Don Alejandro incident and considering my prior relationship with Naropa, I though it prudent to inform the editor of my work and seek a correction; perhaps I could write a piece for their journal to explain the galactic alignment theory. I received a rather surprised apology but no invitation to submit something new.

Years later I found out from Erick that he had never intended to portray the galactic alignment as a direct lineage teaching, and as a result of my complaint a potential collaboration with Naropa had collapsed. It seemed an interviewer had framed the information incorrectly, causing an unfortunate debacle. Meanwhile, 2001, the sci-fi year of Kubrick's *Space Odyssey*, was getting under way. I had been trying to finance a documentary on 2012 with the site of Izapa as the focal point. It was transparently obvious to me that Izapa, as the origin place of the 2012 calendar, should be the centerpiece of any documentary on 2012. Two potential funding sources fell through, so I and my indefatigable friend Jim Reed decided to do it ourselves. With the financial assistance of Visa and MasterCard, we flew to Guatemala and then took a shuttle across the border into Mexico. Jim brought his mini-DV camera and I was armed with maps and diagrams.

It was gloriously hot in the tropical lowlands in early March. We visited the three main groups. I pointed out the orientation of the Group A monuments to the polar Big Dipper, the Group B pillar-and-ball gnomons symbolizing the zenith and the hearth stars of Orion, and the Group F ballcourt's orientation to the dawning December solstice sun. When all was said and done, we had taken some good footage, but as digital technology had quickly evolved the format we had recorded in was deemed not usable for a professional presentation. As of this writing, in early 2009, there has yet to be a documentary production devoted to the importance of Izapa for the 2012 discussion, although I have persistently tried to facilitate one.

When I've done interviews for documentaries, I've gotten verbal agreements that Izapa will be the focal point, but that never ends up being the case. Incredibly, through dozens of 2012 documentary appearances, making direct appeals for inclusion of this material, Izapa has barely been mentioned. I'm used largely as a talking head in someone else's perception of what is central to the 2012 discussion. The origin place of the 2012 calendar has been relegated to the cutting-room floor, while Nostradamus, alchemy, Incas, pole flips, and jet-setting trippers are abundantly portrayed. The one exception, in which my discussion of Izapa was included, was the well-conceived documentary of early 2009 called *2012: Science or Superstition?*

In 1999, I had a falling-out with Lungold when I learned that he had big dollar signs in mind with his tzolkin-themed place mats and was planning to work with a publisher in Mexico that could produce them by the millions. This commodification of the Maya calendar wasn't something I really wanted to be involved in. By the summer of 2000, Lungold had hooked up with a Swedish researcher of the Maya calendar, Carl Johan Calleman. They were traveling through Mexico, setting up the publication of the place mats, visiting the temple sites, and seeking promotional opportunities. I can remember receiving a long-distance call from Ian at the time, afire with an impending deal and how he and Carl were taking Mexico by storm. Their ambitions began to unravel as the summer wore on, until a disappointment with their Mexican agent led to the collapsing of their plans.

Meanwhile, Carl was awaiting my comments on his book *The Mayan*

Calendar: Solving the Greatest Mystery of Our Time. I'd read the book, and it basically took on the audacious and impossible task of proving God. My friend Nicholas Kirsten Honshin, an artist, poet, and mystical philosopher, had pointed out to me with a smile that mysteries could never, by definition, be "solved"—but they could be experienced. This was an apt indication of what emerged as a consistent flaw in Calleman's approach to the Maya calendar and his proposed theology of spiritual transformation. To force-fit spirituality into scientific boxes results in a truncated travesty. The approach should be, rather, to enlarge the conceptual framework of science—of our currently limited mental framework—so that it could directly perceive and embrace the higher metaphysical principles of spiritual teachings.

It's important to share a bit of background so that Calleman's ideas can be understood in proper context. Calleman fell in with the Dreamspell group in the early 1990s while attending the University of Washington in Seattle. My own critique of the Argüelles day-count was available in my 1992 book *Tzolkin*, reprinted in 1994, which Calleman acquired. He could see the value of switching to the True Count and being on track with the traditional Maya system. By 1998 he was writing a book on the subject of the "True Cross" and Maya cosmology. It proposed a notion that the Maya sacred tree, or cross, should be understood as the cross formed by the Milky Way and the perpendicular line that runs through the central axis of the spinning Milky Way. Every spinning body spins upon an axis, and for Carl this was the preferable axis.

His notion contradicted the definition of the Sacred Tree accepted by Schele and other scholars, which was relevant in terms of what naked-eye sky-watchers could actually be viewing—the cross was formed by the bright band of the Milky Way and the ecliptic (the path of the sun, moon, and planets). Carl was utilizing a scientifically valid concept, but it was not in fact a concept utilized in Maya cosmology. The idea of living close to the tree's spinning "axis" had meaning for Carl, and by way of an analogy with the spinning earth and its axis, Carl seemed to believe that people living closer to the earth's poles were somehow more in touch with God or the Creation.

During one e-mail exchange, Carl implied that he had the scoop on the divine wisdom because he lived in Sweden, closer to the north pole. This is an old notion found in theosophy and other occult teachings. The implication, of course, is that equatorial cultures—the Maya, for example—are less privy to the axial wisdom. But the Maya were supposedly the source of Carl's True Cross idea, so if one actually thought through the ideas proposed by Calleman, gulfs of self-contradiction emerged.

I had a problem with these and other assertions evident in his book, and I explained them to Carl in clear factual terms. This caused a backlash, and our ensuing exchanges through the years have always begun with Carl trying in various ways to discredit "my" end date (which is actually not mine in the sense of its being of my own invention; December 21, 2012, is simply derived from the established correlation).[5] As a reaction to our e-mail exchanges, he began to assert a distinction between my approach to 2012, which he claimed was astronomical and therefore "physical," and his own approach, which was "spiritual." I responded that my books were always concerned with reconstructing the scientific (astronomical) as well as spiritual concepts associated with 2012, and that to make artificial distinctions between physical and spiritual was not consistent with an integrated worldview—a nondual philosophy that was a hallmark of both Maya cosmology and the profound insights of Vedanta. The philosophical and conceptual problems that arise when one is stuck in a dualist framework have typified Calleman's approach.

In late 2001 Carl invited me to a debate and we decided to do three written exchanges, to be posted on Geoff Stray's Diagnosis 2012 website. The exchanges were lengthy and revealing. In a nutshell, Carl rejects the December 21, 2012, end date and my end-date alignment theory because it is based in astronomy. He asserted that the Maya calendar has nothing to do with astronomy, and instead it's all about timing a spiritual wave of unfolding. Carl never accepted my clarifications and has persistently asserted the superiority of his exclusively "spiritual" interpretation of the Maya calendar, and thus the priority of his own invented end date, October 28, 2011. In a nondual paradigm, the spiritual transcends the physical, meaning that it includes the physical in a larger whole. So, in this nondual sense, the spiritual domain is indeed superior to the physical. However, a common trap that reveals a misunderstanding of this principle is to make the spiritual and physical mutually exclusive, two forever-separated poles like apples and oranges that cannot mingle. This was the error of dualism in Cartesian thinking, also evident in much Christian dogma, which always results in the fundamentalist attitude that seeks to annihilate the physical, the body, the heathens—the enemy in whatever form it takes.

Calleman's system also asserts a flat-out rejection of the December 21, 2012, cycle-ending date, frequently repeating the mantra that "the archaeologists" got it wrong. His own invented alternative of October 28, 2011, is presented as the true date of the *spiritual* shift, whereas the December 21, 2012, date is simply an inaccurate calendrical marker. His argument in support of his own date is that the day-sign lists for the 260-day calendar begin with Imix. Therefore, 1 Imix must coordinate with the first day of the new cycle and 13 Ahau (the previous day) must correspond to the last day of the current cycle. The argument is facile and reveals a basic misunderstanding of the how the calendars actually work. It applies a "sort of" logic that is much like demanding that we reorder the weekdays alphabetically. It also disregards the many Maya Creation Monuments that coordinate 13.0.0.0.0 with the date 4 Ahau, not 13 Ahau or 1 Imix.

Calleman co-opted McKenna's idea of fractal time acceleration but based his model on factors of 20. The Long Count is a base-20 system and expands into larger multiples by factors of 20, with the exception of the Tun level (which results from the 20-day Uinal multiplied by 18, not 20) and the 13-Baktun cycle, which is generated by multiplying the Baktun level by 13, not 20. So in his theory time unfolds in fractal multiples of the base unit 20, but each higher level in the Long Count is in fact not always generated by multiples of 20. Nevertheless, Calleman assumed that time expanded in this fractal way, and he noted that a big period generated in this way equaled 16.9 billion years, which allegedly approximates the current astrophysical estimate for the age of the universe. Never mind that the current age is now estimated to be at least 18 billion years.

The most egregious problem with Calleman's work is that he follows in the mold of Argüelles in his attempts to evangelize a new, improved, Maya calendar. Argüelles neglected to adopt the authentic 260-day count, whereas Calleman rejects the authentic end date. With the new preordained spiritual shift-date placed on October 28, 2011, Calleman's detailed scheme of portal days and mini-celebration shift-days then proceeds backward in intervals of Tuns (360 days). Followers of Calleman's system heard that, for example, November 12, 2008, would be the Fifth Night of the Mayan Underworld. News flashes went out on the Internet, and Carl wrote a press release or two and did some interviews. The next big one is November 7, 2009, then November 2, 2010, and finally, voilà!: October 28, 2011. And along the way there are other miniportal lieutenant and vice principal days all fitted perfectly into a system as magically rigorous as anything Argüelles devised.

Most followers hardly suspect that the scheme counts down to Calleman's own idiosyncratic end date, and also don't know, or don't care, that the system as a whole has nothing to do with anything the Maya ever followed or believed. Nevertheless, writers such as Barbara Clow and Daniel Pinchbeck have jumped aboard the Calleman wagon without discerning the many difficulties that his system, and approach, present. Clow's 2007 book *The Maya Code* credited Calleman with discovering the concept of fractal time acceleration, disregarding two things: McKenna's pioneering elaboration of the idea thirty-five years ago, and the Hindu Yugas, in which each age unfolds more quickly than the last. That ancient doctrine is, basically, an expression of fractal time acceleration.

The result of the Calleman system has been to further confuse the fundamental basics of the calendar. It's very much in the spirit of Argüelles's confusion of the day-counts. I find this occurrence fascinating. We can scan back over the 1990s quickly and notice that the Dreamspell system arose in 1991. I quickly exposed the flaws of the system, but it wasn't until 1996 that an acknowledgment of its flaws occurred within the Dreamspell camp—and even then it simply triggered a spin-doctoring caveat in which the Dream-spell was emphasized as the new dispensation and preferable Wizard Count. But the admission that the Dreamspell system was at odds with the True Count still followed in the highlands caused a fallout of people away from the Dreamspell camp. Then, as if on cue, Calleman's system arose and asserted an equally flawed perspective, directing disillusioned spiritual seekers into an equally alluring alternative system that was also equally deceptive. The New Age movement was trying to find the words to express a deeper spiritual meaning in the Maya calendar, but was consistently building from flawed foundations.

The brilliant and profound wisdom of the ancient Maya was getting distorted. Professional Maya scholars didn't bother to point out the errors in Calleman's and Argüelles's books. If anything, they simply cast them aside as nonscholars. But the fact is that both Calleman and Argüelles have PhDs. They technically belong in the ivory tower, so why weren't the gatekeepers of academe taking them, their degreed colleagues, to task? Why did it fall to an outsider, who doesn't have a PhD, to call out the errors and expose bad research and flawed models? Why was I doing the scholars' jobs for them? Most annoyingly, I found in my dealings with scholars that they were happy to toss me into the same category as Argüelles and Calleman, unable or unwilling to make any distinction between my work and theirs.

What I actually found in my dealings with professional Mayanists is that they harbored huge assumptions and misunderstandings about the Maya calendar, almost as egregious as those found among popular writers. Few scholars I communicated with understood the correlation debate, or the site of Izapa, or how the Long Count and Calendar Round relate to each other. Likewise, the concept of the galactic alignment has been co-opted and misunderstood. As mentioned earlier, the tendency is for my galactic alignment theory to be received best only if it is delivered through the mouth of a Maya elder. It just makes for better ad copy that way. We saw this in how an interviewer in 2002 framed the collaboration between Erick Gonzalez and me. As if some new viral meme was forcefully trying to insert itself into the 2012 discussion, an identical fiasco occurred a short time later when Stephen Mc-Fadden interviewed Maya teacher Carlos Barrios.

This one has produced far-reaching ripples with disastrous effects, mainly because I decided to take the high road and ignore it. But it festered, morphed, and returned after several years to bite me on the butt. It's both annoying and hilarious that such things happen. The interview expresses the following position regarding "anthropologists" and "other people" who write "about prophecy in the name of the Maya":

> *"Anthropologists visit the temple sites," Mr. Barrios says, "and read the steles and inscriptions and make up stories about the Maya, but they do not read the signs correctly. It's just their imagination. . . . Other people write about prophecy in the name of the Maya. They say that the world will end in December 2012. The Mayan elders are angry with this. The world will not end. It will be transformed."[6]*

And angry they should be. I've been shouting since day one that 2012, like any cycle ending, is about transformation, a new beginning, not a final apocalyptic end. It says so in *The Popol Vuh*. So I'm in complete agreement with Carlos on this. But since many people see my books as being scholarly and me as an (albeit independent) anthropologist or archaeologist, I can't help feeling that the first part of the quote is leveled at outsiders like me who "read the signs." This seems to be the implication, whether it was intended or not; the interviewer's wording is insufficiently clear. In this light, the next passage is all the more distressing:

> *He [Carlos] said Mayan Daykeepers view the Dec. 21, 2012 date as a rebirth, the start of the World of the Fifth Sun. It will be the start of a new era resulting from and* signified by the solar meridian crossing the galactic equator, *and the earth aligning itself with the center of the galaxy.* At sunrise on December 21, 2012 for the first time in 26,000 years the Sun rises to conjunct the intersection of the Milky

Way and the plane of the ecliptic. *This cosmic cross is considered to be an embodiment of the Sacred Tree, The Tree of Life, a tree remembered in all the world's spiritual traditions. Some observers say this alignment with the heart of the galaxy in 2012 will open a channel for cosmic energy to flow through the earth, cleansing it and all that dwells upon it, raising all to a higher level of vibration.*[7]

The emphasized passages are almost direct paraphrases from my books and web pages. A phrase like "the solar meridian crossing the galactic equator" provides an accurate description of what the 2012 alignment is, and I have offered this exact terminology as a clear definition. To what can we attribute this material appearing in McFadden's interview with Barrios, apparently paraphrasing the words of Barrios himself?

One version of the interview contained some source citations. A website called "Great Dreams" was referenced, and I immediately recognized the web page. It was one that appeared around 1999, and its treatment of 2012 included diagrams and direct cut-and-paste sections from an article I had posted on my website in 1995, called "Mayan Cosmogenesis: Cosmic Mother Gives Birth." This article summarized my work on the galactic alignment, showing how it was encoded into Maya traditions like the Creation Myth. I concluded the piece as follows:

Understanding this aspect of Mayan cosmogenesis may also help us understand our own impending millennial milestone. What is going on in the world today? Is this alignment having some kind of influence? The precession of the equinoxes is, after all, primarily an earth rhythm. Whether we call it Mayan or millennial, we are living today in the shadows of a rare celestial juncture which parallels the increasing interest in "New World Orders," "post-historic" thinking, and a major shift in world economic structure and what it means to be human. The Mayan myth seems to remind us that all life springs from the Great Mother. The transformation of cosmic recreation is already occurring. Perhaps we should look closely at this celestial alignment, imagine its meanings, and determine what this transformational shift means for future humanity. For the ancient Maya, on the far-future Creation Day which for us arrives soon, First Mother and First Father join forces to engender a new World Age.[8]

The problem with the appearance of my work on the Great Dreams website is that there were no links to the original source (my website) and my name did not appear. At one point I tried to e-mail the webmaster to seek a clarification, but I never received a response after several attempts. It was only years later when I described the situation as plagiarism, on the 2012 Yahoo Group, that the designer of the Great Dreams website piped up and defended herself, saying that my name and website appeared elsewhere on the website and thus their free use of my work wasn't really plagiarism. Today their 2012 web page has been corrected, but for many years the galactic alignment information on the Great Dreams website seemed to be a general Maya "prophecy" of unknown origin.

As a result, I suspect that either Carlos Barrios or his interviewer, Stephen McFadden, had lifted the idea without, perhaps, being aware of its true source. I confirmed this later on, and communicated with McFadden about the situation. He said he was aware of my work, apologized for the omission of correct citation, and graciously corrected the official version of the interview that is posted on his website.[9] Nevertheless, uncorrected versions of the interview still occasionally sail around the Internet.

Barrios, like Erick Gonzalez, has perhaps inadvertently been accomplice to a way of framing my work in the marketplace that prefers to deliver it through the mouth of an elder. However, Barrios thereafter adopted the galactic alignment scenario as a true expression of one of the so-called Maya prophecies for 2012. He included it in his 2004 book[10] and shared it with author Lawrence Joseph, whose book *Apocalypse 2012* propagated and amplified the McFadden-Barrios debacle. Furthermore, as if unaware of the source of the idea he adopted, he said, "Many outside people writing about the

Mayan calendar sensationalize this date, but they do not know. The ones who know are the indigenous elders who are entrusted with keeping the tradition."[11]

Lawrence Joseph began writing a book about John Lennon within hours of his tragic murder. He boasts on his website that this book was "written, typeset, printed and distributed twelve days after John Lennon's assassination."[12] To such an enterprising soul, 2012 must have been irresistible. How would one begin a book on 2012? Talk to Maya elders, of course. Joseph recounts in the early pages of his book how he flew to Guatemala to receive the Maya prophecy about 2012 directly from Maya teachers, the Barrios brothers, learning that "on 12/21/12 our Solar System, with the Sun at its center, will, as the Maya have for millennia maintained, eclipse the view from Earth of the center of the Milky Way. This happens only once every 26,000 years. Ancient Maya astronomers considered this spot to be the Milky Way's womb."[13] Except for the fact that the Maya have not retained a continuity of this knowledge "for millennia," this is a fairly accurate paraphrase of my theory, including my interpretation that the Galactic Center was mythologized by the ancient Maya as a cosmic womb, a creation place.

Armed with the Maya prophecy for 2012, handed to him by Real Maya Teachers, the author of *Apocalypse 2012* then proceeds to concur with said Teachers to excoriate clueless outsiders, who don't know how to read the symbols. I am mentioned by name as a "cultural imperialist."[14] While my book *Maya Cosmogenesis 2012* was mentioned and wanly dismissed, its primary thesis (that the ancient Maya intended 2012 to target the rare alignment of the solstice sun and the Galactic Center) was left unsaid. Obviously, to mention it would have created a conflict of interest, as Joseph wished to give the impression that the goods were delivered to him by a Maya teacher. This *contretemps* reveals either a shoddy research ethic or intellectual dishonesty in a book that presumes to be "a scientific investigation." I've now had the dubious honor of being plagiarized and excoriated at the same time.[15]

Lawrence Joseph subscribes to the old idea, put forward by Cotterell and Gilbert in *The Mayan Prophecies*, that solar flares will be going berserk in

2012. He frequently points to outdated scientific projections that 2012 will be a year of solar max, never clarifying that such solar sunspot maximums occur every 11.3 years and the one now projected for May 2013 will not be any larger than the one in the 1950s. He's latched on to an alarmist interpretation of the galactic alignment, which he claims came from Barrios, in which the galactic alignment "cuts us off" from the life-force energy of the Galactic Center, like "the power being cut off from homes."[16] This interpretation, however, ignores the rebirth imagery that is associated with the alignment at Izapa. Joseph claims his book is not a doomsday book, that his publisher insisted on the title,[17] yet writes the following in his book:

> The next peak in the planetary tidal force, essentially the sum total of the planets' gravitational pull on the Sun, will come late in 2012 . . . The sunspot maximum, coincidentally also due in that year, will compound the situation, subjecting the Sun to maximum stress. The Sun's magnetic poles . . . are also expected to switch in 2012, adding further volatility to the situation. The resulting synergy of gravitational and electromagnetic pressure on the Sun cannot help but distort and distend its surface, releasing megabursts of imprisoned radiation, quite possibly ones that are far deadlier than any the Earth has encountered since homo sapiens has been around."[18]

Although he tries to conceal it when it is deemed inappropriate, his unequivocally nihilistic position is very common in the 2012 discussion, and shares company with Brent Miller's Horizon Project™, which I'll assess in a moment.

This chapter could easily be expanded into a book-size treatment of these various manifestations, but space prohibits more than a mention of many of them. I can't possibly treat them all in this book, and I'm not implying that all of these researchers play fast and loose with 2012 in the way that others have, nor am I endorsing them. The books of Sri Ram Kaa and Kira Ra, William Henry, Jay Weidner, and Vincent Bridges (*The Mysteries of the Great Cross of*

Hendaye), Sharron Rose, Christine Page, Dr. Willy Gaspar, Gregg Braden, Patricia Mercier (just to name a few)—it's a cornucopia. Geoff Stray's website, Diagnosis 2012, is a comprehensive resource for reliable assessments. For our purposes here, I will discuss a few representative examples.

My book *Galactic Alignment* was published in 2002. The book's very title presented a still vaguely understood concept to the public eye. Within the decade many books, theories, websites, and pseudoscience doomsday models would appropriate the concept, often confusing it with other ideas. David Wilcock began publishing his research and writings online around 1998. His treatment of the Maya calendar mentioned the galactic alignment as occurring in 1999, and drew from the work of Maurice Chatelain and many other writers, from Richard Hoagland to Edgar Cayce. Wilcock integrated many threads of science and ancient metaphysics into his work, and explored spiritual and paranormal phenomenon. As a dream analyst, he has asserted and tracked his own mystical connection to American prophet Edgar Cayce, resulting in a book published in 2004 which asserted that he was Cayce reincarnated.

Wilcock also developed a highly elaborated system of hyperdimensional physics, which he explained during the Global Shift conferences that I also spoke at. His system utilized many ideas, including the galactic alignment and material from the Ra channelings, to explain changes happening in our solar system and the consciousness of humanity. By 2005 he was working with author Richard Hoagland, a regular on the late-night radio program *Coast-to-Coast A.M.* Hoagland adopted much of Wilcock's work and organized several conferences under the banner of 2012.

Hoagland, like Wilcock, draws heavily from hard science—physics, atomic theory, quantum mechanics, and so on—but he was not particularly concerned with the ways that an ancient culture such as the Maya discovered and calculated the galactic alignment and incorporated the concept into their cosmology and teachings. His current 2012 rap involves a belief that secret forces inside the government are aware of 2012's doomsday potential. Hoagland collaborated on a book with Mike Bera about dark matter in the universe. At a conference venue I shared with Bera in 2008, he claimed he and Hoagland were devising an experiment that would test the galactic alignment. He seemed to think, however, that the galactic alignment was an alignment of planets somehow connected to the idea that a lost planet, Nibiru, would be returning into visibility within our solar system in 2012. I asked Mike to elaborate on his work more clearly, but he has yet to send me anything and our e-mail exchanges became locked into a holding pattern. This may seem like hearsay, but I mention it because much in the 2012 discussion is built upon hearsay. Rumor goes down the New Age telephone line and, instead of degrading into even more nonsense than it was when it began, it gets elevated to the status of theory and, finally, Truth. For example, let's look at the Nibiru–2012 connection.

The Nibiru (Planet X) idea comes from Zecharia Sitchin, author of the Lost Chronicles books now running up to some thirteen volumes, who based his radical ideas on ancient Babylonian astrological tablets.[19] He believes that cuneiform references to an "invisible planet" that comes around ("appears") every once in a while to cause havoc is proof that an unknown planet, Nibiru, orbits the sun with a great eccentricity, swinging far out beyond Pluto for millennia before it swings in again. He ties his theory to another idea—that beings on Nibiru meddled with human genetics in the distant past. In recent years, the timing of Nibiru's return has been spuriously connected to 2012.

An examination of Sitchin's work reveals an unfortunate *literalized* interpretation of ancient doctrines. The "invisible" planet that one finds often mentioned in ancient astrological texts is widely known to signify the moon's node. This is an intangible (invisible) point defined by the intersection of the lunar and solar orbits. It defines where eclipses may occur and it precesses slowly around the ecliptic. When it swings around to conjunct the position of sun or moon in the sky, an eclipse will occur. All the factors are there to make Sitchin's interpretation seem valid. The "invisible" point is made manifest after a long hiatus. Eclipses were fearful occurrences during which the sun was disrupted and earthlings were cast into darkness, changed forever. It's scary. In regard to Sitchin's notion of ancient gene splicers altering the species, eclipses symbolize the transcendence of opposites, which in many esoteric teachings triggers spiritual transformation, a new being coming into existence.

I read Sitchin's theory with openness and discernment, and this is what I found. Sitchin offers a literalized interpretation of esoteric teachings, which appeals to the modern materialist mind-set as well as the tendency of modern Occidental religions to interpret scripture, and reality, literally. Sitchin's work typifies the trap of the modern scientist interpreting ancient esoteric doctrines through the lens of materialism. So, instead of insights into the metaphysical teachings connected with the lunar nodes, eclipses, and transcendence, we get Niburian Annunaki fiddling with our genes whenever the Maya calendar says so. The situation is both absurd and hilarious.

For science-oriented researchers, the galactic alignment is a topic of interest but has often been conflated with the orbit of our solar system around the Galactic Center. This confusion indicates a breakdown of rational processing. Furthermore, despite the ideology of proactive spiritual transformation and renewal that the Maya applied to cycle endings, 2012 in the hands of pseudoscience fatalists becomes a literalized doomsday assaulting us from the outside. Spiritual self-actualization is replaced by materialist determinism. Reality gets inverted, concretized, in precisely the same way that Sitchin literalized the ancient astrological doctrine of the lunar nodes.

This unfortunate state of affairs is intimately related to what psychologist and rebirthing expert Stanislav Grof calls "the feeling of cosmic engulfment and no exit" (Basic Perinatal Matrix II in his system).[20] For the person under the influence of this matrix, life appears meaningless and cruel, absurd, dangerous and frightening. Impending doom is perceived as an unavoidable certainty. The fatalistic fear and anxiety that are retained in the body and psyche as a terrifying birth memory gets displaced and projected onto the world, where it sticks on cycle endings because they are conceptually analogous to the intrauterine birth crisis. The dark rift in the Milky Way, instead of being a liberating portal to a new world, becomes the death-dealing receptacle of nefarious killing forces. Choose your metaphor wisely.

Patrick Geryl, a Belgian writer, published a book in 2005 provocatively titled *World Cataclysm in 2012*, followed by *How to Survive 2012* in 2006. His work is about as reliable in terms of factual grounding in Maya tradition as the earlier *Mayan Prophecies* book by Cotterell and Gilbert. And it's unrelentingly, unapologetically alarmist, filled with doomsday visions stated matter-of-factly with absolute certainty. "At the end of 2012, an all-destroying pole shift is waiting for us," he writes on his website. He describes a pole shift in 2012, and how he "came to the staggering conclusion that the Earth will soon be subjected to an immense disaster. The cause: upheavals in the sun's magnetic fields will generate gigantic solar flares that will affect the polarity of the entire Earth. The result: our magnetic field will reverse all at once, with catastrophic consequences for humanity."[21] All of these statements confirm Geryl as the preeminent "predictator" of 2012ology (a predictator is one who asserts their predictions like a dictator).

Like so many other books, Geryl's barely scratch the surface of what the Maya tradition is really about, but liberally reference solar sunspot theories and a veritable grab bag of doomsday scenarios and tack them on to 2012; the details don't matter. The point is: Head for the hills! One might suspect, rightly so, that a book styled in such a way should be taken with a large grain of salt. But it's the kind of thing that the media and scholarly critics love. It provides the easy straw man target, the thing to hold up and say, "See, this whole 2012 thing is a goofy joke." As of 2008, Geryl is spending all his time forming survival groups and leading the call for everyone to leave Belgium and other lowland countries, for the seas will be quickly rising. You could buy the offered survival kits as well as land in South Africa. Hurry up, supplies are limited.

No less alarmist is The Horizon Project™, run by Brent Miller. According to its mission statement, The Horizon Project "relies on multiple sources for each piece of information from resources past and present. If any information does not agree with the rest, it is resolved by scientific committee with all known information. Never before has a research team with this level of effectiveness and capability been utilized solely for discovering answers to life's most crucial questions."[22] The website offers a series of DVDs for sale, and lists Brent Miller, Dr. Brooks Agnew (a physicist), and Michael Tsarion (a "researcher with over 20 years of expertise in the study of lost civilizations and technologies") as The Horizon Project's primary researchers/experts.

Brent Miller, the host of the DVD series, is described as an "expert in ecommerce systems" who has "held executive positions in several New York–based Fortune 500 companies." The first DVD in the series, released in August of 2006, was called "Bracing for Tomorrow."[23] A four-minute trailer offers a teaser statement that the DVD "provides a conclusion that will realize humanity's ultimate fear."[24] The summary states that the DVD "begins with a frightening bang. Newly discovered scientific evidence shows that the world as we know it is about to come to an unexpected end; however, knowing what's coming over the horizon is only the tip of the iceberg; understanding WHY presents a picture far greater than you could have imagined."[25]

As it turns out, an astronomical phenomenon that they call "the galactic alignment" is the reason behind this frightening "unexpected end." They refer to the lost knowledge of ancient civilizations, and how they left behind "major clues that have just been recently discovered" and they "knew of the upcoming inevitable catastrophe . . . The knowledge that was once lost is the missing link that provides a clear understanding of how our world truly operates. Ironically, these clues also inform us that time is running out; sooner than you may believe." The Horizon Project Research Team "will identify some of the signs that are scattered all over our planet and reveal a shocking truth!"[26]

A clip of a Horizon Project DVD hosted by Brent Miller can be viewed on YouTube under the heading "Galactic Alignment in 2012 is Feared to Cause Pole Shift by 2008-2015."[27] The term "galactic alignment" is used repeatedly, as is the "dark rift in the Milky Way," the key centerpiece of my galactic alignment theory. Unfortunately, Miller defines the galactic alignment incorrectly, as being caused by the physical orbit of our solar system around the Galactic Center, above and below the galactic plane over millions of years. This process has nothing to do with the precessional basis of the galactic alignment, as defined on Wikipedia and in my book (which came out in 2002 and was titled *Galactic Alignment*). For many years I've had a page on my website called "What is the Galactic Alignment?"[28] If you Google "Galactic Alignment," the first result is this page. I discuss the distinction between the galactic alignment and Brent Miller's scenario in my book *Galactic Alignment*, on my "Misconceptions" web page, and in an interview I did that is posted on YouTube.[29]

The Horizon Project provides a list of resources used in their research, but, oddly, the book called *Galactic Alignment* (published in 2002, long before The Horizon Project was founded) is not listed. One would think that comprehensive research into the galactic alignment would have included a careful study of the one and only book called *Galactic Alignment*. In fact, none of their sources could provide clear information on the galactic alignment and only one dealt with the Maya calendar (an obsolete 1904 study by Cyrus Thomas). I'm starting to wonder if scientists were really at all involved in the supposedly science-based Horizon Project.

In the DVD, after wrongly defining and describing the galactic alignment, the narrator says: "The Mayans state that the end of each Age, which brings about worldwide devastation, is defined by the world sitting on the dark rift. . . . [I]t is very clear that we are talking about the same event, an event where the earth passes through the galactic equinox."[30] It's frustrating to see the defining terms of my galactic alignment reconstruction being co-opted and distorted in this way. (Not to mention that "galactic equinox" is a meaningless term, apparently meant to indicate the galactic equator.) These distorted appropriations have been the cause of hundreds of accusatory e-mails I've received from people who believe that I, like The Horizon Project, preach a doomsday message.

"How can we know for sure," the narrator asks, "when you should be bracing for tomorrow?" Brent Miller sternly answers: "Computer simulations utilizing the collection of knowledge we have amassed through decades of galactic models and satellite data tell us that our solar system will *definitely* begin passing through the galactic plane in the very near future. The most severe effects that will cause worldwide devastation and a pole shift are most likely to occur, beginning sometime between the years 2008 and 2015."[31]

Although the orbital oscillation above and below the galactic plane is a real process, the scientific model actually places us, right now, fifty light-years above the galactic plane and heading out, as the following Cambridge University publication reports:

> *The Sun is moving upwards, out of the plane of the Milky Way, at a speed of 7 kilometers per second. Currently the Sun lies 50 light-years above the mid-plane of the galaxy, and its motion is steadily carrying it further away . . . But the gravitational pull of the stars in the Galactic (Milky Way) plane is slowing down the Sun's escape. The astronomer Frank Bash estimates that in 14 million years the sun will reach its maximum height above the Galactic disk. From that 250 light-year position, it will be pulled back towards the plane of the Galaxy. Passing through, it will travel to a point 250 light-years below the disk, then oscillate upwards again to reach its present position 66 million years from now.*[32]

The Horizon Project uses hyperbole-filled alarmist language, engages in bad science while giving the impression of being scientifically rigorous, and distorts the galactic alignment information already defined and published. While their efforts may be overlooked as the expected exploitation of fear in the marketplace, the real effects on people who trust "experts" and have little time to fact-check and dig out the truth for themselves are troubling. I've received dozens of e-mails from people exposed to The Horizon Project's misinformation, including distraught mothers of young children, who were beside themselves, not knowing what to do.

Many readers and researchers have apparently been hoodwinked by the astronomical confusions and pole shift rhetoric proffered by Brent Miller, multiplied *ad nauseam* through the Googlesphere. In e-mail exchanges with Gregg Braden I explained how the orbital idea was taken up by various popular writers, from the murky Photon Belt concept of Marciniak in the mid-1980s, to José Argüelles's slightly less murky "galactic synchronization" as defined by him and Brian Swimme in *The Mayan Factor*, to more recent conflations by Michael Tsarion, Brent Miller at The Horizon Project, and others. The earlier sources, including Argüelles, were not presenting the galactic alignment concept but instead something akin to the physical orbit idea, in which our solar system orbits around the Galactic Center and passes through different energy sectors of the galaxy. The later authors often make a loose association between our solar system's up-and-down motion above and below the galactic plane and 2012, the dark rift in the Milky Way, and other elements from my pioneering work. I find it all disappointing, for several reasons:

- According to the scientific evidence, our solar system is nowhere near the midplane right now.
- The orbital process exceeds 250 million years; the galactic midplane passages occur at approximately 60-million-year intervals.
- The passage itself takes roughly 250,000 years.

None of this has any valid basis in Maya traditions and concepts.[33]

And all of this leads ineluctably to the Survive 2012 website (no relation to Patrick Geryl's *How to Survive 2012*). The director of this site says he is just providing all the angles and making survivalist gear available for those who want to be safe. Digital shopping carts and easy-to-use PayPal buttons are provided. Gas masks, water-purification pills, and survivalist food supplies are among the many things offered for sale. Again, the media loves this kind of thing, and as a savvy entrepreneur he was able to get his website linked up to the History Channel's Armageddon broadcasts in January 2009, which included a show linking Nostradamus with 2012 (for which I was interviewed) that completely appropriated the galactic alignment as a pole shift trigger while providing little contextual information about the Maya.[34] I'm now convinced that cooperating with any of these mainstream venues is like handing baby chickens to a fox.

Bruce Scofield is a perceptive researcher, an astrologer who has worked to integrate the oracular insights of the Mesoamerican calendar system and the principles of Western astrology.[35] Aware of the work by Edmonson (*The Book of the Year*), he understood the correct placement of the 260-day calendar very early on, and published his book *Day Signs* in 1991. He reviewed my book *Tzolkin* and followed my work on 2012 as it developed. Suspicious of the calendar system proposed by Argüelles in *The Mayan Factor*, Scofield succeeded in getting Argüelles to share, in a letter of 1989, how he developed his own day-count system. Argüelles wrote that he and a Mexican artist friend working in Mexico in the 1970s developed the placement that he came to follow and would later elaborate in his Dreamspell game.

In short, the letter revealed that Argüelles was either unaware of a surviving day-count or preferred to nurture his own creative interpretation of the system. Once the placement of the day-signs was fixed in his new system, events in the world fell into place and the system appeared to be self-confirming. People thus say that "it works." The reason for this is not rocket science—oracles will respond when you pour energy into them. It doesn't matter that it's fifty-plus days out of synchronization with the calendar followed by the Maya for more than 2,000 years. Said another way, if you say to someone that the number 23 is meaningful, the seed is planted for them to begin noticing it everywhere. The mind will automatically begin selecting 23s out of the environment. Scofield, rightly so, found Argüelles's response to be proof that his system was of his own invention. Later, however, Argüelles claimed it was a direct successor to the calendar in the Chilam Balam books, even though he had noted in his 1975 book *The Transformative Vision* that the Chilam Balam material did not contain much helpful information.

Another thing that the Maya calendar tradition doesn't really contain is a 13-moon calendar. This will come as a surprise to many people who follow Argüelles's 13-moon calendar. The system, as devised by Argüelles, has 13 × 28 = 364 days. Its New Year's Day is always fixed to July 26 (which links it to his Dreamspell system), and you need to add one more day, July 25, to make it work. This is called "The Day Out of Time," which I guess makes it okay. The 13-moon calendar is intended to put us back into synchronization with the rhythms of the moon, the natural cycles of life, to free us from enslavement to the 12-month/60-minute rhythm of artificial clock-time. The calendar you follow will, according to the 13-moon logic, define your consciousness. Solar calendar bad, lunar calendar good. Sounds reasonable so far. But the problem is that the 13-moon calendar does not follow any lunar or "natural" rhythm. Periods of 28 days and 364 days are approximations of lunar cycles, truncating them to roughly fit into a solar year. If you really wanted to synchronize with natural lunar rhythms, you'd pay attention to the waxing and waning movements of the moon and the northward and southward oscillation of the moon's rise positions throughout the year, eventually coming to discern the 19-year lunar extreme cycle. It's worth paying attention to and tracking the celestial cycles and earth cycles that we live within, but you can't get there by following a 13-moon calendar of 364 days, even if you add a Day Out of Time and skip counting February 29.[36] A truly accurate lunar calendar can be created, however. Peter Meyer, the programmer for Terence McKenna's Time Wave Zero theory, did just that; he called it the Goddess Lunar Calendar.[37]

In 2004, the "Road to 2012" conference was organized by Chet Snow. It was a rare venue in which José Argüelles and I would both be presenting. In my two presentations I gave an overview of the spiritual and academic aspects of the 2012 topic and provided a retrospective on the popular 2012 movement.[38] I thus began with Tony Shearer and presented all of the issues with the correlation, Harmonic Convergence, and the galactic alignment. Tony's student, Amaurante Montez, had asked me to give José a copy of the new edition of Tony's book *Spirit Song*, but the opportunity never arose because José appeared only for his presentation and then was gone. It was a bit strange; usually speakers will convene, hang out, exchange ideas, share a panel discussion and field questions from the audience, but José wasn't around for any of that.

It was a great conference in any case, because my friend Geoff Stray from England was also speaking. I hadn't seen him since 1999, and we caught up on all the new books, films, and 2012-related products. Geoff, beyond all other 2012ologists, has taken it upon himself to critique and assess virtually everything on 2012 that has appeared. His task has of late become quite daunting for the sheer volume of products, theories, visions, and films flooding the marketplace. His website, diagnosis2012.uk.co, has been and continues to be an indispensable resource for anyone wanting to get the lowdown on all things 2012. His fact-based reviews are refreshing, accurate, and informative. Geoff tells it like it is. For example, he reviewed *The Idiot's Guide to 2012* by Synthia and Colin Andrews. The books in this series are supposed to give you the simple, no-nonsense info, providing a nonbiased and accurate guide. This Idiot's Guide is a travesty of disinformation, so Geoff offered a corrective guide to 2012 to the authors of *The Idiot's Guide to 2012:*

> *The Andrews couple refer to the system as the "vestigial system" . . . On p. 72, Haabs (365-day cycle) are confused with Tuns (360-day cycle), where it says that the Long Count is the same as the 13-baktun cycle (not true, as there were longer cycles sometimes used), and that the 13-baktun cycle consists of 5,200 Haabs of 360 days each. This will lead to more confusion in what is already quite a complex subject. It is wrongly stated that the end-date of the 13-baktun cycle "is written the same as the beginning date: 13.0.0.0.0 4 Ahau 8 Cumku" (pp. 74 and 114). This reveals that the authors actually know very little about the Maya calendars, and have hurriedly cobbled this book together to meet the deadline of the publisher. . . . The authors have invented their own version of Jenkins's galactic alignment zone, which John Major Jenkins says is from 1980 to 2016. They have also misunderstood Carl Calleman's theories, when they say that, along with Argüelles and*

Jenkins, his theory "has been inspired by the mathematics and astronomy of the Mayans" (p. 170). In reality, Calleman has declared that he thinks the Maya calendar cycles had nothing to do with astronomy.[39]

Geoff has an eagle eye for errors and takes the time to carefully assess what people write. It's unfortunate that the reading public has to be subjected to these kinds of books, which pretend to be easy guides. Geoff's summation is fair: "The book attempts to be a guide for the man in the street to the intricacies of 2012, but has been written by people who obviously knew nothing about the subject before being asked to write the book. There are one or two interesting bits, but it has been ruined by sloppy research, useless proofreading, invented information and quotations, and general confusion."[40]

When I met with Geoff in Tempe in late 2004, he was finishing up his own 2012 book called *Beyond 2012: Catastrophe or Ecstasy: A Complete Guide to the End-of-Time Predictions.* There are only a handful of 2012 books that I would recommend, and this is the top of the list. He asked me to write the introduction to his book in 2004, which I was glad to do. In it I expressed my gratitude for Geoff's unparalleled contribution to clarity and discernment:

Stray has been unbiased in what he has allowed into the pavilion of purview. He is a true pioneer, the first 2012ologist who has sought to collect, survey, contextualize, and comment on the wide spectrum of manifestations related to 2012. Because of his familiarity with all things 2012, he is our best guide into the labyrinths of kaleidoscopic creation and consternation that typify the inner landscape of 2012-land. . . . Stray has used common sense and discerning analysis to critique the contributions, such that basic errors in theories have been identified, always involving internal inconsistencies in the theory itself, rather than by reference to a set of preconceived doctrines of what 2012 "really" means. I appreciate this quality in Stray's book on 2012, because it allows us to categorize the wide spectrum of writings into

fiction and non-fiction, trace the inter-relationships and discern,
sometimes, the shared sourcings between different contributions. A
bit of order has thus been given to the chaos of creativity that 2012
has spawned.[41]

By 2005 I had done hundreds of interviews. The great majority of them had
to contend with interviewers who were approaching 2012 through a net of
assumptions that were hard to unpack during the commercial interruptions
of a typical radio hour. I thus welcomed the free-form late-night interview
sessions offered by Mike Hagan, a smart, courageous, and progressive voice
on the airwaves.[42] Before signing off in June of 2008, he had interviewed
many notables, including Dennis McKenna, Barbara and Dennis Tedlock,
Rick Levine, Elizabeth Upton, Jay Weidner, José Argüelles, Carl Calleman,
and many others.

The five interviews I recorded with Mike explore the entire spectrum of
my work on 2012, and address many of the issues that have arisen in academia, among the indigenous people of the Americas, and in the popular
press. It was great fun to stay with Mike for a few days in February of 2008. I
did an interview with him in studio and a presentation at a nearby locale.
Perhaps because I am from the Midwest myself, I appreciated the smart and
down-to-earth reception of my progressive ideas. I've noticed two extremes
in American audiences—extreme rational skepticism bordering on snobbery
on the East Coast and sensation-seeking New Age gullibility on the West
Coast. These are generalizations that do not speak for every person I've met,
but the Midwest seemed closest to the no-nonsense scrutiny, focused attention, and genuine interest I've also experienced in European venues.

Mass media documentaries have lately gone in the direction of infotain-
ment and have frequently presented 2012 in the most salacious way, doing
little justice to the topic. Independent films have a better chance of doing the
2012 topic justice, because the mass media outlets filter the facts through a
great deal of hype and sensationalizing. Independent film producers are also
concerned with turning a profit and so sometimes aspire to the same stylings

of the mass media, which they believe to be proven formulas for marketplace success. Certain films that treat cutting-edge topics achieve success, such as the *What the Bleep!* movie. The script was framed as an adventure of discovery undertaken by the likable main character, played by Marlee Matlin. We travel with her to learn about quantum mechanics and the implication that we are cocreators of our reality. (This idea was ably introduced in Fritjof Capra's classic 1976 book *The Tao of Physics*, which, unlike the *Bleep!* movie, noted that ancient Hindu metaphysics anticipated the discoveries of quantum physics.)

The *Bleep!* framework of presentation was adopted by Sacred Mysteries film producers Sharron Rose and Jay Weidner for their 2012 documentary film, released in late 2006 as *2012: The Odyssey*. Rose herself was our guide, traveling the country trying to figure out what 2012 was all about. She interviewed various people and spent much time on unexpected mysteries, such as the Georgia Guide Stones and the murals at Denver International Airport. I was interviewed extensively for the film, during which I shared details of the Maya Creation Myth and the importance of Izapa for understanding the origins of the 2012 calendar. I always offer, in these types of interviews, a reading of the Maya Creation Myth in which I highlight spiritual teachings that relate to World Ages and cycle endings, such as the one in 2012. In the lingo of pop culture presentations, this would be called the "Maya prophecy" for 2012. Or, more relevantly, "spiritual teachings" that the Maya believed appropriate for cycle endings—namely, sacrifice, transformation, and renewal. I was a bit disappointed when the film came out and very little of this material was used in the film. Still, at the time it was basically the only thing available that didn't completely hammer the doomsday angle.

Sharron did present Native American wisdom "for 2012," but it came from a non-Maya tradition. The wisdom teachings of the Inca, courtesy of Alberto Villoldo's commendable work, were presented in the film. An Inca prophecy was attached to the Maya 2012 end date and was explained by Villoldo as his Inca shaman friends sat around a fire and did a prayer ceremony. The filmmakers, Rose and Weidner, had traveled to South America to acquire this visually compelling footage of Inca shamans doing rituals in the high Andes. It was apparently strategically difficult for them to visit Maya shamans and temples. Maya cosmology is deep and at times complex, and in my experience filmmakers often limit the story I'd like to tell on the integration of Maya science, spirituality, and mythology. They may use only the portion in which I define the astronomy behind the galactic alignment. Most viewers would likely conflate the Inca with the Maya, and there may be a universal wisdom that the Inca contribute to the ideas of cycle endings and spiritual awakening, but one hopes and expects that Maya teachings would be emphasized in a film about a distinctly Maya date.

In 2007, author and Unknown Country radio host Whitley Strieber published a novel called *2012: The War of Souls.* He had written an article on 2012, which appeared a short time before his book came out, that made connections between Harmonic Convergence and 2012, drawing from ideas found in the Argüelles material. When his book came out, it was exactly what it seemed to be—a horror story flavored with Maya-sounding words and names but with no accurate Maya information at all. The title, "2012," was clearly a marketing strategy. I found it humorous that I was mentioned, along with William Henry and Graham Hancock, as thinkers whom the aliens would have to take out immediately after they appeared on that fateful future day. An alien hit contract was thus put out on my life, at least in the realm of horror fiction. The co-opting of 2012 for a fiction book is not that surprising. What is surprising is that Whitley Strieber would thereafter be called upon to keynote 2012 conferences and speak with authority on 2012 in film documentaries.

Another writer, Steve Alten, wrote a science fiction book called *Domain* that liberally used my alignment theory while getting some of the specifics wrong. This may seem nitpicky, but ideas stick in the public consciousness, and confusion about a new idea such as the galactic alignment can easily be fueled by fictionalized treatments. When I was contacted in the summer of 2005 by 1080 Productions, under contract to produce a 2012 documentary for the History Channel, I was surprised to learn that Alten was on board as a script consultant and writer. I wondered why a science fiction writer who had fictionalized my 2012 alignment research would qualify as a documentary screenplay writer. I should have known that the project was going to be beset with disappointments, but I agreed to participate after getting assurances that the Maya Creation Myth's message of transformation and renewal would get an equal and fair hearing.

On site in Chichén Itzá, the film crew had set up for a night shot in the Temple of a Thousand Columns, a short distance from the famous Pyramid of Kukulcan. Local Maya youngsters had been hired to enact, so they believed, a dance drama. Alten and the director for 1080 Production were codirecting the scene as midnight approached. I listened to them discussing what they wanted to happen: A Maya girl was supposed to be abused, disrobed, and have her heart torn out. An altar was prepared and a fire was kindled. A man with a stone dagger would hover over the girl's chest, flailing the knife downward while the camera picked up the shadow play against the wall. Blood could be added later in postproduction.

Alten pushed his vision of what he wanted to happen in the scene with little sensitivity, and I could feel the centuries of oppression and abuse experienced by the Maya getting replicated and projected onto the girl. It started getting ugly, and I asked if all this was really necessary. The Maya girl, resisting, started crying, and that put a quash on the scene. The half-finished footage was not used in the film. This shocking occurrence was charged with symbolism. The Maya youngsters had prepared a dance, but that wasn't what the directors wanted—they wanted violence, a heart sacrifice, something horrific to underscore the barbarity of the Maya. But that's not what the Maya were about. There they stood, perplexed, being forced into a little skit-fantasy dreamed up by sensationalizing drama kings.

Almost a year later, the film was released and I was surprised at how much of a doomsday message it had. It was as if they chose to emphasize the most salacious possible reading of the 2012 material, favoring fictionalized fantasies rather than straight readings of the Maya Creation Myth. My previous experience, six years earlier with the Discovery Channel, was pleasant by comparison. I immediately began receiving e-mail from viewers accusing me of being a doomsayer. This frustrating turn of affairs inspired me to write a review of the documentary, called "How Not to Make a 2012 Documentary." It was bit sarcastic and cathartic, but right on target.[43]

The History Channel had anticipated by a few months what would be fully fledged in Mel Gibson's *Apocalypto* movie. A fictionalized film, however, can take license with facts in ways that we don't expect a "documentary" will. Still, I was aghast at the brutal portrayal of the Maya in the film as well as the many inaccuracies. Meanwhile, another mainstream film slipped into the theaters and went virtually unnoticed by the justified critics of *Apocalypto*. Darren Aronofsky's *The Fountain* was framed against the backdrop of Maya themes, Maya astro-theology, and spiritual wisdom connected to the symbol of the Maya sacred tree. The movie struck me in three phases, following directly upon my first, second, and third viewings of it. First, I was intrigued and amazed. After my second viewing, I was impressed and awed. After my third viewing, I knew it was a masterpiece. It should be considered on par with Kubrick's *2001: A Space Odyssey*. But it's not for popcorn chasers—you will be rewarded by paying attention, for there is a very specific and clear message that the film conveys, one wrapped in a multilayered tapestry operating simultaneously on three temporal levels. I don't know how he managed to pull it off, but Aronofsky worked a miracle. His message was true to Maya religion and is perhaps the most profound perennial wisdom teaching one can find in any spiritual tradition: Immortality cannot be won by living forever; it is experienced only when one fully embraces death.

In late 2005, a writer named Jon Behak sent me a manuscript for a novel he had written. He said he was a longtime reader of my books and had even acquired a rare copy of my autobiographical spiritual odyssey from 1991, *Mirror in the Sky*. He had written the whole thing in February that year, in a cabin in the San Bernardino Mountains east of Los Angeles. I was the thinly veiled main protagonist. This would normally be a cause for concern, but Behak handled complex issues deftly and wrapped them all in a multileveled mystery that I found very insightful. It reminded me of a cross between Umberto Eco and John Crowley. It was written and sent to me before *The Fountain* movie was released, but in retrospect they are oddly similar—a story operating on several different levels simultaneously, with profound teachings woven in between worldly travel adventures and relationship dilemmas. I'm helping him get it placed for publication.

Gregg Braden, an author who endeavors to integrate science and spirituality, produced a book on 2012 in early 2009.[44] An interesting voice in the self-actualization movement, and a really nice guy, Braden offers another system based on fractal time, a model of spiritual unfolding and history. I was a bit perplexed at his reference to the galactic alignment and magnetic pole shifts. It is reminiscent of math models devised by McKenna, Argüelles, and Calleman. How is it that all these systems operate differently and utilize proprietary concepts and intervals, yet are all believed to be true and accurate? Could it be that the number of possible systems that one could design are virtually unlimited, it's just a matter of imagination? And if they all share with the Maya wisdom teachings a foundation in a universal law, mathematical principle, insight, or teaching, then why do we need to revise or update the Maya's traditional system? Can we patent and claim proprietary ownership over variant versions of a cosmology that is, at its root, universal? This is in fact a tendency of the Western scientific mind-set, to attribute laws and principles to one "discoverer," or name, or personality. Thus, we get Newton's Theory of Gravity. Does he own gravity? Do his descendants get a royalty every time someone falls down? Is Dreamspell, or the Braden Law, McKenna's Time Wave, or Calleman's system sufficiently derivative such that no Maya copyright is violated? This isn't simply about discussing or elaborating Maya calendar teachings, or reconstructing them as I attempt to do, but creatively relabeling them and calling them your own. Perhaps I should create an ornate new categorizing system, such that 1 would be written as an *a*, 2 would be a *b*, the % sign would replace =, and so on. Then I could rewrite Einstein's mathematical formula for the Theory of Relativity and call it "The Jenkins Theory of Spacetime-Energy Non-Absoluteness."

In 2007, Sounds True Publishing took the lead in producing an anthology of writings on 2012.[45] I was closely involved in consulting on this book, and I helped contextualize their contributions. I helped them fill the missing contribution from Argüelles, who was unreachable in Australia at the time, by suggesting they transcribe the audio interview they had made with him back in 1987. The 2012 discussion unavoidably ranges over a broad arena of approach. I was surprised that some contributors simply adapted previously written articles on "human potential" by adding a few references to 2012 here and there. This introduces a problem in the popular treatment of 2012, that of the "insta-expert" who, having gained market share with previous successes, is called upon to comment on 2012 and instantly is hailed as a longtime student of Maya thought and traditions. Or 2012 becomes merely an icon to speak about responsible business practices, with no reference to the Maya or the Maya calendar needed. It's all a bit strange, I must say. Nevertheless, interviewers, journalists, and anthology publishers who take up the 2012 topic do have a difficult challenge.

The publishing industry has been struggling to figure out how to "brand 2012." Sounds True invited me to give a presentation to national marketing reps at the International New Age Trade Show in Denver in 2007. I emphasized what I've been saying for years: A well-documented reconstruction of the 2012 cosmology has been offered, the Maya material says nothing about apocalypse, cycle endings are about transformation and renewal, there are relevant spiritual teachings in the Maya material that speak to the challenges that arise during cycle endings, the Maya prophecy for 2012 has come true (see Chapter 9), and a Maya renaissance is afoot that bodes a larger shift of consciousness, away from the current dominator style of culture (to use the terminology of Riane Eisler).[46] It made sense to them that 2012 could, and should, be engaged proactively and doomsday should be relegated to the back burner. Sounds True continues to publish broad-spectrum offerings on 2012 in print and audio formats. They are a good resource for what people are saying on 2012, with which the public can judge for themselves. This process will at least identify how collective humanity is going to engage, internalize, and shape the 2012 meme for good or bad.

Quetzalcoatl Returns

Daniel Pinchbeck appeared on the 2012 stage in 2006 with his book *2012: The Return of Quetzalcoatl*. The title refers to a basic idea in Mesoamerican religion revolving around the deity figure called Quetzalcoatl (also known as the Plumed Serpent). As Frank Waters explained so beautifully in his book *Mexico Mystique*, this serpent bird represents the integration of opposites. Pinchbeck applied this idea to 2012 and believes that 2012 signals the development of spirituality beyond being fixated on dualisms. This is, of course, the goal of any spiritual tradition. The appearance of Daniel's book took me by surprise, as I had communicated with him by e-mail three or four years earlier. When I received the book, I was glad that Daniel had summarized my work on the galactic alignment and at Izapa. He had visited Argüelles in Portland and found Calleman's theory of interest, and shared a lot of confessional narratives of his personal journey, struggles, psychedelic visions, and observations.

I shared a series of weekend conference events with Daniel in the fall of 2008—in New York, Arkansas, Florida, and San Francisco. Conference engagements can be both intriguing and exhausting, and we didn't have much time to sit on the sidelines and talk. I try to keep an open mind, and Daniel states he is in service of the development of spirituality. It may be my defect, but there's something about Daniel that is enigmatic, that I can't quite grok. He's popularized the 2012 "meme" but doesn't really approach it through Maya traditions or teachings. He has good ideas about community building and economic restructuring but thinks Calleman's problematic system is compelling. He speaks of opening consciousness to transformation, which requires transcending the ego, but wants us to read about his personal history, psychosexual adventures, and visions. He's about my age and we might have hung out in high school; then again, he might have been the guy to slip LSD in my coffee. This contradictory nature perhaps is his embodiment of Quetzalcoatl, the dual-natured serpent bird.

Daniel has made a name for himself as something of a pop icon, speaking at Burning Man, appearing on *The Colbert Report*, and embarking on vision trips to South America. He tells us in his book *Breaking Open the Head* that he was a typical New York City skeptic, suspicious of spiritual things, until his mind was opened with shamanism and ayahuasca (a South American brew made with DMT, a powerful hallucinogen). That book, which appeared in 2002, placed him next in line after Timothy Leary and the late Terence McKenna as an advocate for the transformative power of psychoactive plants. He can be lighthearted, relating the humorous story of his appearance on *The Colbert Report*, when Colbert said, "Daniel, you've been called the next Timothy Leary . . . We just got rid of the last one, why do we need another?"

One effect of his 2012 book was to shift the 2012 topic away from the need to reference the achievements and perspectives of Maya civilization. The "2012 meme" doesn't require them. The debates and confusions caused by Calleman's end date and Argüelles's Dreamspell day-count were quickly summarized and passed by, as if the question of accuracy in representing the 2012 calendar weren't that important. And the truth is, for most people it isn't. So Pinchbeck adopted 2012 as a general icon to springboard the "development of spirituality" with a sense of urgency. His subsequent talks and his Reality Sandwich website have addressed political and economic dilemmas and questions, as well as practical challenges of sustainability. He thus speaks to younger people who are concerned with creating a viable future by adopting sustainable values. This would be, following one of McKenna's ideas, a kind of "archaic revival."

To me, this development was inevitable. The market forces that impel the 2012 discussion were destined to eventually detach it from its roots in Maya tradition. Concern for having the correct day-count, understanding how the Long Count works, visiting Maya temples, and studying the Maya Creation Myth would be superseded by developing alternative fuels, learning how to grow seeds, creating community gardens and eco-villages, and practicing neoshamanism. At first this was perplexing to me, but I now feel more inclined to be grateful that proactive efforts to transform the world into a better, sustainable place for human beings to live are happening. Along these lines, James Endredy's book *Beyond 2012: A Shaman's Call to Personal Change and the Transformation of Global Consciousness* is a good guide into these spiritual, shamanistic, and environmental areas of interest. This is certainly much better than evangelizing one's own inventive calendar system or model of history. And it will free serious research concerned with reconstructing ancient Maya cosmology from having to deal with the impossible question "What's going to happen in 2012?"

This may all lead to the 2012 Big Event, never mind all the debates and details, and perhaps Pinchbeck will be willing to serve the transformation as the 2012 meme leader. I'm glad someone might be willing to do it. You can "Party Like It's 2012" at Harmonic Convergence Part 2, in New York City, Amazonia, Chaco Canyon, Mount Shasta, wherever. But take into consideration that, as Dennis McKenna warned, parking will probably be a hassle.

WHO IS CHARLIE FROST?

Charlie Frost? He's the creation of Sony Pictures, or some subsidiary of them. If you view the trailer for Roland Emmerich's blockbuster doomsday film, called "2012" and starring John Cusack and Amanda Peet (due out in November 2009), you'll see the following words appear while the high Himalayas get smothered by a huge tidal wave: "If the world was going to end, what would governments do to warn you? Nothing."[47] Wow, it's a striking scene. And at the bottom of the page, you can click on two links: One is to "The Institute for Human Continuity." This website appears slick, a cleverly designed backstory about a scientific organization committed to humanity's survival. You can register, and you'll be entered into the lotto for the selected few (144,000; sounds a bit crowded to me) who will be protected from the coming cataclysm. Properly understood, this is viral marketing, a rather clever way to create interactive participation with audiences and gather their personal information at the same time. It's a triple foil: a culture-control operation masquerading as a fake and fun front group that will save you, masquerading as a doomsday movie. A wolf in sheep's clothing in wolf's clothing in sheep's clothing.

The other link (thisistheend.com) will take you to Charlie Frost. You know immediately this is a parody, because it's Woody Harrelson dressed as a cyber-clever Joe Six-Pack, an "apocalypse prognosticator" who is an amalgam of Sean Penn's lovable stoner, Spicoli, and a savvy Prophet of Whatever. He is going to help you understand 2012 and other confusing things. Oh, and don't forget to register your personal information for updates. He's a radical nonconformist stoner type with a Join the Club subtext. And surprisingly smart, too, even through a cannabinated drawl.

One of Charlie's YouTube segments reveals how my galactic alignment/ 2012 theory has filtered into this digitalized corner of pop culture. With blinking, attention-keeping cartoon graphics, Charlie narrates a few items about 2012. "And some say an alignment of planets that happens only once every 640,000 years is going to happen." And the planets are shown all lining up with the earth and sun and the galaxy. So, it's there, in some twisted form, but it's all horribly wrong. I'm reminded of when I corrected an interviewer on this point of understanding the galactic alignment and she laughed, saying, "Well, whatever! There's an alignment of something with something." Yes. Whatever, indeed.

An interesting contrast technique would be to cut right from Charlie Frost to a conversation with, say, David Stuart or some other Maya scholar. This would highlight the absurdity of what's happening in the popular media. I believe the public wants to know what 2012 is all about. If they look at all to the scholars for input on their questions, they will likely receive dismissive comments or invitations to study the Maya material in more depth—an effort the public is unlikely to pursue. Professional academics have largely avoided investigating 2012 and so have very little to say about it. And we certainly shouldn't expect Maya scholars to say anything at all about universal teachings for cycle endings, which could be approached rationally, following the lead of Joseph Campbell and other voices for the perennial wisdom.

So independent writers are left to do whatever they can do, or want to do, with the 2012 meme. The results are pretty messy, as a glance at the marketplace will reveal. It apparently all leads to Charlie Frost. Along the way, trends and tendencies in the popular press can be identified. Following the pattern set by Argüelles, we can see a tendency for popular writers to craft their own unique system or model, complete with proprietary terms and concepts. An ideological lineage can be traced from Argüelles to Calleman to Barbara Clow and, more recently, to the composite calendar system recently created by Gregg Braden. Even Terence McKenna put an innovative time philosophy on the table and connected it with 2012, but he was not influenced by Argüelles. My own work, it should be stressed, is not concerned with creating a new system or model. Instead, on two fronts I've tried to (1) advance a well-documented reconstruction of the original cosmology connected to 2012 and (2) elucidate the perennial wisdom teachings within the Maya Creation Myth, which is also an expression of the 2012 tradition.

The domain of "pop appeal" comprises 90 percent of the 2012 phenomenon. It's not in service to elucidating the deeper, perennial content of Maya cosmology, philosophy, and the 2012 tradition, clearly expressing the core, essential, ideologies of 2012. This could be supported by Maya concepts of transformational renewal at cycle endings and by global parallels in other traditions. I feel it's important to identify the shared metaphysics of spiritual awakening in all traditions, including the Maya, which are especially relevant for cycle endings. This can be done, with good results, if properly framed as an expression of the archetypal, universal level of Maya cosmology. That's what we'll dive into in Part II.

By the way, what is the *modus operandi* behind the 2012 film that Charlie Frost and the Institute for Human Continuity are in cahoots with? It preys on your Basic Perinatal Matrix II! As Stan Grof defined it, this is Sartre's *No Exit* existential hell.[48] It's the high-anxiety stage of the birth process, when the secure womb of constantly increasing gross national product is disturbed by the increasingly intense contractions of unsustainable greed and consumption. There is no tunnel yet, thus no light to be seen at the end of it; just pressure, pressure, pressure, and certain annihilation! One can only hope that the sequel to 2009's doomsday 2012 film will be based on Basic Perinatal Matrix III: *The Rebirth Experience.*

Chapter Six

Doubting Scholars

While it may be ethnocentric to assert that the Maya
were observing astronomical phenomena in the
same way as their counterparts in the West, it is
equally ethnocentric to insist that they were
incapable of such observations, particularly when
their observations and their unique system of
tropical zenith astronomy appear to have led them
to far more accurate calculations than those of any
of their contemporaries elsewhere in the world.
Perhaps it is sufficient to say that the Maya were
observing precession because it was there to be
observed, and because they were uniquely capable of
observing it with remarkable accuracy.[1]

—MICHAEL GROFE

Official commentary on 2012 from academics has been long in coming. There was a small backlog of grudging comments from scholars, elicited by my persistent questions going back to 1991, but they mostly fell into predictably superficial runnels. Several published mentions of the 2012 date recorded on Tortuguero Monument 6 had appeared, going back to 1992, but they treated 2012 circumspectly without engaging the larger implications of that monument.[2] We now know that, when the related inscriptions are considered, the implications of that monument are very great indeed. As we'll see shortly, it records solar and lunar alignments with the dark rift in the Milky Way, in meaningful contexts suggesting a conceptual relationship between the birth of the cosmos and the symbolic birth, or dedication, of the building that housed the monument.

Beginning in 2006, unofficial comments on 2012 increased, resulting from questions forced upon scholars in online e-list groups such as Aztlan.[3] These exchanges, which are archived and readily available, reveal several things. First, consensus trumps facts. On more than one occasion my statements were assailed at once by five or six critics, who called into question minuscule trivia that was laughable but distracting. For example, I referred to Tak'alik Ab'aj as an "astronomical observatory" (the term used by the archaeologists digging at the site), which was countered with the incorrect assertion that there was no evidence for that. Similarly, scholars have doubted the existence of evidence for astronomy in *The Popol Vuh*, as if they had never read Dennis Tedlock's translation. The facts and evidence that I presented in order to engage a rational discussion were trumped by a tacit consensus to deny and distract, regardless of the compelling nature of the evidence I was presenting.

All of this can be tracked and examined in the archival pages of these online e-lists. It got to the point where it seemed a search-bot was waiting, ready to pounce on anything I said. Once, in a spirit of humor on a thread about the amazing complexity of the Nahuatl language, which builds long compound words that rival anything produced in medieval German, I offered my favorite Nahuatl knock-knock joke: "Knock Knock. Who's there? Amatlacuilolitquitcatlaxtlahuitl." (After considerable practice, I can pronounce this word fast.) The joke is, of course, funny before it's even complete because the unsuspecting victim is dumbfounded. The only response to my humorous overture was a dry linguistic correction: "The third t is a mistaken insertion; '. . . itquica . . .' is a so-called preterit nominalization of 'itqui,' meaning 'to carry.'"[4]

Scholars armed themselves with one or two critiques that effectively halted further investigation, at least in their own minds. These stopgap critiques were simplistic and were endlessly repeated, despite my pointing out their fallacious basis. For example, does the fact that the end date falls on a solstice indicate intent? Scholars such as John Hoopes and John Justeson provided an argument for coincidence that plays with statistical fudging to make coincidence seem not as unlikely as one initially supposes. Justeson, for example, explained at a recent conference that a December solstice date is meaningful, but so would be a June solstice, either one of the equinoxes, a zenith passage date, your birthday, the date of your grandpa's hernia operation, and a myriad of other potentially noteworthy dates.[5]

Justeson also said that if the end date was one or even two days off one of these meaningful dates, we would still be duly impressed and allow this measure of vagueness. He ran the stats on all these considerations and found that a 16.66 percent chance existed that a randomly generated end date would be within range of any number of significant dates. That's a 1-in-6 chance, pretty good odds. This is much less than the slim 1/365 chance one assumes upon first glance. Thus, voilà!—the case for the Coincidentalists was improved.

Justeson's argument ably applies a rationalist's thought experiment but ignores several guiding contexts that eliminate other possible dates. To intentionally choose a December solstice date to end a large-Era cycle makes perfect sense, because the end date of a solar year would, by analogy, be an appropriate marker for the end date of a larger World Age era. That the December solstice ends the year is an almost universally attested doctrine around the world, but is especially so, and demonstrated, for the site of Izapa and other pre-Classic sites in the region of the Long Count's origin.[6]

As regards the allowable vagueness, this disregards the fact that there is no vagueness in the de facto cycle-ending date. It does, in fact, fall precisely on a solstice. It may be that they accidentally got it right on target when their astronomical understanding of the tropical year would have only allowed them to calculate it within two or three days, but so what? Why inject uncertainty when the data imply none? The intentional effort to target the solstice still remains as the likeliest possible scenario.

The idea of "accidentally" getting a future calculation more precisely on target than their abilities could support is, however, intriguing. It may help explain the impressive accuracy of the end date's relation to an astronomically accurate solstice-galaxy alignment defined in the most precise scientific way possible—based on Meeus's 1998 date, accurate within 14 years, or 12 minutes of arc. If the Maya's ability to calculate this alignment could only reasonably be limited to 100 years, they would still have a sense for the middle range of that zone, and getting it as close as they did may have been something like a 1-in-5 chance. So coincidence can be argued both ways.

Despite Justeson's well-considered critique, the fact remains that, no matter how you fudge it, the solstice positioning of the end date is beyond statistical chance. His own final stats prove this. A 1-in-6 chance does not mean you can look away. And so rational scholars alert to the dictates of statistics should proceed on the evidence that it's not a coincidence and begin an investigation that generates questions. This was the position I took twenty years ago, with interesting results. As a rational investigator, I've uncovered perspectives and evidence in support of the likelihood of intentionality—at Izapa, in the Creation Myth, in the structure of the Long Count, in rites of kingship, and in the symbolism of the ballgame. I've presented it to scholars with a persistence that has gained me the status of honorary *persona non grata*, and they have largely dismissed it, usually without offering specific critiques. Actually, maybe not the honorary part.

After one particularly exhausting exchange with a bevy of scholars on the Aztlan e-list regarding, for the hundredth time, the relevance of the solstice placement in 2012, an important missive was sent to me privately from Maya epigrapher Barb MacLeod. The subject line read: "not coincidence!" She wrote: "I see the exchanges of the last couple of days as a prompt to share something with you of great importance and relevance from the epigraphic record. It's something I discovered less than a month ago."[7] What she found is revolutionary and lends indirect support to my end-date alignment theory. Barb's open-minded and progressive scholarship has been behind many breakthroughs including, as I mentioned in Chapter 4, Linda Schele's astromythological ideas on the Maya Creation Mythology.

2012 BECOMES A TOPIC
OF ACADEMIC CONSIDERATION

The first treatment of 2012 by a scholar in a journal that other scholars might recognize was Robert Sitler's "The 2012 Phenomenon" in the academic journal *Nova Religio*. It appeared in 2006. He took the twofold approach of assessing the historical record and comments of the modern Maya, looking for references to 2012. He assessed the popular treatment of the 2012 topic in the marketplace as well as my book *Maya Cosmogenesis 2012*, calling it "by far the best-researched of the numerous books that focused on the 2012 date."[8] (By the way, Geoff Stray tells me that my book was the second book ever published that had 2012 in the title; the first was published in 1883, called *Transits of Venus: A Popular Account of Past and Coming Transits from the First Observed by Horrocks A.D. 1639 to the Transit of A.D. 2012.*)

Sitler wrote his article prior to the Tortuguero monument becoming common knowledge, so his article therefore did not treat it and followed the consensus view that there were no references to 2012. He thus didn't see any explicit references to 2012 in the epigraphy of the Classic Period. However, Robert's online "13 Baktun" resource has added the Tortuguero information and various updates from contemporary Maya voices, gathered on his recent trips to highland Guatemala.[9] Upon interviewing modern Maya spokespeople, such as Don Alejandro, he found that whenever they said anything about 2012, it could be traced to modern authors such as José Argüelles. Geoff Stray pointed out this tendency in his 2005 book *Beyond 2012*, which Sitler called "a recent publication that promises to be the most comprehensive book on 2012 to date."[10] Sitler also pointed out that it's not surprising that the Long Count information does not survive, even in traditional areas of highland Guatemala, since the Long Count stopped being carved in stone more than a thousand years ago.

Robert provided an accurate summary of my theory and wrote that "the lack of convincing proof the ancient Maya were actually aware of precession may prevent Jenkins's ideas from ever gaining broader academic acceptance." This assertion is slightly misleading, as there is in fact a great deal of evidence that the ancient Maya were aware of precession. The archaeological work of Marion Popenoe Hatch at La Venta (ca. 1200 BC) and Tak'alik Ab'aj (ca. 200 BC) shows that temples and stone sighting devices were aligned with certain stars and adjusted, through time, to account for precession. Scholars such as Eva Hunt, Gordon Brotherston, and even Anthony Aveni have argued and stated that precessional knowledge would have been par for the course. And today we have new findings, by Maya scholars Barbara MacLeod and Michael Grofe, showing precessional and sidereal-year calculations in the Classic Period inscriptions and the Maya's Dresden Codex.

Geoff Stray registered corrections to Sitler's essay, on the grounds that non-Maya sources of information—intuitive dreams, prophecy, and information from non-ordinary states of consciousness—have also pointed to 2012. A lively exchange between the two ensued, which illustrates how fact-based discussions can and should unfold. In the process, Geoff noted that "academics that are held in such awe often make errors that are repeated by researchers into the Maya calendars. Anthony Aveni's end date of 8 December 2012 was calculated in the Julian calendar, but he failed to state this. This date is equivalent to 21 December 2012 Gregorian.... Aveni places the start at 12 August 3114 BC... this is calculated in the Gregorian calendar, which makes Aveni's dates even more confusing, with the start and end dates calculated in different calendars."[11]

Sitler's look at Classic Period epigraphy suggested nothing directly relevant to 2012. What we seem to find in the Creation Monuments are exclusively focused on the 13-Baktun cycle beginning in 3114 BC. These monuments, however, from Coba, Quiriguá, Palenque, and other Classic Period sites, were carved at least seven hundred years after the Long Count was first committed to stone. They document a Creation paradigm involving the zenith passage of the three hearthstones, stars underneath Orion's Belt. The zenith was thought of by the ancient Maya as a cosmic center, and the Creation of the current era was believed to happen in relation to this cosmic center, symbolized as a throne. It's not that surprising that epigraphy doesn't tell us a lot about ideologies current with the origins of the Long Count, circa 100 BC (or possibly centuries earlier), because mythology and cosmology in that era were conveyed with pictures, a complex iconographic code that epigraphers haven't paid enough attention to.

When scholars look for "documentation" on Maya ideas, they tend to focus on epigraphy. (This was true for Mark Van Stone's 2012 study, published in late 2008 with the Foundation for the Advancement of Mesoamerican Studies.) But iconographic expressions, such as those found at Izapa, should also be allowed. They are, we might say, more relevant than the hieroglyphic writing that evolved centuries later, as they speak more directly for the time and place of the Long Count's origins. Epigraphic texts of the Classic Period, properly understood, might also be a source for information on 2012.

One wonders about the dearth of direct comments on 2012 in the epigraphic record of the Classic Period. I've realized recently that the important information, like all the best in literature, is not overtly stated but is indirectly alluded to. If the devils are in the details, the angels are in the subtext. The solstice-galaxy alignment itself serves as the key to these references, which point to the 2012 date via the sun-in-dark-rift motif. This kind of secondary reference is a common feature of any language. I may talk about "my birthday" and never mention the exact date, but if the context of my words is understood, the secondary reference implies the precise date.

Robert Sitler didn't pursue an examination of early iconography, but he provided a good framework of approach and sincere critique of, as his subtitle put it, "The New Age Appropriation of 2012." He confirmed and explored the complicated interactions between modern authors and Maya elders, scenarios I had experienced firsthand years earlier with Erick Gonzalez, Carlos Barrios, and Don Alejandro. My own response to Sitler's essay addressed "Maya statements" about 2012 and called for iconography to be included as "documentation" that could be read with just as much clarity as epigraphic writing.[12] My intention was to emphasize, once again, Izapa and its carved monuments as important sources for understanding 2012.

TORTUGUERO MONUMENT 6

As 2006 waxed to fullness, Sitler's pointed questioning of epigraphers uncovered a very important textual date from the Classic Period site of Tortuguero, near Palenque. Like the 3114 BC Creation monuments, it was dated 13.0.0.0.0 with 4 Ahau in the tzolkin position. But the Tortuguero monument had 3 Kankin in the haab position, rather than 8 Cumku. This meant that it referred to the current era's cycle ending, on December 21, 2012, rather than the previous 13-Baktun cycle ending, in 3114 BC. It was thus the only known specific date reference to 2012.

13.0.0.0.0 text from Tortuguero,
December 21, 2012.
Drawing by the author

For many years scholars had been saying that we had no references to 2012 in the archaeological record. Since 2012 is the next logical cycle ending, based on the 13-Baktun structure of the Long Count, the point is somewhat moot. My work, for example, proceeded on the assumption that the 13-Baktun cycle represented a standardized era-cycle length for the ancient Maya, and thus 2012 was implied by the plentiful Creation Texts that referenced the 13-Baktun cycle completion in 3114 BC. Michael Coe, Sylvanus Morley, and other scholars had assumed the same; it's simply a repeating structure within a cyclic time philosophy. But now Sitler had pushed the case with scholars on the University of Texas online forum, and epigrapher David Stuart revealed that a few scholars had indeed been aware of the Tortuguero date for some time. Why the date wasn't offered up for discussion long ago, and had to be pried out of the archives, is complicated and fraught with misunderstandings. As events unfolded, I suspect it had to do with not wanting to add fuel to New Age fires. The lapse is not that important; things happen when they will.

David Stuart offered to provide a translation of the text, and of course we all anxiously waited. Following the date phrase and reference to the end of the 13th Baktun, the inscription reads that "*something* (effaced) will occur . . . It will be the descent (?) of the Nine Support God(s) to the (?)." David summarized: "This is it. The term following *uht-oom* is the main puzzle, and largely effaced. The 'descent' reference is highly tentative, too. The enigmatic deity Bolon Yookte' K'uh [the "Nine Support Gods"] has been known for some time from many sources, and I suspect that he (or they) has some tangential relationship to the Principal Bird Deity, as well as war associations. Interestingly, he is a protagonist in the deep time mythology of Palenque, as recorded on Palenque's Temple XIV tablet. A long-lasting character who's still around somewhere waiting, I suppose."[13]

In April of 2006, when the translation was released on the University of Texas online forum, a heated exchange commenced that revealed attitudes on two sides of the discussion.[14] First, within a few days Maya scholar John Hoopes pointed out that Internet sites had picked up on the translation and were hailing it as "a new discovery." David Stuart responded, "I guess I should've known I was creating a monster with that initial post." Geoff Stray responded that in all fairness it certainly did appear like a new discovery to outsiders "because the epigraphers have been keeping the information to themselves, in fear of 'creating a monster.' However, this secretive attitude is not the answer, because it leads to essays by academics like Bob Sitler ["The 2012 Phenomenon"] stating that there are no unambiguous 2012 references in the Classic Maya texts. The closed shop is so closed that the information has failed to reach academics in adjacent fields, such as Sitler, who has a PhD in Hispanic literature, and has only found out about the Tortuguero Monument 6 after writing his essay."

Stuart responded by saying "I'm certain that if anyone had ever posed the question 'Do any Maya inscriptions mention 2012?' to us active epigraphers . . . that we would immediately say, 'look at Tortuguero Monument 6.' " And yet, strangely, he felt no need to offer a correction on the assertions of his colleagues, repeated dozens of times on the e-mail lists he subscribes to, that "there are no Maya inscriptions that mention 2012." Stuart continued: "Frankly, the Tortuguero passage, buried in lots of other data, hasn't been a huge deal to most of us because it is damaged and very, very ambiguous . . . even if the glyphs there were clear and legible, no Mayanist I know honestly believes that the Classic Maya foresaw something that might actually come true in our day and age."

Stuart's last comment suggests he is conceiving of whatever 2012 means through the filter of what many New Age writers say it must mean—a dire prophecy for earth changes and/or spiritual enlightenment that "might actually come true." The possibility that it had any meaning at all for the ancient Maya doesn't seem to come into play. The availability of sparse references to this monument were technically public, if "the 2012 watchers" could afford to travel cross-country to attend conferences and buy expensive conference proceedings, and knew where to look for possible information that they'd been told time and again doesn't exist.

Stray acknowledged that scholars weren't necessarily keeping the information to themselves, but noted that their cliquish exchanges revealed their true feelings—John Hoopes's mock comment, "It's amazing how quickly word gets around the Web (It wasn't me, honest!)," and Stuart's reply, "Thanks, John. I'll believe it wasn't you!"[15] Another well-known scholar elsewhere likened the 2012 people who actively interject their observations and comments on the academic e-mail forums to "a pit of vipers."[16]

I wrote an article on the Tortuguero inscription, pointing out that the mere presence of Bolon Yokte Ku, a usual suspect in Maya Creation narratives, suggested that the Maya therefore thought about 2012 as another type of Creation event, analogous to the one in 3114 BC.[17] I also pointed out that the deity may be present on the important San Bartolo murals recently found in the Petén and on one caiman-tree image at Izapa, both of which involve very early pre-Classic Creation Myth scenes.

More information about the importance of the Tortuguero inscription came two and a half years later from epigrapher Stephen Houston, although his new analysis was claimed to show that the 2012 reference "has nothing to do with prophecy or the supposed, dread events that await us in AD 2012. About that the Maya are notably silent . . . or, truth be told, a bit boring."[18] Of course, he was right on this assessment, but like Stuart he was interpreting whatever meaning might be attributed to 2012 through the filters of what New Age people believe it is about—some kind of "prophecy." The implication, again, is that the Tortuguero 2012 reference doesn't tell us much, end of story. This was a case, as events unfolded, of throwing the baby out with the bathwater.

Houston's analysis, posted on the epigraphy blog he runs with David Stuart, showed that the 2012 date was linked by a distance number to the dedication of a building, probably the sacred enclosure that once housed the monument containing the inscription. Such a practice was common. The Maya would often invoke Long Count dates in the past or future, usually a Katun or Baktun ending, to be present to witness the building's consecration and ritual birth. Deities associated with cycle endings in the Long Count had a special role, as they oversaw the end-beginning nexus that any cycle ending in the Long Count represented. Their ceremonial presence, being invoked for a temple's inaugural birth, was both meaningful and logical.

I decided to reply to Houston's post in the hopes of engaging a dialogue, and wrote:

> Why would they have wanted to link the building dedication to the baktun ending in 2012? In other words, an underlying belief about baktun endings generally, or perhaps the one in 2012 specifically, must

already be present that would explain why the future baktun ending has any importance for a contemporary building dedication. And what might that be?

Is there a seed-planting "foundation" paradigm to building dedication ceremonies that make them conceptually analogous to Creation events? Would 13.0.0.0.0 (in either 3114 BC or AD 2012) have been an appropriate reference point for a building's birth? And would the deities connected with those era-inaugurating Creation events have been considered appropriate overseers to consecrate the dedication? I'd suspect so.

Exploring these lines of thought might help us understand more deeply the cosmological significance of building dedications, as well as how big cycle endings like the ones in 830 AD and 2012 were perceived by the ancient Maya and were intertwined with other elements of Maya ritual. I don't see how these things are boring.[19]

The blog was silent until almost a week later another reader suggested that the Maya might have been interested in cycle endings happening in the near future, but doubted they would be interested in invoking cycle endings occurring very far off into the future. I responded:

I believe the issue under consideration is the relevance of utilizing a big cycle ending (no matter how far off into the past or future it occurs) as a reference point for a contemporary building dedication. In this context, a large cycle ending, such as the one in 2012, would be more evocative of a cosmological Creation event through which the local building dedication would receive an analogous consecration. Nearness in time of a smaller cycle ending, such as a katun ending, would be less relevant than a baktun ending, let alone a 13-baktun ending, which is demonstrably associated with Creation Myth imagery. The metaphorical relationship between "house" (or a "building") and "cosmos" is well demonstrated. Furthermore, Karl Taube

demonstrated a metaphorical relationship between "cosmos" and
"mother."[20]

I suggested that the established conceptual relationship between "house" and "cosmos" could help us understand why a 13-Baktun ending would be an appropriate reference point for a seventh-century building dedication. The analogy between house and cosmos would provide the needed meaning to correlate the "seating" and "creation" of the cosmos with the creation/ dedication of a building. In this light, the 2012 date apparently did have meaning for the ancient Maya—its associated deity (Bolon Yokte Ku) could oversee and consecrate the ritual birthing of sacred temple buildings. There's nothing outlandish about this at all. My observations were apparently not something that Houston wanted to reply to, even though he himself had investigated the symbolic relationship between house dedications and cosmological Creation imagery.[21] If I may state this delicately but bluntly: A logical deduction of great relevance was ignored, or withheld. These guys are brilliant, and I can't believe that they simply didn't notice it. Why they would want to forestall progress on understanding how the Maya themselves conceived of 2012 is baffling.

Instead of being "boring," what the Maya were saying about 2012 on the contrary was rather extraordinary. It meant that 2012 was thought of as a cosmological Creation event worthy of being invoked for a building dedication. In our culture, freemasons played active civic roles and would often be called upon to dedicate a courthouse or other civic building. Often, a cornerstone was laid into the building containing the Masonic year (counting from 4000 BC), a reference to their own calendrical creation moment. What the Maya at Tortuguero were doing is thus not so surprising, except that they invoked a future Creation event, revealing that the 3114 BC and 2012 AD cycle endings were thought to be like-in-kind Creation events. These deductions are pretty straightforward.

The analogy between house and cosmos can also be applied the other way around. Building dedications are typically identified with the *och k'ak'*

glyphs, meaning "his fire entered." Bringing light and fire through the doorway into the building is the ceremonial rite that gives birth to the building.
We can thus easily picture the analogy with 2012: the solstice sun's light and
fire enters the portal of the dark rift, giving birth to a new cosmos, a new era
of 13 Baktuns. As it turns out, a complete reading of Tortuguero's inscriptions, and understanding the role of its seventh-century ruler Balam Ajaw,
leaves little doubt that 2012 was understood by the Classic Period Maya
exactly as I've suspected—as a cosmological renewal signaled by the alignment of the solstice sun and the dark rift.

THE HAMMER OF MAYANISM

Yale graduate Dr. John Hoopes has been active on popular e-list discussion
boards, such as the Tribe 2012 Yahoo group, which he now moderates. I've
had many engaging debates and exchanges with Dr. Hoopes over the years,
and he has had an active interest in all aspects of the 2012 phenomenon for
some time. In fact, he has a particular interest in the popular manifestations
of the 2012 meme, and was initially supportive of Daniel Pinchbeck's book
2012: The Return of Quetzalcoatl as it was about to be released in 2006 (providing prerelease announcements on 2012.Tribe.net). By that time he had
already developed a friendship with Pinchbeck, a burgeoning pop icon, and
had hung out with him at the Burning Man Festival. After Pinchbeck's book
came out, Hoopes wrote that it was "disappointing that Pinchbeck, who
claims substantial research and journalistic skills, did so little homework on
Maya scholarship. His extensive bibliography cites only three references by
academicians on the ancient Maya."[22] The book was apparently not quite
what he thought it was going to be. His conversations with Pinchbeck must
have led him to expect more interviews with scholars and less hype. As it
turned out, the book revolved largely around Pinchbeck's own psychological
adventures and quandaries, the dénouement featuring his Technicolor encounter with the Plumed Serpent, Quetzalcoatl, during an ayahuasca vision.

Dr. Hoopes professes an interest in my research, and indeed has engaged me in discussions on many occasions. No amount of reasoned argument and presentation of evidence seems to sway him from his views. For example, he sides with Justeson on fudging the solstice placement to make it seem not at all that unlikely to be a coincidence. Encouraging me to publish something in a reputable academic journal, Dr. Hoopes believes I can make my case more plausible to scholars. This may be true, but my experiences with academic journals have revealed entrenched resistance, not to mention issues with the perceived implications of my work. The deck is stacked against progress offered by outsiders. The excoriating treatment of Whorf by Thompson is ample testimony to this tendency in Maya studies. Nevertheless, I'll probably stick my head in this guillotine, if only to document, once again, how facts are treated if the implications are unwelcome.

Currently working on his own book on the sociological phenomenon of 2012, Hoopes has contributed to creating and defining an entry on Wikipedia called "Mayanism," which he used to label 2012-related books and ideas that fall under a carefully elaborated New Age profile:

> *Mayanism is a term coined to cover a non-codified eclectic collection of New Age beliefs, influenced in part by Pre-Columbian Maya mythology and some folk beliefs of the modern Maya peoples. Adherents of this belief system are not to be confused with Mayanists, scholars who research the historical Maya civilization.*[23]

I am listed as one of the authors published by publishing houses who promote this Mayanism, and my work is discreetly and more or less accurately handled. His sociological approach provides a valid new framework for approaching the 2012 phenomenon, and the concise summaries of the various topics described in the Wikipedia entry are handled admirably, although I disagreed with the appropriation of the term "Mayanism" from its original context.

I called into question his selection of the term "Mayanism" for his purpose, which takes on a pejorative flavoring.[24] Several years ago I was beginning to use the term in my own writings, following the lead of Victor Montejo, a Jacaltek Maya scholar who survived the death squads in Guatemala in the 1980s, eventually moving to the United States to receive an MA from the State University of New York and an anthropology PhD from the University of Connecticut. He now teaches in California. He had used the term for a pan-Maya identity that shared certain characteristics, universal traits and beliefs and practices that would thus define Mayanism. This proactive use of the term was consistent with the positive use of similar terms, such as "Hinduism," "Buddhism," and "Sufism."

Hoopes had appropriated a term already in use, defined by an ethnic Maya scholar, and inverted it to mean something essentially negative, to corral the host of imaginative New Age doomsday theorists and those who recognize many forms of knowledge, including both that acquired by scientists through discursive analysis and that acquired intuitively as direct gnosis. A definition of gnosis from the vantage point of perennial wisdom teachers such as Suhrawardi, Seyyed Hossein Nasr, or Frithjof Schuon should probably be added to the Wikipedia entry, for as it stands it casts doubt on the merit of knowledge gained through shamanic or visionary means. This is a situation full of irony, since the ancient Maya kings themselves employed visionary shamanism to gain knowledge (gnosis) that conferred upon them the right to rule. Scholars themselves, however, rarely language these facts about Maya philosophy so bluntly, instead preferring to cloak the truth in abstractions. I registered my complaint on Aztlan and to Dr. Hoopes privately.[25] If Wikipedia is the arbiter of reality in any sense, then Hoopes has been successful at co-opting and inverting the term "Mayanism." The endeavor is laudable, but the choice of terminology is misleading and unfortunate.

Hoopes spends a great deal of time moderating many different discussions on the 2012 Tribe website. His interest in 2012 lies not with the possibility of reconstructing authentic beliefs connected with it in the Maya tradition—I doubt he believes there is anything to be found there—but rather he wants to track the 2012 meme as it is interpreted through the filter of pop culture. Thus his interest in "Mayanism" and how such a thing, as he defines it, is manifested in my work, Argüelles's books, Calleman's ideas, and particularly in the recent book by Daniel Pinchbeck.

This arena can be fascinating, and Hoopes has uncovered a very early reference to 2012 in a parody newspaper published by beat writer William Burroughs in 1967.[26] Hoopes also has pointed out that the very first connection between the end of the 13-Baktun cycle of the Long Count and an interpretation of cataclysm appears in Michael Coe's 1966 book *The Maya*. He sometimes slides into conflating my work with the nonsense that floods the marketplace, and I always take him to task for it, clarifying what my primary intentions really are. He seems to have reserved a special category for me—a kind of holding pattern until further notice. The term "syncretism" appears in his Wikipedia entry, but it is used in a way inconsistent with how syncretism has actually occurred in Mesoamerica. He sees it as a blending of two different worldviews, altering the essence of each forever. My comments to him are as follows:

> I believe the term syncretism should be clarified. The connotation currently being utilized is that syncretism is a problematic blending and dilution of Maya tradition in its encounter with foreign elements. However, ethnographers have observed that syncretism largely functions on the surface level of detail—the costume worn by rites, beliefs, principles, and tradition. Christianity, for example, is a thin veneer under which the core tradition is alive and well. It is this core tradition, stripped of superficial surface changes, that I believe should be what "Mayanism" refers to. That's how I intended it when I first used it in 2001.
>
> In addition, "Mayanism" as it is being defined and used in the evolving Wikipedia entry observes that the modern Maya are adapting to foreign (primarily "New Age") influences and adopting new elements. However, this is what the Maya have always done when confronted with foreign influence, although, as stated above, such ad-

aptations and transformations occur on the surface whereas the es-
sential tradition is preserved. It is this essential thing, the core of the
Maya tradition, that should draw our attention.

Furthermore, if the process resulting in this new thing called
"Mayanism" is not really a new process at all, but is what the Maya
have always done, we should steer clear of the investigation taking on
pejorative connotations—serving as a categorical gathering place for
what is perceived as irrational nonsense and so on. Finally, since 2012
is a major focus related to Mayanism as defined on Wikipedia, I ob-
serve that the scholarly analysis of 2012 has been focusing almost
exclusively on the social phenomenon of 2012 (attention going to
what various modern writers are saying and how the collective tends
to think about it and respond to it), rather than the artifact itself as
a viable topic of study (in terms of what function it served in the
Maya calendar and cosmology).[27]

Hoopes has explained to me that my work is often confused with that of
Argüelles or Calleman because we've all been published by the same publisher. Or my work cannot be taken seriously because I frequently speak at
venues that have a New Age flavor. This is understandable but unfortunate, and it doesn't mean that my work can't be assessed carefully on its own
terms, as I've been very patient and persistent in placing it before the eyes of
scholars. One feels one must issue a disclaimer, such as "my presence as a
speaker at this venue does not mean that I endorse the beliefs of its organizers." Hoopes's complaint makes sense from his experience as an academician,
in which only a cautiously narrow range of ideation is allowed. If I were to
give a talk on "metaphysics," it would have nothing to do with the unsophis-
ticated stereotype of the term that he seems to believe it represents. Suffice it
to say here that it has nothing to do with the self-help pop metaphysics that
is associated with supernatural phenomena in the New Age marketplace.

In late 2008, Jan Irvin interviewed Dr. Hoopes on his thoughts about
2012.[28] Being aware of my own work on 2012, he then invited me to respond.

So we ended up having a two-part debate with the potential of continuing. I had the advantage of being the second interview, able to respond to Hoopes's points. But Hoopes was well aware of my theory and so could address my work with that prior knowledge at hand, so it was a pretty even field. Here are a few observations:

Dr. Hoopes addresses what he calls "the common myth that the Maya disappeared." This choice of terminology betrays an attitude that myths are lies, which is confirmed when he later admits that myths may perhaps have some value as moral guidelines. But there was no consideration of the archetypal structure of myths that reveal deeper universal content, as Joseph Campbell, Carl Jung, and Huston Smith have identified. A myth in Hoopes's view, if it has any meaning at all, is merely in terms of ethical or moral guidance. He subscribes to the idea of discontinuity between the ancient Maya and the modern Maya. He says there were "two episodes when the knowledge was lost or changed," referring to the Classic Maya collapse and the Conquest. In both cases, only the surface style of how culture was practiced was disrupted. The deep cultural traditions, which revolve around language, religion, and the 260-day sacred calendar, have been preserved up to the present.

Here we have a confusion of levels. The surface level is perceived by material archaeologists as the only real, empirical level that can be granted one's attention. In the process called syncretism, the Maya adopted the surface details of European culture—seeming to adopt Christian gods, for example—but we've known for a long time that the old ways were preserved underneath. For some scholars, the concept of deeper currents reeks of the ambiguous and unprovable. This distinction between surface and depth again speaks to the original use of the term "Mayanism"—pan-Mayan ideas that we may call archetypal, shared, or universal. One of these, for example, would be the idea that sacrifice is necessary at the end of a cycle to facilitate a successful transformation of the old into the new. It's a universal idea that you find throughout Maya history and different groups. In fact, it's one of those universal ideas that you find at the root of virtually all of the world's religious traditions.

Dr. Hoopes claimed that *The Popol Vuh* is an early-eighteenth-century document contaminated by Christian ideas. This does not appear to be the case, as *The Popol Vuh*'s translator himself, Francisco Ximénez, stated that his intention was to preserve the original sense as precisely as possible (see Chapter 1). He also made a complete transcription of the original documented from the 1550s, and recent translators such as Dennis Tedlock have been able to identify likely typos, but by all appearances it is an accurate copy. The infrequent addition of Christian elements does not affect the overall structure of the doctrine of World Ages in the Creation Mythology section. My assertion that *The Popol Vuh* expresses a World Age doctrine was the nub of my point, leading to our debate, which Hoopes tried to mitigate with his various criticisms. But we can see that they were deflections away from the core fact: *The Popol Vuh* preserves a pre-Conquest World Age doctrine of time. We shouldn't suspect that this was introduced by Franciscan scribes and translators, since Christianity abides by a linear history that ends in the Apocalypse and the Second Coming. Yes, these are doctrines, Articles of Faith, with capital letters.

It was important that Dr. Hoopes, in his interview with Jan Irvin, identified the earliest source for the idea that 2012 is about a cataclysmic event. It didn't come from Argüelles, McKenna, or Waters. It came from Maya scholar Michael Coe, writing in his 1966 book *The Maya*: "There is a suggestion that each of these [time periods] measured thirteen Baktuns, or something less than 5,200 years, and that Armageddon would overtake the degenerate peoples of the world and all creation on the final day of the thirteenth."[29] The use of Christian terminology to describe Maya eschatology is quite surprising. "Our present universe," he continues, is "to be annihilated . . . when the Great Cycle of the Long Count reaches completion."[30] This is the kind of language that Maya scholars today find so offensive, and rightly so. As I've been saying for two decades, the Maya Creation Myth itself does not espouse an idea of a final cataclysmic end to the universe. In a cyclic time philosophy, it's all about transformation and renewal.

ASTRONOMERS AND THE GALACTIC ALIGNMENT

In March of 2007, the *New York Times* contacted me about a piece they wanted to write about 2012. As usual, I provided guidance and observations about what was happening in the 2012 discussion. It was easy to explain the situation with scholars and New Agers. The scholars had barely cared to glance at 2012, and the New Agers were just playing fast and loose with Maya ideas. My own work occupied the unique position of offering new discoveries garnered over fifteen years of rational investigation, as well as a willingness to address spiritual and metaphysical teachings that scholars avoided like the plague. Ben Anastas was given the assignment, and he flew out to interview me.

The timing was good, for I would be introducing a new 2012 film at the Oriental Theater in Denver. The film was *2012: The Odyssey* by Sacred Mysteries. I was interviewed for the film back in 2005. Although I had some issues with the content of the film, namely its lack of focus on the Maya material, it was, at the time, the best thing out there on 2012. Ben and I drove to Denver together and I was able to explain my work in great detail. Being an independent scholar of Maya studies turned out to be an angle they wanted to emphasize, so when the piece came out in July it treated my work accurately and favorably.

As was to be expected, however, they also provided dissenting views. According to Maya scholar and archaeo-astronomer Anthony Aveni, I was "a Gnostic" and I and other Gnostics "look for knowledge framed in mystery. And there aren't many mysteries left, because science has decoded most of them."[31] My agenda, according to Aveni, is to mystify Maya teachings when academia is filled with conclusive answers. This was an odd critique, on two fronts. First, it betrays a complete lack of understanding of my work. Second, even if I were a Gnostic, one wonders by what prejudicial rule of thumb one's religious orientation would disqualify one's intellectual work. One might equally say that a professed atheist's attitude toward Maya religion would be horribly biased. But Aveni did address my galactic alignment theory, albeit through the filter of a modern scientific bias. He said, "I defy anyone to look up into the sky and see the galactic equator." His point acknowledges the precise definition of the galactic alignment that I have formalized in my work: "the alignment of the December solstice sun with the galactic equator." My definition is useful for talking about the galactic alignment in precise astronomical terms, the galactic equator being an abstract dotted line running along the midplane of the galaxy. He then requires that the ancient Maya abide by the terms of this modern definition, and that they too should have thus had an identical concept of the galactic equator. This is an absurd position, and is easily exposed. The astronomical features utilized by the ancient Maya were those of naked-eye sky-watchers. Thus, the dark rift in the Milky Way, which lies along the galactic equator, was the target in their end-date alignment cosmology. This distinction is abundantly clear in my work, including all my books and my website essays.

After the *New York Times* piece appeared, I clarified this point in a private e-mail to Aveni, on the Aztlan academic e-mail list, and in the pages of the Institute of Maya Studies newsletter, which I sent to Aveni.[32] Yet he continued to assert his critique at a talk he gave in the fall of 2008 and again a few months later at the Tulane conference in early 2009, which guaranteed a few chuckles from his audiences.

The issues that astronomers have had with my galactic alignment theory are similarly facile and easy to counter. For example, Dr. Louis Strous, who teaches at the Sterrekundig Institute, University of Utrecht, in The Netherlands and maintains an astronomy website called Astronomy Answers, offered a loaded critique that rendered the galactic alignment completely meaningless. He first defined the alignment incorrectly, by leaving out the important specifying term "December solstice." Then he wrote: "The Sun moves along the whole ecliptic in a year, so it passes through each of those two intersections every year, and not just once every 26,000 years. So, it is not remarkable at all that the Sun passes through those intersections in 2012."[33]

It's hard to believe that a professional astronomer would not understand the precessional significance of the correct definition. One wonders how he could misconceive the definition in such a way as to make it seem like the galactic alignment was not a real astronomical occurrence. This turned out to be a very common happenstance in my dealings with scholars and astronomers. I can clearly say "crab apples are bitter," and someone like Strous will then paraphrase me as saying "apples are bitter" (leaving out the important specifying term "crab") and thus make it seem as if the entire topic is a joke. I've documented similar discussions with other astronomers since 1999, including Stephen Tonkin, who ended up digitally screaming, "Enough! I have already wasted enough time on your drivel" and blocking my e-mail.[34]

From their vantage point, I'm not a scientist and therefore they barely deign to talk with me. And when I point out the fallacy of their analysis, they dig themselves in deeper but resist offering corrections. Author Jonathan Zap has explained to me that this is a classic psychological defense mechanism of debunkers, observing that

> the identical attitude is found in the magazines Psycop and Skeptical Inquirer. A debunker is not a skeptic, but a true believer in a negative. Scientism is their religion, and they have a brittle, neurotic power complex that feeds off of this identification. They are the aristocrats of truth wearing a purple mantle and carry the imprimatur of science (in their neurotic imagination). Those who are representatives of the vast truths and areas of perception that their brittle and hollow neurotic persona cannot bear to engage are the subject of such comic shadow projection that, like a Medieval Monarch who cannot bear even the thought that a commoner should gaze at them or directly address them, the very thought of an actual dialogue with a member of this group makes them squirm with nauseated distaste. You have

violated this man's core psychic intentionality by daring to engage in a rational discourse with him (as they see rationality as their sovereign territory that those not part of their priesthood can't dare to trespass on). You have forgotten what your role is supposed to be in their mind: Passive Straw Man. The esoteric person is supposed to make a series of absurd points, be a cliché or stereotype with no rational ability to engage challenges, and they are supposed to be the monarchs of objectivity, authoritatively casting down idols and buffoons for the general public.[35]

I'm also reminded of the travails of Galileo. He discovered celestial bodies revolving around Jupiter, and a world that *knew* everything revolved around the earth was shocked, not believing it could be true. He invited his critics—various intellectuals and Church officials—to peer through the new telescope and see for themselves, but they all refused. They were afraid they might be infected by demons.[36]

In 2008, I was interviewed on a New Hampshire Public Radio station.[37] The guest prior to me was Dr. Phil Plait, a satirically self-confessed "bad astronomer" who maintained a website devoted to astronomical questions and fallacies. The interviewer asked him what he thought about 2012 and he responded with smug certainty that "I've looked at this a lot and I can say that it's 100 percent garbage." During my subsequent interview I pointed out that, first and foremost, 2012 is a true artifact of the Maya calendar system, so it is incorrect to say that "it's 100 percent garbage." Upon looking at Plait's website I could see that he spent many years responding to inane questions about 2012 and the galactic alignment, every time posed in misleading and incorrect ways.[38] His examination of the 2012 alignment was apparently limited to what his website debates generated, and there wasn't one clear definition of the galactic alignment on it, by him or anyone else, although some tried to point him to my website.

Plait ignored several e-mails I sent in which I offered to discuss with him the galactic alignment and its role in Maya cosmology. He's a good example of a shock jock–style Internet personality who is trying to carve out a career for himself as a scientific skeptic who can explain everything and debunk what he perceives to be unwarranted ideas. Yet, as with Aveni and other astronomers, he simply indulges in a biased attitude, unwilling to respond to the facts and engage in a rational dialogue.

Then there is the issue of how the galactic alignment gets confused with the orbit of our solar system around the Galactic Center, which I discussed in Chapter 4. I'll add here that the sinusoidal orbit of our solar system above and below the galactic plane is ably described by Nassim Haramein in his online video clip "Crossing the Event Horizon," but he, like many others, thinks that our passage through the midplane is occurring around the year 2012.[39]

I can't emphasize this enough: This is a big problem with the 2012

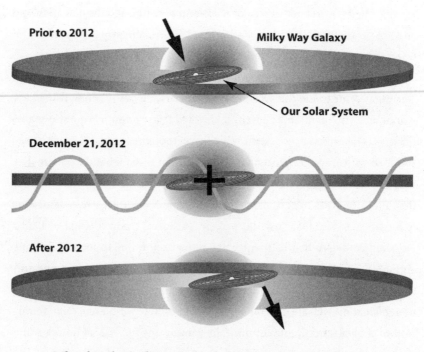

What the galactic alignment is not: the sinusoidal orbit of our solar system above and below the galactic midplane over some 250 million years. Graphic courtesy of Jim Reed

material, and it is unfortunately muddying the waters for the integrity of the precessional basis of the galactic alignment astronomy. Geoff Stray and Zyzygy relate data from no fewer than nine different academic sources for the position of our solar system in relation to the galactic midplane.[40] They found that on average the sources calculate that we are some 64 light-years above the midplane, moving outward, reaching the maximum distance at about 85 light-years. In comparison, our solar system is roughly 25,000 light-years, give or take 2,000 light-years, from the Galactic Center. (I explored the curious connection between this distance and the precession cycle of roughly 26,000 years in my book *Galactic Alignment*, and it was mentioned by Joseph Campbell in his 1963 book *The Flight of the Wild Gander*.)

Meet Waxaklahun Ub'ah K'awil

In the summer of 2007, Jim Reed and I led our second tour to Maya sites. Our group consisted of twenty-two hardy souls of all ages, and our plan was ambitious. We convened in Guatemala City, visited museums, and then struck out for Honduras to visit the ancient site of Copán. It was a five-hour ride in our chartered bus, driven by a good-natured crew of three Guatemalan guys who constantly helped us load and unload our bags throughout our eight-day adventure. For me, the border we crossed near Chiquimula was layered over with many memories, as I'd passed through it several times since 1988, mostly as an unwashed backpack-toting gringo.

Our group was hosted by Flavia Cueva at her family's historic San Lucas Hacienda. That evening, Jim and I gave presentations and many locals showed up. It was a beautiful evening, looking over the Copán River with the ruins just visible in the distance under the glittering stars. The next day we visited the site and observed the famous full-round carving of Copán's eighth-century ruler 18 Rabbit, whose real name is Waxaklahun Ub'ah K'awil. I explained the symbolism on the east and west sides of the carving, one depicting the ruler facing west, over the huge Ak turtle altar. This side, I pointed out, faced the setting of the Ak turtle (located in Gemini) and the three hearthstones of Maya Creation Mythology, where the Milky Way crosses through the ecliptic in Gemini.

And on the other side, the ruler faces east and wears an ornate costume featuring an elaborate crocodile head draped down both sides of his body. It gave the appearance of the ruler standing within the jaws of the crocodile, a vertical pillar of authority growing out of the crocodile's mouth. I pointed out the glyphs on the side of the carving, indicating the Long Count date of its dedication: 9.14.0.0.0 (December 3, 711 AD). I had noticed that on this date the sun was aligned with the dark rift in the Milky Way, the crocodile mouth rising over the eastern horizon. Clearly, the sky reflected the solar king's stance within the cosmic maw of transformation and rebirth.[41]

People in our group roamed freely, as the Maya temples always draw people in different directions. Nearby, Copán archaeologist William Fash, who wrote *Scribes, Warriors and Kings*, was leading a tour. That evening we

The Great Plaza at Copán. Photo by the author, 1988

were hosted and surprised with a slide presentation by another Copán archaeologist, David Sedat. He lives in town with his wife and is known for
discovering the tomb of the female ruler within the buried Rosalila pyramid.
David and I had both appeared in the "Places of Mystery" program produced
by the Discovery Channel, and it was a pleasure to have our entire group
entertained and informed at his home. Some of us were able to experience a
descent into the underworld, at night, with a ritual led by David in his Classic Maya–style *pibna*, or sweat bath.

The next day our group journeyed back to Antigua, where Jim and I
gave another presentation at the Universidad Francisco Marroquin. We were
hosted by Mary Lou and Jay Ridinger, an amazing couple who, in the 1970s,
rediscovered the lost jade quarries of the ancient Maya. They now employ
Maya artisans in the making of jade artifacts and jewelry. Mary Lou gave us
an inspiring presentation on the Maya jade tradition and how Jades, S.A.,
revived the lost tradition. I see my friends Mary Lou and Jay as being engaged
in an enterprise similar to mine—recovering and reviving a lost facet of the
ancient Maya tradition. One encounters endless obstacles, but also breakthroughs. And one discovers, along the way, true friends and allies.

Our group continued into the highlands, visiting the Quiché Maya site
of Iximche, market day in Chichicastenango, beautiful Lake Atitlán, and the
Maya cult deity Maximon. It was fortunate that, when we explored Izapa's
sister city, Tak'alik Ab'aj, Maya priest Rigoberto Itzep Chanchabac was burning incense and doing ritual in front of Stela 5. The ceremonial feeling of
reverence and prayer, making offerings to the sky-earth and the ancestors,
was moving. Our own culture rarely provides opportunities to feel deep reverence for life. We were given a brief tour by the site's archaeologist, Christa
Schieber de Lavarreda. She described for us the line of stones they had found
that pointed to the center point of the bowl of the Big Dipper in the northern
skies. The archaeologists, upon digging deeper, discovered another row of
stones, from an earlier era, pointing to a different star in the constellation of
Draco. They concluded that the people of Tak'alik Ab'aj were tracking precession and had shifted their cosmology as the skies shifted. This was clear evi-

dence that precession was being noticed and tracked, in an area with close ties in the pre-Classic period to Izapa.

After the tour was over and everyone said their good-byes, I stayed in Antigua because Mary Lou and I planned to strike out for Izapa to meet with local officials and give another presentation. With our friend Baldomero driving, we crossed the border into Mexico in under five hours. Little did I know, but a celebration was planned in the town of Tuxtla Chico, near the archaeological site of Izapa. We first met with Rodolfo Juan, our host, in Tapachula. Time was short, so we immediately went to Izapa, where I gave an impromptu talk at the ballcourt. This was "ground zero of the 2012 prophecy," I said, "where the future alignment of the solstice sun and the dark rift was encoded into the mythic narrative carved into the monuments." The next two days were a whirlwind. I was presented with the keys to the city in a formal ceremony in Tuxtla Chico and was made an honorary ambassador of Izapa to the outside world. A press conference happened that evening, and the next day we were front-page news in the Mexican national newspaper. My presentation at the Universidad Valle del Grijalva in Tapachula was well attended, and I was impressed with the students and adults who came out to learn about the astronomical knowledge of the ancient Izapans.

Mary Lou and I were interviewed on a radio program, and I learned of Mam Indians living in the high mountains on the slopes of Tacaná volcano, near the border with Guatemala. We had wondered whether any traditional Maya day-keepers lived on the Mexican side. The answer was "a few." A more precise answer was that a traditional Maya calendar priest wanted to visit Izapa and do ritual, but he didn't know how to go about acquiring official permission. In Guatemala, the Maya Indians have recently been allowed into the archaeological sites, and altars have even been constructed in front of stelae at Tikal, Tak'alik Ab'aj, Iximche, and elsewhere. In Mexico, however, the old rules still apply—no Indian rituals allowed inside the national parks and archaeological sites. I wondered if Izapa could perhaps squeeze through somehow, as it exists in a marginal zone where local powers might trump federal laws. It was an intriguing possibility but would require some patience and behind-the-scenes string pulling.

The day after my presentation at the university, we needed to return to Antigua. But we visited the site one last time and lingered while locals approached, telling us of carved stones they were finding in the fields. We went to the nearby home of a woman who had an Izapa-style potbellied boy, carved of stone with a shallow bowl in the top. I imagined this to be a stargazing device, similar to the vast rectangular pools in the architecture of Palenque, which scholars realized were filled with placid water so the Palenque stargazers could gaze downward into the underworld of the night sky. Another woman told us of some carved boulders on the slopes of Tacaná volcano north of Izapa.

In June of 2009 I was able to visit one of these carved boulders, and I determined that it contained scenes of sacrifice and birth, which very nicely complemented the primary theme found in the Izapan ballcourt. The caiman depicted on this "birth-sacrifice" boulder was carved in the style of Izapa's Stela 25, which is located in the museum in Tapachula. The caiman is cut in half, sacrificed, with three jagged cuts through its body. Stela 25 depicts Seven Macaw holding Hunahpu's severed arm. Hunahpu, below Seven Macaw, is missing an arm and three cuts drip blood. The previously undocumented carved boulder in the mountains above Izapa possibly depicts a version of a Creation Text recorded at Palenque, in which a "Starry Deer Crocodile" (the Milky Way) was sacrificed and cut into three parts that became the three levels of the cosmos: underworld, earth, and sky.[42] The Izapa bioregion itself is divided into three domains: ocean to the south, the narrow plateau on which Izapa sits, and high volcanoes looming in the sky to the north. This tripartite structure is also echoed in the three main monument groups at Izapa. There was clearly more to be discovered in the region of Izapa.

Before we hit the highway for Guatemala we went to Izapa's Group B to observe the no-shadow phenomenon of the solar zenith passage. The date happened to be August 11, one of the solar zenith passage days. We lingered until noon, and the sun was blazing. At the pillar-and-ball gnomons, we watched the shadows disappear as the sun reached the exact center of the sky overhead. On our drive back to Antigua Mary Lou, Baldomero, and I ate fresh cacao, sucking the sweet mango-like nectar off the pods.

That trip was an incredibly demanding nonstop odyssey. Back in Antigua, I assessed the previous ten days and realized I'd given six presentations, a press conference, and a radio interview, not counting two guided tours of Izapa. And as an honored guest entered into the books for all time, I was presented with the key to Tuxtla Chico, renamed for the occasion Izapito, "little Izapa."

MANY SCHOLARS MOVING IT FORWARD

I realize that I can be critical of scholars and New Agers in equal measure, but in this section I want to make it clear that I have been inspired and informed by Maya scholars past and present. Many scholars are doing incredible trailblazing work and are driven by their own love of Maya culture. It's rare for any specialist to become a full-time epigrapher. The new epigraphers are pursuing their interest as a sideline, attending conferences at their own expense, often finding it difficult to get their research published in official journals. It's the digital age, so debates and think tanks unfold today in private e-mails, teleconferences, and on e-list discussion boards. Scholars whose perspectives I disagree with and critique in this book are also the same scholars who have provided insights and breakthroughs. But everything must be assessed with clarity and discernment. As far as I'm concerned, this is how it should be. Blindly following authority figures occurs in academia as much as in New Age cults and anywhere else. Often, a sense of propriety prevents authority figures from being corrected on basic errors. The entire thing is a process, and despite career ambitions professional scholars and independent researchers alike share a desire to understand more deeply what the ancient Maya civilization was about.

Scholars currently doing important work include Susan Milbrath, Elizabeth Newsome, Prudence Rice, Karen Bassie, Julia Kappelman, Victoria Bricker, Barbara MacLeod, Barbara Tedlock, Merle Greene Robertson, Martha Macri, and Gabrielle Vail. Noteworthy pioneers of the past include Tatiana Prouskouriakaoff, Linda Schele, Maud Oakes, Maud Makemson, Zelia Nuttall, and Doris Heyden. Notice that these are all women. A lot of them specialize in hard-core scientific disciplines—archaeology, astronomy, calendrics, and mathematics. They prove that these traditionally male domains are simply not gender-specific. Unlike other high-level disciplines (with the exception, perhaps, of women's studies), Mesoamerican studies is overflowing with brilliant female scholars. I'm not sure why this is so, but I think it needs to be said.

Barb MacLeod is a brilliant investigator with many interests. In addition to consistently offering breakthrough readings of tenaciously inscrutable hieroglyphic texts, she is a passionate aviation stunt flyer and instructor, a guitar-playing singer-songwriter, cave explorer, and artist (she did the Cycle 7 cartoon in Chapter 1). She first traveled from Seattle to Belize in 1970 to explore caves. In a fortuitous occurrence, she soon returned to map out caves for the archaeology department of the Peace Corps. She pursued this for five years, visiting Maya temple sites throughout Mesoamerica while studying the hieroglyphs. Around 1973, she adapted Morley's Long Count table in *The Ancient Maya*, extending it out to December of 2012.

After getting her degree at the University of Texas in Austin, she circulated a series of epigraphic observations in the late 1980s and 1990s called "North Austin Notes." It was one of these, from 1991, called "Maya Genesis: The Glyphs," that spelled out the decipherment of the "three-hearthstone" hieroglyph, connecting it with the three stars in Orion. This is the idea that many attribute to Linda Schele, but in fact it originated with her friend and colleague Barb MacLeod.[43] The connection of this decipherment to Creation Texts at Quiriguá provided a breakthrough revealing Maya Creation Mythology as a metaphor for astronomical features and processes. Now, almost twenty years later, MacLeod has made another breakthrough, called the 3-11

Pik formula, which connects important rites of Maya kingship with temporal "stations" related to the precession of the equinoxes.

Now for the guys. I've always appreciated the work of Dennis Tedlock, Anthony Aveni, Gordon Brotherston, Raphael Girard, Ian Graham (aka "Indiana Jones"), David Sedat, and Michael Coe. The research of these scholars and others that I was immersed in while I wrote *Maya Cosmogenesis 2012* can be glimpsed in my online bibliography.[44] When you are deeply engaged in Maya studies, you feel obliged to speak out at inconsistencies or mistakes. This is part of the process, and my critique of various aspects of Maya scholarship doesn't diminish the respect and gratitude I feel for this unique, committed group of people. And lately there have been some newcomers, rising stars who are building upon previous scholarship and finding some truly astonishing new things. Michael Grofe is one of these; his work argues convincingly for a high level of accuracy in ancient Maya astronomy.

David Stuart was a wonder kid who traveled to Maya sites with his parents and was swept up into the Palenque Round Table craze in the 1970s. Exposed to the hieroglyphic texts as a youngster, he quickly became adept at recognizing text elements and soon began making his own decipherments. Since the 1980s, Stuart has greatly contributed to the revolution in deciphering the Maya script. He and Stephen Houston have collaborated on many decipherments, but neither has any particular sensitivity to potential astronomical references in the texts. Yet they are there to be illuminated.

They wrote a monograph together in the early 1990s that was about place-names—the glyphs used to name sites such as Palenque, Copán, and Quiriguá. A category of place-names referred to what they called "supernatural topography"—that is, locations involved in the Creation Mythology. They wrote, "[J]ust as the deities acceded to high office or gave birth, so too did they live in specific places, ranging from the 'fifth sky' to the 'black hole' . . . the overlap between human and mythological geography would appear to be small."[45] It's quite clear they are conceiving of these "mythological locations" as belonging purely to the human imagination.[46] They are not part of a celestial landscape; they do not see any astronomy in the mythology.

This assumption is unwarranted given the general connection between Maya Creation Mythology and astronomy that was being discussed, at the time, by Linda Schele, and that is now, generally speaking, undeniable. The bias belongs to a general bias, that mythology is an unreliable source of real information. Perhaps it is useful as a codification of moral guidelines, but it does not encode anything so scientific as astronomy. I suspect that when epigraphers develop a greater appreciation for the archetypal dimension of human experience and accept that the Maya culture integrated astronomy and mythology, we'll have some progress on this front.

In early 2008 I began a correspondence with Mark Van Stone, a calligrapher, artist, and student of Maya epigraphy. He was the artist for Michael Coe's important epigraphic guidebook *Reading the Maya Glyphs*. I began by explaining the correlation question, which boils down to the old debate between two end-date choices: December 21 and December 23. The latter date was argued for and defended by Maya epigrapher Floyd Lounsbury, but his argument is flawed, as discussed in Chapter 4. A further point that I've emphasized frequently in online debates with scholars is that the resolution of the issue is supported by the surviving day-count in Guatemala and points right to the solstice in 2012 (December 21). This becomes, then, the vector for the likelihood of the end date being intentionally placed.

Mark and I exchanged many e-mails in early 2008. Later that year, the Foundation for the Advancement of Mesoamerican Studies approved and posted Mark's lengthy, slide-show-style article called "It's Not the End of the World: What the Ancient Maya Tell Us About 2012."[47] John Hoopes called it "The best scholarly background for discussion of 2012."[48] As I read Mark's well-written piece I realized that he had overlooked virtually every clarification I had offered in our e-mail exchanges. I posted a response on Aztlan, providing links to a lengthy critique of Van Stone's essay.[49] The primary problem with the approach of the essay is that it neglected to examine the pre-Classic iconography that would have the most to say about the origins of the Long Count, as the Long Count first appears in the first century BC. Van Stone, on the other hand, had focused his investigation on Classic Period epigraphy and even, incredibly, post-Classic material from Central Mexico, far to the west of where the Long Count was used and centuries after it stopped being recorded.

Mark did emphasize an approach that can produce results. We should expect to find references to 2012 in the Classic Period inscriptions, but epigraphers assume that specific texts complete with dates should be found every time, and that's all that is admissible. This assumption will effectively eliminate information that can shed light on how 2012 was conceived by the ancient Maya. For example, I might write a page of material in which I frequently refer to "my birthday." I never provide the actual date, but use only the secondary reference phrase. Two hundred years from now, a future literary historian could do a little additional research and find the exact date of my birth in an archive somewhere, and thus supply the missing specific date. Likewise, letters of a seventeenth-century French count might refer frequently to "the Border War" and it would take some contextual support from other sources to equate this secondary reference with a war between France and Germany that occurred in 1642 and 1643. The detailed dates could be reconstructed. In Maya history, we have some calendrical references to the era inauguration in 3114 BC. The Creation Mythology associated with this date involves three hearthstones, the zenith, and a turtle. This structural complex becomes a secondary reference phrase, and when it is found in other contexts, without a specific date reference to 3114, scholars accept that it refers to August 11, 3114 BC. The same principle can be applied to secondary references to 2012.

Overall, I believe there is hope for Maya scholars to one day realize that 2012 was an intentional and meaningful artifact of knowledge for the ancient Maya. It's unfortunate that many scholars are locked into responding to the superficial refrains repeated by New Agers or doomsayers—that it's either an ascension or the end of the world. Scholars and pop writers form a perfectly bonded dysfunctional pair, each side unable to see the *ding an sich*, the thing-in-itself, as they are preoccupied and transfixed dealing with each other's projected shadow. Scholars' dismissive interpretations follow from this assumption, and as a result they have been blind to seeing anything of significance. At the first academic 2012 conference, the toughest critic one could imagine, Anthony Aveni, brought all these assumptions and plenty of thoughtful comments to the table. My galactic alignment theory, and the 2012 topic generally, would either be blown to smithereens or emerge unscathed. Let's see what happened.

THE FIRST ACADEMIC 2012 CONFERENCE

The 2012 conference at Tulane University in New Orleans was the first of its kind. Scholars had decided it was high time to address 2012 as an overarching theme. They invited Anthony Aveni, who was working on a book on 2012, to provide the keynote address. My report on the goings-on at the conference is late-breaking stuff, as it happened in February of 2009, while I was writing this book. I've prepared an online resource that will share commentary and audio clips that I recorded during the conference.[50]

New Orleans, for me, is a place of odd memories and experiences. I played guitar as a busker on the French Quarter at age twenty, danced down Bourbon Street with the Hari Krishnas while investigating religious cults, and spent seven days in the New Orleans Parish Prison (the infamous Tent City), and it was a bum rap, I swear. My sabbatical in jail came at the very end of my first trip to Central America. After traveling on a shoestring for more than three months, using money I'd saved working the night shift in a factory for a year, I made my way overland and crossed the border into Texas. There, I made a fateful decision to hitchhike to Florida. The details are irrelevant; suffice it to say that the arrest occurred during Mardi Gras and the charge was "obstructing a sidewalk." The result was that my backpack disappeared with the guy who'd given me a lift. After my release in the wake of a hurricane,

I was able to buy a bus ticket home to Chicago with ninety dollars I had stashed in my shoe. Arriving home with the proverbial T-shirt on my back and twelve cents in my pocket, I lamented the loss of my camera, ten rolls of pictures, my notebook, and assorted mementos. That was the beginning of my career as an independent 2012ologist, and I vowed to return to Central America as soon as possible.

Now I was back in New Orleans. My friend Jim Reed was there too, along with our friend Madison Moore. It was good to have a few allies on hand, as I planned to storm the ivory tower, much the way I had done in 1997 at the Institute of Maya Studies. I knew what Aveni's critique entailed, and had noted that in his other public comments he harbored ideas not unlike those of the astronomers I discussed in the previous section. In periodic news items on 2012, which I too had been interviewed for, Aveni and other scholars typically dismissed the whole thing as meaningless. In a CNN interview David Stuart said: "There is no serious scholar who puts any stock in the idea that the Maya said anything meaningful about 2012."[51] By the time 2012 arrives this assertion will be proven incorrect, as the new evidence is already at hand.

I was curious if scholars really believed that the cycle ending in 2012 was meaningless for the ancient Maya, because the news media typically framed their presentations as "New Age kooks versus the scholarly voices of reason." There was little room for the kind of work I've been presenting—an intentional effort to reconstruct forgotten beliefs connected to the Long Count calendar and the 2012 cycle endings. In fact, it's fair to say that Aveni and others were content to address their comments to the silliest far end of the New Age fringe. They could simply say, "The Maya didn't believe the world is going to end in 2012." Of course, I've been offering that correction too, for many years. But Aveni was only beginning to rationally investigate the evidence for something else going on, and it was clear that he would resist the suggestion.

Barbara and Dennis Tedlock were giving a presentation, which promised to say something specific about 2012. The other speakers, including Marc

Zender, Matthew Looper, Victoria Bricker, Markus Eberl, and John Justeson, only obliquely dealt with 2012, if at all. However, their presentations were fascinating, and I was greatly inspired to renew areas of research I'd been neglecting. Oddly, Robert Sitler, the first scholar to publish a peer-reviewed article dedicated to 2012, was not invited to speak. Aveni's Friday-night keynote talk would be the focus of official comments on 2012. An open panel on Sunday would provide another opportunity to ask some pointed questions.

Weeks before the conference, I had prepared an outline of what I considered to be key points that any scholarly treatment of 2012 should cover. I sent this to Aveni as a heads-up, as I was concerned that he would not sink his teeth into the real issues. The first fact that is obvious to anyone who spends a little time with the Long Count is that the end date falls on a solstice. This implies an ability to accurately calculate the tropical year more than 2,100 years ago. Despite my heads-up, as it turned out Aveni mentioned this fact but conveniently avoided addressing the implications. It took my direct question after his talk, as an audience member in a huge auditorium, to force the issue to be considered.

Items I listed as essential, which I sent to Dr. Aveni:

- The likelihood of intent suggested by the solstice placement of the 13-Baktun cycle-ending date in 2012
- The calendar correlation
- The place and time of the Long Count's origins
- The relevance of Izapa to the Long Count's origins
- The galactic alignment theory with respect to the significance of the archaeo-astronomical symbolism in the Izapan ballcourt
- The question of ancient knowledge of the precession of the equinoxes and its accurate calculation

Critics of 2012 spend much of their time responding to the exaggerated media hype that asserts "the Maya predicted the world will end in 2012." We (and scholars, especially) should be addressing our questions to 2012 as an intentional artifact of the ancient calendar, and explore how this date and ideologies possibly connected with it manifested in Maya cosmology.

When I decided at the last minute that I could get away for the conference, I xeroxed 100 copies of a four-page document that I intended to hand out at the conference.[52] On Friday, we attended other talks in the morning and afternoon. One noteworthy thing happened in Markus Eberl's talk. It was a basic introductory class, the first of the weekend. In describing the Long Count, he presented the famous image from Coba, with its twenty-four place values set to 13. This image is often used to imply that the 13-Baktun cycle is meaningless because there are much greater cycles in the Long Count. This perspective avoids the fact that most Long Count dates are recorded with only five place values, meaning the Baktun level is for all practical purposes the highest. During the question session, my friend Dave Shaeffer from Antigua triggered a realization about Markus's presentation of the Coba Creation stela. Dave pointed out that his slide cut off the bottom of the image, where the explicit date of the stela is found. It is in fact a Creation Text, so the final date, despite the huge abstract levels that precede it, ends up at 13.0.0.0.0, 4 Ahau 8 Cumku, August 11, 3114 BC. The monument is all about that date, the inauguration of the current era of 13 Baktuns. There was a subtle way that the information was selectively presented which avoided dealing with the importance of a 13-Baktun cycle in Maya Creation Mythology.

During a break in the afternoon I bumped into Aveni in the foyer. He said, "Oh, you're here—you sent me your six points and said you weren't coming!" This was indeed true at the time I'd sent them to him. I should mention that Aveni and I appeared in a recently released documentary together, called *2012: Science or Superstition?* I've had serious issues with many of the documentaries I've been involved in, some of which micro-edited my words to make it seem as if I advocated the 2012 doomsday position (if I had a team of damage-control spin doctors, or could afford lawyers, they would have been on that right away). But the new documentary really did a nice job of accurately treating my work while providing reasonable critiques. These were provided by Aveni, and I could see that he was willing to address the question of the galactic alignment. His Tulane talk covered much of the same ground as his comments in the documentary.

Harvey Bricker gave a long introduction, with funny slides taken during vacations they had shared and satirical jabs, all in good fun. He called Aveni an interdisciplinarian who was the perfect person to address the 2012 topic. I was a bit surprised at the constant humorous references to "end of the world" ideation, as if that was all it was about. It seemed that scholars were just as imprisoned by that doomsday framework as the media and many popular writers were.

Aveni began right off with his Google results for "Maya 2012 Creation": 281,000 hits and growing by the month. It was, indeed, "a very hot topic."[53] He said he wanted to discuss the "event" that "will occur" on "the winter solstice of 2012" from three vantage points: what latter-day prophets are saying about it, what it might have meant for the Maya, and what cycle turnings generally mean and have meant for cultures.

He mentioned Geoff Stray's website but called it "Dire Gnosis" (the crowd tittered); Geoff's site is actually Diagnosis2012.co.uk, and he tells me that he originally had the logo read "Dire Gnosis" as a pun. Realizing that some people were taking it literally, he explained on his website that "there is a whole complex of meanings wrapped up in the Dire Gnosis logo . . . The word DIRE, although it can mean calamitous; dreadful; ominous, can also have a meaning of URGENT as in 'dire need.' Thus, the words 2012: Dire Gnosis mean 2012: Urgent Knowledge."[54] Stray's website has been the go-to resource for all things 2012, providing detailed critical reviews of many books, theories, and movies. More so than any other investigator, including Aveni and myself, Geoff has been tireless is providing clear, informed, careful, and accurate reviews of almost everything that has appeared on 2012.

Aveni read from the jacket blurbs of books by Lawrence Joseph and Daniel Pinchbeck. He allowed various popular writers to indict themselves with their own statements, and it's true that the hyperbole in Pinchbeck's writings as well as Lawrence Joseph's book is easy to spot. For example,

Joseph wrote that 2012 will be "more catastrophic, tumultuous, and revelatory than any other year in human history—it will make you think twice about your retirement plans." And he quotes Daniel Pinchbeck as writing that his metaphysical opus reveals "secret thoughts on suppressed dimensions of being embedded in Maya 2012 philosophy that can save the world from impending environmental disaster."

We might suspect that Aveni chooses the most outrageous selection, guaranteed to entertain his audience. It's an old *modus operandi* that harkens back to Eric Thompson's treatment of Benjamin Whorf, taking the weakest points and "worrying them to death," as Michael Coe said. But I'm not surprised that pop writers get this treatment from Aveni, because of late there's been a tendency to do very little actual research into Maya traditions. It's as if a subparadigm has been created that can just quote mutually supporting New Age sources. Or 2012 just gets adopted as a pop icon, removed from its roots in Maya tradition. For researchers, writers, and journalists, there's actually a lot of fascinating Maya source material to sink their teeth into.

Aveni then came to my work, and mentioned that I was in the audience and provided him with a list of six essential points, joking that he was glad to have me on his dissertation committee. Aveni's genuine sense of humor alternated with no-nonsense observations. "Jenkins," he said, believes "the Maya knew the winter solstice sun was slowly moving toward the center of the galaxy and when it passes the galactic plane we too will connect with our cosmic heart." He mentioned my emphasis on the dark rift as a birthplace and my interpretation that the Maya conceived the Galactic Center as a "womb of creation." So far so good, but then he said that I believe "this is all recorded on Stela 25" (from Izapa). He belabored the image as my proposed key to the alignment, which it isn't, then he correctly pointed out that I see it as encoding an oppositional relationship between the Polar Center and the Galactic Center. Stela 11 is the carving from Izapa that I've presented as an image of the alignment of the December solstice sun with the dark rift in the Milky Way, for reasons I explained in Chapter 4. Without really passing judgment, Aveni quickly moved on to his next subject.

Next he quoted Lawrence Joseph saying that "the world will be thrown out of kilter" on December 21, 2012. A full-course menu of catastrophic scenarios was laid out by Joseph in purple prose that would give Poe pause. In a CNN interview, Joseph claimed his book wasn't really cataclysm oriented, that his publisher insisted on the alarmist title (*Apocalypse 2012*), but his own words sure give the impression that he had doomsday on the brain.[55] Aveni next reported that Dr. Calleman believes "the harmonic coincidence attending the seminal moment will constitute nothing less than a spiritual awakening, an enlightenment that demonstrates the progress of evolution." The "seminal moment" for Calleman comes not in 2012 but on October 28, 2011, according to his system.

The second area that Aveni wanted to address involves what people believe the Maya may have thought about 2012. He says these ideas can be criticized on astronomical and cultural grounds. On astronomical grounds, he claimed there was no evidence they were aware of precession. Apart from the evidence at La Venta and Tak'alik Ab'aj that I previously mentioned, there is now breakthrough information from MacLeod and Grofe, which Aveni glossed over disparagingly. He ran through some quick comments on the eclipse table in the Maya's Dresden Codex, the use of Copán ruler 18 Rabbit's double-serpent bar, and described Long Count numbers going into the deep past on Copán Stela B. He stated that these were "not forward-looking ideas but backward-looking ideas, connecting rulers into deep time," making a point that the Maya did not look into the future. However, in the Tortuguero texts as well as at Piedras Negras and even in the corpus of texts from Copán he mentioned, future cycle endings are in fact frequently referenced. For example, Copán's dated inscriptions project backward and forward, making calendrical analogies between Yax Kuk Mo's fifth-century reign and the future close of Baktun 10 (in 830 AD).[56]

On cultural grounds, he said the ancient Maya weren't forward-projecting. In fact, they did use both forward and backward projections in their Creation Texts. Many scholars, such as Matthew Looper, understand quite clearly the analogical relationship between the period ending of the previous World Age (in 3114 BC) and other period endings, great and small, throughout Maya history: "Zoomorph P and Altar P' [at Quiriguá] were commissioned by Sky Xul as the primary commemorative monuments for his third period ending festival on 9.18.5.0.0 [September 13, 795 AD]. As a celebration of cosmic renewal, the period-ending was considered to be a replay of the events of cosmogenesis, which occurred on 4 Ajaw 8 Kumk'u [13.0.0.0.0 in 3114 BC]."[57] All cycle endings would have been treated as like-in-kind events in which sacrifice and new dedications were performed.

Next, Aveni claimed that the Milky Way was never represented by the Maya as a tree, an opinion that many Maya scholars simply don't agree with. The Lacandon Maya, to give just one example, believed that the clump of the nuclear bulge where the Milky Way crosses through Sagittarius and Scorpio was the "roots of a giant tree."[58] Aveni produced the famous image from the last page of the Maya Dresden Codex, which shows a flood pouring over the earth from the mouth of a giant sky-caiman. He compared this flood image to prognostications given in the Chilam Balam books, and Aveni believes these "prophecies" are simply free-floating "metaphorical frameworks"—sort of like moral guidelines—rather than "transcendent" messages that would apply to all humanity as some kind of universal truth. Again, one senses a resistance to accepting the archetypal dimension of the human psyche that does offer a "universal" or "transcendent" level on which these kinds of ideas have meaning. The idea of a cleansing "flood" is not only a universal occurrence geographically speaking, but more important it is a universal (in Aveni's conceptual usage, "transcendental") idea that has meaning for each and every human psyche—death itself will be the great flood.

Aveni stated that in the early days of Christianity, a religion he calls "Gnosticism" prevailed that believed in an essential unity of all faiths. He opined that such a view is outdated, a kind of idealistic superstition that should not be entertained today. He was, I think, trying to describe the Perennial Philosophy, which is not so much a historical phenomenon as a depth perception that acknowledges the underlying essential unity of religious teachings, at their archetypal core, while the exoteric forms and dogmas of

religion always appear in changeable garb. This is an essential unity that transcends formal differences, best understood through initiation into a level of
consciousness that can integrate the superficially different exoteric forms by
seeing their shared root. Direct experience confers gnosis—a knowledge not
limited to the statistics and data of surface reality but that embraces an integrative higher viewpoint conferred by direct inner realization, or illumination; aka, gnosis.[59]

I wouldn't expect Aveni to appreciate the scholarship and insights of
the Perennial Philosophers, since *Publishers Weekly* correctly identified him
as a writer who "presupposes a readership that embraces a scientific-materialistic worldview."[60] It is surprising, however, that he misrepresents the
widespread phenomenon of Gnosticism, since he wrote several books on the
occult, the roots of astronomy in astrology, and magic. His approach to
those subjects can be summarized as a belief that people fall prey to those
subjects because of their human failings and unwillingness or inability to
approach life responsibly and think rationally. This is similar to the scien-
tistic attitude that religion and spirituality were developed only after enough
grain was stored in the tower for people to have time to ponder intangibles
(i.e., to exercise their imaginations). The deck is so stacked against the in-
terdependency of subjective and objective domains that one wonders how
anyone with this attitude can accurately represent cultures, such as the Maya,
that are rooted in a nondual vision of the cosmos. Carl Calleman denies the
physical realm of astronomy that can provide objective data; Aveni denies the spiritual realm that can provide direct gnosis. And never the twain
shall meet.

On the precessional and sidereal-year calculations that Michael Grofe
found in the Serpent Series of the Dresden Codex, Aveni asserted there is very
little agreement that there are precessional calculations in the Dresden and
he believes "such details are unnecessary in a talk about apocalypse." This is
a diplomatically cautious statement that lets him off the hook. Scientists are
often in great disagreement about facts, how to interpret facts, and how many
facts are needed in order to qualify as evidence. A lack of consensus among

experts does not mean there is a lack of evidence. The evidence usually gets overlooked or marginalized for years, without critics ever once actually dealing directly with the evidence. This is clearly the case with Aveni's unwillingness to assess Grofe's work. Precession is, after all, a central issue in the 2012 alignment theory. Furthermore, the theme of the Tulane conference was 2012, not apocalypse. Aveni must see those two terms as being synonymous.

He stated that there was no evidence that the ancient Maya thought anything about the next creation (in 2012). Although this assertion was presented in no uncertain terms, it is a demonstrably false statement because of the text on Tortuguero Monument 6, which references 2012 as a Creation event and evokes the deities present at that 13-Baktun shift to consecrate a local building dedication. The building's birth was anointed with a symbolic nod to the cosmos's future rebirth. That is *something!*

Did the Maya know about precession, about the galaxy? Aveni takes a scientific definition of the galaxy and says no. This is like saying ancient people didn't know about sex because they didn't know about the genetic code. He requires that they had a spiral dynamic visual concept of the galaxy on par with modern scientific models. He describes and defines the galaxy's center and midplane (equator) with scientific concepts and terms, and assumes a much greater need for precision than my theory requires. He has said that the alignment could be seen to be valid for five hundred years; ignoring the more precise dark rift and the middle range of the Milky Way's width that could indeed be extrapolated.

At one point, Aveni showed a composite photograph of our Milky Way and asserted that the nuclear bulge of the Galactic Center was not compelling at all for anyone looking up at it. He seemed to ignore the fact that the nuclear bulge region was already demonstrably significant for the ancient Maya, due to the fact that the Crossroads and the southern terminus of the dark rift are located within the bulge and play a significant role in the Creation Mythology. He also used a fairly poor photograph of the Milky Way to illustrate his point, which was quite apparent and should have insulted the intelligence of his highly intelligent audience—if they were willing to see through his ruse.

His interest in dismissing the visual significance of the Galactic Center was revealed in this ploy. In the clear night skies near the equator, the Milky Way explodes with distinction and definition, many dark cloud features are readily apparent, and the nuclear bulge looks even more like a puffy, bulging, and pregnant serpent or other animal than it does when viewed from temperate latitudes. That's why the Inca see a mother and baby llama in that area. Furthermore, Aveni did not entertain or apparently consider that the ancient Maya probably had a greater acuity of vision than do modern humans. Progressive Maya scholars such as Barbara MacLeod now see inscriptional evidence for the ancient Maya tracking Uranus, which the majority of modern people would not be able to pick out with the naked eye even if they were shown exactly where it is. The boundaries of the Milky Way, much wider in the nuclear bulge than on the opposite side of the sky, would have been obvious to them.

There are other good examples that reveal Aveni's dismissive attitude toward 2012 and 2012 authors.[61] The real clincher came at the end of his talk, in an exchange we had during the Q & A. After almost an hour, he had failed to address the most compelling first step that a rational investigator would take in examining 2012 (one that I had included in the six points I had sent to him and that he acknowledged receiving). I was surprised and disappointed, and realized I'd have to make a stand so that, at least in a thumbnail sketch, the audience members would have a chance to work with the facts of the matter.

Aveni completed his talk with a quote from Shakespeare, to the effect that we should look within for the solution to our problems, not to the stars. Eric Thompson used quotes from classical philosophers as epigrams in his books, a habit that bothered Michael Coe. I think it's nice to use thoughtful philosophical sentiments to change the pace of thought. The similarity between Aveni and Thompson, however, is more than epigram deep. It seems to me that Aveni is the new Thompson, the new gatekeeper who will always insist on more evidence and never believe you have enough.

After the applause died down, the crowd was invited to speak. I asked my question: "Well, that was a lot funnier than I thought it was going to be [*laughter*]. Apart from all the millenarian distractions, I think the most pressing question in this whole 2012 thing is: *Is the 2012 cycle ending an intentional artifact of the calendrical tradition?* And in one of your very first slides, you showed that the end date is December 21, 2012, which is an accurate December solstice. I'm surprised you didn't revisit the idea first put forward by Munro Edmonson over twenty years ago in his *Book of the Year*, where he wondered, 'Hmm, the 13-Baktun cycle ends on an accurate solstice . . . I really doubt that that's a coincidence.' So it suggests that there is some kind of intentionality built into the placement of the end date, and so how should we go about exploring how that manifests in Maya ideology and eschatology?"

> Aveni: "Yeah, I agree with that, and I have noted that they started the Long Count on, or within a day or two of, the day of zenith passage . . . John Justeson's looked at that. I don't doubt that they might have done it."

The placement of the zero date in 3114 BC on an accurate zenith passage date at a specific latitude does not require much in terms of astronomical calculation—it's simply the observation of no shadows at high noon, and it doesn't shift with precession. The end date's location on the solstice, however, implies an accurate knowledge of the tropical year, to at least an impressive several decimal places.

> JMJ: "I'm talking about the end date in 2012."
> Aveni: "I don't doubt they may have placed the end date of the cycle on the solstice. The theory that they did is that pre-Classic sites are more solstitially oriented, so there's nothing unique about Izapa, nor about its ballcourt in terms of its alignment . . ."

Izapa is the only ballcourt that points right at the December solstice sunrise, and Izapa is the only site that contains a coherent fugue of carved monuments that can be read with a high degree of comprehension as to their intended mythological and astronomical meaning. Aveni referred to a paper he wrote in 1990, which wasn't published until 2000, which he said showed how the pre-Classic period "was the beginning of the calendar." But in it he never stated that the solstice alignments of the early sites he examined made them a likely locus of the Long Count calendar's origin.[62]

> Aveni: "However, I will not, and have no desire to, take that argument any further and bring in the galaxy—that's where I totally push back, because I think this concept of what a galaxy is, is totally alien to Maya thought."

He claims that some have accused him of "dumbing down the ancestors" and admits that he is "employing an idea [of the galaxy] that comes from Western science that doesn't have anything to do with the Maya."

> JMJ: "But they were aware of the Milky Way, right?"
>
> Aveni: "Sure they were."
>
> JMJ: "Well, that's the galaxy."
>
> Aveni: "But it's not a tree . . ."
>
> JMJ: "Well, they didn't have to have the same concept of it as modern science does . . ."
>
> Aveni: "They don't, but then you start talking about the plane of the galaxy and the center of the Milky Way galaxy . . . Why do you speak about the center of the galaxy? Would they know that it was the center of the galaxy—it's perceived as a blanket of stars and gas that goes across the sky."
>
> JMJ: "Well, there's evidence that they thought about that part of the galaxy as a center because it's where the Milky Way crosses over the ecliptic, and crosses symbolize the idea of cosmic center—on thrones and in Maya cosmology in general."
>
> Aveni: "I suppose, but I don't see it as an emphatic point in the calendar; we can talk more about that outside."

As for the ancient Maya conception of the nuclear bulge of the Galactic Center as being, in fact, a center, my "Open Letter to Mayanists and Astronomers" of 1999, which I had posted on the Aztlan discussion board, presented the evidence for this concisely:

> Among the modern-day Quiché Maya, the dark-rift is called the xibalba be. *This means "road to the underworld." In the ancient Maya Creation text, the* Popol Vuh, *this same feature serves as a road to the underworld and is also called the Black Road. Associated iconography with the "underworld portal" concept includes caves, monster mouths, and birthing portals. . . . This demonstrates that the Maya understood the region of the Galactic Center as a source-point or birth place. The cross formed by the Milky Way with the ecliptic near Sagittarius has been identified at Palenque, among the Quiché and Chortí Maya, and elsewhere as the Mayan Sacred Tree. In the* Popol Vuh, *it is the Crossroads. The cross symbol, according to accepted epigraphic and iconographic interpretation (e.g., on thrones), denotes the concept of "center" and usually contextually implies a "cosmic" or "celestial" center. The concept of "cosmic center" and the principle of world-centering was important to Mesoamerican astronomers, city planners, and Maya kings—kings who symbolically occupied and ruled from the "cosmic center." Thus, the Maya, via the Sacred Tree/Cosmic Cross symbology, understood the region of the Galactic Center to be a center. Center and birthplace—understandings that are true to the Galactic Center's nature.*[63]

I had one more important point to make.

> JMJ: "Okay, but one last thing—do you think that when the Long Count was first put in place, say 2,200 years ago, did those sky-watchers have the kind of astronomical sophistication to have a really good estimate for the tropical year, because they would have had to."

Aveni: "I think that they did; they certainly could have. They were working toward an understanding of the haab (365-day year) and I think, and I've written about this in *Skywatchers of Ancient Mexico* (first edition), that they probably were aware of the slow drift or movement of the stars against the background at the horizon, although I think there's no way you can assume awareness of a 26,000-year cycle."

My own theory, in its basic form, doesn't require that they were aware of the full 26,000-year cycle. However, both MacLeod's work with the 3-11 Pik formula in the inscriptions and Michael Grofe's work on the Serpent Series provide evidence for an accurate knowledge of long-range precessional intervals. But Aveni skimmed over brief mentions of their work. They are nothing more than "a coincidence with the numerology of 72 years." He believes those intervals and dates were probably relevant as stations but "doesn't get" MacLeod's connection of those precessional stations to the base date. Okay, progress—he simply doesn't understand what MacLeod has found.

My turn was up and he went on to other audience questions. It should be pretty clear that Aveni's comments are well presented, but he didn't really offer a serious consideration of the evidence that 2012 was meaningful to the ancient Maya, and that meaning revolves around the alignment of the solstice sun with the dark rift. That's the bare-bones scenario. Perhaps a public talk is not the appropriate place for such information, although that's what the Tulane 2012 conference organizers promised.

I followed up on his invitation to speak with him "outside" on Sunday, during the break in the panel discussion session. His gregarious nature made it difficult to have a calm conversation, and he began getting upset when I talked about the unique nature of the Izapan ballcourt's alignment to the solstice horizon. He was, however, very generous in offering me the citation for the article he published on solstice alignments at Izapa and other pre-Classic sites, called "Water, Mountain, Sky."

After the conference I went to Tulane's library and found it in an obscure volume, and xeroxed it. Sure enough, he had been to Izapa in 1990 and measured the horizon orientation. He had the hard data on Izapa and other sites, and concluded that a solstice-oriented calendrical cosmology was prevalent during the pre-Classic in southern Mesoamerica. And, it should be added, these solstice-oriented sites belonged to the Isthmian cultural sphere that gave rise to the earliest Long Count dates. He stated specifically that the ballcourt was aligned to the solstice.[64] His data corresponded well with my own data and measurements.[65] It is important to now have the published measurement data to refer to, but his observation that Izapa was oriented to the solstice is, after all, implied in the maps from the Brigham Young University studies.[66] His data nevertheless lend support to my work, especially in consideration of the unique arrangement of monuments in the Izapan ballcourt.

I have said for years that scholars mistrusted my own measurements and observations at the site, and that no one seemed to have previously noted it. Aveni apparently did in 1990, but his paper wasn't published until 2000, two years after my book *Maya Cosmogenesis 2012* was published. He began his essay with a statement I really liked, which implies a sensitivity to taking into account the entire environment, including astronomy, when interpreting the conceptual factors that the ancient Maya embraced when designing their towns: "Much of Mesoamerican ceremonial architecture is interpretable as an ideological 'text' that makes manifest in the work of humankind the observed principles of cosmic order that the people acted out in their religious temples."[67] If this attitude was carefully applied to Izapa's monuments, and how they are oriented to solstices, volcanoes, and celestial features (which are indeed part of the "environment"), Aveni would see that my work is based in the same interpretive strategy that he subscribes to.

My overall experience of the conference was very positive. I can't recount all the personal discussions with the Tedlocks, Harvey Bricker, Matthew Looper, David Stuart, and other speakers; it was abuzz with intriguing and exciting ideas. Dennis Tedlock answered my correlation question in no uncertain terms with full-throttle support for the December 21 correlation, saying, "We wouldn't even be having this conversation if Lounsbury hadn't made that mistake."[68]

I met in person many students and scholars I'd not met before, including Carl Calloway, Matthew Looper, Mark Van Stone, Lloyd Anderson, John Justeson, Marguerite Paquin, Marc Zender, Allan Christiansen, and David Stuart. I was heartened by the efforts they had made to understand Maya civilization, and I realized that a great deal of progress and new discoveries have happened in the last ten years. I'd been a bit out of the loop with the new information, and realized I needed to renew my studies, and what I would find would likely lend new support for my end-date alignment theory.

This new support would come sooner than I thought. Probably the most important meeting I had at the conference was with Michael Grofe. I've mentioned that Barbara MacLeod, Michael, and I had been in e-mail and phone communication for almost a year, working out the details on a documentary concept. It now seemed clear that I had allies that were willing to entertain the possibility that the solstice 2012 placement, as well as the end-date alignment, was not a coincidence. I was impressed with Michael's PhD dissertation, in which he had courageously mentioned my work. To do this in a dissertation was probably not advisable, as my work is generally cast aside by scholars. However, he treated my ideas fairly and accurately, and offered an entire reconstruction of the Serpent Series numbers, showing precessional calculations of great accuracy. This was really good breakthrough scholarship. Other essays he sent me were equally compelling, rigorous, and insightful. Barb and Michael's open-minded attitudes have rekindled my confidence after many years of misunderstandings, plagiarism, and time-wasting debates.

Something happened after my meeting with Michael Grofe at the Tulane conference, and I began to suspect there might be another way of deciphering references to 2012. I scanned my astronomy software, looked at other dates recorded at Tortuguero, and exchanged e-mails with Michael. Together we started finding patterns, and within a few weeks a truly unsuspected vindication of my work unfolded. Beyond any sense of personal satisfaction, these new discoveries open up a greater understanding of how the ancient Maya thought about 2012, which in my view has lasting meaning for two reasons: (1) this is the best way to approach understanding 2012; (2) these results will survive all the trendy 2012 models and millennial madness. Here is what we found.

CHAPTER SEVEN

THE GALACTIC
ALIGNMENT THEORY: UPDATE

It's not a coincidence.

—BARB MACLEOD

The newest of the new discoveries emerged immediately in the wake of the Tulane conference. But they occurred on the fringes, in open-minded exchanges among Barbara MacLeod, Michael Grofe, and me. They were driven by a breakthrough in a documentary film on 2012 that I'd been collaborating on for almost three years with Warren Miller Films. In 2006, I was invited by screenwriter and project director Hans Rosenwinkel to present my work at the Warren Miller Films offices in Boulder. I gave presentations and for two years the script was worked and reworked, being recalibrated with my ongoing feedback. There was interest at *Nova* and PBS in funding the project. It seemed to be hovering in no-man's-land when Barb MacLeod e-mailed me in January of 2008 with her findings on the 3-11 Pik formula. She alerted me to the good news by her subject line: "It's not a coincidence!"

Barb's findings began with data recorded at Tikal, first noted by Matthew Looper.[1] Barb's close examination of these data revealed a consistent application of periods of time separated by 8,660 days. Usually these occurred in steps of three and were rooted in a Calendar Round position prior to the era Creation of 3114 BC. Barb next noted Nikolai Grube's realization that identical parallel dates were generated if the base date was shifted forward 11 Baktuns.[2] The three date stations occurred at 8,660-day intervals, but when combined equaled precessional steps of just under 72 years, the number of years in one degree (or day) of precessional shift. (The "circle" of Maya calculation may use 365 degrees, or days, rather than the 360 used in Western geometry.) The locations of each precessional "power station" in time were significant because of their precessional resonance with the base date, the era Creation. She calls this precessional mechanism the "3-11 Pik formula" and finds evidence for it in the inscriptions of Copán and elsewhere.[3]

Not simply an abstract mathematical operation, this calendrical and astronomical framework was utilized in rites of Maya kingship. When a king passed through one of these temporal power stations, he gained added authority and power. Kings would often pass through two power stations during their reign, but only a few would live through three. The passage represented a cosmological relationship, via precessional resonance, with the Creation event. Furthermore, these 3-11 Pik references often appear in combination with vast distance numbers and cycles of deep time. Barb's work suggests that precession was not only accurately calculated by the ancient Maya, but was used in a widespread paradigm that related kings to era-inauguration dates and the Creation mythos.

Her findings are well documented and are revolutionary in their implications. They provide support for my end-date alignment theory on two fronts. First, her theory utilizes the base date of the 13-Baktun cycle, in 3114 BC, as a reference point for its intervals. Second, the method requires an accurate estimate for the rate of precession (if not the full precessional cycle), which was built into the Long Count at the time of its inauguration. The apparent lack of accurate precessional calculations made by the ancient Maya was one of the critiques against my theory asserted by Aveni; now that critique is challenged by Barb's findings. And she is not alone in finding accurate precession calculations in the ancient Maya Long Count inscriptions.

Barb introduced me to the work of Dr. Michael Grofe, a rare Mayanist who has a deep understanding of both astronomy and epigraphy. He received his bachelor's degree from the University of Miami in 1993, his MA from the California Institute of Integral Studies, and his PhD in Native American Studies from the University of California at Davis in 2007. Michael had worked under Martha Macri and Matthew Looper as a graduate student, and he became interested in the calendrical bones from burial 116 in Tikal, including the 3-11 Pik calculation as discovered by Looper. In a 2003 research paper[4] Michael had similarly proposed that the 3-11 Pik formula suggests a precessional calculation, which later prompted his correspondence with Barb in 2008 when Looper brought Barb's paper to his attention. Barb and Michael had both reached similar conclusions independently, which says something in itself. Grofe's work on precession is amply documented in his PhD dissertation, called *The Serpent Series: Precession in the Maya Dresden Codex.* His work deduces a methodology used by the ancient Maya astronomers for calculating sidereal positions of the moon, planets, and the sun, and thus precession, using eclipses and asterisms like the Pleiades. First and foremost, Michael's pioneering work presents evidence that the Serpent Series in the Dresden Codex contains a Distance Number formula strongly suggesting that the Maya had achieved a very precise calculation of the sidereal year and the rate of precessional drift. Since then, Michael has also found epigraphic evidence in Tortuguero's 2012 text (Monument 6) and at Palenque that identifies solar and lunar alignments with the dark rift, lending a great deal of direct epigraphic support to my controversial end-date alignment theory.[5]

I quickly realized that the film documentary needed to include these breakthroughs. The script had already gone through another revision, based on conference calls incorporating Anthony Aveni's now obsolete critique[6] and other scholars as voices of reason who would cast doubt on the precessional basis of the galactic alignment theory. With the new material by MacLeod and Grofe, the film script went through yet another round of changes. Forward motion was followed by hovering.

THINGS THAT GO BUMP
IN THE DARK RIFT

After Tulane, Hans announced that a funding deal with PBS was imminent. I was called upon to be filmed, summarizing in short order the importance of my own as well as Grofe's and MacLeod's work. I thus needed to refresh my mind with their key ideas, and had two long phone calls with both of them. In setting up the call with Michael, I decided to share my plan to analyze the Long Count dates from Tortuguero, looking for precessional intervals and relevant astronomical alignments utilizing, for example, the dark rift in the Milky Way. I knew that only a small portion of the Tortuguero Monument 6 text had been translated, and I believed that it might be possible to identify secondary references to 2012 via the astronomical image-complex of the galactic alignment. Instead of finding specific 2012 date references, we might find secondary contextually meaningful references utilizing the "sun-in-dark-rift" statement. This would be similar to the known use of tripartite monuments to designate the solar zenith and the hearthstones in Orion—an astronomical image-complex that refers to Creation narratives connected to 3114 BC.[7] The inscriptions might be found to consistently reference the dark rift as an alignment locus for the sun, moon, eclipses, or planets. Dates of the sun's alignment with the dark rift during the Classic Period would be particularly compelling if they were used in meaningful ways that implicated the end date's like-in-kind alignment (albeit utilizing the *December solstice* sun).

This is where the *newest* new discoveries come into play, ones that require further study by Maya scholars. In broad outlines, they comprise what I would call smoking-gun evidence for the hypothesis I put on the table fifteen years ago—that the ancient creators of the Long Count system intended the 13-Baktun cycle end date in 2012 to target the rare alignment of the solstice sun and the dark rift. I described in Chapter 6 how Tortuguero's 2012 inscription was used to consecrate a building dedication. It was meaningful because a building (or a house) is a microcosm of the cosmos. That alone shows that 2012 had meaning for the Classic Period Maya. What follows are several equally important recent findings.

The Long Count dates and inscriptions from Tortuguero were described in Sven Gronemeyer's study of the site, and Geoff Stray had made available a PDF of the study on the Tribe 2012 website.[8] Although Sven's work was in German, one could at least track the Long Count dates and look up the astronomy. I noticed a solstice date and a 3 Kankin haab date, which is the haab date of the cycle ending in 2012, perhaps suggesting an intentional haab resonance. I also noticed that a very important Katun ending, 9.14.0.0.0, was recorded on Tortuguero Monument 2. This was intriguing because the date also occurs on Stela C from Copán. An astronomical alignment that happened on that date is conceptually analogous to the 2012 alignment.

In 2000, at Jim Reed's invitation, I published an article in the Institute of Maya Studies newsletter in which I pointed out that on the Long Count date 9.14.0.0.0 (December 3, 711 AD), the sun was positioned in the dark rift in the Milky Way. In addition, the figure on Stela C was the ruler 18 Rabbit, and he faced the eastern sunrise, where the sun with the dark rift were rising, together. He was wearing the caiman regalia, composed of two caiman jaws draped around his front and back, the upper and lower jaws of the caiman giving the appearance that he, the solar ruler, was within the jaws of the underworld monster. In other words, 18 Rabbit was posing as the sun in the dark rift, an alignment that was happening on 9.14.0.0.0.

The Stela C image is symbolically reminiscent of both Stela 25 and Stela 11 from Izapa. Stela 25 depicts a caiman whose mouth and fangs are very similar to the caiman on 18 Rabbit's regalia. Stela 11 shows the solar Ahau standing in the cosmic frog's mouth. The similar frog on Stela 6 is positioned such that a figure in a boat is sailing into or out of its open mouth. This suggests that the mouth of these cosmic frogs were portals to the underworld, analogous to the dark rift in the sky. Stela C at Copán, therefore, confirms the astronomy of the date carved on its side: The mouth of the caiman represents the dark rift in the Milky Way.

This can be stated bluntly: Copán Stela C, perhaps the most famous carving of the eighth-century Copán ruler 18 Rabbit, depicts the ruler as a solar god aligned with the dark rift in the Milky Way. Curiously, the context of the scene is transformation. That the date is also recorded at Tortuguero is intriguing. Kings at Copán and elsewhere were very interested in showing their rulership over period endings and Long Count periods. As we can see, the astronomers at both Copán and Tortuguero were aware of the concept of the sun aligning with the dark rift. The precessional shift between 711 AD and 2012 AD is 18 degrees, or "days." This may be significant because it provides a precessional shift-interval that is commensurate with 360, a key number in the Long Count. It is also 1/400th of a Katun. I shared this with Michael Grofe, and he was intrigued. A few days later, he dropped the bomb on me.

In spending a few late nights examining the astronomy connected with dates in Tortuguero's inscriptions, Michael identified a date on Monument 6 (Long Count 9.10.11.09.06) that occurred just a few days after an eclipse in late May of 644 AD. It was a total lunar eclipse, so the moon was opposite the sun, right in the dark rift. As the moon was blocked out by the earth's shadow, the outlines of the Milky Way became visible. This was a way to identify when the sidereal position of the sun would come around and likewise be aligned with the dark rift—exactly a half-year later. (The sun's alignment with the dark rift is, in fact, what is recorded and indicated with the 9.14.0.0.0 date.) In the ensuing 67 years between 644 and 711 another day or degree of precessional shift would have occurred. The link seems to indicate an interest in precessional drift.

But we haven't gotten yet to the bomb. Michael is an epigrapher, having worked for years as a grad student under Macri and Looper, compiling the new catalogue of Maya hieroglyphs and the Maya Hieroglyphic Database Project. He can read the inscriptions, and he said the text associated with the eclipse date could very well be read as an "eclipse of the moon in the celestial caiman."[9] Like Stela C from Copán, it indicates that the dark rift was envisioned as a portal into the celestial caiman! Michael also pointed out that there are crossed bands in the eyes of the caiman glyph, significant as a symbol for the cross formed by the Milky Way and the ecliptic (which targets the southern terminus of the dark rift). I e-mailed him back with the further observation that the next date in the hieroglyphic corpus from Tortuguero, the Tun ending from Jade Celt 1, was 174 days after the eclipse text—the eclipse half-year period, indicating when the next eclipse was likely to occur.

THE KING AND THE DARK RIFT

Michael responded that evening with a report that he had just completed a thorough examination of the text on Monument 6 and couldn't believe what he had found. He said he was tracking the events in the life of Balam Ajaw, the king who ruled when Monument 6 was dedicated. It was apparent that the king had a special relationship with Bolon Yokte, the deity who appears on the 2012 date and has transformation and warring attributes. Balam Ajaw was somewhat of an aggressive reformer, transforming his kingdom through waging wars on neighboring kingdoms. These kinds of rulers typically saw themselves as following a divine mandate, blessed by the culture heroes and creation deities. In the same way that Pakal, the king of Palenque, and 18 Rabbit, the king of Copán, created propaganda monuments that placed them into mythic narratives with cosmological Creation events, Balam Ajaw claimed Bolon Yokte as his totem and 2012 as his cosmological mandate. He, too, would create a new world, a new kingdom, through the auspices of his tutelary creation deity. In the same way that 2012 could be called upon to consecrate a house or building dedication, it could also be invoked to confer blessings and legitimacy on a *royal* house.

This scenario makes sense, but what Michael found really nails it to the wall: Balam Ajaw was born between November 28 and December 8, 612 AD (one of the dot-and-bar sections is eroded), with the probability being for December 3. This means, importantly, that he was born when the sun was precisely in the dark rift. These hierophanies did not go unnoticed in the Maya world. Wars were timed with Venus movements, eclipses had their auguries, and we've already seen that the dark rift was depicted in the iconography in specific ways involving birth and transformation themes. Balam Ajaw's birth, and therefore his identity, was seen to have a special connection with the Creation events—not those of 3114 BC as at Quiriguá and Copán, but those of the future cosmogenesis event, in 2012. That sounds reasonable enough, but the smoking gun lies in recognizing the only reason why this would be so. And that is because the astronomical configuration of his birth was analogous to *what they knew* would be happening in 2012: the solstice sun in the dark rift. The key that makes the 2012 scenario unique is that it involves the solstice sun, but the parallelism was clearly compelling enough for Balam Ajaw to claim a special relationship with 2012 and the deity connected with it, Bolon Yokte Ku.

Michael found further support for the above precessional calculation elsewhere in the text from Tortuguero Monument 6, which mentions another date on an exact winter solstice on 9.10.17.02.14, as well as another pair of dates separated by 137 years, 9.03.16.01.11 and 9.10.15.01.11, which place the sun in the exact same sidereal position, while the tropical year has shifted by two days.

Dr. Aveni, in his talk at Tulane, said there was no evidence that the Maya made forward projections in their calendrical calculations and rituals. This is abundantly untrue, the best example being how Pakal, the king of Palenque, noted a special connection he had with a 20-Baktun cycle ending, one that comes to pass in the forty-eighth century AD. He found it useful, as a political stratagem, because it just so happened that the date of his own coronation (his ritual birthing as king) fell on the same day in the solar year that this far-future cycle ending will fall on. He, like his contemporary Balam Ajaw, cast himself into the narrative of creation to increase his status in the eyes of his subjects. Both used their own "birth" event as a connection point to the cosmological birth of a large period-ending, understood to be a World Age birth. He may have done this as a copycat to what Balam Ajaw did, also perhaps one-upping the Tortuguero king by using a larger cycle of 20 Baktuns.

It Happened at the Black Hole

The king of Copán, 18 Rabbit, did something a little different with the dark rift. After showing himself on 9.14.0.0.0 as the sun-king in the dark rift, he erected a series of stelae in the great plaza of Copán. His Maya name, Waxaklahun Ub'ah K'awil, references the deity K'awil. In the many inscriptions he recorded, he honored a ritual involving K'awil performed by one of his lineage ancestors on a Baktun ending, 9.0.0.0.0. Other inscriptions infer that he likewise wished to claim the next Baktun ending, in 830 AD, as his own. Since he ruled in the early eighth century, that would be too far off for him to live through, but he nevertheless needed to relate himself to cycle endings and their attendant creation imagery. His entire corpus of inscriptions, building dedications, and activities are astounding and require thorough investigation.[10] What follows provides more evidence for the role of the dark rift in transformational creation imagery, with a special focus on the motif of sacrifice that the Maya believed was necessary at cycle endings.

Waxaklahun Ub'ah K'awil's namesake, K'awil, is the deity associated with God K and the planet Jupiter. Helen Alexander writes that God K "is the power behind conjuring, transformation, and transcendence in Maya ritual practice; he is the essence of the *och chan*, the bearded dragon of *Xibalba*; he is the essence of the sacred dance that empowers the Maize God to dance out of *Xibalba*; he is the essence of human royal power that allows mankind access to the cosmos from the heavens down to earth and into *Xibalba* itself."[11] A strange event brought this king's forty-three-year reign to a sudden, perplexing close. In 738 AD, just after he made the final dedication on his new ballcourt complex at Copán, he was captured by K'ak Tiliw, the king of nearby Quiriguá, and held prisoner. No resistance, no Copán militia was sent to rescue him. On the solar zenith passage day, May 1, he was marched into the Quiriguá plaza and decapitated. This ritual sacrifice was reminiscent of the beheading of One Hunahpu by the lords of the underworld in *The Popol Vuh*. The event is recorded in four surviving inscriptions at Quiriguá and Copán. The most official report, from Quiriguá Stela F, reads: "He is decapitated, Waxaklahun Ub'ah K'awil; under the supervision of K'ak Tiliw, it happened at the Black Hole place."[12] The black hole? Years ago, in a review-essay I wrote on place-names and Maya Creation Texts, I concluded that the hiero-

Hieroglyphic text from Quiriguá Stela F describing Waxaklahun Ub'ah K'awil's decapitation and apotheosis at "the black hole," when Jupiter was aligned with the dark rift in the Milky Way on May 1, 738 AD. Drawing by the author

glyph translated as "black hole" probably represented the dark rift in the Milky Way.[13] So I suspected that something relevant happened in the dark rift on the day of his decapitation. Looking at astronomy software, there it was, the 'most appropriate possible astronomical configuration one could imagine: Jupiter was perfectly aligned with the dark rift. Waxaklahun Ub'ah K'awil's head, Jupiter, the dark rift, transformation, sacrifice, Creation Myth themes, are all wrapped up in this event.

Most strikingly, because of the odd circumstances of this important event in Maya history, namely its providential timing, we must entertain the possibility that the Copán King went willingly into the black hole and his sacrificer was accomplice to a historically enacted mystery play. Waxaklahun Ub'ah K'awil's apotheosis ensured his legacy by laying him to rest in the heart of heaven. We think of the Passion of the Christ as a mystery play full of drama and theological significance. These events at Copán may have had a similar powerful purpose and meaning for the ancient Maya. If Jesus could willingly go to the cross, Waxaklahun Ub'ah K'awil could willingly drop his head into the dark rift. As we can see, calendrical inscriptions indict meaningful astronomical configurations intimately involved with the end-date alignment theory.

DARK-RIFT GLYPHS

The "black hole" glyph can clearly be identified with the dark rift. The controversial half-eroded glyph next to the Tortuguero 2012 inscription is identified, with fair confidence, as containing a "black" element. Scholars, such as Susan Milbrath, believe that the dark rift is associated with skeletal maw imagery.[14] The Black Hole glyph, for example, is miniature shorthand for skeletal jaws, also sometimes identified as incised bones. An entire range of hieroglyphs can now be suspected as being related to the dark rift and the nuclear bulge of the Galactic Center (see cloud center glyphs, page 274).[15] These are found in meaningful ballgame contexts and in relation to other monuments dated 9.14.0.0.0 (sun in dark-rift date) at Tikal, Calakmul, and Dos Pilas.

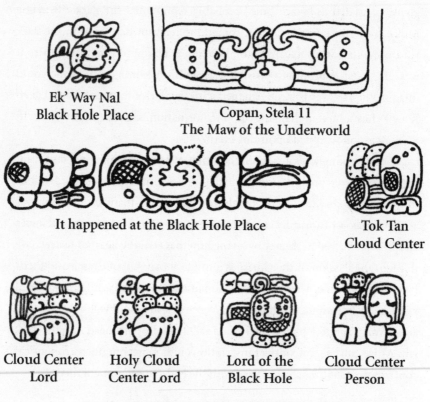

Ek' Way Nal
Black Hole Place

Copan, Stela 11
The Maw of the Underworld

It happened at the Black Hole Place

Tok Tan
Cloud Center

Cloud Center
Lord

Holy Cloud
Center Lord

Lord of the
Black Hole

Cloud Center
Person

Portals to the Underworld and the Cloud Center Place.
Drawing by the author

Yaxchilán provides a special example for a probable dark-rift association in its place-name, *Pa' Chan*. Translated as "broken sky" or "sky cleft," epigraphers think it represents jagged mountains along the horizon or refers to the fact that Yaxchilán is situated in a dramatic hairpin loop of the Usumacinta River. It is recognized that Yaxchilán is just about halfway between the source and mouth of the Usumacinta River, placing it in its "middle." This great riverine highway of temple sites flows roughly north-south. In many places in Indian America and in fact around the world, rivers were seen as earthly counterparts to the celestial river, the Milky Way. The sacred Urubamba in Peru, the river flowing through Rabinal in highland Guatemala, and the great

Ganges in India are just a few examples. It would be surprising if the Usumacinta did not have this meaning for the Maya. In this context, Yaxchilán's location in a hairpin coil of the earthly Milky Way is reminiscent of the dark rift's situation between two white branches of the Milky Way. Since the dark rift's mythological meanings include hole, cave, cleft, portal, road, birthplace, and maw, to say it could be thought of as a "sky cleft" is not at all far-fetched. Could this be the meaning of Yaxchilán's hieroglyphic place-name? Maybe. It sounds more reasonable, given these considerations, than its representing jagged peaks along the horizon.[16]

The dark rift was a significant reference point in so many different meaningful contexts it boggles the mind. When the sun, moon, eclipses, Jupiter, or other planets aligned with it, Creation imagery occurring at cycle endings, building dedications, transcendence and transformation, death and rebirth were evoked. I suspect that other inscriptions will yield secondary references to 2012 via the astronomical image-complex of "sun in dark rift." The epigraphic code for this will probably involve the many dark-rift glyphs combined with a "sun" infix or prefix. I argued in earlier work that the upturned frog-mouth glyph (which means "to be born") relates to the dark rift. Significantly, it is prominent in the iconography at Izapa and is found in its later hieroglyphic forms in Classic Period inscriptions.

We shouldn't forget that this new evidence augments my previous work, which argues

QUIRIGUÁ, STELA F

The Black Hole event,
end of 13 Baktuns

Tikal Stela 16
9.14.0.0.0 ended at the First Maw
Hole (the portal to the underworld)

The Black Hole Place in Maya inscriptions.
Drawings by the author

for the end-date alignment being encoded into ballgame symbolism, the Creation Myth, birthing symbology, and king-making rites. The "integrative continuity" of the entire picture virtually eliminates the possibility that all of these connections are pure chance. This work may perhaps find its best ally in good old-fashioned common sense: "Given the integrative continuity of its monuments, sculptures, calendrics, and alignments, is it possible that Izapa *does not* have anything to do with the precessional convergence of Milky Way and solstice sun?"[17] Thankfully, Barb MacLeod herself said the obvious: "It's not a coincidence."

Michael, Barb, and I continue to collaborate on various investigations relating to precessional astronomy. I am learning to decipher the hieroglyphic inscriptions, which I had previously left to others. The findings of other scholars are starting to converge, adding more support to my end-date alignment theory. It doesn't matter whether or not the alignment directly causes some kind of change or transformation. That never was central to my work, although by route of coincidence or providence the unprecedented events occurring in today's world are undeniable. The galactic cosmology I identified at the heart of the Maya Long Count can now be shown to be more deeply interwoven into core Maya traditions, important historical rulers and astro-theological rites than I ever dreamed it would be. The dark rift, the womb of creation, the sun's sacrifice and rebirth at the end of the cycle, has meaning in direct proportion to the depth that you meditate on it. For me, it is enough to know that such a beautiful vision once existed and has now been pulled out of the shadows.

The entire history of the 2012 story in Part I, from the rediscovery of a lost civilization to the vicissitudes of reconstructing lost pieces of a massive cosmological and cultural puzzle, to appropriations by New Age inventors and the endless resistances of academic gatekeepers, has led us to the cusp of 2012 and we are now seeing ancient Maya cosmology for what it truly was. Its ultimate orientational nexus was the rare galactic alignment. However one wants to limit the fact of this by paring down the definition, that nuts-and-bolts fact remains. This is the bare-bones conclusion: A precession-based galactic cosmology was pioneered in ancient Mesoamerica more than 2,000 years ago.

Now we have to attend to the Big Picture and the real interesting 2012 question: *What does it mean?*

PART TWO

2012 AND

THE BIG PICTURE

Temples at Waxactun, Guatemala.
Photo by the author, 2008

PART TWO. INTRODUCTION

Mental facts do function both singly and together, at once, and we finite minds may simultaneously be coconscious with one another in a superhuman intelligence.[1]

—WILLIAM JAMES, *A Pluralistic Universe*

In Part I we surveyed the 2012 story from several different angles. We addressed the Eurocentric Western world's discovery of Maya civilization, its often denigrating judgments as well as its efforts to reconstruct forgotten traditions, including the Long Count calendar. We addressed the accelerating popular appropriation of 2012 and surveyed the claims of the most prominent model makers, systems designers, doomsayers, and New Age writers. We took a concise look at my own effort to investigate 2012 and reconstruct buried ideas and a lost galactic cosmology. We summarized what some of the modern Maya themselves say about 2012, and will explore contemporary Maya views in greater detail in Chapter 11. We took a look at the media, a barometer for collective hysteria and misconceptions that also tends to feed fear-based marketing exploitation. We gave a fair hearing to scholarly critics of my theory and other ideas that have been attached to 2012, and heard a revealing account of the first academic 2012 conference, held at Tulane University in February 2009. Finally, the latest breakthroughs in understanding how the ancient Maya thought about 2012 were announced, including new information on Tortuguero, Copán, and the link between sacrifice and renewal in Maya thought.

And where do we stand as of mid-2009? At first glance, it seems we are essentially where we were ten years ago, twenty years ago, or thirty years ago. The majority of scholars do not believe that anything relevant to ancient Maya beliefs can be found in this date. Likewise, skeptical pundits in pop culture dismiss 2012 wholesale as a "hoax" or "100 percent garbage." My work, which has offered a rational investigation of 2012 with an eye to re-constructing original beliefs connected with it, is ignored, co-opted, distorted, or dismissed. Twenty years, however, is a short time when it comes to acknowledging new discoveries that threaten the fundamental assumptions of Western culture. In Chapter 8, and all of Part II generally, we'll explore these fundamental assumptions and compare and contrast them to the alternative—perennial wisdom that many civilizations, including the Maya, have taken for granted.

Acknowledging threatening ideas can take decades. Usually the pioneers who pestered the status quo die in poverty, forgotten. Many of the trouble-makers that modern science honors as trailblazers (Kepler and Galileo among many) were kicked into the gutter by the leaders of their day. After the mere formality of acknowledging unwelcome information comes accepting their merit and then integrating what they offer. In this light, 2012 is definitely not just about one day in 2012; it is about a sea change that probably won't bear fruit for many decades. But I believe that 2012 could be seen by future histo-rians as a temporal marker of a great renaissance that will raise a submerged continent of consciousness that has been suppressed by Western science and culture.

With the historical survey of Part I bringing us up to the cusp of 2012, how can we quickly summarize the current state of 2012ology? Generally, popular writers are largely underinformed on the details of Maya traditions. The latest pop manifestations of the 2012 meme—in movies, novels, and cosmic models—have basically cut themselves loose from any obligation to reference Maya tradition at all. Or if they do, they propagate stereotypes and clichés. Systems designers craft their own idiosyncratic models based on catchy marketplace ideas such as fractal time or natural time or spiritual wave-time, thereby creating cut-and-paste syncretic schools in the same way that theosophy and anthroposophy did, diluting the great teachings of the ancient Orient. On another front, the doomsday theories, as Geoff Stray pointed out in his detailed analysis of virtually every doomsday theory, are not based in facts and are internally inconsistent, irrational, and/or inaccurate. Meanwhile, scholars up until very recently have failed to address 2012 as a valid artifact of Maya tradition worthy of investigating in a rational way and instead have reactively responded to the silliest assertions in the popular marketplace. As a result, scholars and New Agers are basically locked in a staring contest, both failing to see the thing-in-itself.

New Agers largely indulge in irrational assertions. By irrational I don't mean to minimize feeling and intuition, but intuition guided by higher wisdom needs to be discerned from mere personal feelings and opinionated preferences. Scholars, too, indulge in irrational dismissals of evidence at hand, or refuse to engage in rational deductions that threaten their beliefs. As we saw in Chapter 4, a rational investigation leads to the evidence with which we can offer a reconstruction of the nuts and bolts of a lost Maya cosmology attached to the astronomy of 2012. But most scholars, as well as most New Agers, have seen little value in this, or distrust it without understanding it.

A breakthrough is needed. As we explored earlier, breakthroughs require a shift in consciousness. I believe that a rational analysis of the evidence can result in a compelling and accurate reconstruction of ancient Maya cosmology. That's what I've offered in my work. Beyond that reconstruction, a deeper understanding of the 2012 material is possible, but it requires a shift in consciousness to a more inclusive perspective. I earlier described three levels of approach to understanding cultural ideas and traditions, especially the complex and deep material connected to the Maya calendar: nuts-and-bolts reconstruction, investigation of underlying universal symbols, and direct experience of the universal principles thereby identified. We've already covered Level I, and now we are going to open it up to Level II.

At this stage we are still within the realm of objective investigation. Beyond this rational investigation we will find in Chapter 12 not another irrational level, but a transrational level. The transrational level of consciousness includes rational processing. It can do rational processing; in fact, it has *perfected* the art and faculty of ratiocination and has moved beyond it to an integrative and synthesizing faculty, which is called in various philosophical traditions the *intellectus*, the *noetic* faculty, or the *buddhi* mind. All of these terms relate to an inner faculty that each human being has, one that allows a direct perception of the essence underlying manifest reality. This is a perspective that revives the "big picture" in order to integrate the microcosm and the macrocosm, physics and spiritual science (metaphysics).

For now, we need to hang out with the second level for a while, the level at which we rationally investigate the universal content of Maya philosophy. This angle of approach has been neglected. We've been assuming that the Maya material is completely culturally relative and we should only approach it objectively. This approach is not fully satisfying. The important questions are: Does 2012 mean anything for us? Why should we expect it to? Does the 2012 material have any value for us today? We might reconstruct a galactic alignment cosmology encoded by the ancient Maya into their calendar, but so what? And what of their beliefs about cycle endings, such as the one in 2012? Can we find anything in their traditions that speaks to us directly as human beings, that provides a "prophecy" or "insight" for 2012? And if we do, why should we believe it is accurate and has meaning? These questions are really what drive New Age pop writers, but we've observed that instead of going deeper into the perennial wisdom, or Perennial Philosophy, that underlies Maya teachings, they invent syncretic new systems and models, or indulge in irrational self-aggrandizing fantasies. This is clearly the wrong approach. Their desire to tap into something deeper, something meaningful to all human beings, is laudable, but they've been going about it the wrong way.

The first aspect of the fulfillment of the Maya prophecy is covered in Chapters 9 and 10, with surprising results: The Maya prophecy has come true! But that's just the first part of the Maya prophecy. Our reconnection with the big picture is the second part of the fulfillment of "the Maya prophecy for cycle endings," which will be explored in Chapter 12. Today, many self-styled prophets assert "what's going to happen" in definite terms, saying "this will" take place and "that will" occur. I call them *predictators*. In my discussion of Maya prophecy we will see that prophecy isn't intended to dictate predetermined events. The deeper symbolic content will be addressed, one that allows for and empowers free-will choice. This is how we can pierce into the heart of the inner meaning of these teachings. A deeper vision and a bigger context is necessary.

I've always been interested in these deeper questions, and I believe that Maya cosmology opens a door into profound insights—insights into science and spirituality that should be meaningful to any human being, but especially so now as we approach 2012. To state it bluntly, the Maya seem to have understood the nature of cycles, integrating celestial cycles with cycles of culture and consciousness here on earth. They achieved a profound metaphysical understanding of life and understood why and how era-2012 would signal a time of great change. This is my belief, an unavoidable conclusion from having been immersed in academic research while being sensitive to the universal, or archetypal, content of the Maya material. Part II will explain what I mean by this. We'll explore the bigger picture of 2012, the profound implications for our modern world in crisis, and why Maya wisdom teachings speak to what modern civilization is experiencing.

Most books that covered the material I did in Part I—the approach of an objective survey—would not dare venture into this area, the domain of "soft" science, comparative mythology and philosophy, and something barely talked about in academic circles, except among a small cabal of brilliant and underappreciated philosophers. It's rarely discussed in the universities, is outside the box of progressive West Coast experimental colleges, and has been smothered by personality-driven gimmicks in the spiritual marketplace. That is the Perennial Philosophy, also known as the Primordial Tradition. It is about time this framework of understanding is embraced, as it helps us understand so much of what 2012 means in the larger sense.

My investigation of the larger perennial context of the Maya's teachings for cycle ending (for 2012) has nothing to do with Atlantean New Age fantasy. Those who believe so are distracted by their own issues and projections and ignore what I'm actually saying. This work isn't some kind of theosophical assertion hinging on faith, but an identification of the archetypal and perennial content of Maya spiritual teachings. Ironically, scholars themselves often skirt the fringes of languaging a universal level within Maya teachings, but use abstract and clinical terminology—as if speaking gingerly about it will make it less objectionable. Even so, if this area of my interest be deemed irrelevant by scholars, it shouldn't interfere with my breakthrough work on the 2012 alignment, which received a long-awaited, late-breaking boost from, of all places, academia itself.

The Big Picture is thus an integration of the objective and subjective approaches. This book is really a two-fer, a two-for-one offering that embraces and shows the intimate interrelationship between subjective experience and objective analysis, between science and spirituality. Why is this relevant? Because when these two domains are forcibly kept apart, the result is the crisis of the modern world. And when our consciousness allows them to integrate, the pathway through to a sustainable future opens.

> When you see a pearl on the bottom,
> you reach through the foam and broken sticks on the surface.
> When the sun comes up,
> you forget about locating the constellation of Scorpio.
>
> When you see the splendor of union,
> the attractions of duality seem poignant and lovely,
> but much less interesting.[2]
>
> —Rumi, "Sheba's Throne"

CHAPTER EIGHT

SACRED SCIENCE AND PERENNIAL PHILOSOPHY

> *I want to speak about one of the basic laws of*
> *Mount Analog. To reach the summit, one must*
> *proceed from encampment to encampment. But*
> *before setting out for the next refuge, one must*
> *prepare those coming after to occupy the place one is*
> *leaving. Only after having prepared them can one go*
> *on up. That is why, before setting out for a new*
> *refuge, we first had to go back down in order to pass*
> *on our knowledge to other seekers.*[1]
>
> —RENÉ DAUMAL, *Mount Analog*

This is where we turn everything upside down, so let me start with the conclusion to this chapter: *The essential spiritual teachings within the Maya Long Count calendar belong to a universal Perennial Philosophy.* This conclusion will seem, especially to Maya scholars unconcerned with cultural comparisons, like an unwarranted step toward a New Age interpretation of Maya tradition. It's not. There are plenty of statements by Maya scholars that suggest the same thing. Maya archaeo-astronomer John Carlson, for example, compared the Mesoamerican tradition of fourfold city planning oriented to celestial coordinates to similar practices in Asia.[2] That's a tangible example; in regard to ideological parallels scholars usually do not utilize appropriate terminology from the interdisciplinary field of comparative mythology that allows us to state the connections bluntly.

Joseph Campbell's archetypal mythos would be helpful here. In this regard, the Maya king's voluntary sacrifice in bloodletting rites is symbolically parallel to a Minoan king's willingly acquiescing to his own sacrifice at the end of his reign.

James Frazer wrote of these royal rites of "putting the king to death" when the king's powers began to fail or when his appointed tour of duty was complete.[3] His season of rule was seen to reflect the natural seasons of change, and the king selflessly acknowledged the high truth that death and life go together. His sacrifice would ensure the continued prosperity of the kingdom that he had served. Clearly, this distant Old World paradigm parallels Maya cosmovision—not by route of ancient boats circling the globe, but via a shared human psychology, what we could call a "higher common factor" of truth from which all ancient cultures drew their sacred teachings. I suspect scholars tend to dance around directly admitting a universal ur-mythos for precisely the reason stated above, that it sounds like a New Age generalization. Succumbing to this tendency does not, however, do justice to Maya tradition that partakes of, in its essence, the same great spiritual wisdom that animates the core of all of the world's religious traditions. For scholars, identifying differences is more defining than seeing parallels; the academic categorizing reflex is built upon distinctions, which automatically tend to whitewash any sense of "universally shared" ideas.

The problem is that exoteric forms of religion (and scholarship) conceal, to the uninitiated eye, the esoteric principles that religions and cultures universally share. For example, the Long Count calendar expresses a World Age doctrine, a fundamental doctrine of all cultures that have adopted a cyclic time philosophy (which covers virtually every cultural tradition save one—the Judeo-Christian). The 13-Baktun cycle ending is a period ending, and there are other smaller period endings within the Long Count calendar. The Maya perceived these period endings as being connected to astronomical cycles, big and small, as well as the life cycles of royal lineages (sometimes running upward of twenty generations of dynastic successions) and the overall life cycle of city-states. With the fall of the Classic Maya civilization around the Baktun 10 period ending (830 AD), some scholars suspect that Maya civilization rose and fell according to a life cycle based on their Long Count calendar. The 13-Baktun period endings, in 3114 BC and 2012 AD, would obviously have been incredibly important for the ancient Maya, the alpha and omega of a grand cycle of human and celestial unveiling.

What did the Maya teach about period endings? What did they do at period endings? Following a cyclic time philosophy, they saw period endings not as final ends, as a linear time philosophy would, but as times of transformation and renewal. The inscriptions are filled with period-ending rites involving sacrifice and transformation. Even today, the modern Maya do ceremonies at cycle endings within the tzolkin-haab calendar. The role of human beings during such times is to consciously facilitate a successful transformation and renewal by willingly sacrificing the dross of the old cycle, sacrificing the illusions that will not be useful in the new cycle. They invoke the day-sign deity of the next cycle, feeding it with prayer and incense, while the old day-sign, ruler of the passing zeitgeist, undergoes a metamorphosis. Fire ceremony has always been the quintessential medium for sacrifice and transformation.

The spiritual teachings for Long Count cycle endings are thus easy to identify, and can be stated as a three-part process: sacrifice, transformation, and renewal. The Maya shaman facilitates the transformation in the role of Sacrificer. On a deep symbolic level he is also the Sacrificed, for his effectiveness is contingent upon his ability to set aside his personal ego so he can be a conduit for a higher purpose. The process is one of individual spiritual transformation in service to a larger analogical transformation of humanity and culture. Change springs from within, beginning with the free-will act of sacrifice made by the individual. These ideas of spiritual transformation at the end of a cycle can be identified at the core of all of the world's great religious traditions. Whether it be located at the end of a cycle of time or the end of a mortal life, the decision to relinquish illusion defines the future state of the individual soul and the world at large. Notice here that free-will choice is a key.

The intent of these traditions is to initiate the spiritual seeker into a higher level of being, a state of unified consciousness. Attachment to limitations is what gets sacrificed and transformed, recentering the being on a new identity locus, one that is timeless and eternal, rooted in the Divine Ground of all manifestation. Huston Smith in his books *The Primordial Tradition* and *The Religions of Man*, Aldous Huxley in his book *The Perennial Philosophy*, Alan Watts in his book *The Supreme Identity*, Joseph Campbell in his *Hero with a Thousand Faces* and in his four-volume *Masks of God* series—to name just a few of the better-known scholars—identify Buddhism, Hinduism, Islam, Confucianism, and Christianity as having this transformational intent at their cores. They all belong to what is referred to as the Perennial Philosophy. It's about time that we nominate the Maya for admittance into the Perennial Philosophy, as their tradition not only possesses all the hallmarks of this perennial vision but also provides an astro-theological piece that has been buried in the other traditions and has remained, until now, shrouded.

What Is the Perennial Philosophy?

In 1946, philosopher and novelist Aldous Huxley wrote a brief introduction to a new translation of the Hindu sacred text the Bhagavad Gita. The way he framed it, as an expression of universal wisdom, doesn't seem that surprising to us today, but at the time it was a radical notion. In four doctrinal points that he called "the Perennial Philosophy in its minimal and basic form," he elucidated the underlying reality of a universally relevant framework of "first principles" that inform all spiritual traditions at their deepest core.[4] His point was that the ideas contained within the Bhagavad Gita, properly understood in their archetypal and symbolic context, were expressions of that perennial wisdom.

Regarding symbolism, a symbol is not a sign in the same way that myth is not a lie. Ananda Coomaraswamy, art historian and philosopher, wrote:

> *Symbolism is a language and a precise form of thought; a hieratic and*
> *metaphysical language and not a language determined by somatic or*
> *psychological categories . . . symbolism can be defined as the represen-*
> *tation of reality on a certain level of reference by a corresponding*
> *reality on another . . . traditional symbols are the technical terms of*
> *a language that transcends all confusion of tongues and are not pecu-*
> *liar to any one time and place. Indeed, they are the language of the*
> *philosophia perennis.*[5]

This understanding of symbolism opens up for the rational mind a whole new way of thinking about the reality of ancient myth, archetypal psychology, dreams, and visions. And luckily, an entire cadre of intelligent thinkers have talked about it. Seyyed Hossein Nasr, for example, simplified Coomaraswamy's intent when he wrote, "The symbol is the revelation of a higher order of reality in a lower order through which man can be led back to the higher sphere."[6]

In this light, the Bhagavad Gita was, to Huxley, a sacred text that had something of great symbolic significance to say to modern people. Let's remind ourselves of the ingrained sentiments toward Hinduism that were still in vogue when Huxley was writing this in the late 1940s. First of all, prejudicial Americans were likely to conflate Hinduism with the "Japs" who had just dropped bombs on Pearl Harbor. Second, scholars of religious history were still prone to think of Hinduism as a polytheistic animism filled with superstitions, certainly not a tradition that shared any wisdom with Christianity. Yet Huxley's point was precisely this, that Hinduism, Buddhism, Islam, and Christianity all share a "Highest Common Factor."[7] But in order to see this, you must pierce into the esoteric core of the tradition, beyond the exoteric cultural veils of dogma. The symbolic narrative of myth, although utilizing culture-specific deity names and scenarios, points beyond itself to an underlying (or "higher") reservoir of gnosis. Here are Huxley's four definitive points of the Perennial Philosophy, through which all these traditions are linked:

1. The phenomenal world of matter, things, and individualized consciousness are temporary manifestations of an underlying Divine Ground, which is unconditioned, unquantified, infinite, and eternal. All partial realities within the manifest world of form take their being from this Ground, without which they would be nonexistent.

2. Human beings, limited within the state of individualized consciousness (ego consciousness), can deduce that such a Ground exists through rational inference, but it requires a shift of consciousness to directly experience its existence through a direct intuition, or gnosis, that is superior to discursive reasoning. This immediate, nondual awareness is known to mystics throughout the world as a union of the knower with the known.

3. The glimpse of this ultimate center and source of all manifestation is accessible to all human beings and places the limited ego consciousness into correct relationship with the unlimited Divine Self. Each human being possesses this double nature, "a phenomenal ego and an eternal Self."[8]

4. The highest spiritual purpose and most fully actualized potential of each human being is to realize that the limited ego is a temporary extension of the eternal Divine Self. What should naturally follow from this realization is the organization of life and human culture around this truth, with decisions and goals being made in deference to this unitary, whole-consciousness perspective.

The Perennial Philosophy, the essence of all the multifarious variations on enlightenment, shamanism, religion, and spiritual awakening, cannot be made more succinct and clear. The early appearance of Huxley's words, some sixty years ago, renders moot 90 percent of the subsequent New Age blathering on spiritual transformation. It's just window dressing. Huxley's definitive book *The Perennial Philosophy* appeared in 1945 and established what should have been a central reference point for everything that came later in the human potential movement. Some writers and teachers did pay homage to the Perennial Philosophy, but many did not. It is said that Western philosophy is a series of footnotes to Plato. Likewise, and more lamentably, the New Age movement is largely a series of increasingly bad paraphrasings of Huxley. In fact, since the spiritual marketplace is today driven by personality, the cult of ego, we can observe that Huxley's clear exposition of the Perennial Philosophy has not only been forgotten but inverted. Instead of meeting the challenge of transformation via self-sacrifice, transcending the ego and awakening the higher wisdom, we flock en masse to see the latest Oprah-approved spiritual entertainer at the local megaplex Event Center.

Nevertheless, throughout the 1950s other standout books appeared that complemented Huxley's early exposition on the Perennial Philosophy. One of great significance was *The Supreme Identity* by Alan Watts. In his foreword he thanks both Coomaraswamy and French philosopher René Guénon for their work on reviving the Perennial Philosophy. I consider myself lucky to have stumbled across a used paperback of this book at a bookstore in the early days of my quest for knowledge. The Chicago suburbs in 1980 was not exactly a place where you'd expect the perennial wisdom to be found, let alone take root. But by age sixteen I'd already exhausted readings in science, having had my inner Carl Sagan soundly trounced by Fritjof Capra's *Tao of Physics*. I then began reading of inner realities via Carl Jung and Joseph Campbell, so I was well-primed when Watts's *Supreme Identity* leapt off the bookshelf at me. That was the best $1.50 I've ever spent.

The great nondual principle of Vedanta was instilled in me at the time, with all its multifarious ramifications. My own soul was rooted in the world soul. The inner depth-psychology worlds within me were reflected in the outer appearance of nature, including earth processes and astronomical cycles. Symbols were not "signs" but doorways to higher consciousness; entire sets of data were linked in ways not apparent to linear processing. Matter emerged from spirit. Consciousness was not, as Darwinian evolution required, an "epiphenomenon" of material combinations, something that

294 THE 2012 STORY

popped out of matter. The subjective and the objective were one in a higher space, a higher state of consciousness that could be directly glimpsed. And at age seventeen, it was; my mind and heart were opened. The conclusions generated through empirical science were of a lower order of reality in comparison to *knowing* in this direct unitary sense. Real understanding could be gained only by looking within. By age eighteen I was a meditating vegetarian doing yoga daily—all things that Midwest suburbia circa 1982 didn't take kindly to. As for college, I did not, as Mark Twain said, want it to interfere with my education.

In the so-called progressive colleges today, the Perennial Philosophy is not well represented. The evolutionary spirituality of Jesuit scientist and philosopher Teilhard de Chardin has taken center stage. The lingo of quantum physics has been creatively mapped onto Oriental metaphysics in a syncretism as problematic as Madame Blavatsky's newfangled ancient theosophy. Buzzwords are trademarked as the proprietary New Thing in the hopes of shelf-life stamina and surefire profits. New designer systems promising the integration of science and spirituality put the cart before the horse: Instead of integrating the more limited approach of physics into the larger framework of metaphysics, it appropriates the higher truths of ancient mysticism as the latest findings of science. For example, unlike Fritjof Capra's groundbreaking *Tao of Physics*, the recent *What the Bleep!* movie neglected to identify its quantum conundrums as the highest truths of ancient nondual Oriental mysticism. Similarly, efforts are made in the marketplace to simplify, rename, and dumb down the profound truths of ancient metaphysics to fit into the narrow confines of modern consciousness and scientific boxes, when the whole point is to help enlarge consciousness to directly perceive those profound integrative truths. The tacit mandate that authors are supposed to follow, to write to a third-grade reading level, is never once indicted for creating and reinforcing that level!

Why is this important? And why is the Perennial Philosophy discarded or scoffed at? It's important because it identifies the underlying cause of the crisis of the modern world, and it's scoffed at because modern consciousness is held prisoner by the values of self-serving egoism. Modern consciousness has been flattened into a superficial and materialistic plane which perceives only that narrow domain. There is no depth, there is no vertical transcendence, there is no higher perspective. Such terminology is virtually heretical in the secularized discourse on politics, psychology, sociology, and even religion. Especially religion. Only in marginalized corners of the discourse on human transformation, and notably among Traditionalists (students of the Perennial Philosophy), have these perspectives been kept alive, but they are always in danger of being commodified and subsumed into consumerist culture. (When will the Coomaraswamy action figures appear?) If embraced, they are popularized and diluted, rendered trendy and impotent by the spiritual marketplace.

Traditionalist philosopher René Guénon called this situation "the reign of quantity."[9] The logical consequence of this worldview is, as John Zerzan says, "the twilight of the machines."[10] And a twilight it is, for the materialist illusion leads to an unsustainable situation, the fading of delusions of grandeur, an impossible impasse as dangerous as a top-heavy tower built on faulty foundations. The modern world is now having to face the fact that its dream of endless scientific and cultural progress, driven by an endlessly expanding gross national product, is not a dream or ideal at all, but a delusion. Isn't it odd that the American dream shrinks as the GNP grows? This "myth of progress" is hung upon a linear time-philosophy that is unique to the Western Judeo-Christian mind-set. And this mind-set is held thrall by self-serving egoism. Jungian analyst Monika Wikman said it well:

> Part of our modern delusion is that ego consciousness is now completely in charge of all life. This fantasy resides at the bedrock of all our modern problems, such as the worldwide ecological crisis, as the separatist ego greedily runs off with its plans for life, no matter that the planet may perish in the process. The devastating effects of the split between ego and Self mysteries, felt in every region on earth, are wake-up calls to which we must attend. . . . Although ego con-

sciousness is indispensable, it is not the ruler of psychic life, or life on the planet.[11]

Ego consciousness goes hand in hand with the linear-time assumption of Western civilization, because the ego cannot accept a time in which it would need to relinquish its sovereignty for the sake of renewal. For it, only half of reality is real. Time doesn't move in cycles between two complementary extremes; day doesn't need night and life must deny death. Time is merely the unchanging stage upon which the fulfillment of ego's bottomless needs are pursued.

It is not possible to encapsulate all the brilliant philosophical insights of Traditionalist writers. The insightful words of Guénon, Coomaraswamy, Marco Pallis, Frithjof Schuon, Joseph Campbell, Alan Watts, Aldous Huxley, Huston Smith, Seyyed Hossein Nasr, Titus Burckhardt, Lord Northbourne, Kathleen Raine, Stella Kramrisch, Annamarie Schimmel, Whitall Perry, Wolfgang Smith, and Martin Lings have been augmented by new voices such as Estefan Lambert, Timothy Scott, Peter Kingsley, Patrick Laude, and Roger Sworder.[12] The Perennial Philosophy also informs the work of popular writers such as Peter Russell. Small publishers such as Fons Vitae, World Wisdom Books, and Sophia Perennis have endeavored, with little expectation of profit, to reprint the old titles and publish new ones in this underappreciated genre. In this chapter the salient points of the Perennial Philosophy will be covered and they will be referenced frequently throughout the rest of the book. As far as I can tell, they offer the only sane explanation of, approach to, and solution for the crisis of the modern world, regardless of whether or not we are comfortable with connecting that crisis with 2012.

SACRED SCIENCE VERSUS PROFANE SCIENCE

We have to be very careful with terminology. What does the phrase "sacred science" mean? Why is such a phrase necessary? First, sacred science revives a sense of awe and reverence for nature, a sacred participation between object and observer. "Normal" science—or shall we say "profane" science in contrast to "sacred" science—assumes the only real part of the universe is the physical domain of matter, forces, and the laws that govern them. Everything in this worldview can be reduced to and explained by these physical laws. Spiritual "realities" are, by this definition, not really real.

The phrase "sacred science" is necessary in order to highlight the idea that, from the viewpoint of an underlying spiritual center, historical "progress" is a devolution. Modern science and secular pop culture offer a profane and desacralized worldview. Earlier humanity saw the universe animated by living and conscious beings occupying many levels in a multidimensional ecology that was ultimately unified by the principle of the center-origin. Modern science identifies this previous modality as inferior and superstitious. But let's revisit this and take a careful look at the assumptions underlying these judgments, and the consequent implications for cultures that believe one versus the other. Ancient cultures living under the guidance of sacred sciences did well enough to recognize the physical surface of appearances, which is the sole concern of modern science. But it also went beyond the veil of appearances to recognize and embrace other modes of knowing and being—not simply what we would call intuition and feeling, but parallel, coexisting ontological domains: the plant kingdom, mineral kingdom, elemental beings underlying physical transformational processes (such as fire). These domains were incorporated into the daily worldview, what we might call a depth-psychological folk wisdom that provided meaningful participation in an ultimately unfathomable and beautifully mysterious cosmos.

The universe is a multidimensional place. Likewise, the human mind is multidimensional and integrates sensory data with perceptions from what in traditional sacred sciences are referred to as spiritual faculties. For example, in ancient Tibetan teachings (which is the perfect example of an ancient sacred science), there are five levels of the human being, each of which corresponds to energy centers residing along the spine called *chakras*. These five levels process increasingly subtle information from the physical environment as they ascend upward (earth, water, air, fire, space). Above them, two more chakras exist. The sixth is associated with the so-called third eye. When this center, or subtle sense faculty, is opened, consciousness is able to transcend, or integrate, dualities. Conflict generated by the interplay of dualities in the world can be "seen through." People in this mode tend to not become entangled and limited by identifying themselves with only half of reality. There are plenty of people in the world today who can access this level of consciousness, though it is not a perspective that factors into the values of modern politics and trans-national economies. Many ancient cultures were informed, in their philosophies and religions, by this nondual perception of the world.

A sacred science acknowledges the highest level of consciousness (the subtlest level) as the most real, while a profane science denies that level's relevance and validity because it belongs to a nonmaterial domain. Profane science will say it is ambiguous because it is "subjective." Here we find another distinction between profane science and sacred science (or Perennial Philosophy): Modern science is inverted in relation to sacred science. In the profane desacralized view of modern science, physical matter is the most real, the only part of the universe that can be analyzed and tested with consistent results. In a sacred science the subtler higher levels of consciousness are more real. This is not a matter of one opinion versus another opinion; it is a question of a more complete cosmology (a more sophisticated ontological understanding of reality) versus a less complete cosmology that is true only within a relatively narrow subsection of the big picture. Science values and hones in on precision, whereas sacred science zooms out for the big picture, with comprehensiveness (and comprehension) as the goal. The more subtle and spiritualized that consciousness gets, the more it can embrace and interpenetrate lower levels, denser domains, of the universe. In this way, a comprehensive grasp of the whole can be realized.

On a scale of progressive rarefication from material to spiritual, Tibetan and Hindu sacred science identifies five sheaths or levels of human consciousness. Lama Anagorika Govinda explained this doctrine in his profound book *Foundations of Tibetan Mysticism.* In this scenario, the five levels of consciousness crystallize around our innermost core, the Divine Ground, which is itself immaterial. Each successive sheath is denser than the last. From highest to lowest the five levels are: the inspiration body, the depth-consciousness body, the thought body, the pranic (breath) body, and finally the physical body. The inspiration body is nourished by joy, or ecstasy. It is the subtlest of the sheaths and therefore penetrates all the others. In other words, the sheaths are not separate levels, building consecutively around a solid nucleus, but rather have the nature of interpenetrating forms of energy. The densest, like large pebbles in a sand sifter, cannot occupy the same space as the subtler levels. So, too, the limited worldview of science, informed and defined by the faculties of physical sense perception, cannot penetrate into the subtle domains perceived with the subtle faculties. In fact, the subtle faculties are likely to be obscured by the exclusive focus of the grosser faculties on material sense perception. Not so the other way around, however. When the consciousness shifts to awaken the inner faculties of subtle sense perception, the outer world doesn't simply disappear. Why? Because the inner sense perceptions embrace the data received by lower physical impressions, but places them in a larger, more inclusive, context. This is, essentially, what sacred science offers to a world hoodwinked by profane science—a larger, whole, perspective. As long as we identify ourselves with denser aspects of our totality, then we are subject to the laws of matter.

Why is this relevant to the Maya calendar? Quite simply, the doctrine of World Ages is a version of this same doctrine. Each successive World Age brings about a more perfect reflection of divinity within humanity. As it says in *The Popol Vuh*, humanity is transformed at each successive level, or Age, to more fully honor the spiritual being of the creator, Heart of Heaven. Comparative mythologists, such as Joseph Campbell, are adept at seeing beyond the culture-specific garb and terminology, to identify the universal ideas that link seemingly diverse doctrines from around the world. The World Ages of Mesoamerican cosmology are spatiotemporal versions of the ancient Oriental sacred science of the five spiritual centers of the human microcosm.

Implicit in this doctrine is the recognition that this microcosm is a miniature reflection of the macrocosm.

We have to be careful here not to fall prey to false conceptual opposites. Descartes's error was to apply mathematical plus-and-minus values to nature, resulting in the separation of mind and body, or spirit and matter, into unrelated oppositional domains. The error has cascaded into a sanctioned and institutionalized misconception of the spiritual domain's relationship with the material plane: The relationship between the two conceptual domains of matter and spirit is not one of rigid dualities set apart and reflecting each other as in a mirror. Instead, one must imagine a vertical conduit running from material manifestation at the base up through increasingly refined levels to unconditioned, nonmaterial spiritual essence. Each successive level moving upward transcends the level immediately preceding it. Transcendence, however, is not to be thought of as being "above" in a separating sense. Transcendence is inclusive of that which it transcends.

The ultimate level of pure spiritual consciousness thus embraces the more material domains of the universe. It is, by definition, unconditioned, limitless, unbounded, timeless, infinite, and eternal. It is, after all, the unmanifest ground state from which the material world of appearances springs, which is a realm in which everything that arises must eventually pass out of being-ness and back into the infinite source, like clouds disappearing back into the underlying blue sky from which they were born.

THE PRE/TRANS FALLACY

There is another way of thinking about the many levels of consciousness. Three stages of psychological development can be identified, and are particularly useful for clarifying the problems that the modern mind-set has with the ideas so central to the Perennial Philosophy. The three stages can also be thought of as states of consciousness, and they are: prerational, rational, and transrational. Nietzsche, in his essay called "On Scholars," presented this idea allegorically. The prerational state is analogous to that of babies, who have not yet learned to process reality in a linear, sequential fashion. Their immersion in the unitary ocean of feeling is a kind of blissful oneness, but it is bereft of the ego sense through which external data can be related to a sense of individual identity. This categorizing and processing of external reality is the province of the rational stage, which requires a more or less concisely formulated ego with which external data can be measured, analyzed, and rationally categorized. This second state is inherently limited by the dualist framework that it requires—an observer and the observed. The being has fallen out of oneness, out of paradise. The unconscious unity of the prerational state has achieved a conscious relationship with the objects of sense perception, predicated on the fiction of the ego. The ego is a good thing, a natural development. As Terence McKenna used to say, we need the ego, otherwise we'd be likely to put food in the wrong mouth. The third stage is a logical development that leads beyond logic. It is the transrational position, or state, that perceives ego within a larger field of a unitary whole. It's not that the ego is annihilated (that would be a return to the prerational state), but that the ego is transcended, is placed in a nondual relationship with, well, everything else—nature, the world, other egos.

In terms of psychological development, the transrational state perceives connections between "things" that are not contingent upon the cause-and-effect framework utilized by rational processing. We might say that the rational state is logical, while the transrational state is analogical. An analogy made between, say, the form of a river delta viewed from above and lung alveoli takes on great meaning. Though labeled a mere poetic metaphor by the rational mind, to the transrational mind such a parallel reveals an underlying universal ordering principle that is there, exists, is evident to the perception, but cannot be explained by good old-fashioned Newtonian science.

It's not simply that geological erosion and tissue formation are governed by the same mathematical laws, but that different orders or domains of reality are united by a common principle, as in "as above, so below." The critical key here is that the transrational position includes the rational position—

transcendence includes that which it transcends. It should not be a threat to the rational mind, because it is the logical higher viewpoint in the rational mind's development. Thus, *meta*-physics (metaphysics), as the term itself suggests, is the larger cosmological viewpoint of which physics is merely a small subset.

This three-part model should make sense, especially to the rational mind, but unfortunately a confusing fallacy is all too common. Philosopher Ken Wilber calls it the "Pre/Trans Fallacy" and explains:

> The essence of the pre/trans fallacy is itself fairly simple: since both prerational states and transrational states are, in their own ways, nonrational, they appear similar or even identical to the untutored eye. And once pre and trans are confused, then one of two fallacies occurs: In the first, all higher and transrational states are reduced to lower and prerational states. Genuine mystical or contemplative experiences, for example, are seen as a regression or throwback to infantile states of narcissism, oceanic adualism, indissociation, and even primitive autism. This is, for example, precisely the route taken by Freud in The Future of an Illusion.[13]

Why does the pre/trans fallacy relate to the topics of sacred science and Perennial Philosophy? We have three levels, or states of consciousness. The middle state is occupied by rationalists. It is they who, in our culture, are the arbiters of what is admissible and it is they who are called upon as experts, "voices of reason." The garden-variety rationalist falls prey to the righteous prejudice that the rational intellect is the highest and most desired development a human being can strive for. As Wilber said so well, "Rationality is the great and final omega point of individual and collective development, the high-water mark of all evolution. No deeper or wider or higher context is thought to exist. Thus, life is to be lived either rationally, or neurotically (Freud's concept of neurosis is basically anything that derails the emergence of rational perception—true enough as far as it goes, which is just not all that far)."[14]

They believe that beyond reason is nothing, or perhaps faith, which is judged a weak recourse of those who have failed to apply rational processing. This is why we have a contentious and misleading debate between "faith and reason," as if faith was merely a kind of god-sanctioned feeling, a basically irrational personal conviction tolerated only because it provides a safe illusion for the intellectually deficient. The typical rationalist intellect does not see faith as a transrational certainty forged by direct experience of the transcendent. In fact, often it is not; in the modern world faith is very often merely blind faith, uninformed by direct gnosis. What blind faith replaces is knowing, direct gnosis of that which lies beyond the limited purview of rationalist science. In this formulation, we have the prerational, the rational, and the transrational. We can see how easy it is for the rationalist mind-set to mistake the transrational as a form of the prerational.

The Maya spiritual teachings connected with 2012, in their deepest transrational implications, are not likely to get a fair or accurate treatment by scholars limited to rationalist reductionism. Again, it's important to note that transrational processing of ancient metaphysical wisdom teachings is not the same as prerational. Transrational includes rational processing; it can do rational process just as well as the exclusively rationalist intellect. It admits into its consideration integrative ideas and cosmological perspectives—doctrines, one might say—that science would reflexively dismiss or reject. As an example, let's take astrology, a hugely misunderstood topic that scientists just love to skewer. The only way that science can think of critiquing astrology is on its own terms—that of scientific cause and effect. Thus, Jupiter's position and movements are identified as being gravitationally irrelevant, since a paper clip two feet away from you exerts as much influence on you as Jupiter does.

Now let's consider the acausal basis of astrology, which explains astrology via the principle "as above, so below" (or "the macrocosm reflects the microcosm"). The outer realm of planetary motions and the inner subjective realm of the human psyche do not need to be linked through the cause-and-effect zinging of gravity waves or energy from one to the other. The connection is not even one of "effect" but of resonant unfolding because both realms, the subjective and the objective, spring from the same source and unfold with the same rhythm. Jung called this "synchronicity, an acausal connecting principle."[15]

The basic tenets of astrology, such as extroverts in solar signs and introverts in lunar signs, were proven by the statistical analyses of Jung and parapsychologist J. B. Rhine,[16] which should mean something to scientists, but the main point is that scientists should not be expected to embrace an acausal connecting principle because it is, by definition, beyond the limits of their worldview. It isn't the realm of physics, it's the realm of metaphysics, which nevertheless includes physics in a larger cosmo-conception. Metaphysics, in the topsy-turvy interpretation of science, is mistaken for an irrational approach to reality, when in fact it is transrational. Here, again, we see the pre/trans fallacy at work, sanctioned by scientism.

A FEW WORDS ON ATLANTIS

In my book *Galactic Alignment* I identified how precession angled the earth's North Celestial Pole toward the Galactic Center some 12,000 years ago. This happened to be the era of the previous galactic alignment, when the June solstice sun was aligned with the dark rift in the Milky Way. Plato's account of the fabled sinking of Atlantis, in his *Timaeus*, dates that sinking to 9,600 years before his time, thus about 10,000 BC, or 12,000 years ago. Since then, the effect of precession shifting the direction of the North Celestial Pole has caused the nuclear bulge of the Galactic Center to slowly reach lower and lower meridian transits in the southern sky. It has, in effect, been sinking, and the observation is relevant for northern latitudes. Eventually, from the latitude of Greece, for example, the Galactic Center no longer rose above the southern horizon; it sank below the horizon. I believe that Plato's Myth of Atlantis refers to this precession-based process. Intriguingly, Atlantis-as-Galactic Center will one day "rise again" when the North Celestial Pole reaches the other extreme—pointing away from the Galactic Center. In my investigation of these astronomical processes I discovered that these extreme points are keyed to the eras of the galactic alignment. At the time of the June solstice–Galactic Center alignment of Plato's 10,000 BC, it began "sinking." With the December solstice–Galactic Center alignment of era-2012 "Atlantis" will begin to shift upward once again, reaching higher and higher meridian transits in the southern sky. The Galactic Center timing of these eras are generalized, because the nuclear bulge of the Galactic Center is quite large. The important thing to understand here is that the turnabout points are keyed to the galactic alignment eras, an idea that occurred to me in my investigation of Old World precessional cosmologies.

The Atlantis legend makes more sense as an astronomical process than as a literal sinking and rising of a physical continent. I believe, however, that the astronomical metaphor can be extended to the domain of spiritual cycles. Remember, the principle of "as above, so below" is merely another way of stating a modern notion of quantum mechanics, that *subject and object are inseparably linked.* The Primordial Tradition, or Perennial Philosophy, observes cycles of forgetting and remembering that consciousness on earth undergoes. It progressively forgets its true, multidimensional nature, and later resurrects or remembers this true Self. In this way, we might think of the rise and fall of Atlantis as a metaphor for the forgetting and remembering of the Primordial Tradition. Our craving to raise a physical sunken continent is a displaced desire to awaken our spiritual true natures.

In this view, the Primordial Tradition is a state of mind rather than a long-past Golden Age or ancient physical location. As a state of mind, the Primordial Tradition is accessible to any person or culture, at any time or place, without the aid of direct transmission through lineage or Atlantean antecedent. The current pop-culture quest to trace fragments of compelling "evidence" back to some Atlantean ur-civilization misses this point, and is evidence for the overliteral preoccupations of Western "modern" conscious-ness. An incredibly low-minded manifestation of this is the mass media's treatment of Maya and Egyptian archaeology, revealing an inability to see anything beyond treasure hunting, gold artifacts, and scary mummies. The deeper truth of our search for lost "artifacts" is our desire to make visible a knowledge or mind-set that is more comprehensive and fulfilling. As with Shambhala, which faded into invisibility as humanity lost the ability to see it, the Primordial Tradition fades but reemerges in places conducive to dis-covering and appreciating its profound depth and wisdom. This explains the ancient Maya's isolation and independent genius, which nevertheless had tapped into the same doctrines also found in ancient Vedic and Egyptian cosmology. Transoceanic voyages are not required for this parallel emergence of the same insights.

The quest for lost Atlantis or Shambhala arose as humanity descended into an increasingly dense and materialistic age. It's not that Atlantis or Shambhala lies hidden in some remote valley or underwater grave. The point is that humanity has forgotten how to be in that place where "Atlantis" or "Shambhala" did and always will reside. We may find engines in the sands of Egypt, stone computers in the jungles of Guatemala, and gears in Paleolithic encrustations of lava, and this may—indeed, should—create awe and wonder among scientists and the interested public in general. But it shouldn't distract us from laying aside our own civilization's faulty materialist obsessions to truly learn from the high metaphysical teachings offered by ancient civiliza-tions, including those of Egypt, Vedic India, and the Maya.

COPERNICUS AND THE SPIRITUAL ILLUMINATION OF THE CENTRAL SUN

Jeremi Wasiutynski offered, in his magisterial book *The Solar Mystery*, an in-depth reevaluation of the influences that drove Nicholas Copernicus to formulate his heliocentric model. He noted that, within the history of science, the current understanding is "hampered by false preconceptions" and "the prevailing ideas concerning the motives of Copernicus's creative work are inadequate."[17] The symbol of the sun fascinated the great minds of the Renaissance, including Copernicus, Ficino, Pico della Mirandola, da Vinci, Michelangelo, Thomas More, Campanella, and Giordano Bruno. They were all inspired by the new translations of ancient Greek philosophy that contained profound ideas that challenged Christian doctrine. As hermetic philosophers entertaining ancient "pagan" notions, they danced on the fringes of heresy and their true agenda had to be cloaked in secrecy. For them, the sun had to be returned to the center of a spiritual metaphysic, reviving a superior esoteric cosmology they believed was taught in the ancient Greco-Hellenist Mystery Schools as well as Plato's Academy.[18]

A group of initiates in Italy strove to realize the paradigm of the ancient solar religion. Copernicus was one of them. He sojourned to Italy in the 1490s and joined a milieu of thinkers and artists who were being transformed by the philosophical works of the late-Byzantine Neoplatonist philosopher Gemistos Plethon.[19] The connections between Copernicus and key players in this movement, which was in fact destined to trigger the sixteenth-century renaissance of ancient Greek science and ideals, are quite compelling. The period was awash in political and cultural tumult. Byzantium had just fallen to the invading Turks, and intellectuals and other refugees were fleeing to Italy. There, the painter Giorgione and others were all ears and were greatly influenced by Neoplatonic and hermetic principles, one central idea being that the outer sun was a symbol of an inner sun, which as the central conduit of spiritual illumination offered salvation as well as intellectual wisdom. The ancient mystery cults of Greece placed this sun at the center of their divine cosmos; why, then, was the external sun relegated to the outskirts? This line of thought led its investigators in two directions. For Giordano Bruno, it led to being burned at the stake. For Copernicus, it led to being hailed as the godfather of modern science.

In his book *The Solar Mystery*, published two years before his death at the age of ninety-eight, Wasiutynski wrote that his primary task was "to reconstruct and interpret a complex of historical facts related to the working of the solar mystery in the minds and lives of some of the leading creative representatives of the Renaissance, united by unknown secret bonds."[20] Copernicus emerges as a misunderstood figure whose real intention, in its original essentially mystical formulation, was diametrically opposite to what eventually happened with his work. Copernicus "was highly conscious of the crucial significance for human life of his transformation of the image of the world . . . [but] the way in which he was called to usher in the modern history of mankind has certain paradoxical and tragic features which have become fully apparent only now."[21]

Copernicus was devoted to a romanticized past in which spiritual mysteries had been realized by great sages and philosophers. In his effort to revive and "prove" the principles at work in this metaphysic of solar illumination, he unintentionally undermined the very foundations on which he was building. Wasiutynski explains that this dislocation occurred because he attempted to represent the *modus operandi* of a high order spiritual revelation in a lower order of consciousness—namely, that of a nascent materialist science. This is, of course, the same problem we have in much of the modern scientific-academic treatment of ancient Maya teachings: force-fitting a multidimensional nondual cosmology into the confines of a shortsighted linear flatland.

Copernicus had been an initiate in a solar brotherhood that erupted in Italy in the 1490s. His own vision of the world was recentered upon the transcendent spiritual sun of direct gnosis, but when he tried to turn it into a tangible model and present it to a profane world, trouble ensued. "By disclosing to the profane world the ruling power of the Sun in the universe [in a way that was] accessible to the science of his time, Copernicus definitively diverted the profane mind from that transcendent principle—the Solar Logos—which he himself had directly experienced as mystically present in the Sun."[22] That this would occur, inadvertently against his own intentions, must have quickly become apparent to him, for although his great work was mapped out by the year 1520, he resisted releasing it and delayed its publication until a fan, Rheticus, facilitated its publication shortly before his death in 1542. The Copernican Revolution, as a new way of mapping the universe, was what the swine did with the pearls thrown before them. Cosmology (cosmos-logos = knowing the cosmos) was trumped by cosmography (cosmos-graphing = mapping the cosmos).

And here we are at a new juncture, in which a galactic cosmovision devised by ancient pagans (the Maya) threatens the superiority complex of modern science. At the same time, if properly understood as an expression of perennial wisdom, 2012 offers to inspire and possibly awaken spiritually sensitive seekers. It offers something that has been winnowed out of modern civilization, something that just might be more sophisticated than anything achieved by the modern world. How will Western civilization respond to this breach in its self-image? Not surprisingly, it will call it doomsday and try to make you fear it, judge it, or dismiss it. It will try to render it impotent by distorting all the facts, or turn it into a Saturday-afternoon distraction with a variety-pack of entertaining movies. In this, which is already happening, it enslaves 2012 to the small-minded agenda of empiricism and materialism.

The problem, as usual, is looking in the outer world for that which can only be found within. Wasiutynski, who in his thinking combined analytic exactitude with intuition, wrote:

> As long as men will seek spiritual inspiration in some artificial temple rather than in the archetypal temple whose dim mirror-image is Nature, the products of their creative work are not likely to be immortal. But the desire of Life was bound to raise mighty waves in the mythical substratum of European civilization to break the crust by which the preservers of external traditions protected themselves against the Eternal Revelation.[23]

Let's hope that the galactic cosmology of the Maya doesn't get treated like Copernicus's heliocentric cosmology did. How many different ways must the stubborn ignorance of the Western world be handed the perennial wisdom on a silver plate before it stops, lets go, and simply opens up? I hope that future historians will read this and chuckle to themselves, for the right reason. Time will tell.

THERE IS NO ABSOLUTE TRUTH: EVERYTHING IS RELATIVE

Read that heading again. If you buy that, you missed a great joke. Also, the White House is red and I am not my not-self. All funny, but this isn't about semantic games. Our culture is rooted in an absurdity which can be summarized as the belief that "there are no absolutes." The doctrine of relativism is the primary critique against the Perennial Philosophy, which is predicated upon an absolute source and center of all manifestation. Source and Center are the absolute first principles of the Perennial Philosophy, the necessary consequence when you start your philosophy with nothing. The commandment that there are no absolutes is the talisman thrust at the Perennial Philosophy, but it's a logical conundrum. Philosophically and conceptually, it just doesn't work. You can't have relativism without an absolute reference point. "No, no," says the convert to relativism, "it's all relative." Absolutely.

By the way, it's funny that our mainstream culture uses the word "absolutely" as a catchphrase or space filler that is synonymous with saying "I agree with the opinion you just expressed as if it were a profound universal truth." An interviewer asks, "Do you think that Big Foot has anything to do with crop circles?" The interviewee obligingly responds, "Absolutely . . ." and proceeds to unwind a series of wild assertions. We can add "absolutely" to the list of our culture's inverted malapropisms along with "myth" and "symbol."

Rather than being an abstract point of questionable worth, a whole range of related confusions, some having very practical implications, falls under the dominion of this issue. Time and eternity, life and death, limitation and limitlessness, free will and determinism—if these ideas are correctly understood, a sustainable worldview and civilization result; if misunderstood and inverted, the crisis of the modern world results. You can't have time without the timeless within which time happens. The two are indeed intimately related—one is the projected externalization of the other. As Plato said, time is the moving image of eternity. According to an old idea, time is the fourth dimension. That might have sounded compelling in the 1880s when Edwin Abbott was writing about the fourth dimension in his classic book *Flatland*, but it's the third dimension that is time-bound. One dimension up is the fourth dimension, which is beyond time—the timeless. Eternity is not a long period of time; it is the cessation of time. Or, we might say, time is a small subset of the fourth dimension, which underlies time *in potentia*.

Here's a good one: If everything is relative, then nothing is relative. Neither of these concepts has anything to do with quantity, though we tend to think of "everything" as "a lot of things." I can remember laughing at the logo used by a local building supply company, emblazoned in big letters, announcing that they stocked "More of Everything!" More of everything? How can you have more of everything? That's like having less than nothing. Similarly, one wonders why we even have words like "fuller" and "emptier." If a glass of water is full, it cannot be made fuller. Likewise, when my bank account is empty, which it usually is, it cannot be made emptier, unless you call it going into debt. These conceptual mind-benders are as absurd as expecting something that's dead to get deader. It leads to amusing assertions such as "all people are equal but some people are more equal than others." If life lives, does death die?

I'm belaboring these conceptual paradoxes because they are a good way to prime the rational mind for a higher perspective that is there, but it denies. It reveals a nondual state of consciousness that more accurately reflects the true nature of reality—a paradoxical integration of opposites. And the big linkup is between the Absolute and the Relative. These terms easily transpose into "timeless and time" (or "eternity and time"). The phenomenal world is constantly moving in time; eternity is the unmoving center of time. Traditional cultures live at the center; Western desacralized civilization has colonized the periphery. When you deny the transcendent center, you evict yourself from it. The eye of a hurricane is unmoving while the motion happens around it. But neither would exist without the other.

Philosophically speaking, or perhaps we should say *metaphysically* speaking, the appearance that all the phenomenal world is endlessly changing, its individual elements constantly coming into being and falling back into nonexistence, suggests an unchanging ground. The poets and mystics of the world have seen through the illusion of impermanence, the *maya* of the phenomenal world, to the underlying ground state. In accepting and embracing death, they touch immortality. This nondual perspective is the essence of the Perennial Philosophy. Revived by René Guénon and Ananda Coomaraswamy in the 1920s and '30s, it was identified with Vedanta and Oriental *dzog-chen* teachings. Its ultimate goal is the direct experience of the nondual state. As such, it is initiatory but demands allegiance to no creed, for its only purpose is the awakening of the true nature, the divine eternal consciousness within souls that are overly attached to egoism, the mind being clouded, as it says in *The Popol Vuh*, like breath on a mirror. This primordial tradition can never become obsolete. Perennial wisdom can be forgotten but will eventually spring forth again. Universal truth can be ignored, but it cannot be thrown out for long.

These ideas are surprising and unpopular to modern science. We will see in the next chapter how intimately Maya teachings and Maya prophecy are connected with these ideas. The Maya worldview is much more akin to these perennial ideas than to those of modern science. Modern science and the entire modern mind-set, which the average person has been deeply indoctrinated into, has a hard time enunciating, let alone appreciating, the true depth of Maya thought. As if that wasn't problematic enough, the debunking style of scientism that attacks the 2012 topic merely results in travesties of misinterpretation and misconception. There's just no way, according to this prejudice, that the ancient Maya can have anything important to tell us.

The assumptions and orientation of the modern world are diametrically opposed to the values of traditional cultures and a traditional spirituality that is rooted in the perennial wisdom. The transcendent location where the perennial wisdom resides has been denied by modern science and the modern secular culture of consumerism. The ego has arisen to run indispensable cultural institutions that were once, or ideally can be, informed and run by selfless principles in which the good of the whole is the primary objective.

If this sounds far-fetched and impractical, these values were in fact outlined and made law some 230 years ago, the authors being the founding fathers of the United States of America. Even before Thomas Jefferson died he lamented the rising power of aggregate capital (what we today call "big business"). He believed that the principles and ideals of a free democracy had already met their match and begun to erode. By the early twentieth century, John Dewey observed that "politics is the shadow cast on society by big business."[24] And by the early twenty-first century AIG would receive billions in taxpayer bailout money while still giving its executives million-dollar bonuses. We are definitely not in Kansas anymore, folks.

What happens to a culture that forgets the center, denies the transcendent perennial wisdom, and becomes married to an antitraditional philosophy in which ego, consumer materialism, and self-interest run the show? What happens is the fulfillment of the Maya prophecy for 2012.

CHAPTER NINE

THE FULFILLMENT OF THE MAYA PROPHECY

I am great. My place is now higher than that of the

human work, the human design. I am their sun and

I am their light, and I am also their months . . .

my light is great. I am the walkway and I am the

foothold of the people, because my eyes are of metal.

My teeth just glitter with jewels, and turquoise as

well; they stand out blue with stones like the face of

the sky.[1]

—SEVEN MACAW, *The Popol Vuh*

We've already looked at the Maya Creation Mythology, known as the Hero Twin Myth or *The Popol Vuh*, and discovered that it expresses the Maya's World Age doctrine. There are many Ages or cycles, and therefore many cycle endings, but the dynamics of each cycle ending are essentially the same. In the four previous eras alluded to in *The Popol Vuh*, the cycle ending always exposes an error in the activities, thinking, or understanding of humanity, leading to a corrective sacrifice followed by transformation and renewal as the next cycle begins. That is the fundamental structure of cyclic time, especially in relation to how human beings experience it.

The central story line of *The Popol Vuh* involves the exploits of the Hero Twins, and this narrative provides more intimate details of what happens as a cycle ending nears. Although not explicitly stated, the narrative applies to 2012, because mythic narratives are not historical accounts; they occur in the numinous space-time that was, is, and will be. The teachings are relevant "during cycle endings" and therefore apply to any cycle ending, including 2012. We can suspect that the Hero Twin story might speak to us, since we are living during the 2012 cycle ending. In other words, the Hero Twin story is a perennially recurring mythic drama, populated by archetypal characters, and we should be able to relate to its contents. This will be especially true if we can pierce the veil of the surface detail in the myth and get to the symbolic core of the story.

Getting to the heart of the message is important. Similarly, the "prophecy" in the story is a predictable general state of the world at the end of any World Age. It doesn't concern itself with specific details on when and where earthquakes or asteroids are going to hit. Its symbolic or archetypal content may or may not reflect what is happening in our world. This is a test we can put to the Creation Myth. What is the Maya prophecy for 2012? Does the scenario for the cycle ending recorded in *The Popol Vuh*, that primary document of Maya prophetic philosophy, find confirmation in the events of the modern world? Is the ancient Maya prophecy for 2012 coming true? Let's find out.

THE MAYA PROPHECY FOR THE END OF THE CYCLE

As we explore the teachings and prophecy in the Creation Myth, we need to remember that the end of the Age, as scheduled by the Long Count calendar, falls on December 21, 2012. The Long Count is the calendar part of the World Age doctrine expressed in mythological terms in *The Popol Vuh*.

The Hero Twin narrative in *The Popol Vuh* contains several important characters. There is One Hunahpu, a primary solar lord. He has a brother, uncles, parents, and grandparents, who are all more or less organized around his adventures. Even his twin sons, the frequent focus of action in the myth, are really just his helpers or subidentities. They are on his side, part of his archetypal purpose.

Another main figure is Seven Macaw, a bird deity who squawks loudly, proclaiming he is the real lord of the world. His lesson involves the dangers of hubris. He has a son, Zipacna, who figures in his own vignette, but Zipacna's lesson is simply a reiteration of Seven Macaw's lesson, so the two figures merely symbolize the same persona. Similarly, all of the Lords of Xibalba belong to the category of characters that, like Seven Macaw, embody an energy of deception and limitation, and oppose the divine destiny of One Hunahpu. They aren't called the Lords of Darkness for nothing.

The female figures in the myth are indispensable for the manifestation of One Hunahpu's destiny. A Creator Grandmother models the first humans from corn dough. A maiden named Blood Moon is magically impregnated by One Hunahpu and becomes the mother of the Hero Twins. One Hunahpu's mother provides the house and home where he, his brother, and his sons are raised. It provides the stable background to many of the events, a central "hearth-place" reference point.

There are supernatural deities, too. Heart of Heaven is an overseeing figure, suggesting the importance of the concept of "cosmic center" in the myth. A falcon deity serves as a messenger for Heart of Heaven and may represent the Aquila constellation. Called Xic ("hawk") among the modern Quiché Maya, this constellation lies on the Milky Way, just north of the Galactic Center. A trinity of deities in another section of *The Popol Vuh* become lineage founders, the totemic figureheads of family clans among the modern Quiché Maya. They seem to represent three aspects of Heart of Heaven, special local "centers," each being sovereign over his own domain.

Generally, amid the panoply of minor characters and side adventures throughout the myth, we can identify two sides: the characters helping One Hunahpu's rebirth and installation as the new ruler, and the characters who serve deception and darkness, exemplified by Seven Macaw's vain and false rulership. The chiefs of the two respective teams are clear: One Hunahpu and Seven Macaw. So who are these figures and what do they represent? One Hunahpu is a solar lord. Maya kings are solar lords who symbolically occupy the center of the cosmos. Their throne symbolizes the cosmic center. In Maya

philosophy, they are earthly representatives of the higher wisdom that emanates from the cosmic center. As kings, they are responsible for the suste-
nance of the kingdom by protecting and channeling the energy and wisdom
of the divine center. Their identity is interfused with a higher purpose. Their
consciousness is centered in the soul's essential nature, which is limitless and
eternal.

Maya philosophy shares with many wisdom traditions the idea that the
deepest identity of a human being is the supreme identity found in one's
eternal and infinite source-consciousness, the undying transcendent center
from which the manifest world springs. In Hindu religion, for example, the
eternal soul of the individual is called *Atman*, whereas the eternal soul and
source of the universe is called *Brahman*. In a state of higher consciousness,
of realization of truth, the Hindu yogi experiences the previously hidden
truth that Atman and Brahman are one and the same. Maya kings have also
been initiated into this knowledge, and One Hunahpu is the mythical archetype of this kind of awakened person.

Seven Macaw is a bird deity, a false sun, who proclaims his divine nature
but is in fact something else. He is the ego. The ego identity centered in ego
consciousness serves a purpose in the life of humanity, but should be held in
right relationship to the eternal soul. The ego complex belongs to the individual self, the mortal and ultimately passing identity of this life. Many problems arise in the world when ego assumes the mantle of the eternal soul and
projects itself as an invincible figure, all-knowing and indestructible. Ego is
a mask, and the modern world confuses the mask with the real person. Seven
Macaw squawks and deceives humanity, magnifies himself as the true sun,
and tries to take the place of One Hunahpu (the eternal soul).

The drama in the story begins when One Hunahpu journeys to the
underworld, encounters the Lords of the Underworld, is deceived and gets
his head cut off. The meaning of this is profound, and is identical to the
story of Quetzalcoatl's fall among the later Aztecs.[2] The perfect divine being,
the consciousness aware of its eternal source, loses itself and forgets its divine
nature. A spiritual darkness then falls over the world. In the absence of the

divine wisdom's guiding presence in the world, ego gets a promotion, over-steps its proper place, and proclaims itself as the true self. Worldly power takes center stage and spiritual wisdom is handed a mop to clean up ego's messes. Everything then becomes inverted and the world falls further into deception and ignorance. In the Christian tradition a similar insight is found in the myth of the Fall, when humanity forgets how to live in the egalitarian partnership and harmony of Eden where God's presence is directly known. After the Fall, the eternal nature of the soul is forgotten.

Meanwhile, the eternal soul cannot really be killed, it can only be eclipsed and hidden by the ego, so One Hunahpu works behind the scenes to facilitate his own rebirth, his own reappearance on the stage of history. He magically conceives his twin sons, who later come to the underworld to retrieve his severed head and set things right. But first the Hero Twins must deal with Seven Macaw, whose self-serving vanity causes much suffering in the world. It is when spiritual darkness maximizes at the end of the cycle that Seven Macaw wields the greatest power. He's perfected the deceptive techniques of controlling humanity through glittery distractions and fearmongering. But it's all smoke and mirrors, a deception of appearances, for within he is rotting out.

The ego cannot survive being alienated from its source, the eternal soul, even though it has banished the eternal soul from its consciousness. It's a paradox destined for disintegration or resolution. The twins feed him his own weakness, his own hubris and ignorance, reflect back to him his own falseness, and Seven Macaw is tricked. Unwilling to consciously sacrifice his illusions of supremacy, he must suffer the blows of fate, so he withers and fades into the background. Ego must ultimately learn to accept having a proper relationship to the higher eternal soul—to One Hunahpu.

Now the twins illustrate the power of self-sacrifice—the act that Seven Macaw could have done to save himself from so much suffering. They trick the Lords of the Underworld by throwing themselves into the fire, burning themselves up, having their bones ground up and thrown into the river. The Dark Lords, envious, imitate their amazing feat but are destroyed. The

twins, however, become fish and
are reborn as themselves. They had
identified themselves with their
eternal essence and therefore do
not die; they can come back again
fully aware of themselves. This illustrates how ego does not survive
the transforming fire of eternity,
but the eternal soul does. The eternal soul *is* the transforming fire
of eternity. It all depends on what
part of your nature your consciousness is located in.

*The fall of Seven Macaw at the hands
of the Hero Twins, Izapa Stela 2.
Drawing by the author*

Throughout these dramatic
adventures the ballgame was being
played with One Hunahpu's head
as the ball, the twins against the
Dark Lords. The demise of Seven
Macaw and the Dark Lords, and
the illustration of self-sacrifice by the twins, is the precondition to One
Hunahpu's body getting reconnected with his head, and he is thus reborn.
The eternal soul gets revealed as the true center and source, and One Hunahpu
takes his proper throne in the center of the sky-earth, reunited with Heart of
Heaven.

This striking story encodes universal spiritual truths. And the prophecy
for 2012 is, simply, this: *As 2012 approaches, self-serving egoism will be ruling
and ruining the planet, deceiving people.* The world will be suffering because
the consciousness of humanity is disconnected from its eternal transcendent
source and root. Within the throes of egoism, consciousness resists opening
to the transcendent perspective. Ego will usurp the role of the eternal soul
and then everything becomes inverted, distorted, and increasingly degraded.
Our world is indeed ruled by this situation. God is dead; we try to make bod-

ies stay eternally young, science is the world's religion, and individual personalities in the entertainment biz are elevated to godhood. They are, in fact, called stars, while the stars themselves have become products: Suburu is the Japanese word for the Pleiades. The opposite was true for the ancient Maya and other ancient cultures, for whom the stars were deities.

Most dangerously, megalomaniacal egoism's destructive and ignorant agenda is nauseatingly apparent in the political sphere today. The Maya prophecy for 2012 is literally verified in a person who appeared, ruled, and ruined so much while seeking to exercise great control over humanity, all in service to his own selfish purposes. The prophesied appearance of Seven Macaw came to pass, and his name was George W. Bush.

THE EMISSARIES OF SEVEN MACAW AT LOOSE IN THE WORLD

That was a bit hyperbolic, for there are many Seven Macaws at loose in the world. Big ones and small ones, we meet them at our jobs, in our families, everywhere. The dog-eat-dog, king-of-the-hill, climb-the-ladder, look-out-for-yourself, utter selfishness of Seven Macaw has become the template, the prerequisite, the membership badge, for succeeding in our debased modern culture. They are the sadistic petty tyrants who seek and find positions of control. As we will see, the Seven Macaws in the world today are both human and nonhuman, and George W. Bush has achieved distinction in exemplifying Seven Macaw to an unprecedented degree. And let us not neglect vice president Dick Cheney as well as Karl Rove, who played significant roles in the Bush II administration. I nominate them all, without hesitation, as the fulfillment of the Maya prophecy for 2012.

The goal of Seven Macaw is to rule and control humanity and magnify his own wealth and appearance in the world. Seven Macaw's goal is accomplished with three primary tactics: lying, distraction, and fear. Seven Macaw lies to his subjects regarding his appearance, qualifications, and ability. In truth he is inept and unqualified, so he must lie. He magnifies himself by associating himself with greatness. He declares, "Look at me, I am the sun!" Going hand in hand with the lie are the distracting ornaments that Seven Macaw wears and flashes, blinding his subjects with superficial glitter. This has the effect of driving the lie in, deluding his subjects by distracting them with flashy clothes and symbol-laden regalia. If Seven Macaw pulls off his deception, his subjects will be left with a feeling of awe, that he is powerful, a force to be reckoned with and *feared*. Fear is the third key ingredient in the accomplishment of Seven Macaw's goal of control and subjugation.

As a perfect example of all of the above, let us recall the events of May 1, 2003. In a widely televised and well-executed propaganda stunt, President George W. Bush landed on the USS *Abraham Lincoln* aircraft carrier at sea, as copilot aboard an S-3B Viking jet. Moments later he emerged from the jet in full flight gear, helmet tucked under arm. After strutting across the deck and waving to the cameras, he proceeded to shake hands with the prearranged observers. Although many questions lingered about continuing violence in Iraq, the failure to locate weapons of mass destruction, and the whereabouts of Saddam Hussein, President Bush gave a nationally televised speech later that day under a banner that read "Mission Accomplished," saying "major combat operations in Iraq have ended."

Since this brazen announcement, total coalition fatalities (up to May 2009) have exceeded 4,270.[3] Clearly, combat operations have not ended, and the mission has not been accomplished, unless the mission was to establish a permanent presence in Iraq. This is a distinct probability, considering that the United States has been funding and building an extravagant new embassy on the banks of the Tigris River, very close to the heart of Baghdad.[4] A fortresslike compound the size of Vatican City, it sits on 104 acres and will have its own defense force and self-contained source of power and water.

Although the flight suit stunt was a fairly transparent publicity ploy, commentators in the media fell for it and reiterated, indeed amplified, the propaganda deception it was intended to implant in the minds of Americans. Talk show host Chris Matthews said, "Here's a president who's really nonverbal. He's like Eisenhower. He looks great in a military uniform. He looks great in that cowboy costume he wears when he goes West."[5] Later that day, on MSNBC's *Countdown with Keith Olbermann*, Chris Matthews continued, "We're proud of our president. Americans love having a guy as president, a guy who has a little swagger, who's physical, who's not a complicated guy like [former President Bill] Clinton or even like [former Democratic presidential candidates Michael] Dukakis or [Walter] Mondale . . . Women like a guy who's president. Check it out. The women like this war. I think we like having a hero as our president. It's simple."[6] Former Nixon administration official G. Gordon Liddy, after viewing the footage, said that Bush's flight suit made "the best of his manly characteristic" and "Al Gore had to go get some woman to tell him how to be a man. And here comes George Bush. You know, he's in his flight suit, he's striding across the deck, and he's wearing his parachute harness, you know—and I've worn those because I parachute—and it makes the best of his manly characteristic. . . . He has just won every woman's vote in the United States of America. You know, all those women who say size doesn't count, they're all liars."[7]

On the May 4, 2003, edition of CBS's *Face the Nation*, host Bob Schieffer and *Time* columnist Joe Klein rhapsodically pontificated:

> Schieffer: "As far as I'm concerned, that was one of the great pictures of all time. And if you're a political consultant, you can just see campaign commercial written all over the pictures of George Bush."
>
> Klein: "Well, that was probably the coolest presidential image since Bill Pullman played the jet fighter pilot in the movie *Independence Day*."

These are actual quotes from the mainstream media. Ann Coulter and Wolf Blitzer also contributed gems to this chorus of adulation and high praise. If there was any margin of misunderstanding in the intended effect, the right-wing cheerleaders in the mainstream media were at the ready to literally tell the viewing audience what they should think of it. They were very effective and devoted servants of Seven Macaw. How could a leader with such an impeccable "manly characteristic" be guilty of, say, initiating an illegal war of aggression?

An unfounded, unprovoked war of aggression against another sovereign nation is a crime against humanity, according to the U.S.-led international charter drawn up by prosecutors at the Nuremberg trials. It was noted that those who initiate a war of aggression bear individual criminal responsibility, both for waging an unprovoked war and for the various wartime crimes that follow. During the first Nuremberg trial in 1946, U.S. Supreme Court Justice Robert Jackson respected this legal guideline and secured the conviction of more than a dozen of the most prominent Nazi leaders. The most damning charge, resulting in eleven death sentences, was "initiating an unprovoked war of aggression against sovereign nations."

In the effort to secure support from Americans for the impending war, a deception was foisted upon the American people. After the trade towers went down on 9-11, a false connection between Saddam Hussein and the Osama bin Laden/Al-Qaeda front in Afghanistan was asserted and repeated by the Bush administration and in the mainstream media. This was yet another conscious strategy of obfuscation designed to pull on the patriotic heartstrings of honest Americans. It's a time-hallowed strategy in the playbook on how to control public opinion, and it doesn't matter if the facts are ignored or distorted.

Manipulating and deceiving people and foreign governments is easy as long as you are able to effectively launch one very powerful weapon: fear. Seven Macaw strikes fear into the heart of his subjects and thereby keeps them trembling and under his spell. The propagandists, such as Karl Rove, knew that one need only repeat, repeat, and repeat the method. The words "terror" and "terrorists" were thus endlessly repeated by Bush, Cheney, and Defense Secretary Donald Rumsfeld, literally hundreds of times in a given speech. If you can keep the public in shock trauma, you not only control them better, but you can pass all kinds of crazy self-serving legislation that wouldn't have a chance otherwise.

In the aftermath of World War II, Hermann Göring, Hitler's Reich

Marshall, gave his Nuremberg prosecutors a simple lesson in mind control, saying, "The people can always be brought to the bidding of the leaders. This is easy. All you have to do is tell them that they are being attacked, and denounce the pacifists for a lack of patriotism and exposing the country to danger. It works the same in every country."[8] These are tactics that were employed by the Bush administration.

Perhaps more disturbing is how marketing advertisement gurus have adopted similar mind-control strategies, scaring people into buying more insurance, bigger cars, and the latest cell phone widget, often in the name of greater convenience for the consumer. This is the realm of created wants, and now the pharmaceutical industry encourages consumers to diagnose themselves, visit their doctor, and literally tell the doctor what to prescribe. This was unthinkable as recently as the mid-1990s. These fear-based tactics distract people from being alive to the moment and they ignore what their self-serving rulers are up to, since they are so busy chasing security, consumer fads, mindless entertainment, and other empty behaviors dictated by the advertisement media. It keeps consciousness stuck to the surface of reality and discourages deep reflective thinking.

Another big industry, the movie biz, is complicit in crafting public opinion and conveying stereotypes and attitudes to American consumers that benefit warmongers in Washington. This may sound far-fetched to the skeptic, but it is demonstrably what is happening. Even the President of the Motion Picture Association, Jack Valenti, has observed that "Washington and Hollywood spring from the same DNA."[9] This is no baseless comment, as some Hollywood films are produced in cooperation with the U.S. Department of Defense.

Since the 1990s, an increasing number of Hollywood movies have portrayed the glories of war, and even are consciously designed to elicit racist attitudes in the public mind. For example, the 2000 film *Rules of Engagement* was written and produced by a former Secretary of the Navy, James Webb, who later became a senator from Virginia. This film portrays Arabs during a military occupation in Yemeni, even a little one-legged Arab girl who initially elicits our compassion, as conniving terrorists. The ensuing brutal massacre of civilians by U.S. troops is thus depicted as justifiable, necessary, even heroic.

As author Jack Shaheen points out in his book *Reel Bad Arabs: How Hollywood Vilifies a People*, Hollywood films have consistently avoided depicting the humanity of Arabs, and killing these stereotyped Arabs is presented as an entertainment spectacle having no moral implications.[10] The success of these movies lies in their effect, often unconscious, on public sentiments. The message is that Arabs, even the most innocent-appearing of civilians, should not be trusted. It is not hard to see how this plays into the permanent war that warmongers and profiteers in Washington tried to set up and sustain. That *Rules of Engagement* was written by Department of Navy Secretary James Webb should alert us to the truth of these connections between Hollywood and Washington. His role in producing *Rules of Engagement* identifies him as an emissary of Seven Macaw. His next movie, *The Kingdom*, continued the mind-control agenda.

The key ingredient for making deceptive propaganda effective, as Hitler's propaganda minister Joseph Goebbels said, is repeat, repeat, repeat: "If you tell a lie big enough and keep repeating it, people will eventually come to believe it. The lie can be maintained only for such time as the State can shield the people from the political, economic and/or military consequences of the lie. It thus becomes vitally important for the State to use all of its powers to repress dissent, for the truth is the mortal enemy of the lie, and thus by extension, the truth is the greatest enemy of the State."[11]

These are the tools of social engineering in the kit bag of all Seven Macaws. The goal is to serve a runaway fetish, an addiction: total world domination. Along the way, they kill and control people, destroy nations, amass wealth, and enslave Third World populations. The methods used are lies, fear, and distraction. As Michael Parenti wrote, "There's only one thing that the ruling classes have ever wanted." And that is: "everything."[12] All the rewards and none of the burdens. We need to remember that behind these media agendas and corporate policies are people making decisions that affect our lives. In the hierarchies that define modern society, the head of each level is merely a smaller and more local version of the chief, the head honcho, whose archetypal identity we have already identified. Seven Macaw and his agents are everywhere.

It is really not that surprising to find historical figures, such as George W. Bush, embodying a predictable archetypal role at a predictable moment in the life cycle of a civilization. Seven Macaw is the code name for self-serving megalomania. Legions of tyrants always appear at the later, degraded phases of a civilization. The later Caesars come to mind, and in particular Caligula, whose corruption in the decadent demise of the Roman empire is legendary. At those moments when the power structure of self-serving nihilism begins to quake, the ego tries to appropriate everything for itself. Thus, in a last-ditch attempt to get more of everything, a rampant out-of-control destruction of everything ensues and the world ends up with nothing. By the end of George W. Bush's second term the situation was out of control and Americans, even conservatives, were starting to see the real agenda behind the Bush-Cheney administration.

The election of Barack Obama promised a complete reversal of the Bush trajectory. Between March and November of 2008, something close to a miracle happened in American politics. Barack Obama, a little-known senator from Chicago, captured the sentiments of what a great majority of Americans were feeling. It was time to come together, stand up to power and corruption, and change the course of the nation. Obama spoke eloquently and rose to the challenge of taking on the Republican power structure fearlessly and with conviction. On November 4, the vote was decisive and historic. An African-American took the highest position of power in the United States. On an archetypal level, the self-serving egoism of Seven Macaw was defeated.

Obama soberly reminded Americans that there was much work to be done and a long road stretched ahead of us. He steadfastly called for all to work together in a spirit of unity with a common goal—to make a better, more sustainable world. If the definitive downfall of Bush-style politics was a manifestation of the Maya prophecy of the rise and demise of Seven Macaw, it's hard not to see Obama as the fulfillment of the second part of the Maya prophecy—namely, the restoration of the true ruler and the emergence of a unity consciousness represented by One Hunahpu.

In his first year in office, Obama has had to deal with an extremely difficult national crisis involving the economy, jobs, real estate, health care, education, bank failures, and minority rights. Many ready-and-willing critics in the right-wing media assail him daily with jabs and distractions.[13] They have no interest in reform, and are already planning for a Republican victory in the 2012 election. If ousted, Obama will be the sitting lame-duck president when the 13th Baktun reaches completion on December 21, 2012. The alternative is for his first term to become a success, he gets reelected, and we truly enter a hopeful new era just as the next World Age, according to the Maya, arrives.

But the powers that be are making Obama's attempts at reform difficult. The media, as mentioned, are picking apart everything he does. The banking institutions continue their unconscionable behavior despite the new president taking them to task for it. But also, strangely, Obama himself has made concessions to the same powers that designed and benefited from the Bush agenda. In fact, Obama the president has been doing things we never would have expected from Obama the candidate. For example, in June of 2009 he dissolved the Office of Thrift Supervision, created to regulate banking conglomerate AIG and take account of what it did with taxpayer bailout money (apart from giving some of it as bonuses to its top executives).[14]

Obama has also selected some dubious characters for top advisory positions. Seven Macaws have been invited into Obama's administration. Take, for example, top White House economic adviser Lawrence Summers and Obama's Treasury secretary, Timothy Geithner. Summers was one of the leading voices of radical financial deregulation in the Clinton administration, policies that led to the current subprime-loan crisis. Geithner, as head of the New York Federal Reserve, ignored Wall Street's collapse and then advocated propping up Citigroup and AIG with taxpayer dollars. Today, both Geithner and Summers blame the current crisis on the same unregulated derivatives markets that they once championed.[15] This reversal may simply be paying lip service to a public expecting reforms, as it's quite possible that financial industry lobbyists will succeed in subverting any real application of oversight and regulation of banking practices. The quick fix currently being applied to the crisis, that of printing more money to bolster failing industries and banking institutions, undermines the dollar's worth in the not-too-long run. So are Geithner and Summers reformed, or are they implementing a different kind of rhetoric while picking more taxpayer pockets? And what are they doing in the Obama administration, anyway?

Zbigniew Brzezinski is a partisan Democrat, an elder master gamesman of economic strategy whose activities as Jimmy Carter's national security adviser helped to create the Afghan mujahideen (from which the Taliban and Al-Qaeda emerged). These events were glamorized in the movie *Charlie Wilson's War*.[16] He has been a frequent speaker at conferences of the Bilderberger group (a nonpartisan affiliation of wealthy and powerful families and corporations), and now, at age seventy-eight, has been appointed Obama's foreign policy adviser. He is a lifelong committed architect of The New Order in which wealthy global elites control the world and its populations. In his book *Between Two Ages*, Brzezinski wrote of the increasing impact of technology on society. He called this the dawn of the technetronic era, and envisioned future scenarios characterized by "the gradual appearance of a more controlled and directed society. Such a society would be dominated by an elite whose claim to political power would rest on allegedly superior scientific know-how. Unhindered by the restraints of traditional liberal values, this elite would not hesitate to achieve its political ends by using the latest modern techniques for influencing public behavior and keeping society under close surveillance and control. . . . The emergence of a large dominant party . . . could accelerate the trend toward such technological managerialism."[17]

This future plutocratic world of elites omnisciently controlling the world's population is eerily similar to the scenario in George Orwell's famous book *1984*. Thomas More's classic *Utopia* derived the term "utopian" from the Greek for "nowhere," underscoring the irony of Brzezinski's ideal all-seeing future Big Brother state, surely a dystopia to the average human, reaching its tentacles *everywhere*. The grand chess game he sees himself playing reveals a Machiavellian mastermind, and now, in his new role as foreign adviser to Obama, he is perhaps positioning himself for checkmate.

These facts may seem surprising to many who voted for Obama. His influences, however, have been a matter of public record. Politicians influenced by the Chicago School of Economics, the so-called Chicago boys, are allied with a neoliberal economic strategy. It is neoliberal because it advocates a free (liberal) global marketplace. As such, its proponents recommend the kind of unregulated business practices that have gotten us into trouble. Milton Friedman, a neoliberal strategist and patriarch of the Chicago School of Economics, believed that free markets are the best way to design a world economy. Obama lived in Chicago and launched his career within the pressure cooker of hard-boiled Chicago politics, and his economic values, not surprisingly, resemble those taught in the Chicago School of Economics. For example, in a press conference of June 17, 2009, Obama shared his policy toward oversight and regulation of big business, the absence of which led to the banking and subprime-mortgage crisis: "I believe that our role is not to disparage wealth, but to expand its reach. Not to stifle the market but to strengthen its ability to unleash the creativity and the innovation that still makes this nation the envy of the world."[18]

Even if Obama was 100 percent committed to everything he promised during his campaign, he'd have as much chance of changing the course of globalization as a tugboat would have of saving the *Titanic* three minutes before it was impaled by the iceberg. Historian and political activist Howard Zinn wrote: "Obama was and is a politician. So we must not be swept away into an unthinking and unquestioning acceptance of what Obama does. Our job is not to give him a blank check or simply be cheerleaders. It was good that we were cheerleaders while he was running for office, but it's not good to be cheerleaders now. Because we want the country to go beyond where it has been in the past. We want to make a clean break from what it has been in the past."[19] And to do that we have to get to the root causes of why things happen the way they do. Why is health care failing? Why are our banks bankrupt? Obama himself once said, "It's not enough to get out of Iraq; we have to get out of the mind-set that led us into Iraq." Yes, that's true; we need to identify and deal with the psychological or ideological source of the problem. But Zinn rightly asked, "What happened to that Obama?"[20]

THE PATHOLOGICAL HEART OF THE HYDRA

An unresolved and festering dark side poisons American politics. Bush is no longer president, but there is a larger Seven Macaw threat at loose in the world today. Seven Macaw is a many-headed hydra, and removing one head will not do him in. The stated intentions of Obama have so far proven ineffective against a much more deeply rooted systemic problem. He is morphing before our eyes into yet another political figurehead molded by Big Money and the military-industrial-informational complex. He either had this up his sleeve all along (since when can politicians ever be trusted?) or he has been taken hostage by the forces of globalization. The Hero Twins had it easy; we have a more difficult task. We must speak truth to power and identify the entity that lies behind all Seven Macaws, one that has its tentacles embedded in our own lives.

The heart of the many-headed monster is that strange nonhuman institution that has been granted immortality: the corporation. The corporation is today's dominant institution. We can't pass a day without interfacing with corporations; they are deeply interfused in our lives, from schools to banks to news sources to jobs, gas stations—they are literally impossible to avoid. Mythologist Joseph Campbell noted that the highest buildings in a town reveal the priorities and dominant institutions of a culture. In the Middle Ages, it was the high steeple of the Church.[21] Today, it is the high skyscraper of the corporate banking institutions that runs the world.

Corporations can be traced back to 1712, to a community-held water pump in England designed to pump water out of a coal mine and thereby increase productivity. With the industrial revolution in the early nineteenth century and the mechanizing of the textile industry, the corporation became an idea whose time had come. But early corporations had a very narrow legal mandate. There were limits placed in a corporation's charter, and its owners and shareholders were liable should anything go wrong. The corporation was basically seen to be in service to a public good, a temporary gift granted by the government. Local and national governments gave very little actual power to the corporation, and extensive licensing and oversight was required. Corporations had certain privileges but no rights.

Then came the railroads. People moved west by the thousands, and banks saw they could capitalize on funding the dream of a transcontinental railway. Corporations grew in size. And they grew hungrier. The societal changes wrought by the Civil War were craftily utilized by corporate lawyers to give undue power to corporations. After the Civil War, the Thirteenth Amendment granted freedom to slaves. A lingering conception of slaves as property made it seem odd to grant freedom, human rights, to property. After a co-opted court case in 1886, this murky conceptual shift was applied to the idea that a corporation was the property of its shareholders, and some deft and illegal maneuvering in the courts between 1886 and 1895 set up a series of decisions and precedents that resulted in corporations being given all the rights of a human being but none of the responsibilities.[22] You can't throw a corporation in jail, and it can live forever. It became a "legal person" that could buy and sell property, borrow money, sue and be sued in court.

As the twentieth century dawned, the first millionaires began to appear. J. P. Morgan, the Rockefellers, and the huge megacorporations such as the railroads and steel manufacturers started to muscle into the political arena. Big industry could wield power in a democratically elected Congress. Lightning had been shot into Frankenstein's monster. Along with big corporate industry came the Big Wars, engines that fed on and drove industry. Early observers of these events, such as social philosopher John Dewey, were largely marginalized or reviled as socialists. Meanwhile, in the 1920s a flush of illusory wealth flowed through American culture and lulled people securely under Seven Macaw's spell. This was due not to the inherent sustainability of the corporate industrial model but to the perfection of techniques for extracting, refining, and utilizing resources in the New World—mainly oil and iron. The stock market crash of 1929 was a temporary wake-up call. FDR's liberal social reforms were effective solutions to the Depression of the 1930s and promised a more egalitarian style of culture, but were quickly superseded by World War II, Korea, more temporary wealth and big cars in the 1950s, Vietnam, and the continuing feeding frenzy of the corporate monster.

The legal status and rights of corporations were now well established. What was the abiding purpose of these person-corporations? Noam Chomsky stated that "corporations were given the rights of immortal persons, but special kinds of persons—persons who had no moral conscience. You expect a human being to care about others but corporations are designed by law to be concerned only with the financial interests of its stockholders."[23]

And the bottom-line financial interest of the stockholder is how to make as much money as possible. Some companies do good for the community and for people, but the lingering problem is always the trajectory dictated by the bottom-line profit motive. Publicly traded companies are structured and required by legal, court-decided mandates to place growth and profit above competing interests—including the public good. Therefore, a corporation can behave against the public good, and will even be protected by law in doing so. If an environmental law prevents a corporation from polluting, it can lobby and change the law, or simply pay the fines and continue polluting, continuing to cause health problems for human beings living in the affected areas. This happens constantly in the corporate arena. If it is more cost-effective to pay fines than to reengineer its pollution controls, then the courts will agree that it is within its rights. The courts then become a type of servile legal monstrosity, in essence being paid off by Seven Macaw.

The halcyon days for corporations were amplified by a brilliant technique for maximizing profits. All businesses have two parts of the profit equation to deal with: expenses and income. If income exceeds expenses, you have a profit. The profit motive demands as much profit as possible. If some or all of the expenses could be pushed outside of the accounting tally, in effect forcing someone else to pay them, then you've just made a killing and really maximized your profits. In the legal jargon of corporate accountants, this technique is much used and is called "externalizing." It's an effort to externalize, project, or coerce someone else to cover your costs. Corporations have learned to do this by getting in bed with politicians. Huge amounts of money now go to lobby efforts, which are able to finagle tax breaks and loopholes, financially beneficial legislative decisions, and what is referred to as "corporate welfare," meaning the government—that is, your tax dollars—will defray costs incurred by big companies. We, the taxpayers, become the ones who pay for the externalized costs of huge corporations.

Since the brief turmoil and human rights breakthroughs of the 1960s, the business world has increasingly moved toward megamergers and huge umbrella-like corporate entities, no longer limited to any particular nation. It's gone transnational; national boundaries are meaningless in the modern corporate culture. And today, our world is heading toward the ultimate wet dream of the corporateer: globalization, one world government— that is, the one Mega Company that rules the world.

And here's the ten-trillion-dollar question: If a corporation is a person, what kind of person is it? That is the question asked by Joel Bakan in his 2005 book *The Corporation*, recently made into an informative documentary. Bakan decided to examine case histories in the activities of various corporations, performing an analytical diagnosis of sorts. Using specific examples, Bakan found that corporations exhibit the following personality traits:

- A callous unconcern for the feelings of others
- Incapacity to maintain enduring relationships
- Reckless disregard for the safety of others
- Deceitfulness: repeated lying and conning for the benefit of self-interest

- Inability to admit and feel guilt
- Failure to conform to social norms with respect to lawful behavior

Each one of these diagnostic traits is demonstrated by numerous examples from case histories. For example, corporations have a strategy of periodically locating to different Third World countries, tapping the human resources there until workers begin to demand better pay and working conditions. Instead of engaging in negotiations, corporations typically close down operations in that locale and relocate. This demonstrates an inability to maintain enduring relationships. As another example, corporations are willing to pay huge amounts of settlement money for damages and deaths, but do not admit guilt or release apologies to those affected. This demonstrates a callous unconcern for the feelings of others and an inability to admit and feel guilt. Corporations behave outside of social norms by willingly breaking laws and paying the fines, as long as the fines are more cost-effective than solving the problem—regardless of the deadly nature of the problem.

The official diagnosis of such traits and behavior is: psychopath. Corporations are the type of person who cannot be trusted or relied upon, the type of person who is very, very dangerous. This psychopathology of corporations is driven by a self-centered and self-serving narcissism. The implications of this approach to understanding the diabolical nature of corporations is staggering. How did the corporation gain such power and become such a Frankenstein monster? The turning point appears to be the moment when personhood was granted to corporations, when the Promethean spark of life was injected into a formerly lifeless body.

Thom Hartmann traced the origins of this magical moment in the history of big business and reveals that it was based on a total deception. In his book *Unequal Protection* (2004), Hartmann traces the first judicial decision, which later served as a precedent, to the 1886 case *Santa Clara County vs. Southern Pacific Railroad*. In it, the U.S. Supreme Court ruled that the state tax assessor, not the county assessor, had the legal right to determine the taxable value of fence posts along a railroad's right-of-way. That's it. Doesn't sound too groundbreaking, does it? In the case's summary headnote, however, the Court's reporter wrote something that had no legal precedent and didn't have anything to do with the case. He wrote: "The defendant Corporations are persons within the intent of the clause in section 1 of the Fourteenth Amendment to the Constitution of the United States, which forbids a State to deny any person within its jurisdiction the equal protection of the laws."[24] That Court reporter happened to be J. C. Bancroft Davis, a former railroad president. Hartmann points out that the Court ruled no such thing. The presiding chief justice wrote elsewhere that they had not discussed "the Constitutional question," and nowhere in the decision itself does the Court say corporations are persons.

Nevertheless, corporate attorneys quickly adopted the language of the head note and began to quote it as legal precedent. Hartmann writes: "Soon the Supreme Court itself, in a stunning display of either laziness (not reading the actual case) or deception (rewriting the Constitution without issuing an opinion or having open debate about the issue), was quoting Davis's headnote in subsequent cases. While Davis's *Santa Clara* headnote didn't have the force of law, once the Court quoted it as the basis for later decisions its new doctrine of corporate personhood became the law."[25]

And such is the artifice by which Frankensteins are created. This all happened very quickly, under the cloak of deception. Even the president of the United States was aghast and perplexed at the growing power of the big companies. In his annual address to Congress in December 1888, President Grover Cleveland observed, "As we view the achievements of aggregated capital, we discover the existence of trusts, combinations, and monopolies, while the citizen is struggling far in the rear or is trampled to death beneath an iron heel. Corporations, which should be the carefully restrained creatures of the law and the servants of the people, are fast becoming the people's masters."[26]

Exxon/Mobil, Monsanto, Microsoft, Nike, Pfizer, Telecom, and the AIG are just a few of the megacorporations that now rule the world, monopolize the resources of small countries, act with impunity, influence political process, broadcast propaganda, manufacture consent, and by law can live forever. Their birth certificates were forged. They and their Seven Macaw managers and governmental policy-makers are the fulfillment of the Maya prophecy for 2012.

Chapter Ten

Ending the War on Us

If you're lucky you'll come to a crossroads and see
that the path to the left leads to hell, that the path to
the right leads to hell, that the road straight ahead
leads to hell and that if you try to turn around you'll
end up in complete and utter hell. . . . Then, if you're
ready, you'll start to discover inside yourself what
you always longed for but were never able to find.[1]

—Peter Kingsley,
In the Dark Places of Wisdom

The corporation and the government have an intimate relationship. They need each other, and are as interconnected as light and shadow. One tells you to open your pocket, while other picks it. Government, which in a democracy is supposed to represent the people's interest, is getting fat by charging the people interest. The absurd equation of representative democracy says we told government to do that to us. As for the corporation, its diagnosis as a pathological entity is now clear. Joel Bakan asked the reasonable question, and the case histories gave him the answer. Given that we can now understand the personhood of the corporation to have a diagnosis of narcissistic pathology, what kind of relationship does it have with government?

THE CODEPENDENT CORPORATION

Psychotherapist and social commentator Anne Wilson Schaef examined the relationship between addictive behavior and larger social institutions in her book *When Society Becomes an Addict.* This approach is relevant to the question because the biggest corporations in the world are addicted to oil. Her previous book, *CoDependence,* laid the groundwork for understanding codependent and addictive behaviors in a larger context, tracing the convoluted ways that dysfunctional people tend to create dysfunctional corporations.

Based on Dr. Schaef's work, I suggest the following: An institution or corporation is composed of its internal units, no matter what unassailable abstract identity it is granted by the courts or adopts as its mission statement. In others words, a corporation will in practice be a reflection of the mind-set of its internal units. In this real world, a corporation will express the basic dynamic of its constituent parts. Schaef found that the behavior and inter-relationships of workers in many companies follow a pattern. Rather than the objective professionalism that we might expect, workers were instead found to create, experience, and sustain extremely dysfunctional and code-pendent workplace relationships.

Very few people are mature enough to maintain a completely profes-sional and objective workplace ethic. A veneer of professionalism may exist, but it usually hides deeper dysfunction. Workplaces, in fact, often serve as the stages on which we unconsciously try to work out deep-set personal is-sues and problems. The hierarchical structure of companies allows and rein-forces a dysfunctional tendency, as the corporate environment encourages and offers status, power, control, and advancement within the constantly shifting possibilities of the modern work world. Typical Pavlovian strategies of reward-stimulation-gratification are routinely employed by the upper management, confusingly combined with poorly concealed favoritism and nepotism. The end result is a type of employee-employer relationship that is untrusting and codependent.

The employee's job is to enable the corporation in its vices and distorted self-image, and vice versa. The employee may be charged with the responsibility of facilitating the corporation's vices, such as its need to externalize its costs so as to maintain high profits, setting up an ethical dilemma if the employee has any conscience. The employer enables the employee's vices in providing opportunities for power plays and personal gain at the expense of others, or perhaps merely in providing money for addictions. Apart from vice fulfillment, the employer at least promises to fulfill the employee's need for money, security, vacation time, fair treatment, health benefits, and so on. Thus, the employee expects the employer to take care of his or her basic needs. After all, that's the deal, that's why a person sought the position in the first place.

For the corporation, an employee's needs are costly. They are on the "expenses" side of the profit equation, and it's a cost that many corporations have learned how to externalize. Wal-Mart, for example, grew fatter by encouraging its employees to apply for Medicaid rather than providing a decent health program. The corporation will always try to squeeze more out of its workers, provide for them less, while the employee feels its long-term loyalty should be increasingly rewarded with time. Corporations are essentially duplicitous, with the mouth assuaging employees' insecurities while the hand is picking their pockets. To make this metaphor even more tortured, the duplicitous corporation that picks your pocket is made up precisely of you and others like you. It's no wonder that doctors are prescribing more antidepressant drugs than ever.

This entire structure is unhealthy, dysfunctional, and codependent. My interpretation begs the question: If a company is seen as an aggregate of its components, and the people within it are basically codependent, then what is the company codependent with? The corporation, as an aggregate of dysfunctional and codependent persons, needs someone or something outside of it to take care of its projected garbage, its externalized costs. In practice, a whole spectrum of targets have been used—entire groups of people, Third World countries, minorities, and so on—but there is one well-known entity that has become the primary codependent partner for corporations. That is government. Through their huge lobby efforts, corporations coerce governmental policy-makers into legislating tax breaks, loosening environmental laws, and creating other benefits so that profits can be maximized and costs can be covered by someone else. This externalizing technique requires an intimate connection between corporations and the government. In what is known as corporate welfare, government covertly arranges for someone else to cover the externalized cost of big business. That someone else is, ultimately, you, the taxpayer.

So we have a vicious circle in which corporations, including one that you may work at, is designed to be in a codependent relationship with another entity, the government, who manages your tax dollars and hands them over to your employer. In time you can only give less to your employer. This results in a certain prospect of diminishing returns for the corporation, otherwise known as sucking you dry. The corporation is a huge cannibalizing virus, feeding on itself until it is dead. This vicious circle lies at the heart of the flawed thinking that drives Western civilization: We are killing ourselves in order to thrive. The result is short-term profit for some and inevitable impoverishment for all. The holistic nature of the system has been disregarded, and the efficacy of the system can be maintained only with lies and deception. Eventually, the charade must end.

Our economic system is failing because it is built upon faulty premises. The circularity of supply-and-demand economics would be hilarious if its consequences weren't so tragic. Note the unfortunate paradox of the "Coal Miner's Riddle," which is being played out time and again in so many parts of the world:

Daughter: "Daddy, I'm cold."

Coal miner: "That's 'cause we ain't got no coal."

Daughter: "Why not?"

Coal miner: "'Cause I'm broke, can't afford it."

Daughter: "How come?"

Coal miner: "They let me go at the coal mine."

Daughter: "Why?"

Coal miner: "Because there's too much coal."

We in the modern world live in a global crisis at a crossroads. Despite the illusion of security created by temporary bursts of wealth driven by resource control, our behavioral choices have set up institutions that are destroying the world and making it uninhabitable. Why is it that human beings are manifesting this self-destructive drive to dominate and consume the world at any cost?

THE WAR AGAINST NATURE

Divisive self-serving politics driven by egoism has created a schism in the collective psyche. The artificial construct called the ego has its uses, but to organize an entire civilization around its gratification has led us to a precipice. One of the many ways in which this manifests is a destructive attitude toward nature. Territorial expansion, land parceling, habitat destruction and species extinction, resource drainage—all of this reveals the impact of Western civilization. And to be clear, this attitude is particularly rampant in the brand of Western civilization practiced by American policy makers and corporations. All of the Americas. North America, including Canada, has more regulatory laws in place than do Central and South America, where pollution and wilderness eradication is rampant, but North American companies exploit loopholes such as energy and pollution credits, which they trade among themselves like baseball cards.

With Seven Macaw running the show, nature itself is a threatening and dangerous "other." Worse than that, philosopher Seyyed Hossein Nasr observed that for modern man,

nature has become like a prostitute—to be benefited from without any sense of obligation and responsibility toward her. . . . It is precisely

> the "domination of nature" that has caused the problem of over-
> population, the lack of "breathing space," the coagulation and conges-
> tion of city life, the exhaustion of natural resources of all kinds, the
> destruction of natural beauty, the marring of the living environment
> by means of the machine and its products, the abnormal rise in men-
> tal illness and a thousand and one other difficulties.[2]

Like an addict compulsively seeking the next fix, running unconsciously on automatic pilot, the Seven Macaw system tries to bring everything under its dominion and control. But this is a monster of our own creation, a direct consequence of deputizing ego as the sole sovereign of All Reality. We feed and enable Seven Macaw. WE have been waging a war on nature, on life itself, and therefore, without even knowing it, on ourselves.

As the old saying goes, "You can drive out Nature with a pitchfork, but she will speedily return." This anecdote from the Middle Ages has two readings. It's like one of those magic diagrams in which the eye perceives either a candlestick or two faces looking at each other. The first, literal level, is that of a typical householder trying to keep their yard tidy. Mowing and weeding and trimming branches is a constant task, for nature will always encroach into the little domain of order that you try to maintain. This approach to nature assumes a separation of the human being out of nature, a particularly acute development among societies where the individual ego is accentuated. In this process, the human being is artificially abstracted from nature, as if it is not part of it. To the extent that the artificial ego is the fulcrum of the identity, this is true. The ego doesn't belong to nature, it is an artificial construct. This situation is not "normal" in two senses: One, it leads to the problems sketched above, and two, traditional cultures (meaning virtually every culture apart from those that embrace the values of Western civilization) have had a more integrated relationship with nature. World history as seen through the lens of Western scholarship diminishes this fact, preferring to emphasize the demands of survival and the products of material culture. Here modern historians are attentive to the lowest common denominator, a reductionist approach that wouldn't dream of even trying to identify the "highest common factor" spoken of by Huxley and the Perennial Philosophers. As a result, ancient people are turned into struggling parodies of our own materialist agenda who couldn't manipulate the environment in the superior way that the modern world can. We developed out of them and are in all ways better, and better off. This is, in its essence, the myth of progress. And it is a myth in the sense that the modern mind sees a myth, as a lie, a fiction, an untruth.

The aboriginal Dreamtime is perceived by the modern mind, wrongly, as a prerational stage of development. What if, instead of a prerational stage, the Dreamtime is really a transrational state? An awareness of the subtle earth lines and fields, conscious interactions between human beings and seasonal cycles, reflected in astronomical movements, initiatory traditions that cultivate higher wisdom—what if human cultures before the advent of city-states and hierarchical monotheism lived within the space of this Dreamtime, a transrational state of consciousness rather than a prerational state? Something very curious that happened in Australia, about 3,000 years ago, suggests this is so.

The aborigines of Australia are noted for not developing and using tools. They have historically been nomadic gatherers shifting from region to region with the changing seasons. Archaeologists consider tool use a sign of civilization, a development out of a more primitive state. About 3,000 years ago, tool use did begin to develop among the aborigines. Artifacts survive that tell a story, one with a surprising twist. Tools and technology began to spread from group to group and then, suddenly, it stopped. The tools stopped being made. Why this odd turn of affairs? Wouldn't any human culture welcome the develop of technology? Robert Lawlor, in his book *Voices of the First Day*, has suggested a plausible explanation based on his deep work with the Dreamtime denizens of Australia. Lawlor suggests that the ancient aborigines realized that tools and technology would lead them down a road to a place where the Dreamtime did not exist. Projecting meaning onto abstract artifacts, the creation of categories and labels, the whole process, would draw a veil over the grand, holistic, transrational domain of the Dreamtime. They made a rational decision to not limit their minds to the domain of material objects and their clever uses, to not leave the Dreamtime. I suspect that all human populations once lived within the Dreamtime state, what we might call a multidimensional or holistic state of being.

This fascinating scenario tells us much about the modern world's assumptions and biases, and exposes the myth of progress—the belief that the modern world is in all ways more sophisticated and evolved than our ancient ancestors. We have our stereotypes of grunting cave dwellers that preclude us from accepting this scenario. This is, interestingly, yet another example of the power of abstract image-objects (stereotypes) to delude and occlude direct perception of reality, of the thing-in-itself. From the Dreamtime perspective of transrational consciousness, history has been regress, not progress; we kicked ourselves out of Paradise.

Driving out nature with a pitchfork is like banishing ourselves from the Dreamtime. This is the deeper meaning of the adage. It's a declaration of a fiction, an abstraction, a lie. We do, in fact, live here on earth, within its multiple fields of energy and seasons. It is our home; we emerge from it and return to it. To have a transcendent or transrational perspective is not to deny the body of the earth and the life that it gives, but to embrace it fully and honor it with reverence. The ego resists this because it sees in it a chaos it can't control, a future dissolution of itself that it can't prevent, and a sovereign being much larger than itself. Resisting this at all costs, the ego envisions leaving the earth, jettisoning itself into outer space, which it believes is a further developmental step toward eternity. Nasr wrote:

> The sense of domination over nature and a materialistic conception
> of nature on the part of modern man are combined, moreover, with
> a lust and sense of greed which makes an ever greater demand upon
> the environment. Incited by the elusive dream of economic progress,
> considered as an end in itself, a sense of the unlimited power of man
> and his possibilities is developed, together with the belief, particularly

well developed in America, of boundless and illimitable possibilities
within things, as if the world of forms was not finite and bound by
the very limits of those forms.[3]

Consider the promotional campaign of NASA in the 1990s, a poster showing that well-known sequence of Darwinian evolution from hunched proto-ape to erect, well-shaven, Modern Man. The words read: "What makes us the most intelligent species on earth is knowing we must leave it to survive."[4] Sadly, such a goal of Darwinian technocracy is just one more step of abstraction *away from* eternity, a catchy new formulation of the same ego-based pathology that has led us, and the earth, right into the crapper.

But you cannot banish forever what is part of yourself. And time comes around in the seasons of change when the renewal of the full potential of the human mind, and human society, will be the choice made by those who are conscious.

PARTNERSHIPS AND DOMINATORS

We are told that human beings emerged from the primates some eight million years ago. Our understanding of evolution and our attitudes toward it are informed as much by vague stereotypes as by science. The image of our ancestors as grunting uni-brow ogres in caves does not reflect the truth. Human beings living during the Neolithic Magdalenian period in Europe (ca. 17,000–10,000 BC) had arts, trade, music, and burial rites.[5] If language is an indication of the level of mental sophistication, why is it that the most ancient language, Sanskrit, is many times more complex than modern English? The Aztecs are frequently portrayed in the media as atavistic savages, and many unsuspecting viewers accept this portrayal without question. How is it, then, that the Aztec language, Nahuatl, is more nuanced, expressive, and adaptable than English, capable of producing meta-concept compound words running over a hundred letters?

We are told that human beings are basically male dominated, hierarchical, and aggressively territorial, just like our closest genetic cousins, the primates. We see our own civilization's propensity for endless war in the violence and alpha-male dominance observed in chimpanzee populations. It seems to be an obvious fact of nature that we would retain instincts and behaviors forged through millions of years of evolutionary biology. Our institutions and foreign policies are indeed oriented toward the chimp goal of dominance and setting up control hierarchies. Chimpocracy (primate politics) reigns in religion, business, families, and politics. Domination is a core principle at work on every level of our civilization. Why is this? Is it really because such behavior is hardwired into our genes, courtesy of our close cousins the chimps?

Certainly there are, and have been, populations of human beings who live peacefully and cooperatively among themselves and their neighbors. The Australian aborigines, as mentioned, rejected warfare and tool use to remain living in the seasonally shifting unity consciousness of the Dreamtime. Why does it thus seem we are fated to be, on the whole, aggressive dominators? Is it evolutionary fate, or a choice? Is it our nature or our training? Individual human beings and small groups are certainly capable of compassion, caring, egalitarian sharing, and mutually beneficial problem solving. Why, then, are our largest and most prominent social institutions compelled to abide by the driving force of aggressive imperialism, self-interest, and territorial resource domination?

Social historian Riane Eisler studied and wrote a great deal about the development of dominator styles of culture in her book *The Chalice and the Blade.* She found that history, as commonly understood, begins with the advent of the dominator style and the subsequent control of resources with the development of city-states in the Middle East. But this particular mode of culture is not the norm; it does not faithfully represent the larger span of *Homo sapiens'* presence on the planet, which stretches back some 200,000 years.

Prior to the advent of "the dominator mode" in about 5000 BC, there was a lot going on. This earlier phase was simply labeled "prehistory" and until the work of archaeologist Marija Gimbutas wasn't acknowledged or explored by historians because the cultural groups in that period behaved very differently from the later dominator cultures. Eisler called these cultures "partnership" cultures, and in many ways they exhibited traits and behaviors the very opposite of the dominator cultures. An emphasis on peaceful relations, cooperative strategies, expressive art, pottery, painting, poetry, mutually beneficial trade, religious rituals at birth and death, even early script has been identified. A pantheon of animal, sky, and earth deities centering on the archetype of the Great Mother as a transformational mystery is a key to understanding these early partnership cultures.

Eisler observes that the partnership style is evident in human societies for the great majority of the human presence on this planet. The dominator style that has typified the recent 5,000 years, increasingly and globally so into modern times, is an exception. Or, let us say, it's not the only option. These two different cultural styles represent two poles of behavior that human beings are capable of expressing and formalizing into the defining institutions and attitudes of entire civilizations. The partnership style tends to organize around reverence and awe for the principle of an ever-renewing Great Mother—Nature in all its multiple aspects, experienced as a sacred unity. Human beings in this mind-set perceive themselves as participating in the great mystery play of life and being. The dominator style, on the other hand, is organized around male gods and rulers, man-made laws wielding punitive control, and hierarchies of power structure. In this mind-set, nature is artificially divided up into separate conceptual parts that can be owned and controlled. In this view, separate states of being and the different domains of nature are not perceived from the larger perspective of a unifying whole. An abstract division has taken place and the sense of the whole has been lost. This is, again, humanity ejecting itself from Eden, from the Dreamtime.

Although gender is evident in these two styles, Eisler takes the high road and her terminology, partnership and dominator, is intended to remove gender from the equation. This is an important distinction. A common mistake in understanding these ideas is to think the choice is between patriarchy and matriarchy, in which matriarchy is simply the old male power structure and tendency to dominance wearing a dress. The partnership mode, however, is fundamentally different from the dominance mode. Compared to the dominator mode, it is far more compassionate, humane, relational, communicative, integrative, and selfless.

If we remember our previous discussion of the dialectic between Seven Macaw and One Hunahpu in *The Popol Vuh,* we might begin to suspect what these two modes of culture are really about. Seven Macaw is about ego and gives rise to the modern crisis that is fueled by a narcissistic pathology. One Hunahpu represents the consciousness renewed by reconnection with the source and mystery of life, consciousness returned to right relationship with the One, the whole. The return of the partnership style, after the demise of Seven Macaw, is one manifestation of the second part of the Maya prophecy for 2012. But it requires that human beings choose to make it happen, choose to sacrifice the illusions of pathological ego dominance, and work to remake themselves as well as the world at large.

A lingering question remains: Why do these two tendencies in human beings exist?

DIVEST THE CHIMP, AWAKEN THE BONOBO

Let us return to the chimps. Not too long ago, evolutionary biologists considered the savannah baboon to be the closest living cousin of human beings. That primate had adapted to the same ecological conditions that prehumans faced when they descended out of the trees and entered the plains and savannahs. The search for the common ancestor, the point at which human beings diverged, was loaded with mystique and meaning. Darwin's theory of evolution, and the taxonomic categorizing of genus, species, and subspecies into related family branches, dictated that the primates were our closest living ancestors.

Among the primates are several species that also bear close relations to human behavior, and behavior was indeed considered to be a relevant indicator. With the work of Dian Fossey and Jane Goodall, in the 1970s the chimpanzees became the preferred model. Traits not observed in the baboons were present among the chimps, including pack hunting, tool use, food sharing, power politics, and primitive warfare. This occurred before the breakthrough perspectives of Marija Gimbutas and Riane Eisler were given credence, when male aggression and dominance were assumed to be defining, hardwired characteristics of human societies. This trait is observed in both baboons and chimpanzees, so the assumption of male superiority among all of the common human ancestors was not threatened. Indeed, the chimps provided classic examples of male power politics.

The chimps received support from advances in DNA testing, in which it was determined that they shared 98 percent of the genetic heritage of human beings—as close as a fox is to a dog. But another primate was lingering on the sidelines, one that was causing hushed whispers among the primatologists. The bonobo is as closely related to human beings as the chimps are, but their social behavior is markedly different.

Frans de Waal has pioneered a clear understanding of this new kid on the primate block, after years of observing bonobo groups. The results are startling and upset cherished notions of human nature. The bonobo species is best characterized as female-centered, egalitarian, and peace-loving, one that substitutes sexual contact for aggression as a means of conflict resolution. De Waal framed the larger sociological implications of his findings in an article he wrote for *Scientific American*: "At a juncture in history during which women are seeking equality with men, science arrives with a belated gift to the feminist movement. Male-biased evolutionary scenarios—Man the Hunter, Man the Toolmaker, and so on—are being challenged by the discovery that females play a central, perhaps even dominant, role in the social life of one of our nearest relatives . . . the bonobo."[6]

Bonobos are roughly the same size as chimpanzees. It is an entirely distinct species within the same genus as the chimpanzees. The role of sex in bonobo social relations is central, whereas in other species sex is a distinct, circumscribed behavior. Like human females, the bonobo female remains sexually active continuously. Bonobos engage in virtually every type of part-ner combination, and engage in sexual contact much more frequently than do other primates. The behavioral separation between sex and reproduction is a unique trait that bonobos share with humans.

Although engaging in sex for reasons other than reproduction is a defin-ing human behavior, there are some people, mainly religious fundamental-ists, who decry this practice as amoral. Such puritans are usually very well connected with the political and corporate culture of the Seven Macaws, who seek to control humanity. For them, the freedom of choice, personal empow-erment, and fulfillment that are practiced in a sexually diverse culture are dangerous.

In physique, the bonobos are observed to be much more graceful than the chimps. They have a flatter, more open face than the chimps, with a higher forehead, making them look more like humans. In our own biased aesthetics, they look to us more intelligent than the chimps. Whereas bono-bos in captivity can use tools, in the wild they tend not to. Instead they spend time in creative play, food gathering, and sharing tempered with frequent sexual exchanges. These exchanges should not be viewed as a type of excessive pathology, for they serve a purpose. They establish nonviolent, readily acces-sible, mutually beneficial reciprocity as a means of conflict resolution and social cohesion. We might say it is a nonmaterial currency that has value in establishing a pact of egalitarian partnership. It is practiced in the atmo-sphere of nonpossessiveness and nonaggression, constantly shifting and being renegotiated. It is not simply a utilitarian adaptive strategy in the Dar-winist reductive sense—often it is simply part of the play that maintains af-fection and relationship.

Bonobos evince a greater emotional sensitivity than the chimps and a surprisingly wide spectrum of emotional responses and expressions. Young bonobos make "funny faces" in long pantomimes, alone or while tickling each other, and are more controlled in expressing emotions than the chimps. Joy, sorrow, excitement, and anger, and surprisingly human nuanced com-binations occur during a typical day. Bonobos also are very imaginative.

De Waal observed captive bonobos engaging in a "blindman's bluff" game, in which the eyes are covered with a hand or leaf and the bonobo stumbles around, bumping into others, navigating the unknown space as if with the inner eye. De Waal writes that they seem to be "imposing a rule on themselves, such as 'I cannot look until I lose my balance.' Other apes and monkeys also indulge in this game, but I have never seen it performed with such dedication and concentration as by the bonobos."[7]

Although it may seem laughable to say it in such blunt terms, the bonobo prefers love, not war. Earlier we discussed the difference between partnership and dominator modes of culture. I believe it is possible and appropriate to emphasize the connection between the bonobo style of society and the ancient human partnership society identified by Riane Eisler. If we are committed to the myth of progress—the idea that the modern world and modern humans are more advanced than in former times—we must ask ourselves how the modern fixation with the dominator mode is more advanced than the egalitarian partnership focus of "prehistory." Clearly, the assumptions of our mainstream anthropologists and historians are flawed, and this problem must be explained. The chimp example of aggression being hardwired into our humanness is challenged by the gentle bonobo, who is as much a part of our genetic heritage as the chimps. The image of the club-wielding Neanderthal, so ingrained into the collective imagination, is a joke, a propaganda stunt designed to buttress a kind of social Darwinism that justifies Seven Macaw's dominance fetish.

ENDING THE WAR ON US

The war on nature, on our inner bonobos, on the partnership mode of culture that held humanity steady for five hundred centuries, is essentially a war on ourselves. How do we end the war on us? The following suggestions all fall under the heading of "easier said than done." The more difficult challenge of how we do it will be taken up in Chapter 12. For now, the writing is on the wall. We need to stop working for Seven Macaw. We need to embrace our shadows, integrate our lower and higher selves. The indigenous societies have been a screen for Western civilization's shadow projections for too long. These exemplars of living within a multidimensional ecology of nature, of practicing partnership, of forging mutually beneficial alliances, need to be honored and included as leaders and decision makers. The territorial imperialism that we have used to colonize the New World must shift to behaving as if we live here. When Cortés landed in Mexico in 1519, it was like foreground meeting background, like form meeting its essence. It could have been a harmonious "East meets West," but it wasn't. On some level this unresolved situation still haunts the subconscious of America, where selfish lifestyles usurp a disproportionate amount of the world's resources. The only way out, it seems, is to embrace our full beings; divest ourselves of selfish greed and resurrect the unity consciousness exemplified by One Hunahpu reborn. The kind of human being we will be is a choice, is generated and reinforced by our behaviors and the principles we want to install at the forefront of our society's institutions. The high principles of the American democratic experiment have been overtaken by a coup. Our founding fathers have had their heads cut off and hung in a tree while self-serving plutocrats magnify themselves, clinging to the shreds of control and power in a world gone trendy.

It is a simple step to see that the two choices have their own distinct consequences. The partnership mode held humanity steady for tens of thousands of years. It is a choice that results in a long-term sustainable world. The dominator mode, on the other hand, leads us ineluctably and relatively quickly to the brink of destruction. It seems as if we accidentally fell into the ego-based dominator mode, but perhaps forgetting our connection to the whole is part of the process. Now we've gotten the message. We know what it is like to live in a debased world disconnected from its eternal root. With all our information and data and historical perspectives set out on the table, we should now be able to make an informed and conscious choice about what kind of world we want to live in. Instead of a return to something in the past, and rejecting everything in the world around us, we can choose to make a new synthesis. We can adopt the best advances that the modern technological world offers, but combine it with a social style of relating that values peaceful conflict resolution, nonmaterial systems of exchange, nonviolence, and mutual respect for all beings.

The world is in a crisis. Systems need to be transformed, social activism is called for, but the new synthesis demands a spiritually centered and inspired social activism. We must do the inner work while engaging in the outer transformation creatively. There is a revolution afoot, a quiet transformation led by conscious people, emissaries of One Hunahpu. They believe that a sustainable world can be made now, and the future looks bright. Not to be cast as idealistic Pollyannas, this is the realm of inventive Americans, innovative young people intent on divesting from the Seven Macaw system and establishing community-based economies, mutually beneficial trade alliances, blending high tech with low impact while placing an emphasis on human fulfillment where it matters—in the hearts and minds of conscious human beings making peace.

The Maya possessed an insight into cycle dynamics and conveyed these ideals in their Creation Mythology. At the end of each cycle, a transformation and renewal can occur. But only if a sacrifice is made. This big "if" in the Maya prophecy exists because they understood the principle of individual free will, rejecting fatalistic determinism. They understood that nature inevitably cycles through phases of increases and decrease, day and night, awakening and forgetting. There is every reason to believe that 2012 represents midnight in the precessional seasons, the end of the phase of increasing darkness and the first glimmer of increasing light. Year 2012 is not about apocalypse, it's about *apocatastasis*, the restoration of the true and original conditions. Galactic midnight is upon us, but we are turning the corner, and this is the perfect time to set intentions for the next round of the human endeavor. Each person can choose where they want to be, inwardly, regardless of the circumstances of the outer world.

There's reason to believe that change is already happening. Amazing things are happening in grassroots communities, and we should try not to be distracted by negativity. It is usually the artists and visionaries who anticipate and intuitively extrapolate what is coming up for humanity around the next bend. In her conflict-resolution work, Corinne McLaughlin facilitates communication and bridge building in business and politics.[8] Social activist Charlene Spretnak envisions a future humanity seeing beyond its current limitations: "The knowing body, the creative cosmos, the complex sense of space—all these are asserting their true nature as we increase our abilities to see beyond the boundaries of the modern worldview."[9] We can't expect all of humanity to wake up and respond to the challenge of returning balance to the world, but it's likely that a significant portion will.

We've been examining the Maya prophecy for the years leading up to 2012. The second part of the prophecy is where free will comes into play. The biggest free-will act we can do, right now at this crisis-filled juncture, is to sacrifice our inner Seven Macaws—that is, our attachment to the illusions that keep our consciousness fixated to domains of limitation—and stop feeding the monster that is generating a debased, controlled, deceived world. We can pull the plug and simply not reinforce a world generated by the illusions of Seven Macaw. This is a core truth that the world resists embracing, and it requires that we take responsibility ourselves for making the change.

CHAPTER ELEVEN

THE MAYA RENAISSANCE

Hopefully, with the revitalization of Mayan culture,

the elders and the Aj K'ij, or Mayan priests, will,

once again, be seen as religious leaders and not as

witch doctors. They are the spiritual guides who

know and understand the ancient Mayan calendar,

a tool they consult for the appropriate time to

petition the supernatural beings for their blessing

and to give thanks.[1]

—VICTOR MONTEJO, *"The Road to Heaven"*

When I first traveled to Guatemala in the mid-1980s, I was blissfully unaware of the genocidal atrocities that were occurring. I had read about the highland Maya, still following the 260-day calendar, and happily tramped around traditional villages such as Momostenengo, Santiago Atitlán, and Todos Santos. The Maya rites and new cultural vistas I encountered were all bewildering to my young eyes, and it wasn't until halfway through the trip that it dawned on me—I was wandering in a war zone.

The shock of realization happened on a bus trip through the Petén jungle of northern Guatemala. I'd just visited Tikal and was making my way to the contested Belizian border, which I'd heard might be shut down by the Guatemala army. The bus itself was the typical ramshackle affair, packed to the brim with Maya campesinos and assorted characters, so I had to climb onto the roof. The four-hour ride through the dewy scrubland would have been pleasant, as I nestled down into sacks of corn chips, except for the annoying fact that every hour the bus stopped and we were all obliged to get out and present our belongings and identification to malevolent-looking machine-gun-toting soldiers. I was the only gringo on board. At the third checkpoint, three travelers, young men, were yelled at and dragged away. I wondered why they had passed the previous inspections unscathed, whereas at this one they became targets. That was a question that was never answered; it has no answer. Genocide follows no reason.

The genocide in Guatemala was brought to the attention of the American media by Jennifer Harbury, whose Guatemalan husband, Efrain Bamaca Velasquez, had been "disappeared" under mysterious circumstances. Under the threat of death she investigated his kidnapping and was able to trace, by herself, a sequence of events that clearly indicted specific officers in the Guatemalan military.[2] She held out hope that he was alive, but after filing lawsuits and digging deeper, she eventually discovered that he had been brutally tortured, murdered, and dumped in a shallow grave along with a few dozen other unfortunates. The tragic fact that Harbury humanized with her story was that her husband was one of hundreds of thousands of untold stories. Fathers and brothers, sisters and mothers, were kidnapped from their homes or as they walked on roads, corralled into army trucks, and hauled away, never to be seen again.

Harbury, a heroine for calling attention to a story that the U.S. media refused to report on for years, used to sit in front of the governmental palace in Guatemala City for weeks on end, sleeping and sitting in one spot in a hunger strike. That's what it took to draw the media's attention and to get answers. It took years, and she spent hundreds of thousands of dollars, to expose what was obvious to anyone who knew how international politics worked: Bureaucratic governmental leaders in Guatemala had ordered the killing of Maya peasants to clear the land for transnational development of prized export crops, such as coffee and sugar. The Zapatista rebellion in nearby Chiapas, Mexico, was launched precisely when NAFTA (the North

Amercian Free Trade Agreement, which would result in the appropriation of indigenous lands) went into effect on January 1, 1994.

During my early trips to Central America, in 1988, 1989, and 1990, my attention shifted to human rights issues. I fancied myself to be a footloose journalist masquerading as an anthropology student, hitchhiking through war-torn Nicaragua just after the Sandinista ousting of 1990, living and working with the highland Maya in San Pedro, while continuing to explore the Maya ruins. I researched and studied the history of Central America. The CIA-led coup of democratically elected Guatemalan president Jacobo Arbenz in 1954 was the seed that developed into the murder and disappearance of more than 200,000 Maya Indians in Guatemala throughout the 1980s. Four hundred and forty villages were wiped off the map, making way for international companies to appropriate the land for export crops.

Arbenz wanted to return some of the Chiquita Banana landholdings, which were not being farmed, to the Maya farmers they had originally been taken from, for subsistence farming. That's why they got rid of him. Entire Maya communities, such as Batz'ula on rich arable land in the highlands, were having their legal land grants rendered null and void, while the army intimidated and murdered men, women, and children, forcibly relocating the survivors to distant camps in the cold altiplano or pushing them across the border into Mexico. By 1994, when NAFTA was launched, the genocidal tactics had abated but the result was a national health issue—tens of thousands of Maya Indians were displaced, trying to live in marginalized areas or survive in government camps. Many refugees moved to the dumps of Guatemala City, where they foraged for food scraps and various items, such as plastic bags and paper, which they tried to resell on the streets. Glue sniffing became an epidemic among children as young as five years old. In 1994, I flew to Guatemala with relief supplies for the community of Batz'ula, including medicines, clothing, and viable seeds. The need was immense, and I felt helpless amid a national crisis involving the Maya people I had grown to love.

My earliest writings were journalistic pieces published in my brother's

Chicago-based newspaper, *Scenezine*, reporting on my travels and the political injustice endured by the Maya. Some of these observations and experiences also appeared in my first book, *Journey to the Mayan Underworld*, in 1989. Throughout the nineties, a sea change in the Maya world was astir, one that promised better times ahead. In 1992, the five hundredth anniversary of Columbus's "discovery" of America was trumped up in the media, greatly to the dismay and outrage of Native American rights activists. This of course galvanized the Columbus defenders, mainly Italian Americans who didn't really understand Columbus's true motivations. The romanticized image of an intrepid explorer charged by God to open up an empty hemisphere for European exploitation was alive and well. Oh yeah, there were two-legged creatures occupying the "new" world. Savages, of course, heathens; theologians doubted they had souls. I can remember going to a talk by political commentator Michael Parenti, and he read from Columbus's journal. Reporting back to the Spanish Crown on the nature and demeanor of the "Indians" (he thought he was in India), Columbus said they were gentle yet robust and healthy, good natured, loving and kind, trusting—they'll make great slaves. That was not the Columbus being celebrated in 1992.

OUT OF THE ASHES

An inspiring and courageous Maya woman emerged as a galvanizing figure in the 1990s, introducing the outside world to the stark realities of being Maya. Rigoberta Menchú was born in 1959 and spent her early years like many Maya peasants, traveling between her highland village and farming cooperatives where she worked on the coast. Notorious for unethical practices that kept their workers in debt, these slave-labor fincas, or farms, have come under international ridicule. Throughout the 1970s civil unrest in Maya communities was growing, spurred by unjust treatment by the Guatemalan government. Any effort to organize themselves was called communist, and civil patrol forces—often poorly supervised local regiments of the

National Army—were armed to supervise the Maya in their remote villages. This threat of violence within their midst caused a great deal of tension among Maya townspeople, as one might imagine, and they sought to organize themselves so as to have a stronger voice when petitioning the government for reform.

As a result, in a typical turn of events Rigoberta's family was accused of joining guerrilla efforts and her father was imprisoned and tortured. In 1979 Rigoberta joined, along with her father, the Committee of the Peasant Union (CUC). Within three years her father, brother, mother, and other relatives were killed as a result of government backlashes against Indians who wanted to empower themselves through organizing. She had taken an active part in Maya rights demonstrations for several years, but then had to go into hiding, and eventually she fled Guatemala for Mexico.

In 1984 her famous biography, *I, Rigoberta,* was published and translated, to international acclaim. Although some of her recollections on details have been called into question, her shocking story drew attention to the genocidal tactics employed by the Guatemalan military, working in the interests of transnational corporations who sought the use of traditional, legally held Maya lands. Through the following years Rigoberta has been celebrated as an outspoken advocate for Indian rights and multicultural reconciliation. In an amazing contretemps that rocked her home country, in 1992 she was awarded the Nobel Peace Prize. She used her $1.2 million cash prize to create a foundation in her father's name to fight for human rights for indigenous people. Her efforts resulted in the United Nations declaring 1993 the International Year for Indigenous Populations. Since then she has educated people about the Maya and human rights internationally. In 2007, she ran for the presidential office in Guatemala but withdrew before voting commenced due to violence against her constituents.

Another Maya leader who emerged from the genocidal tumult of the 1980s is Victor Montejo. His journey from a Jakeltek Maya village in the Guatemalan highlands to a PhD-holding chair of the Department of Native American Studies at the University of California is impressive and inspiring.

His story embodies the themes of death and resurrection, and he has become a primary voice for the renewal of Maya culture.

In September of 1982, he was a young schoolteacher in his home village in the Guatemalan highlands. In order to fulfill their "objective" of discouraging community self-determination, the Guatemalan army launched a series of murders against alleged leftist sympathizers, including Victor's brother. They effectively unleashed an episode of terror and violence that obliterated most of the village and its citizens. Victor himself was taken prisoner and endured a night of horror that he later described in his published testimonial:

> [They] lifted me up by my arms, then dragged me outside, past the pillar I had been tied to and across the patio to the rim of a foul cesspool filled with mud, water, and garbage. As they held me at the rim I heard a muffled cry rise from the depths and a head broke the surface, struggling to free itself from that horrible captivity . . . "T-t-take me out or shoot me, but don't leave me in here," he wailed pitifully. One of the soldiers leaned over the rim the man was clinging to and hit him in the face with his rifle butt, sinking him once again into the dark murky waters of the pit. "Shut up, turd . . ."
>
> All at once a piercing scream tore through my thoughts and caused my heart to pound violently; it was like a howl from the world beyond. The soldiers had become so inured to these hair-raising screams, not one of them stirred in his bunk. They all kept on snoring, impervious to what was happening in the adjoining torture chamber.[3]

Montejo survived that terrifying night and was later reunited with his wife and children. He soon learned that his name was on the death list and he, like thousands of other Maya refugees, fled Guatemala. By 1989 he had received an MA from the State University of New York at Albany, and by 1993 an anthropology PhD from the University of Connecticut. He held teaching posts at Bucknell University, the University of Montana, and the University of California, and he received a Fulbright scholarship in 2003. In that year, back in Guatemala, he was elected congressman by popular vote and was appointed vice president of the Commission on Indigenous Affairs by the Guatemalan National Assembly. In 2006, he sponsored and helped pass a law designating a National Day for the Indigenous Pueblos of Guatemala.

His books range widely over poetry, folklore, politics, anthropology, and Maya traditions. In his "brief" résumé he lists his many areas of experience and expertise: social, political, and cultural anthropology, specializing in the indigenous peoples of the Americas; Latin American diaspora, human rights, migration and transnationalism, comparative ethnic and religious studies, and native worldview and knowledge systems. As a political activist and community leader he has been involved in indigenous community development, rural and sustainable development, cultural/economic/political self-determination, cultural resource management, and poverty-alleviation strategies.[4] His other accolades and activities are too numerous to mention, but I'd like to focus on two things: his defining use of the concept of "Mayanism" and his discussion of the "Baktunian" movement, revealing the role he sees 2012 playing in what he calls the "Maya intellectual renaissance."[5]

MAYANISM AND THE BAKTUNIAN MOVEMENT

In Chapter 6 I discuss the appearance of the term "Mayanism" in a new Wikipedia entry, where it is used as a blanket term to refer to the New Age appropriation of 2012 and Maya concepts. I pointed out that using it in this way conflicted with the proactive use of similar terms, such as "Hinduism" and "Buddhism," and distorted Victor Montejo's original use of the term. In 2001, no less reputable a source than *The Oxford Encyclopedia of Mesoamerican Cultures* listed an entry called "Pan-Mayanism," consisting of a cultural entry by anthropologist Kay Warren and a political entry by Victor Montejo. Neither entry gives the slightest indication that Mayanism, or Pan-Mayanism, has anything to do with the New Age appropriation of Maya traditions. Montejo observes that a new identity for the Maya is forming as the twenty-first century begins, one that involves "reorganizing themselves and making alliances among distinct Mayan organizations in order to reach a consensus on how to negotiate with the government of Guatemala on behalf of their communities."[6] Acknowledging common goals, beliefs, and identity is at the root of this development.

Kay Warren, in her cultural section of the Pan-Mayanism entry, notes that "indigenous activists have confronted powerful stereotypes" and in response "Mayan-identified activists have created hundreds of organizations and institutions in the 1980s—including research institutes, publishers, training centers, libraries, and training groups—to identify the vitality of indigenous language and culture."[7] Out of this process a Pan-Mayan identity is emerging, one that is predicated on shared beliefs, customs, and values among many different Maya groups speaking different languages. A truly universal level of Maya tradition has been found in this process. This Mayanism highlights the common values and goals of diverse Maya communities, based on the core elements they all have in common.

Some of these shared qualities and values are elaborated in Montejo's article "The Road to Heaven: Jakaltek Maya Beliefs, Religion, and the Ecology." While his Oxford entry on Pan-Mayanism focuses on political struggles, this article is much like a companion piece that explores folklore and religious beliefs. He states that the theories advanced to explain the "primitive religions" of indigenous people are unsatisfactory. Early anthropologists were likely to explain Maya traditions as a product of magical thinking and superstitions, a laughable belief in ghosts and protective prayers motivated by a fear of the unknown. This is the typical view of scientism toward indigenous practices, and Montejo rightly observes that "Western scholars have tried to explain indigenous religiosity from a Eurocentric point of view."[8] He identifies the reference point of *nature* as a common thread of indigenous Maya beliefs, one that might be considered the hinge point of Mayanism. Cycles in nature, patterns in the sky and in agricultural rhythms, life cycles of animals and plants and human beings were all joined under the unifying umbrella of nature, Mother Earth and Father Sky, or as the Quiché Maya say, "all the sky-earth."[9]

"Earth and Heaven," Montejo writes, are "the generators of life and happiness."[10] This viewpoint provides a reference point for a pan-Maya identity and a satisfactory framework for a correct understanding of the term "Mayanism," stated in the work of a Maya intellectual and professor of anthropology who provides "an indigenous perspective," arguing that a "concern for the natural world, and the mutual respect this relationship implies, is constantly reinforced by traditional Mayan ways of knowing and teaching." Importantly, he formulates his thoughts on this pan-Maya basis of Maya spirituality in terms of what we could call a realized Perennial Philosophy: "For indigenous people, the environment and the supernatural realm are interconnected. This holistic perspective of human collective destiny with other living creatures on earth has a religious expression among indigenous people."[11] I interpret this as coming from the perspective, or value position, in which ego is already placed in right relationship with the unitary consciousness; Seven Macaw has successfully been transformed into One Hunahpu. The fourth point in Huxley's elucidation of the Perennial Philosophy, in which the purpose of human life is to live in the awareness of eternity, has been achieved. Paradoxically, this can occur only when the full life-and-death whole is embraced, something indigenous cultures are much more adept at than Western Eurocentric cultures, which deny death and thereby drive their citizens less elegantly toward it.

Victor Montejo's book *Maya Intellectual Renaissance* is an important resource for understanding the political, mythological, and social implications of a burgeoning Maya revival. He specifically suggests that the 2012 cycle ending is a critical component of this process. Framing the entire discussion within the emergence of a new Maya leadership taking the world stage (e.g., Rigoberta Menchú), Montejo explains "the present revitalization of the Maya culture in terms of its place in history, as occurring in the 'prophetic' cycle of time, the oxlanh b'aktun."[12] The word "oxlanh" means 13, and "b'aktun," or "b'en," refers to the Baktun period of the Long Count. Montejo points out that the phrase "Oxlanh B'en" was found in a Jakaltek Maya folktale he documented and translated, called "El Q'anil: Man of Lightning":

> . . . But in Oxlanh B'en, when the war breaks out
> We ourselves will come back as we are now
> And nobody else will act in our place
> Then, we will finish off the enemy.[13]

The context of the phrase makes sense, and Montejo believes it is a late reference to the 13-Baktun cycle ending. This is pretty interesting, but as for the literal meaning of the story, we should always take this kind of information with a grain of salt, not placing undue emphasis on it as a literal, inviolable prophetic utterance. Information like this gets filtered through a dozen storytellers over many centuries, and each adds and subtracts his own energy and thoughts. The idea of the final line, that "we will finish off the enemy," takes on political urgency or threat to enemies of the Maya. Its metaphorical meaning seems to derive, however, from the scenario in *The Popol Vuh* when the Hero Twins defeat "their enemies," the Dark Lords of Xibalba, at the end of the story, thus ushering in the new cycle and the rebirth of their father.

Historically, the Maya have often reasserted their self-determination at cycle endings in the calendar. The Caste War in the Yucatán, for example, was driven by a prophetic voice coming from the "Talking Cross" at Chan Santa Cruz toward the culmination of a Calendar Round. Today, as the end of the 13-Baktun cycle approaches, Montejo suggests that the Maya renaissance is a part of a millenarian phenomenon he calls the "b'aktunian movement."[14] This movement, which grows with the emergence of Pan-Mayanism, will inform and define the true Maya identity. I see this as a *true* identity as opposed to *new*, because the process seems to be more about a revival, an awakening, than the creation of something new. New elements, however, will unavoidably come into play as the Maya integrate themselves, as they always have, with new environmental and political realities, so a bit of both perspectives must be acknowledged. The *true identity* can be understood as existing at the essential core, while changing patterns of outer identities morph along the surface.

Change at the husk (the surface) and the seed (or core) is the essence of a beautiful paradigm of time that the Tzutujil Maya call *jaloj kexoj*. Spirit (*k'ex*, essence) and matter (*jal*, form) unfold in tandem. The priority of the seed-identity is necessary in the same way that spirit has priority in informing the ever-changing patterns of material forms. The Tzutujil Maya doctrine of jaloj kexoj goes hand in hand with another conception called "Flowering Mountain Earth"[15] in which reality grows, like a flowering mountain, outward from the spiritual essence as it becomes all the many things of manifest existence. Mayanism is concerned with the collectively shared seed-identity, and the Baktunian Movement is concerned with reestablishing and maintaining correct orientation between ego and Self, between matter and spirit, between indigenous and colonial mind-sets, to empower Maya leaders. This formula is similar to the mandate obeyed by ancient Maya kings—establishing within themselves an integrated shamanic conduit between sky and earth, between this world and the other world, and through that role they were empowered as political chiefs.

Montejo writes that "Prophetic expressions of the indigenous peoples insist on the protagonist role that new generations must play at the close of this Oxlanh B'aktun (thirteen B'aktun) and the beginning of the new Maya millennium. The ancestors have always said that 'one day our children will speak to the world.'"[16] And, again, the role of 2012 in Montejo's conception is clear:

This millennial or b'aktunian movement responds to the close of a great prophetic cycle . . . the great prophetic cycle of 400 years in the Maya calendar. For the Maya, this is not the close of the second millennium or 2000 years after Christ, but rather the close of the fifth millennium according to the ancient Maya calendar initiated in the *mythical year that corresponds to 3114 B.C. [correction of typo in original]. . . . The b'aktun includes the global concept of time and the regeneration of life with new ideas and actions. In other words, the theoretical b'aktunian approach leads us to understand the effect of human ideas and actions on all that exists on the earth and their effects on the environment and cosmos.*[17]

Montejo's observation not only helps us understand the concept of Mayanism (in which the spiritual values taught in *The Popol Vuh* are realized) but also helps us understand the indigenous attitude toward nature, one that is sustainable and diametrically opposed to the dominator style of colonial Western civilization. The Maya Renaissance can and should have a wider sphere of impact, one that speaks to the global crisis created by unsustainable, nature-destroying practices that need to be transformed at their roots in the collective consciousness.

Other scholars doing parallel work in elaborating the values of the "pan-Maya movement" include Garrett Cook and Robert Sitler. In his book *Renewing the Maya World*, Cook explored Maya rituals of renewal, identifying modern traditions as survivals of ancient rites. This means that, as I explained elsewhere in the book, the modern Maya do indeed retain ceremonial period-ending practices intended to facilitate transformation and rebirth. What Cook calls the modern "millenarian myth" of the modern Maya is simply another way of talking about the end of a great cycle, much like the role of the World Age in the ancient *Popol Vuh*. As such, Cook writes that "the millenarian myth depicts world transformation as a sunrise."[18] Importantly, the modern performances and ceremonies that are designed to depict and facilitate this "world renewal" are traceable back to the archetypal structure of *The Popol Vuh*. In his own comparative methodology, Cook outlines a five-step functional process in this Creation Myth, which is essentially identical to Joseph Campbell's hero's journey: engagement or contest; imprisonment; emergence or rebirth; reengagement; and defeat (of enemies).

I'm sure that my previous identification of Maya teachings as being part of a perennial wisdom tradition, or universal mythic pattern (Chapter 8), struck some readers as highly dubious. But here we can see a Maya scholar outlining the same position. This is a problem I've encountered frequently in academic work—the facts are presented but the obvious remains unstated. Cook writes: "The Twins' Xibalba episode, read as a script for a performance, is the prototype for a major Quichean rite of renewal."[19] (By Quichean Cook means the modern Quiché Maya who preserve the perennial essence of the ancient *Popol Vuh* teaching.) At the end of the rite the Hero Twins sacrifice themselves, as Quetzalcoatl did, by throwing themselves into the fire. This self-sacrifice, as we will explore more deeply in the next chapter, is the key to successful transformation and renewal. Are these not central ideas within the Perennial Philosophy? These ceremonial rites are intended to be observed at cycle endings, and the primary metaphor is the sun, which moves through many cycles of birth and death on different temporal levels, from the day cycle to the year cycle to, by analogy, the larger World Age cycle. Clearly, these contemporary "millenarian" ideas could be mapped onto the 2012 cycle ending, and Victor Montejo has himself adopted this rather obvious approach.

Among Maya day-keepers, spiritual guides, and political leaders, this is a time of great debate and intellectual tumult. How do they think about 2012? Is it consistent with these rites of renewal, or do some speak of doom? Robert Sitler, professor of modern language and literatures and director of the Latin American Studies program at Stetson University, has had a passionate interest in the Maya since early adulthood. He has described a spiritual experience he had at Palenque with his future wife, June, in the 1970s, as the launching point for his career. It is rare for an academic scholar to have integrated his spiritual inspirations with his professional vocation. Robert was the first scholar to publish a detailed treatment of the 2012 phenomenon (in 2006), and he has continued to record and document contemporary Maya attitudes about 2012.[20]

Sitler's work with the contemporary highland Maya reveals, not surprisingly, an entire spectrum of thoughts and ideas. My hope is that the voices which express ideas congruent with the ancient message of sacrifice, transformation, and renewal be elevated above all others because they retain a continuity with the ancient perspective. Anyone spewing unalloyed dooms-day should be suspected of engaging in a cheap and easy knockoff of the ancient wisdom, in the same way that newspaper horoscopes don't accurately reflect the profound nondual astrological principle of "as above, so below." This is not to exclude statements that are tempered with warnings and ob-servations about the crisis facing the world. That is inevitably part of the package, but notice that many of the following statements address both the dire situation at hand as well as possibilities for healthy change. Free-will choice is an implicit undercurrent. As Maya leader Don Alejandro points out, 2012 was prophesied as a time of change and a new dawn, but the "task to be finished" involves human engagement and choice:

> We have several prophecies concerning the time we are living in, and it is in fulfillment of the Prophecies that we are here today. I will men-tion some of them:
>
> "At the time of the 13 Baktun and 13 Ahau is the time of the return of our Ancestors and the return of the men of wisdom." That time is now.
>
> Another one says: "Arise, everyone, stand up! Not one, nor two groups be left behind the rest." This prophecy is in reference to all: rich or poor, black or white, men or women, indigenous or non indigenous, we all are equal, we all have dignity, we all deserve respect, we all deserve happiness; we all are useful and necessary to the growth of the country and to make a nation where we can live with respect among the different cultures.
>
> The Prophecy says: "Those of the Center, with their mystical bird Quetzal, will unite the Eagle of the North with the Condor of the South; we will meet because we are one, like the fingers of the hand." This prophecy means that the Indigenous People of the North and the Indigenous People of the South, through those of the Center, will come together to strengthen the recovery of the ancestral science; recovery

of our identity, art, spirituality and Cosmo-vision on life and death that the different Cultures have. . . .

According to the Maya Long Count Calendar, we are finalizing the 13 Baktun and 13 Ahau, thus approaching the YEAR ZERO. We are at the doorsteps of the ending of another period of the Sun, a period that lasts 5,200 years and ends with several hours of darkness. After this period of darkness there comes a new period of the Sun; it will be the 6th one. In each period of the Sun there is an adjustment for the planet and it brings changes in the weather conditions and in social and political life as well.

The world is transformed and we enter a period of understanding and harmonious coexistence where there is social justice and equality for all. It is a new way of life. With a new social order there comes a time of freedom where we can move like the clouds, without limitations, without borders. We will travel like the birds, without the need for passports. We will travel like the rivers, all heading towards the same point . . . the same objective. The Mayan prophecies are announcing a time of change. The Pop Wuj, the book of the Counsel, tells us, "It is time for dawn; let the dawn come, for the task to be finished."[21]

Don Alejandro has emerged as a leading voice among the modern Maya, bridging political office and religious duties. As one can see, there are many ideas and some unfamiliar concepts presented in his narrative. In August of 2008 he was appointed Ambassador of the Native Peoples of Guatemala by President Cocom. In an irony that would have been impossible to conceive of in the 1980s, President Cocom himself had gone through the shrine initiations to become a day-keeper. It is not unheard of for "outsiders" to be initiated into the calendar tradition in this way. Barbara and Dennis Tedlock, for example, went through the process in the 1970s. And since there are five levels of day-keeper initiation, leading up to the highest "Mother-Father" position, the process continues and deepens over many years.

A curious prophecy of a Yucatec Maya man, recorded in 1930, seems to preserve a vague recollection of the timing of the end of the 13th Baktun:

> *I guess I'll tell you the story of beautiful holy Lord for you to hear, because I have read the testament of beautiful holy Lord, where he says [that in] 2000 and a few more years it will end on earth. But if they have been very good Christians on earth, he will not end it. . . . He begins to diminish, beautiful holy Lord, His merciful grace [corn], the end of the road. . . . It is left, they are just looking one another in the face, no one is going to win the fight, hunger is going to win, truly. It ends, then, the fight like that. Hunger is going to finish it. Amidst that, whoever remembers there is a beautiful holy Lord, he makes a prayer in the cornfield, a harvest ceremony. Thus he makes it for beautiful holy Lord, He throws out blessings, beautiful holy Lord, there is corn in the fields.*[22]

José María Tol Chan, a Quiché day-keeper from Chichicastenango, spoke in 2006 with Dr. Sitler about how he saw 2012:

> *It is an event that has already begun, there are already signs. If humans don't correct our course in the face of these events we will be off-balance in the moment the event appears, a very strong event in comparison with what we have experienced. Humans more than ever should pay close attention to all the events that disturb balance. They are teachings that we living beings should extract from the stages through which we pass. It's not that we are arriving at a zero hour in 2012, it's already beginning. That is, just as in a day we begin at dawn, and as we approach noon the sun beats down harder; just as in the afternoon the forces of the sun start to calm down until experiencing night. In the passing of a day we experience degrees and effects of heat and at the same time we experience the energies that influence our lives. This date is the same way and I dare say that 12*

years previous to 2012 we have been experiencing different stages of
a sacred effect that can turn harmful if we lose human wisdom and
there will be 12 years after in which the effects also will arrive. 2012
is just the high point of the story.[23]

Perhaps the best perspective is short and sweet:

As the elders said, everything is going to change. The world will be
changed by that memorable date. Our children will have a different
world view. The time will have passed and other beings will inhabit
the universe.[24]

In 2007, Jim Reed and I were leading a group of twenty-two adventurers to
Maya sites in Honduras and Guatemala. When we arrived at the important
site of Tak'alik A'baj, a ceremony was taking place in front of Stela 5, led by a
spiritual guide from Momostenengo named Rigoberto Itzep Chanchabac.
Afterward we sat and talked briefly before our groups went their separate
ways. He exuded the kind of humble integrity and depth of understanding
that I'd seen before among the Maya day-keepers. We were told that the
Maya "day-keepers" had decided that they would prefer to be called "spiritual guides." A year after this fortuitous meeting Don Rigoberto was present, along with dozens of other Maya spiritual guides and their families, at a
well-attended conference in Antigua, Guatemala, called "La Profecía 2012
Maya: El Amanacer de una Nueva Epoca." It was organized and sponsored by
my friends at the Jades, S.A., Museum and artisan factory, in coordination
with the grand opening of their Museum of Maya Cosmology. Admission was
free, and no moneymaking concessions were allowed. It was truly an effort
to bring together many different voices in a noncommercial environment of
oneness. It can be a challenge for Maya traditionalists and outsiders to come
together and discuss what is fundamentally a Maya concept and tradition,
the 2012 calendar, which many people from different backgrounds are writing and talking about.

The specific issues around the 2012 date are compounded by the fact that the Long Count was historically lost, although, as I've emphasized, cycle-ending traditions of renewal are very much alive and well. In the ideological mess that 2012 has become, opinionated assertions are mixed with spiritual truths and philosophical doctrines. Not least of the issues has been my reconstruction of the origins of the 2012 cosmology at Izapa. The modern Maya may find it unusual, strange, and even irrelevant to their concerns, even if it is true. My hope is that a space of reconciliation and unified vision can be achieved between my work and the leaders in the Maya renaissance. Beyond that small concern is the larger issue of the reconciliation of the Western and Indigenous minds. The value systems connected with these two mind-sets are in many ways diametrically opposed. I believe the pathway through to a healthy and sustainable future, for the world at large, is not for the indigenous mind to adapt itself to Western values. That results in the same problem of trying to fit the vast vision of ancient metaphysical wisdom into the small box of materialist science—it can't work that way. The only way that unification can happen is for the Western paradigm to revive its own "indigenous" wisdom, which we could call "original mind" or even "buddhi mind." In this regard I am inspired by the words of Don Rigoberto:

> In a passage from the sacred book Pop Wuj, in one of the lines it says, "nor are they condemned by justice." When it speaks and says this, they are making a prophecy that there was going to be a Western judgment against the Maya; this is a reality. Today the laws of the Americas are foreign to the Maya cosmovision. These laws are violating the legitimate rights of the Maya. Another interpretation enters in that the ideological power of the West in its entirety might expire forever in 2012. "As long as the sun walks, as long as there is light, our existence will never be lost." Thus says the passage in the sacred Pop Wuj [The Popol Vuh].[25]

Don Rigoberto performed a ceremony on the final day of the conference in Antigua. We were to have an informal gathering to discuss issues pertaining to the conference. There had been an expression of some bad feeling around the Western appropriation of 2012, around big-money Hollywood movies, and around conferences excluding the Maya voice. The Antigua conference itself, however, was designed as a free event; no profits were made and, in addition to my presentation on Izapa and one by Georgeann Johnson on the participatory function of the Maya ballgame, three delegations of Maya spiritual guides were hosted at the nearby Concepcion guesthouse and presented their views to the audience of close to a thousand attendees at the conference. It was, overall, a great success. Thirteen people showed up for Don Rigoberto's fire ritual, and as with all rituals of renewal the theme was about sacrificing or letting go of negative thoughts, feelings, and energy. This was an enactment of the fire transformation of cycle endings—throw the illusion into the fire![26]

Maya voices include political leaders, spiritual guides, as well as more philosophical writers in Maya traditions. Robert Sitler is currently translating the work of Gaspar Pedro González, who emphasizes that an important voice for the modern Maya is the ancient book *The Popol Vuh*. In his book *El 13 B'aktun*,[27] he emphasizes the same reading that I have made of *The Popol Vuh*, piercing into the archetypal level of meaning: At the end of the cycle, self-serving egoism (Seven Macaw and the Lords of Darkness) must be transformed into a new being of light and consciousness (One Hunahpu as unitary mind). González writes:

From the perspective of contemporary Maya, 2012 constitutes a very important point in the history of humanity since time is a variable that greatly influences the life of the planet and everything that exists on it. Human beings do not exist by coincidence or by a work of chance. They are part of a plan to carry out a mission in this part of the universe. The world is still not totally finished in its creation and perfection; this human creature has a role to play in the world and its preservation. One could say that the life of the planet depends on human beings and what they do in their existence.[28]

González publishes from within the Maya context and his life experiences that began in Xibalba, the archetypal Maya underworld, alongside the Ajtxum, the spiritual guides, who preserve authentic Maya identity. I see him as a Maya philosopher who offers both well-reasoned research and insights into Maya teachings presented in the genre of allegorical fiction. Often it is the latter medium that is more effective than nonfiction research in conveying profound truths.

It must be said that, not surprisingly, there are other alleged Maya leaders who are more showmen than shamans. The fact is that you are going to get this anywhere. All statements and work must be assessed with discernment. We often expect prophecy to be about time-stamped visions of specific events that "will happen." This is the cartoon version of prophecy. I believe that prophecy is best understood as an evocation, an ecstatic calling into being, of the highest possible outcome. This is the role of a true prophet. Of course, there are "dark prophets" (as there are also "dark shamans" or "black magicians") who will try to call into being with their apocalyptic nihilism the darkest possible future. It is good to be aware of possible worst-case scenarios, but we should not pour our energy into envisioning them and projecting them into manifestation with our fears.

THE MAYA RENAISSANCE WRIT LARGE

A great undercurrent is at work in the Maya renaissance that 2012 is shining a light on: We are still trying to work out the integration of Western and Indian modes of being. This is not really Occidental versus Oriental, as two exclusive opposites on equal footing. Ideally, that makes for a nice symmetry, but it isn't really the way it works. The fact is that the Western mind comes from the more shortsighted and limited perspective of self-interest. It sees the foreground, the details, and can manipulate things with great advantage. Said bluntly, it is stuck in a narcissistic and adolescent phase of psychological development. The Indian mind, or indigenous mind, perceives the entire underlying gestalt, the big picture, and is oriented more toward the good of the whole and maintaining balance with a sustainable value system. As you can see, these two minds are not on equal footing. This isn't about an "East-meets-West" dialectic. It's more of a lower mind (irrationalist/ego-based) versus higher mind (transrational *original mind*, Dreamtime mind, heart-mind, whole-consciousness mind). Again, it's Seven Macaw versus One Hunahpu.

This is not meant to denigrate the Western mind, although I tend to emphasize its failings precisely because it is so oblivious to taking responsibility for the ecological, political, and economic crises of the modern world that it has spawned. Lost in consumerism and the pursuit of personal gain, the Western life philosophy is acutely developed in the United States of America. Hollywood and the cult of personality are egregious expressions of this state of affairs. In this, something has gone terribly wrong, because the high ideals upon which the United States was founded did not have this scenario in mind. "Life, liberty, and the pursuit of happiness" were meant to empower the individual for Self-actualization (capital *S* in the Jungian sense, in contrast to the lowercase *s* used when "self" is synonymous with the ego). The spiritual component of this was not hidden behind a mandate requiring the separation of church and state, but was encouraged by that separation! The church was not to meddle in the worship of ethical freethinkers. Today, America is dealing with many of the same problems that the founding fathers struggled with. They are all issues resulting from the ego's desire to control— to control people (slavery), resources (global capitalism), and nature for personal gain.

It's fascinating that a forgotten esoteric code can be read in the monuments of our nation's capital. New information has been uncovered by William Henry, who visited Washington, D.C., many times and was able to view art, rooms, and sculptures normally closed to the public.[29] George Washington, after his death, was apparently conflated in the public imagination with Jesus Christ. His representations in the art commissioned through several presidencies repeatedly implies he was mythologized as the American liberator or Savior. He opened the way for the realization of the highest ideal of America, a place where human beings could live fully actualized lives. William Henry observes that a French painter by the name of Constantino Brumidi was hired in the 1860s by the White House and completed many striking murals in the style of Renaissance painter Raphael. One discreetly depicts the famous Aztec Sunstone, with Montezuma and Cortez standing in front of it in poses of happy welcoming, greeting each other as long-lost brothers. This is history rewritten as it *should have been*, expressing the ideal underlying template that history, so far, has failed to fulfill.

The traditional Kogi Indians of Colombia preserve ancient lore about their long-lost brother who fled from the pure homeland. He got lost in the world, in his own pursuits and ambitions, and forgot the true world. The Kogi elders believe that the white European colonists represent the descendants of that long-lost brother. But the reconciliation is difficult because of an inversion of values and an inability of the lost brother to recognize the preservers of the true world.[30]

Hermann Hesse's novel about the lives of two friends, *Narcissus and Goldmund*, paints a beautiful story of the two ways, or paths, that a person can follow. One leads into life's experiences of excitement, love, grief, and loss. The other renounces the world and seeks the quiet places of contemplation, keeping the soul pure and undisturbed by life's travails (and joys). In their occasional meetings throughout their lives, each comes to lament his own chosen way and wish for what the other has. But it is too late to turn back time, and each experiences a kind of epiphany in their very different deaths, dying as they had lived life and reaping the rewards and grieving the losses of their chosen paths.

If we make the analogy to our Western-versus-Indian discussion, Hesse's story suggests that the Western and Indian mind-sets are each missing something the other has. A gesture of reconciliation is necessary. I hesitate to state, in tangible terms, what this might be. I don't think it is a tangible thing. Perhaps it is simply "peace." Neither side has it, and it can only be found with and through the other. That said, it is blatantly apparent that the Western mind could have learned a lot from the Indigenous mind in regard to having a healthy and sustainable relationship with nature. Respect and reverence for nature is a hallmark of indigenous societies; for Western civilization, not so much.

What does the West bring to 2012? What do the Maya bring to 2012? Western science's access to the tools of archaeology and information can offer a reconstruction of the true original 2012 paradigm, which was lost and forgotten by the descendants of its creators, as well as a framing of that as a perennial wisdom. My own mind, as a Western-educated mind, sees value in this. The Maya bring to the 2012 table a ceremonial rite of sacrifice, the skills required to facilitate the needed transformation and renewal. Together, a long-overdue fusion can be possible. We need a shared ceremony, a mystery play to enact, in which both sides sacrifice themselves and rebirth each other. Hearts and minds united, body and spirit humming together, evoking the great alchemical union of opposites at the end of the cycle. This hypothetical mystery play, or hierophany, reminds me of the union of the solar and galactic levels suggested by the galactic alignment.

Terence McKenna proposed that a shamanically driven "archaic revival" is needed in the West to radically derail the pathologies of egoism that are destroying the planet.[31] He believed that the root of the Western mind partakes of the same holistic gestalt that tenuously survives in indigenous corners of the planet, and that the shamanic practices of high Maya civilization in the Classic Period can inspire and awaken our own dreams of returning to our long-lost perennial homeland. And to return is not to regress, for we've come around the globe armed with something new: the direct experience that an ego-directed civilization isn't what it's cracked up to be. Terence believed we could get recentered in true and sustainable values by "following in Maya footsteps." In his introduction to my book *Maya Cosmogenesis 2012* he wrote:

> Collectively, as the 21st century dawns, we feel the ennui and exhaustion of the millennia-long practice of Western religion, politics, and science; we encounter the pollution and toxification that is the legacy of our particular style of being in the world. And we also find, among the endless bric a brac of the spiritual marketplace, the cosmogenic calendar of the ancient Maya. Can their temporal alchemy, which failed in the time of their own cultural climax and left their cities empty by the coming of the Conquest, work for us? Can the Maya dream of renewal at the conjunction of winter solstice and galactic heart valorize and redeem our civilization? I believe that it can play a significant part, and that part of the resacralization of the world that must accompany any valorization of post-historical time involves the recognition of the deep power and sophistication of the aboriginal mind—not only the ancient aboriginal mind but the contemporary aboriginal mind as well.
>
> As we awaken to the power of the moving sky, as we awaken to the powers that inform and illuminate many of the plants that have found their way into aboriginal medicine, as we struggle with the vastness of the universe of space and time and our place in it, as we do these things, we follow in Maya footsteps. In doing so we should celebrate the wisdom of the Maya, ponder its depths and wonder after its most persistent perception: that the world is to be born at last on December 21, 2012 A.D.[32]

What is needed in the Western world is our own renaissance, our own revival of our true identities, beings who live in the awareness that the earth is our homeland, and *nature is us*. The war on nature that Western civilization has been waging has been a war on our humanity. The world's problems have been generated by a limited state of consciousness called narcissistic egoism. And problems, as Albert Einstein said, cannot be solved by the same level of consciousness that made those problems. A higher state of reconciliation must be achieved. The transrational perspective must be opened. From that higher domain, which ego will find already populated by Indians, mystics, and Australian aborigines, the problems can be solved. It just may be that 2012 will contribute to a renaissance that ultimately has international and global implications. If we entertain for a moment that the word "Maya" means the larger consciousness of the Maya mind-set, future historians could very well identify era-2012 as the trigger point for a Maya Renaissance, a renewal of high ideals and a larger consciousness through which the world's troubles can be approached with some hope of reconciliation and solution. A nice thought, but as always, time will tell if we can and *will* do it.

Here's the nub of the issue that leads us even deeper into the 2012 mystery: How do we get there?

CHAPTER TWELVE

RESTORING THE BIG PICTURE

The Meta-universe does not subject beings to great
suffering to become self aware only to have them
dissolve into the great All. Instead we are learning
the skills to function as ethical, self-referencing
beings in the infinite ecologies beyond our material
cosmos.

—DUANE ELGIN, *Awakening Earth*

W e've established that a larger perspective, or self-concept, is necessary in order to do two things: actualize our full potential as human beings and effectively address and transform the crisis of the modern world. Both aspects involve reorienting the relationship between ego and this higher perspective, and I've emphasized that this goal is a deep principle within the Perennial Philosophy, which is also the essence of Maya spiritual teachings for cycle endings. The crisis, caused by a limited ego consciousness running the show, prevents the transformational breakthrough of awakening to the larger, trans-ego perspective. The entire dynamic and challenge is clarified by a deep archetypal reading of *The Popol Vuh*. The relationship between Seven Macaw and One Hunahpu embodies this spiritual teaching, tempered by the principle of sacrifice, of surrendering attachment to illusion. On another level, which we left behind in Part I, the rebirth of One Hunahpu at the end of *The Popol Vuh* Creation Myth is a metaphor for the solstice sun's alignment with the dark rift in the Milky Way. I framed my overall approach to 2012 with three stages—the tangible nuts-and-bolts reconstruction, the identification of universal perennial wisdom in the Maya material that relates to cycle endings (2012), and finally the possibility of directly experiencing profound integrative truths. This last stage, which we'll explore here, strives to open the mind and heart to a direct revelation of higher gnosis, the bigger picture. This is important because, according to the Perennial Philosophy, all true knowledge comes from an ecstatic connection with the transcendent.

How to Do It and What to Do

So we have a complete package, but one final item needs to be addressed. How do we transcend the ego and gain the initiatory glimpse of direct gnosis? How do we restore One Hunahpu's head, his unity consciousness? In Chapter 9 we saw that the Maya prophecy for cycle endings involves the appearance of the vain and false ruler, Seven Macaw, controlling humanity through fear and deception. In laying out striking parallels in world politics that would be amusing if they weren't so gravely true, we saw that the archetype of megalomaniacal egoism, in individual leaders as well as in corporate mandates, is indeed ruling and ruining the planet. The Maya prophecy for 2012 has come true. But, as *The Popol Vuh* reveals, that's only the first part of the prophecy.

The Hero Twins succeed in sacrificing Seven Macaw and the other lords of darkness; they were challenged to sacrifice the hegemony of egoism fueled by illusion to pave the way for the resurrection of One Hunahpu, the awakening of a higher unity consciousness beyond ego. The metaphor speaks truly for the crossroads that humanity finds itself in today. Will we sacrifice our attachment to the illusions of limited consciousness drawn over our eyes by self-serving egoism? Can we recognize that this is an essential key to facilitating world renewal, for creating a sustainable future? And then, how do we do it? Let's look at these one at a time.

First, will we sacrifice our attachment to illusion? Well, this is a free-will choice and a possibility for each individual. The point, however, is that our civilization's ruling institutions need to be reformed upon the principle of selfless service. This is a tall order, and I believe the effort will be impossible unless the people inside of the effort are engaged in their own simultaneous inner process of transformation. You can't just expect to put a bandage on transnational corporate feudalism and expect it to heal. Political institutions must change from within. No amount of legislative machination, or activists demonstrating, or more violent means of terrorism, will help unless the root spiritual cause of the world's dysfunctional structure is corrected. To fight the world's external problems in this way is like shadowboxing—one tries to hit phantoms. Instead, a kind of spiritually centered social activism is necessary. This begins to sound like the grounded earth-based spirituality of the Maya, who, rooted in the earth, could look out to celestial spheres with deep knowing. The structures of culture thereby congeal around stable foundations. Rooted in a spiritual center, civilization can flower. Rooted in the shortsighted agenda of ego, it is doomed to collapse.

Second, can we recognize that sacrificing the monopoly of egoism is essential for facilitating world renewal? Well, there is only one being on the planet who would disagree: Seven Macaw. In explicating the profound teachings of the Perennial Philosophy I've tried to make the case on rational grounds. Intellectuals will have to do some soul-searching to determine if they agree or disagree, and carefully discern what is motivating their decision. I suspect that those who believe self-serving egoism should continue to run the world, as some kind of benevolent automatically self-regulating over-being within global capitalism and politics, are probably hearing the demented whisperings of Seven Macaw. And they are probably motivated by the fear of annihilation, because they confuse ego with Self, and consequently ego's loss of power is seen as a mortal threat. Ego fears losing; the Self does not.

Third, how do we do it? How do we embrace the big picture? How do we put ego back into correct relationship with the unitary Self, and how do we actively midwife the renewed world that unfolds from that fundamental shift? How is One Hunahpu reborn? This is the second part of the Maya prophecy for era-2012, and is the focus of this chapter.

TURNING IT ALL INSIDE OUT

Our playbook should be *The Popol Vuh*, which elaborates in archetypal terms the process of transforming Seven Macaw into One Hunahpu, utilizing the necessary key, which is: sacrifice. Yes, a big scary word with lots of blood and violence oozing out. But all the world's religions and metaphysical systems of spiritual transformation agree: Sacrifice is the key. Preferably self-sacrifice, for the simple reason that if we don't do it, the universe will do it for us. The former method can be quite exquisite and fulfilling while the latter alternative is not so pretty. Luckily, the thing that needs to be sacrificed is the thing that runs the show at the end of the cycle: illusion. The macabre interpretation of sacrifice is unnecessarily literal. So far, so good. Unfortunately, illusion is deeply entangled with ego, and unraveling the ego-illusion mess can seem as difficult as untangling a fifty-pound knotted ball of yarn.

A long laundry list of methods and techniques for freeing the ego-identity from the tangled knot of illusion is well known, including yoga and meditation, sacred plants and shamanic healing work, and devotional prayer or chanting. I personally believe that developing a meditation practice is a very good thing to do—and best of all, it's free! Vipassana meditation (breathing meditation), in particular, can have beautiful and profound effects on one's life. We want to bring a presence of mind to our actions and awaken a deeper field in which the results of our actions can be directly perceived and felt. We shouldn't expect to sustain this mode of consciousness constantly, but an initiatory glimpse of the deep interrelationship between our thoughts and actions and the larger field of other beings and nature can radically change how we behave in normal consciousness.

For example, if one experiences (by whatever means) a spiritual opening in which one feels, for a second or a minute, a deep compassion for all created beings and a deep knowing that all life is interdependent and connected, your lifestyle and behavorial choices are going to reform around this conviction. I'm trying to ease into this slowly, so I used the word "conviction," but really the experience is more of a revelation of truth than a decisive commitment to a particular belief. The experience imprints the soul with a deep knowing, a true vision of the way reality operates. This doesn't mean peace and harmony and the lion lying down with the lamb. As Joseph Campbell said, "No, the lion is going to eat the lamb, but that is the way of nature."[1] This is being in the Tao, the flow, allowing the thing-in-itself, including the thing that you are, to be. Talk to your friends, coworkers, and family members. You might be surprised to discover, after a little gentle prodding, how many people will say they have had an experience something like this at some point in their lives.

HEALING MODES OF BEING WHOLE

There are many ways to awaken a sense of wholeness, of being and acting in congruence with the unfolding of life. This effort is predicated on the understanding that the tower of ego is an unsatisfactory place to be, that it has gone rogue, turned pathological, dislocating human beings from their humanness. There are many ways to catch a glimpse of essential wholeness, the unity consciousness of One Hunahpu restored, and different temperaments will benefit from different approaches. I'll discuss three methods representing three broad categories: sacred plants (initiation/transforming), meditation (knowing/being), and service work (action/doing). Ideally, all human beings should have some direct experience with all of these areas.

In the first example (sacred plants), the concept of initiation is centrally important. Sacred plants and shamanic techniques of transforming the consciousness are not the only methods that can result in an initiatory experience; others include any safe initiatory process that supplies the seeker with a death-rebirth journey in which the egoic reference point is temporarily suspended. I've chosen sacred plants (psychoactive tools of shamanism such as peyote, psilocybin mushrooms, ergot) for two reasons: (1) they have a prominent role in the 2012 discussion, both popular and academic; and (2) they informed the beginnings of Western philosophy.

Shamanic rites of initiation are intended to induce a transformative death-rebirth experience for the initiate. Purification of irrelevant dross, negative thoughts and emotional patterns, and unhealthy intentions is the goal of these rites. In addition to the all-encompassing rite of passage induced by the use of sacred plants, which Stanislav Grof likens to a death-rebirth experience, these traditional ceremonies usually also involve fire transformation. From Siberia to Amazonia, shamanic fire ceremonies follow the same patterns and share the same intentions.

> *The [shaman's] mastery of fire also often includes control over symbolic actions, especially initiation rites that "cook" candidates or subject them to the heat of incubation. The shamanic master of fire is responsible for transformative processes burning at the core of spiritual life: the symbolism at the center of the hearth or social units, community groups, all civilized life, and the cosmos itself . . . the shamanic experience of consumption correlates directly with ecstasy. Consumption by fire signifies the death inflicted by supernatural powers during ecstatic trance. Ecstatic death consumes the spiritually awakened or inflamed human being, who is transported to an illumined state of consciousness.[2]*

Subjecting initiates to "the heat of incubation" pertains to the spiritual heat that transforms; the imagery here is reminiscent of that used in alchemical transformations. Fire is, after all, the great transformer. These shamanic rites survive primarily in indigenous societies that draw time-tested methods for transformation from the storehouse of *what works*. Curiously, their practices directly parallel initiatory trials in Western mystery schools and Roman Mithraism. A long lineage of more ancient wisdom schools goes far back to Egypt (for example, the Hem-Shu school), not to mention shamanic schools in ancient China. These effective transformational rites survived as an underground stream of esoteric knowledge, passed down as ancient lore to initiates who would visit their shrines and oracles. The oracle at Delphi, for example, was one of many conduits of initiatory wisdom that were visited frequently by Plato, Socrates, and other Greek thinkers. Historically, Egyptian mystery schools influenced Greek thought as a result of pre-Socratic philosophers having interactions with Egypt and the Middle East. These visits by Greek thinkers to the founts of ancient Egyptian wisdom triggered the Greco-Hellenic renaissance. The mysterious figures of Parmenides and Pythagoras occupy an early place in the formulation of Greek philosophy, prior to Plato. Western philosophy and politics, it should be recalled, look to Greek philosophy as their prototype.

For the Greeks, oracles served much as shamans do for indigenous societies, as intermediaries between this earth realm and a supernatural higher source of knowledge and information. The oracle at Delphi was associated with a goddess and snake cult, evoking the Hindu doctrine of the kundalini "serpent energy" that rises and awakens spiritual seekers. The primary mystery religion in the Greek world was enacted annually at Eleusis for more than a thousand years. It finally succumbed to the destructive intolerance of Christianity around 300 AD. The practices of this fascinating initiatory school were shrouded in mystery and its participants were forbidden to reveal what they had seen inside the Mysterium (the Sacred Theater). Its graduates were the founding minds of Western thought, including Plato and Socrates and many other Greek philosophers and statesmen. Modern scholars interested in the role of psychoactive plants in religion have successfully reconstructed long-lost aspects of the Eleusinian Mysteries, finding that the sacrament used in the visionary mystery play enacted at Eleusis was a psychoactive elixir called the kykeon.[3] One of these authors, Carl Ruck, has gone on to explore more examples of the use of psychoactive substances in connection with Christian symbolism and the Greek Classical world.[4] The larger implications of the forgotten sacraments of religion are admirably explored in Irvin and Rutajit's *The Pharmacratic Inquisition: Astrotheology and Shamanism.*[5]

Stated simply, at Eleusis the founding fathers of Western philosophy and science were radically informed by a vision induced by a psychoactive elixir whose chemical analogs are components of LSD. They all experienced initiatory visions that were described as an illumination from within, a revelation. A teaching story or mystery play was performed, which may have been the famous Myth of Demeter that involved the origin of the seasons and the necessity of sacrifice to the chthonic underworld lords so that light, the sun, could return every spring. Sound familiar? Sacrifice, transformation, underworld lords, and renewal are all present in this mythos, echoing the archetypal outline of the Maya's Hero Twin Myth. Plato wrote of underlying "Ideas" (equivalent to archetypes) that are the essences behind all created Forms. He thus anticipated the existence of inner psychological archetypes more than 2,300 years ago.

There are strange stirrings in the other writings of Plato, however, that suggest a reactive counterresponse to his mystery religion experience. Another thread of Greek thought was the striving for order, to schematize nature and the mystery of life, and this truly was the beginning of the Western descent toward modern reductive science. Plato (born in 427 BC) was preceded by the mysterious figure of Parmenides, who was active around 475 BC. He was a shaman-poet who experienced a mystic initiation in a Plutonium (the cave-chamber of Pluto, lord of the underworld), and there in the darkness he saw the light. He wrote an ecstatic anagogical mystery poem that has lost much of its original sense and transformative punch through dozens of translations. Parmenides was not unlike a Maya shaman who descends into a cave to engage the underworld journey and, there in the darkness, awakens the inner vision to perceive the intangible truths that underlie manifest reality.

Classical scholar and Perennial Philosopher Peter Kingsley has recovered the long-lost true story behind the teachings of Parmenides and, most unfortunately for the history of Western thought, how he was misunderstood by Plato.[6] Kingsley argues that a fundamental misstep occurred at the dawn of Western civilization. The esoteric initiatory mystery teachings of Parmenides were appropriated and distorted by Plato and Aristotle, who merely demystified his words. This desacralization of reality has become the defining hallmark of Western politics and secular humanism. What's wrong with the essential Mystery? It belongs to its own ontological category of experience, so why should one even attempt to demystify it? You can't solve a mystery, but you can suck the transformative power out of it by labeling it "not real." Kingsley encourages Western science and philosophy to back-engineer its true origins and reinstate the original Parmenidean teaching, that in the darkness of the fecund womb of the initiatory cave, true knowledge awaits one who sincerely seeks to understand reality. This is how Western science and philosophy can reclaim its nondual roots, to awaken its forgotten indigenous mind.

Kingsley convincingly has shown, with deep scholarship and a clear voice, that we have gotten it all wrong, we have been sold a lemon; Western philosophy is rooted in a coup. Plato appropriated Parmenides, who journeyed in the Plutonium, the mystic initiatory cave of darkness, the womb of the unmanifest plenum of infinite potential. His experience was like that of a Hindu yogi or Buddhist monk, seeking the spiritual source in, as Kingsley said, "the dark places of wisdom." This dark place of wisdom is a womblike environment and is the source of all manifest existence, the place where in deep meditation you can find the higher space of source consciousness and an integration of the formless ground with the forms of manifest reality.

Author Anne Klein speaks of this in her book *Meeting the Great Bliss Queen*. She observes that in Buddhist traditions

> *the womb that is an "expanse of reality" is a ubiquitous matrix, participating in and pervading all that is born from it. It is never left behind as is the maternal womb of contemporary Western description. In contrast, most Jewish and Christian traditions understand*

God to have created the world ex nihilo, *that is, from a nothing that,
like the maternal womb, is left behind. In Buddhist understanding,
there is no dead space left behind when existence manifests. The womb
of the expanse is an ever-replenished resource, and the wish to renew
association with it is not regarded as regressive but potentiating.*[7]

Here, "expanse" might as well be called "source." The "renewed association"
with it is a movement toward transrational reintegration of ego with source
rather than prerational dissolution of ego.

We can't be sure to what extent Parmenides was using sacred plants in
his underworld journeys, but the essential initiatory intent is there. And certainly, as mentioned, the Eleusinian Mysteries clearly show that something
akin to psychedelic shamanism informed the founders of Western science
and philosophy.

Sacred plants also played a central role in the astro-theological concep-
tions formulated at Izapa, an origin place for the Maya Hero Twin Myth
and the Long Count calendar that were both defining traditions of the Classic Period Maya florescence. Stela 6 at Izapa, for example, depicts a huge toad
with its head arched back, its mouth opened upward. This is the "to be born"
icon standardized later in Maya hieroglyphic writing. Dangling on the end
of his outstretched tongue is a little human figure in a boat. This clearly
represents a shaman taking a journey into the mouth of the frog, a symbol
for the underworld portal or cave. Most interestingly, the frog has been identified as a *Bufo marines* toad, whose shoulder glands secrete a substance
containing the powerful hallucinogen 5-Meo-DMT. To clinch the association,
the carving shows the "vision scrolls" coming out of the toad's dotted shoulder glands. This means the toad was a source of vision, of entry into the
underworld. And remember, the night sky was seen to be the underworld
flipped upside down every night. The shaman, like an astronomer, was an
explorer of "the underworld," the celestial realm.

Ritual mushroom stones were also found in the areas around Izapa, and scholars believe that a mushroom cult existed during the pre-Classic period when Izapa was thriving. The central role played by cacao in Izapa's economy and ceremonial use of sacred mushrooms should not be overlooked. Psycho-active mushrooms were traditionally mixed with a cacao beverage, probably because cacao contains MAO inhibitors that potentiate the effects of DMT and psilocybin. The South American psychoactive elixir called *ayahuasca* is a mixture of a DMT-containing plant with an MAO inhibitor, to enhance and lengthen the initiatory healing journey. The DMT can thereby be con-sumed orally, giving a longer-lasting effect than when smoked. I've suggested that cacao could have been the MAO donor that Izapan shamans may have

A meditating Maya. Photo by the author, 2001

combined with a prepared form of the toad secretions, or the mushrooms, making a drink we could call *cacaohuasca.*

My point here is that the visions induced by sacred plants must have informed the profound cosmology pioneered at Izapa, which integrated precession-based astronomy, the 2012 calendar, and the metaphysical teachings of the Hero Twin Mythology.[8]

The second method I outlined above for realizing the big picture is meditation. This method is actually helpful for the shamanic journeys undertaken with sacred plants, as the ability to focus intent and open consciousness can make all the difference between positive and negative experiences. But it's not about controlling the experience, it's about letting go and opening up to what is there. In shamanic journeys as well as in the deepening process of meditation practice, one encounters unresolved issues of personal emotional history. Deeper still, familial and ethnic baggage appears, and beyond that collective human karma and transpersonal material. Meditation is a centering practice, a mindfulness generator, a letting go into the moment and being present to the now. It deepens the consciousness to directly perceive the underlying field, the realm of subtle insight that lies behind the veil of manifest appearances. We do not annihilate the world in meditative practice, we awaken the faculty with which we can see through the impermanence of form. All manifest reality is an ever-changing domain of shifting forms and appearances, which is real to the extent that we can see their basis in the unmanifest Ground, the eternal and infinite source that we may call source consciousness. This unquantifiable and unconditioned consciousness is not something we evolve, but something we revive, or awaken. It's always there, has always been and always will be. We've just clouded our vision of it with ego's distractions and Seven Macaw's fixation on glittery ornaments, the things of surface reality.

Letting go in meditation is an important practice for setting aside, or transcending, the nagging dictates of ego. Sitting with one's inner thoughts, not engaging in outward activity, deepening the sense of being present to Nowever, awakens the timeless. We open to eternity and directly understand that eternity is at the root of time. Going to the center is like awakening your inner One Hunahpu. I find it amusing that the English word *hurricane* is derived from variants on One Hunahpu's name. The Maya deity Hun-rakan (one-foot) is associated with God K (*k'awil*) and the Quiché Maya god named Tojil. They are one-footed and spin upon the Pole Star. Readers might recall that Seven Macaw, as the Big Dipper, spins upon the Pole Star, suggesting that Seven Macaw and One Hunahpu are two facets of the same entity. And they are: Lower self and higher self are two parts of the whole being, called Ego and Divine Self in the Perennial Philosophy. More subtly, a transformational ethos is at play here, for from a certain perspective Seven Macaw (ego-focused identity) is meant to transform into One Hunahpu (unitary selfless identity). We must go to the center of the hurricane, the eye of phenomenal change, to transcend the chaos! And in so doing we find that we are the source and center of the tumult.

As we do these things our relationship with the world changes. As our identities become centered on our true Self, and we consciously restore ego to its proper function as a temporary extension of the true Self, our relationships will change. And we find that we slowly shift from acolyte of the mysteries (a student or initiate) to teacher. We are granted an esoteric PhD as we

Heart of Heaven, from a late Classic Period vase. Drawing by the author

climb the degrees of inner gnosis. We begin to take on the identity of *conduit* rather than *recipient*, conveyor rather than container.

Christopher Bache is a teacher who has observed the transformational cocreative process between himself and his students as he has deepened his spiritual journey. With subtle insight he notes that his own state of awareness can trigger understanding in his students. And he has noted the potential problems of transference that are common in the psychoanalytical field, in the give-and-take between therapist and client. Sometimes the teacher becomes the student; in fact, Bache notes that teaching is most effective when a nondual or nonhierarchical relationship is established.

Bache has openly shared his pursuit of self-awareness using the tools of psychoactive plants. He understands that modes of consciousness define modalities of knowing, and this has little to do with learning in the commonly understood sense. He writes of the change that any person on a journey of spiritual awakening is likely to undergo. Not surprisingly, the initiatory death-rebirth experience, occurring at ongoing levels of deepening integration, is essential, and at some point the person's orientation to the transcendent wisdom shifts:

> When an individual's death-rebirth experience is concluded, therefore, he or she does not detach from the species-mind, as if that were possible, but rather his or her therapeutic role, vis-à-vis the species mind, shifts from that of providing cathartic release to that of infusing transcendental energies into the collective psyche.[9]

Which is to say that a person does not leave planet earth upon establishing a connection with the transcendent source consciousness. Once the ego-self is sufficiently transformed, it no longer requires cathartic initiatory release into the transcendent; instead, the person becomes a channel for "infusing transcendental energies" into human culture. Here let's recall Joseph Campbell's definition of myth: "Myth is the secret opening through which the inexhaustible energies of the cosmos pour into human cultural manifestations."[10] A person becomes a leader, a source of genuine insight. The Maya king was shamanically elected into office in this way, his ruling power conferred by his ability to infuse higher wisdom and guiding insight into his kingdom. In comparison, democratic elections are mere popularity contests. Our political figureheads should not, however, be given the power that we can establish for ourselves in the process of awakening our true selves. We should not elect Best Ego but rather the True Conduit. And we can recognize the true conduit to the extent that we have become true conduits ourselves. A true conduit once said:

> The person who has not courageously confronted the basic unreality
> of conventional structures—including both individual and collective
> egocentricity, including as well the very notion of a substantial uni-
> verse—can never sincerely Love the Real or long intensely for the Real,
> much less become Reality.[11]

That was Ramakrishna, a Hindu saint who in many ways inspired and guided the West's initial encounter with Vedanta. René Guénon's book from the 1920s, *Man and His Becoming According to the Vedanta*, framed this nicely in the context of the Perennial Philosophy, whose cause was soon taken up by Ananda Coomaraswamy and Aldous Huxley. In some quarters there has been a tendency to psychologize the Perennial Philosophy (particularly in the psychology of Carl Jung and his students), and some writers have suggested that "subconscious" terminology confuses higher states of integration with lower states of unconscious nonintegration.[12] The goal of both Jungian psychology and the Perennial Philosophy is, however, wholeness and integration. Bache draws from Jung's psychological terminology, and his genuine insights need to be understood in this light:

> [I]f we are a holon functioning as a part within a series of ever-
> enlarging wholes, then the death-rebirth dynamic may have different
> functions for different levels of reality, all of which are being realized

simultaneously. *From the perspective of the smaller holon, for example, the effect of death-rebirth may be liberation into that which is larger, while the effect of the* same *transition from the perspective of the larger holon may be to allow it greater access to and integration with the smaller field. An event that functions as an "ascent" from below may simultaneously function as a "descent" from above.*[13]

The transcendent illumines and informs the individual consciousness to the extent that it can descend into, open, and see beyond the filter of ego. (This, I believe, is the deeper meaning of the epigram to Chapter 8, taken from René Daumal's philosophical fable *Mount Analog.*) Here we find the suggestion that depth process is really an awakening to higher truths. As with any encounter with nondual concepts, polarities of height and depth are easily conflated. But the nondual truth in this is that knowledge, which science traditionally accepts only as coming from outer sense data, is ultimately rooted in the most inner recess of the being, the transcendent source-center. This can also be conceived as the highest heaven. As one of the Perennial Philosophy's most insightful voices said: "The traditional universe is dominated by the two basic realities of Origin and Center, both of which belong to the realm of the eternal."[14]

A DAY IN ETERNITY

I wouldn't be able to say these things with such conviction if they hadn't been galvanized by direct experience. Here I'd like to share an experience that reoriented my entire being, at a young age, and has led me along the path that is my life. This kind of treatment, being about the most subtle level of direct gnosis, will always fall short of providing what it talks about. It simply can't; words and concepts can't be used to convey what ultimately must be directly experienced for oneself. The closest I can come is to relate a personal experience in language that is a bit freed from tedious discursive constraints.

Meditation and sensory isolation go hand in hand. A useful tool that can help deepen meditation and the awakening of the inner light is the sensory isolation tank. These devices were developed in the 1960s by scientists who were doing research on consciousness. They enjoyed a brief spate of popularity in the 1980s as "relaxation tanks," because they provide a completely dark environment protected from light and sound, with the surrounding water and air at body temperature. You float on an 80 percent Epsom salt solution, which keeps the body buoyant and the head above water even if you fall asleep. In this environment the consciousness can withdraw its attention from the five physical senses to awaken inner vision, the dormant faculty of gnosis that perennial philosophers call *intellectus* and mystics call the third eye.

Dolphin scientist John Lilly wrote about his visionary experiences inside of isolation tanks, using LSD as a catalyst. At age nineteen I was inspired by the intrepid adventures of Lilly, which I had read about in his books *The Center of the Cyclone* and *The Deep Self*. At the time I was very into yoga, meditation, fasting, and breath work. It was an extreme phase of purification, identity exploration, and engaging transformative inner work. Being resourceful, I sought out a facility in Chicago called Spacetime Tanks that advertised its "relaxation" services and "state-of-the-art" isolation tanks. After four or five trial experiences without pharmacological help, I had become comfortable with the process and made friends with one of the clerks there, and decided to propose my experiment. I had logged some experience with sacred plants, although I had lately eliminated mind-altering substances in deference to yoga practice, seeking clarity of mind. Nevertheless, I believed in the transformative power of these substances and decided to experience what Lilly was talking about—they weren't called "consciousness-expanding" for nothing. I would be combining my ability to go into a meditative state, which I had developed as a result of daily meditation practice, with the isolation tank and a good dose of quality LSD.

It was a fine spring day in early June. I cultivated a sense of gratitude and reverence while I disrobed and settled into the warm environment of the isolation tank chamber, closing the door. Lying back, supported by the buoyant body-temperature saline solution, I began to let go. I breathed deeply, gently, working out some body kinks. I was already comfortable with the process, having had a few previous experiences in the tank. This time, of course, I was aware that within forty-five minutes or so the LSD would start having an effect. Pure darkness, at this point, appeared like a flat screen with no depth, but by the end of my voyage that flat screen would be radically enlarged. Images and sounds of the day, of driving into Chicago, popped into my mind. I breathed and let go. It took fifteen to twenty minutes before this sensory detritus of the day's impressions began to fade and an inner vista began to dawn. My heartbeat was present for me; my rhythmic breathing took on a distant, autonomous quality. I allowed myself to disengage from fidgeting and readjusting my body; there was nothing really to do in this regard, I told myself as I was floating in a perfectly safe ocean of comfort. The quietude was complete.

My mind began to seek reinforcing boundaries of my body, which usually come from pressure, gravity, and contact with clothes or a chair. But here there were no sensory signals to be found, so my mind decided that no body limitation existed and began to reach beyond. The mind, I found, has the innate capacity to reach outward into many dimensions, including time, but it is usually quashed by sensory signals that define boundaries. Not so in the tank. Relaxation indeed! My mind began opening like a thousand-petal lotus. Excuse the cliché, but that's the perfect metaphor. I became aware of presences on the fringes of my consciousness, which seemingly drew near as my mind ventured outward, expanding into multidimensional space. I heard a conversation between two people, an everyday chat that I imagined was happening somewhere else in the building where I lay, or perhaps another building nearby. Other beings were sensed in other directions too, at the same time, although direction really had no meaning because I was becoming a manifold multidirectional awareness. My inner observer seemed to remain intact, and I suspected the psychedelic was taking effect, although I experienced no distortions of perception with which it is usually associated. No melting walls or dripping colors or demon faces or elfin laughter; I felt those were all distortions that would happen only if I was trying to engage outer reality—at a party or rock concert, for example—or if my system was also trying to process other chemicals, such as marijuana or alcohol or even food. (I had fasted the previous day and that morning ate only an orange.)

Instead, pure expansion of mind into a boundless space occurred. While the spatial infinity emerged from the shadows (for that is how I felt it occurring), time also dissolved. I sensed an intensity growing around me, a throbbing urgency that may have been my own blood coursing through my veins, or some endocrinal system kicking in, but all that got left behind as I telescoped out onto a quick succession of larger cosmic viewpoints. The previous domain, which I thought was immense, was quickly seen to be a mere speck on a stick on a tree in a forest on an island on a planet in a galaxy, which was only one galaxy of trillions. A kind of apotheosis or upward-expanding experience that was intimately involved with my very being, my sense of self, accelerated. Suddenly the darkness simply wasn't dark anymore, but light, pure unmodified light that spread in all directions and through me. Boundless, infinite, and eternal: I am. Or rather, I had once congealed out from this and was now returning into it with some semblance of a memory-making self-consciousness that was nevertheless quickly being subsumed into the light. I suppose, in retrospect, that the light was also love, but at this stage the experience was very much a pure-light illumination, perhaps the "dawning of the clear light" spoken of in the Tibetan Book of the Dead.

I was at an attenuated stage of experiencing an ultimate vision of reality; I could see within it the process of history and time, of the creation of the manifest cosmos and created beings, and in one fell swoop the purpose and destiny of humanity unfolded before me and was gone, imprinting me with a knowing that would take a million books to adequately convey. I have preserved in my notebook something that sounds as banal now as it was profound then: "The purpose of life is to grow!" The mystic identity of "Thou Art That," of identification with the All, began to turn into a feeling of intense ecstasy, of love. Oceans of tears streamed from my heart while a thousand emotions flooded my being in quick succession. Washing over the entire kaleidoscopic panorama was a feeling that God is All, All is God, All is Love, love is all you need, love is all you are. I felt a universal compassion for all beings—these words come to mind now, but I am aware of how trite they must sound and how inadequately they convey the inner ecstasy that my immersion in bliss conferred. I'm condensing this recollection from my notebooks, and at this point I wrote "and then I disappeared."

Who knows where I went; full identity immersion in eternity extinguishes the "little I" and nothing can be brought back. But there are a million dimensions of being between heaven and hell, between ego and eternity. What I recall next is that, far from any sense of connection with my body or my ego identity, I awoke within a dream in which I was a Chinese man around the turn of the last century. This wasn't, however, merely a hallucination. In fact, nothing in this experience could really be rightly called a hallucination. I lived out the life of that man. I was that Chinese man and experienced every little thing he had, day after day and year after year. I had first memories, fell in love, got married, had kids, experienced heartache and a million other things that we all register through our lives, and I grew old and died. It wasn't a speedy overview, either, like a flashback in a near-death experience—it happened in real time. And what I brought back to document when I wrote it down in my notebook was not names and details, but karmic impressions, defining moments, wounds and joys. These are the things that define us.

I then was released into a transhuman realm of being, and I drifted into imagistic reveries involving primordial forests and vast expanses of geological time that occurred as a life cycle of some higher being that I also was. Imagine the life cycle of an entire grove of redwood trees. Some of these groves have been in existence for millions of years. If there is some higher entelechy or ongoing "beingness" of this grove of trees, think of the repository of memories that it holds, or roots, into the earth! Wonder upon wonder unfolded in cosmogonic symphonies before my inner eye. Eventually, my full stride of bold forward motion began to ease. The long journey started to downshift. Ever so subtly, shadows started to creep in; odd angles and question marks began distracting me. I was decelerating now and was about to "come down" into my ego-identity as John. Family faces began appearing, personal thoughts, pathos, compassion, memories, events, disappointments, personal traumas—in broad sweeps I became reacquainted with the knot of karma that is my current incarnation. I could bathe the causal knot of each experience in a compassionate kiss as it passed by, embracing many things that were squirreled away in the recesses of my psyche. I felt this reintegration was a very important part of the entire experience, in which I could recalibrate my identity and reconfigure priorities, goals, motivations, and intentions for my life.

As I was drawn back to the local galaxy, to earth and my waiting body, I remembered I was lying in the isolation tank, a vision box for my underworld journey. I also felt I had never really left my body; I had, rather, explored the cosmic contents of it. Humor percolated into my mind; I began to feel reconnected into my body, and after a while I decided to move a finger. Then a hand, then an arm. The exquisite feel of muscles contracting and blood coursing was as physically pleasurable as the previous mental and spiritual ecstasies I had soared through. After much stretching and moving, getting reestablished into the physical space of my body, I sat up in the box and opened my eyes. Or at least I thought I was opening my eyes. There was no difference between open and closed. I was, in fact, staring out into limitless velvet depths of infinitude. My mind was opened down to the ultimate ground, which was no ground at all but a boundless depth. I was in awe; as the jaw drops in wonder at some fascinating sight, my mind was dropped open in a reverential awesomeness that no word could express. And it was more than some philosophical idea of an alive and bright plenum of infinite space and time. My eyes were actually gazing upon eternity. It was there, always; that, for me, was all I needed to know.

I lay back again and gently glided down into a peaceful reentry as the magic chemicals were processed out of my bloodstream. As I became curious about revisiting the world outside, which was surely going to be brand new to my reborn soul, I reflected back over my visions and experiences and felt I was returning from an immense adventure through time and space. In certain respects it felt as though I had sat down in the tank perhaps thirty minutes earlier (whatever "thirty minutes" means), but when I soon extracted myself from the tank I noted that five hours had passed.

The experience deeply affected me. It was completely different from the several psychedelic trips I had previously undertaken. I walked around north Chicago neighborhoods for a few hours to get anchored back into embodiment. My body seemed newly reborn, as did my mind and soul. I had a few awkward interactions with the hustle and bustle of what seemed an insanely overmechanized world—cars, bikes, trucks, buildings, planes flying overhead. It was a bit jarring, but also edifying, as it taught me how the consciousness closes, puts up a barrier of protection, when violence, noise, and angst-filled disturbances occur. It's doubtful, I thought to myself, that the modern life of humanity allows people to keep even the slightest sliver of spiritual consciousness open.

I sat in a park, drank water, and ate an apple I had brought with me, which was truly nectar. My senses came alive and my body lapped up its juicy flesh. Wow. I wrote what I could recall in my notebook, and by that evening I was none the worse for wear. My notebook concludes with an odd pronouncement, a kind of philosophical muse that echoes some key ideas from *The Popol Vuh*. At age twenty in 1984, however, I had no knowledge of *The Popol Vuh*:

> *In the beginning the gods drew a veil over the eyes of humanity like breath clouding a mirror. Now with that mind mirror polished, the entire universe of form appears clear while the light of eternity shines through.*

I don't advocate LSD use or suggest this experiment should be repeated. What I would like to convey is that the infinite and eternal Divine Ground is our own source-mind and soul, and it underlies and gives rise to all manifest form. To catch a glimpse of this truth is the birthright of every human being, is not impossible, and radically reorients the ego to an awareness of realities much greater than it could ever imagine or hope to rival. Ego's job is to be an ego, not stage a coup on eternity.

To connect all this with some topics previous explored, realizing a unity consciousness within is completely congruent with the partnership mode, investing in our inner bonobo while divesting ourselves from chimpocracy, reviving the aboriginal Dreamtime, and opening up the transrational perspective. We might call it an integration of East and West, but a transformation of the lower self into higher self is probably a better way to think about it. In addition, assuming that this kind of initiatory experience of nonlocal immersion in eternity is what the "transformation and renewal" of 2012 is about, then many mystics, visionaries, shamans, and spiritual seekers have already been to 2012.

GET DIRTY AND JUST DO IT

I've saved the best for last. Of the three "methods" for realizing or building the Big Picture, the practical is probably the most important. Undertaking works in service to a greater good is essential for building a foundation for a civilization that honors the whole and desires a sustainable way. We can all offer our unique talents and gifts to this effort. I feel that my writings, guided tours, and conferences are my "activist" offering. Priorities and interests can shift, however, and the unfolding process of self-actualization can activate other abilities and projects. Our outer work in the world reflects, in some way, the inner work we are engaged in. It is precisely through this synergy of inner and outer that both domains receive nourishment and actualization.

I tend to be cerebral, engaged in thoughts and creative mental processes. Writing is also a very introverted process that can only be done alone. Imbalances in the inner being, by reinforcing exclusive focus on one area of the self, need to be tempered by engaging the opposite. Psychologically and energetically, this is equivalent to embracing the shadow. To ground my cerebral tendencies, I recently decided to take up a very tactile and physical pursuit. This wasn't really a decision but more of a half-conscious groping for wholeness. It was, as Joseph Campbell would say, "following my bliss." Loved ones might see it as a radical departure from your habitual patterns and can become alarmed. Some people seem to do an about-face, and often the intuitive effort to find wholeness is aborted before it barely begins. A straitlaced practical accountant may take a singing class to express a long-repressed aspect of his being.

For me, the turnabout in the deepest seat of my behavior was to take on physical challenges and invite earth and iron into my elemental life. It was a big, long-term plan that started as a small little voice. The more I pursued it, the more I felt I was paving the way for a new kind of future for myself, one that led beyond 2012 and one that divested me of the cultural matrix that imposes limits and controls. It doesn't need to have a practical component, it just has to open up dormant parts of the brain. Instead of sitting in a chair and tapping away endlessly on a keyboard like a crazed woodpecker spewing private monologues, I sank my hands into clay. I carved wood, and I began to draw again. I resuscitated my ancient ten-speed bicycle and grounded myself with vigorous rides, reviving my inner sixteen-year-old who loved riding for hours along the Prairie Path in suburban Chicago.

And then a new path inside of that opened up, one that I doubt would have presented itself had I remained stuck in habitual patterns. My friend Stevyn Prothero told me of an old print shop going out of business in my old neighborhood in Denver. I was curious. The dying art of hand-set letterpress printing was already on my radar. Between 1880 and 1940 thousands of printing machines were produced, and they could be operated by hand or foot. Typically, the operator hand-set the type and images in a metal frame, mounted it in the press, inked up the rollers, and pumped the foot treadle. Clang, clang, clang! The beast's maw opens and closes as you feed each page in by hand, to be inked and pressed into the metal type. True printing! You can design pages with ornaments and use different-colored ink, handmade paper, and then bind your books by hand. It appealed to my sense of doing things off the grid as well as producing something of quality. The craft-guild ideals of William Morris's Kelmscott Press, or the Roycrofters, stoked my imagination. Our modern marketplace, especially books, have gone down in quality in terms of both content and design ethic, while the primary goal is to sell, sell, sell! The reign of quantity has smothered the value of quality.

As a writer, this concerns me. In my youth I produced my own books. I enjoyed designing intricate book covers and page content, then going to Kinko's with it. My original self-published version of my book *Tzolkin*, of which I sold an edition of sixty copies, contained forty pages of fold-out calendars and a color day-sign chart. This was well before my letterpress interest blossomed in 2007. Throughout my writing career, in retrospect, it seemed that my more creative side was being eclipsed by the editorial mandates and design limitations of the commercial publishing world. So my escape was to save one of the monstrous Chandler & Price platen presses from the scrap yard. Reviving the ancient art of letterpress printing was not unlike reviving the lost cosmology of the Maya.

I was surprised to find a community of like-minded printing enthusiasts who were happy to initiate me into the Black Art. Stevyn and I wrestled with a ton of iron, loading up a rental truck with "the beast" and other paraphernalia. I strategized a work space in my one-car garage and even got some tips from Lloyd O'Neil, the master printer in Denver, who was folding up his shop after fifty years. There aren't too many of these around anymore; almost all of them have now succumbed to offset and digital printing. What I love about this is that without once plugging into the grid you can produce a book-as-art, just as medieval illuminated manuscripts were a feast for the senses and an invitation to go deep into an experience that the book's contents could trigger. Sacred art was designed to transport the viewer into a state of consciousness that could directly apprehend the mysteries they symbolized. So, too, a book could open up vistas beyond the surface meaning of words printed on a page.

My little print shop has opened new relationships in my community with artists, designers, other letterpress fans, authors, and poets. Everyone was excited about the underlying motivation and value that the enterprise creates. And they met it with innovative new enterprises of their own. Our entire American culture is feeling a deep upwelling urge to turn the boat around, to begin doing things differently than our culture wishes us to do. Conspicuous consumption can be rebuffed with creative generosity, dog-eat-dog economics can be mitigated by community-based sharing; dominating others can be diffused by building mutually beneficial partnerships.[15]

These are all real things that real people can do. My brother Bill lives on the outskirts of Los Angeles in a little urban valley where chickens and coyotes dwell. His hillside property contains some open land and two small houses. He devised his own system of powering his needs with solar panels, with a minimal investment. Today, his roof is covered with them and he feeds surplus energy back into the grid. He is starting to grow corn and other crops. But he isn't some back-to-nature nonconformist—he works as a soundman for movies. He has created a sense of independence from the endless niggling ways that the matrix seeks to deceive us and suck our money, time, and energy away, to be used for its own profit.

I live in northern Colorado, where a great deal of innovative sustainable living practices are being developed. My own "bliss following" merged with others doing their own bliss following, and I believe this is the way through to a healthy future. It comes out of the heart to transform the culture; the larger institutions of society must be transformed by grassroots change. I now see myself as belonging to a community network of farmers, beer brewers, solar panel innovators, wind-power pioneers, alternate-fuel inventors, poets, musicians, writers, artists, festival organizers, traders, and health-food entrepreneurs. All are more than willing to divest the chimp and awaken the dormant partnership style of culture that has been submerged like some sleeping Atlantis under the illusory world of Seven Macaw. This, I believe, is the Maya renaissance writ large, the transformation of colonial values of territorial domination into the archaic partnership value of sustainable community-building. The guiding rudder of this process is the nurturing of higher consciousness, of reconnecting our little selves with the whole. In a time of global crisis, consciousness is the ultimate adaptive strategy.

In this chapter I outlined three methods for connecting with the big picture, each of which has an initiatory focus and intention. Importantly, there is one key to the effectiveness of any method one chooses to employ: *None of these methods work without the humble attitude of self-sacrifice, or ego transcendence.* It is often noted that "humiliation" is a central part of traditional initiation rituals, which is a term applied to the ceremonies by modern anthropology. It's a loaded word, a value-judgment term, which is inherently biased and misleading. The inner experience of what is labeled "humiliating" might actually be one of freedom, a liberating exaltation. Things look very different when you see things from the inside with the eye of the heart, not from the externally directed ego. The Big Picture appears when correct spiritual relationship between ego and Self is restored. The crisis of the modern world is an outward projection of a wrong state of affairs within the soul of humanity. This is fundamentally an inner work. Simultaneously, the outer work of political reform, cultural renewal, and innovative community-based solutions for food, fun, and energy can be pursued. But that outer work is most effective when inner progress is happening.

CHAPTER THIRTEEN

AFTER THE PARTY

Finish it.

—IZZI CREO, *The Fountain*[1]

This has been a guide through the many varied aspects of the 2012 discussion, and I hope that facts mixed with food-for-thought have seasoned a soul-stew that satisfies. Despite what the pundits of propriety assert, 2012 has meaning on virtually every level at which it appears. Critics who assert that "it's all nonsense" are missing the point. Such a statement is misleading—first of all because 2012 is a true artifact of the Maya calendar tradition. It is explicitly recorded on Tortuguero Monument 6, with related inscriptions connecting it to a whole host of meanings and beliefs. If we see 2012 manifesting on the level of spirituality, it can there have meaning too without violating Maya traditional beliefs about cycle endings. If we take a long, hard look at its use on the level of mass media doomsday rhetoric, that has meaning as well, because it reveals the shadow projection of our own culture's secret worship of death, destruction, and violence. These unhealthy prejudices, linked to a linear-time philosophy of questionable philosophical merit and an atavistic lust for destroying nature, perhaps need to be projected and exposed before healing and wholeness can occur. Our sick civilization apparently needs to use 2012 as a cathartic purge before the higher aspects of the spiritual teachings it points to can be benefited from. And that may simply be the way that it needs to be.

The 2012 date may also be a rallying cry for the indigenous mind and soul to reassert itself on the world stage—among all human beings of all ethnic groups because we are all indigenous to earth. The Maya renaissance, already under way, may just be the spark of a wildfire that may spread around the world, igniting the dormant primordial mind that has been layered over with materialism and abstractions. This renaissance can be phrased in many ways. It is essentially about throwing illusion into the fire of sacrifice, returning ego to its proper place as a satellite of the Divine Self (not the other way around), and awakening a higher consciousness through which the world's intractable dilemmas can be solved. If, as Terence McKenna said, consciousness does not loom large in the future of the human race, what kind of future is it going to be? And if the awakening of consciousness, a turnabout in the deepest seat of the collective soul, does not occur, then no amount of legislation, electing new leaders, or applying bandages is going to help.

Scholars and New Agers should move their thoughts beyond the prerational and rational stages of psychological development. They have become locked in a staring contest, failing to see a higher level of consciousness where their dualistic standoff can be reconciled and a direct experience of transformation and renewal can occur. According to the perennial wisdom at the root of the recovered 2012 teachings, the key to facilitating that renewal is, as it is for any cycle ending, sacrifice. This isn't rocket science, it just requires taking a step in the right direction and doing what needs to be done.

As for my own work to recover the lost cosmology connected with the origins of the 2012 calendar, there is more evidence for it now than there was fifteen years ago when I first put it on the table. Recent breakthroughs by scholars themselves are supporting a simple idea: The 13-Baktun cycle ending in 2012 was intended to target the rare precession-caused alignment of the solstice sun with the dark rift in the Milky Way. That's the "end-date alignment theory" stripped down to its basics. I suspect that this work will continue to matter, and to be added to, long after 2012 has passed. I never intended or expected it to be conflated with misconceived apocalyptic madness, or enlisted into serving a dozen different doomsday devices. But I did suspect that it was generally on target and would one day be subsumed into Maya studies, with or without credit to its originator.

It's likely that many of the curious people entering the 2012 topic are not going to care much for those details. They hear tell that 2012 is about transcendence, tripping, a new generation's reimagining of Woodstock Meets Burning Man. If people are merely wanting to know where the party is going to be, they should think twice about the impact their celebration is going to have on the sacred sites they'd like to visit, and double-check if their intentions are congruent with what 2012 is really about—transformation and renewal. I don't mean to rain on anyone's parade, but if the end-of-time party planners invite Eternity (you'd think they would, right?), they better make sure there will be enough room in the parking lot. I hear Eternity will be bringing some friends.

WHERE ARE YOU GOING TO BE?

This is one of the more hilarious and perplexing questions that I am supposed to respond to. I've given as many answers as times it's been asked. What can you say? "I don't know, I can't predict the future." "Right here." "In the Now." "Everywhere and nowhere." How about this one: "I've already been there." The reasons I'm not playing that game are many. First off, someone has to clean up after the party. That ensures that class divisions (worker bees serving party monsters) will survive the shift. Second, I've tried to envision what the ultimate cool "end of the world" partay would look like, and my mind meanders over various absurd scenarios. Let's see . . . I could parachute into the Great Ballcourt at Chichén Itzá, ritually deflower a virgin, and throw her into the cenote while 100,000 people throng around the Pyramid of Kukulcan. I could wear a top hat and be the ringleader of the 2012 circus, a cosmogenesis carnival replete with requisite freaks and fantasias.

No one should be on center stage! Any expectation of me personally is antithetical to the ego-transcendence that I believe is a central idea in the 2012 spiritual teaching. I may be the ultimate party pooper when I explain that I've never seen the specific day as having any predetermined or inherent significance for those who are around to experience it, apart from its being an authentic calendrical artifact. And having to be somewhere at a specific time in order to experience eternity—I don't know, it seems as counterproductive as consumerism has been to Christmas. The last thing I'd want to deal with is an event the Seven Macaws of mass media could have their way with.

Perhaps it is better to say where I don't want to be. The scenario I'd like to avoid is thousands of seekers descending, Harmonic Convergence–style, on Maya sites that shall remain nameless. The postparty cleanup and repair that a tug-of-war between anarchist apocalyptarians and ascension acolytes would entail is too much to contemplate. The violations of local laws, confrontations with misunderstanding officials, and the bad mojo generated with local populations are not things that party planners are likely to anticipate or even care about. These are real concerns. It could be the biggest crazy party you ever wished that you never went to. Sex, drugs, and rock 'n' roll are probably not going to be applicable as a hoped-for salvation. If they are, then 2012 really will be a time-travel portal, as some have suggested. Many might be expecting to party like it's 1967, even if they weren't yet alive in that "summer of love."

It should be clear by now that no one should be future projecting to December 21, 2012, waiting around for "the thing to happen." To plan a gala affair on that date is the least productive behavior I could imagine, but it is bound to happen. So, what can we expect? Well, we can expect the typical media exposés, crass condemnation by clueless commentators, and throwing the entire 2012 baby out with the bathwater. The mere presence of the all-seeing eye of Big Brother would likely bring about a buzz-kill, and the Eschaton, the transcendental object at the end of time, could decide to remain in hiding. Even good intentions have a built-in catch-22. If we focus all our collective conscious energy on having an ego-transcending mind-orgy of blissed-out oneness on December 21, 2012, we are likely to catalyze the opposite collective shadow—a lunatic with a dirty bomb who will also be counting down the days, seeking to keep Seven Macaw in power.

Something new and surprising may nevertheless emerge. Let's remember that *emergence* is attended by a sense of emergency, and this is a hallmark of spiritual awakening. We may even call it a crisis, a crossroads, a collective crucifixion as we ride the wave of earth's apotheosis, awakening to the sacredness of the living sanctuary that our ancestors simply called "home."

> *Whenever a profound experience of change is about to take place, its harbinger is the motif of death. This is not particularly mysterious, since it is the limited view and appraisal of oneself that must be outgrown or transformed, and to accomplish transformation the self-image must dissolve.*[2]

Clearly, the pathway through to the other side is to embrace death rather than fight it. This was the beautiful and profound message of Darren Aronofsky's movie *The Fountain*, which deftly wove Maya themes together with this perennial teaching: *Eternity cannot be found by living forever; it is found only when death is embraced.* This is what was meant in the movie by Izzi Creo's mysterious refrain: "Finish it." The specter of death does not have to breed fear; it invites, rather, a meditation on mortality and a fuller appreciation for life. The paradox of this advice is well known to spiritual guides who facilitate the rebirth passage for people in crisis. The advice applies to 2012, which is the screen upon which the urgent fear of world cataclysm is being projected. The psychodrama of personal dissolution is a microcosm of larger portents.

Psychologist John Weir Perry observed the process: "In times of acute and rapid culture change, visionaries undergo the shattering experience of seeing the world dissolve into a chaos and time whirl back to its beginnings . . . dissolution of the world image is the harbinger of change. Expressions of cultural reform are explicit."[3] The crisis of change is throbbing with urgency; we feel the impending juncture of something awesome and profound on the horizon, but when, when, when? Death or birth? Both processes are utterly and completely interwoven, and if you embrace their *hieros gamos*, or sacred

The 13 numbers and 20 day-signs in a mandala.
Drawing by the author

marriage, your passage to a new reality is ensured. Yes, an old world fades, but a new one appears. Here we see how the term "apocalypse" is best understood in its original etymological sense: it means "unveiling." What is unveiled, or revealed? The *dang an sich*, the thing-in-itself, that which is, was, and will always be: Reality.

Individual renewal and world renewal must happen in concert. Both share the same representative image: the *mandala*—the image of center, source, wholeness, oneness. To the extent that the world image is a projected dream of the inner psyche, the burden of successful world renewal lies with the individual. We decide, and we make it or break it. We may prefer to sit around, "waiting for 2012 to happen," and avoid the responsibility for *being the change* that needs to happen, but that completely misses the point. If we don't do it before the 2012 party, it will be waiting for us afterward.

> And now the rope of time runs out
>   unweaving the wrongs
> Till nothing's left but loosening strings
>   and without doubt
>   all the things
> Dissolve into the sea of songs[4]

—John Major Jenkins

Appendix One

Glossary of Terms

1 Ahau.   The Sacred Day of Venus. Occurs every 104 haab (26 days less than 104 years) when the cycles of Venus, the tzolkin, and the haab coordinate on a Venus morning star rising.

4 Ahau.   The day in the 260-day tzolkin calendar that coordinates with both the zero day and the completion day of the 13-Baktun cycle.

Ahau.   One of the 20 day-signs in the 260-day tzolkin calendar. Has multiple meanings, including "solar lord" and "blowgunner."

Anagogical.   Perceiving or accepting that symbols have a higher or larger reference to other sets of meanings, beyond a literal and specific denotative meaning. The etymology of the term means "upward-leading."

Anagogue.   A neologism derived from the term *anagogical* (see entry). By analogy with the relationship between *pedagogical* and *pedagogue*, an anagogue is a person who teaches or believes in the anagogical interpretation of symbols.

Apocalypse.   From the Greek, Ἀποκάλυψις (*Apokálypsis*), meaning "lifting of the veil" or "revelation." In modern usage it has become synonymous with a fated catastrophe.

Apocatastasis.   From the Greek, meaning the restoration of the original and true conditions. Implies a doctrine of degeneration through time followed by regeneration, which may apply to the world generally or to conditions within humanity, including spiritual awareness.

Astro-theological.   A worldview espoused in many ancient cultures, including the Greek and Maya civilizations, founded on an intimate relation between the human world, spiritual teachings, and astronomical cycles. It often resulted in the alignment of temples with meaningful astronomical horizons. See, for example, *The Earth, The Temple, and the Gods* by Vincent Scully, Jr.

Baktunian movement.   A term used by Maya scholar Victor Montejo in reference to the modern renaissance of Maya culture heralded by a renewal at the end of the Baktun (in 2012).

Bloodletting rites.   A sacrificial practice of letting blood from the tongue, earlobes, or penis by ancient Maya elite.

Buddhi, buddhi mind.   Buddhi is a feminine Sanskrit noun derived from the same root as Buddha (*budh*—to be awake; to understand; to know). The word signifies a transpersonal faculty of mind higher than the rational discursive mind that is approximately equivalent to "intuitive intelligence" or "higher mind," but is more properly identified as *gnosis* (direct inner knowing). It is "that which knows"—that is, able to discern truth from falsehood.*

Calendar Round.   A period of 52 haab (18,980 days) representing the synchronization of the 260-day tzolkin and the 365-day haab.

Chac Mool.   A reclining deity holding a bowl in its belly to receive sacrificial offerings. Associated with the New Fire ceremony and the movement of the Pleiades. Many large and small stone carvings of Chac Mools have been found.

Classic Period.   The period of the Maya florescence and sudden decline, from 200 AD to 900 AD. The beginning of the Classic Period used to be set at 300 AD, but defining characteristics have now been identified for an earlier date.

Correlation.   The coordination of the Maya time system with the modern Gregorian calendar. This effort began in the late 1800s, and Joseph T. Goodman published a breakthrough in 1905 that was later confirmed but adjusted slightly by Juan Hernandez Martínez and J. Eric S. Thompson. The issue was settled by 1950, resulting in 13.0.0.0.0 correlating with December 21, 2012.

Creation Myth.   Specifically used in this book to refer to the Maya *Popol Vuh,* also called the Hero Twin Myth.

Cycle-ending date.   The date that falls at the end of a cycle; a term used intentionally to avoid confusion caused by the term "end date," which has often been mistakenly taken to mean a final ending.

Dark rift.   A visual feature, caused by the thick accumulation of interstellar dust along our galaxy's midplane, that lies along the lengthwise body of the Milky Way, beginning within the nuclear bulge of the Galactic Center (between Sagittarius and Scorpio) and extending northward to Cygnus.

Day-count, count of days.   Refers to the 260-day cycle (the tzolkin).

Day-keeper.   An initiated priest, or spiritual guide, who counts the days of the 260-day tzolkin calendar, says prayers and makes offerings at shrines, and is adept at using the calendar as an oracle.

Desacralized.   A term describing something that has been drained or shorn of its sacredness.

Dresden Codex.   One of the surviving Maya books.

Eclipse half-year.   An ideal period of 173.3 days between eclipses; used in Maya calculations and almanacs.

Ecliptic.   The 14-degree-wide band that encircles the earth and along which the planets, moon, and sun travel. It is, astronomically, the plane of our solar system.

18 Rabbit.   The approximate English translation of the name of the Copán king who ruled between 695 AD and 738 AD and erected the many carvings in the Grand Plaza. His name in the Mayan language is Waxaklahun Ub'ah K'awil.

End-naming practice.   The Maya practice of naming a Long Count period by the day in the 260-day tzolkin that its last day falls on. For example, we are currently in the 4 Ahau Katun because this Katun's final day falls on 4 Ahau.

Entelechy.   According to Aristotle, an entelechy is the condition of something whose essence is fully realized; actualized in its totality. In some modern philosophical systems it is a vital force that motivates and guides an organism toward self-fulfillment.*

Epigrapher/epigraphy.   Epigraphy is the study of inscriptions or epigraphs engraved into stone or other durable materials, or cast in metal; the science of classifying them as to cultural context and date, elucidating them, and assessing what conclusions can be deduced from them. A person who does this study is called an *epigrapher.**

Epiphenomenon.   A consequent or secondary phenomenon derived from a previous existent. For example, mind is thought by some thinkers to be an epiphenomenon of matter.

Equation of Maya time.   13.0.0.0.0 = 4 Ahau = December 21, 2012.

Eschatology.   The study of the ultimate ends of the world, or universal process; an ultimate spiritual state of being. Some historical religious traditions, such as the Essenes of Qumran, are thought to have realized their eschatological ambitions, and thus its members lived in a state of awareness of ultimate reality, a "realized eschatology."

Eschaton.   The end state, or ultimate condition or object, that emerges at the end of time. See *eschatology.* Used by philosopher Henry Corbin and popularized by Terence McKenna.

Fractal.   Is generally a rough or fragmented geometric shape that can be split into parts, each of which is (at least approximately) a reduced-size copy of the whole. A property called *self-similarity.* A mathematical fractal is based on an equation that undergoes iteration, a form of feedback based on recursion.*

Fractal time.   The application of fractal geometry to time. The concept was elaborated by Terence McKenna in his Novelty Time Theory. The concept has since been adopted in various forms with varying intervals and periods by other writers.

Galactic alignment.   The alignment of the December solstice sun with the dark rift in the Milky Way. This definition highlights astronomical features that are compelling to naked-eye sky-watchers, past and present. For a more technical definition, one can replace "dark rift in the Milky Way" with "galactic equator." This alignment takes place within the boundaries of the nuclear bulge of the Milky Way, also perceptible to naked-eye observation, known as the Galactic Center.

Galactic Center.   The center of a spiral galaxy. Our own galaxy's center lies between the constellations of Sagittarius and Scorpio. Astronomers tend to conceive of the Galactic Center as a precise point, which is misleading because galaxies have slightly different gravitational, visual, and electromagnetic centers. In addition, some spiral galaxies, such as our own, have two closely connected centers. A more realistic conception, which is congruent with how the central part of the Milky Way is perceived by naked-eye stargazers, is that of a "nuclear bulge," which is a wider and larger zone of brighter stars as compared to other parts of the Milky Way. For example, the opposite part of the Milky Way in Gemini is very thin and diffuse, as that is the direction looking out of the galactic disk.

Galactic synchronization.   A term coined and a concept used by author José Argüelles, defined by Brian Swimme in his introduction to *The Mayan Factor*. It is related to, and perhaps developed from, the Photon Belt concept (see entry). It is astronomically unrelated to the galactic alignment.

GMT.   The original Goodman-Martínez-Thompson correlation, proposed in 1927 by Thompson: JD 584285, making the cycle-ending date fall on December 23, 2012. (JD refers to the Julian Day designation.)

GMT-2.   The adjusted Goodman-Martínez-Thompson correlation number, finalized in 1950 by Thompson: JD 584283, making the cycle-ending date fall on December 21, 2012.

Gnomon.   A shadow-casting device, often a vertical pole, used to measure the sun's movements through the day and year.

Gnosis.   A knowing conferred by direct inner experience. See *buddhi mind, Primordial Tradition*.

Gnostic.   A term applied to religions that cultivated direct initiatory awakening to wisdom, as opposed to obediently following exoteric dogma.

Haab.   Period of 365 days used in Mesoamerican calendrics. Same as the "vague solar year."

Hermetic.   A magical and religious movement stemming from the teachings of Hermes Trismegistus. Generally, Hermetic philosophies are based on a conviction that comes from a direct initiatory experience of the deep interconnection between subjective and objective domains. The hermetic adage testifies to this: As above, so below. This refers not only to an interweaving between sky and earth, but also of microcosm and macrocosm, subjective and objective. Standard definitions of the word "hermetic" as pertaining to secrets, obscurity, and unrevealed information are superficial.

Hero Twin.   Hunahpu or Xbalanque; one of the two sons of One Hunahpu in *The Popol Vuh*.

Hero Twin Myth.   Generally, equivalent to the Creation Myth and *The Popol Vuh*.

Specifically, pertains to the section of *The Popol Vuh* that involves the Hero Twins and their adventures.

Hun.   One.

Hunahpu.   One of the Hero Twins of *The Popol Vuh*. Refers to the day-sign Ahau, and therefore, as Hun-ahpu or One Ahau, to the Sacred Day of Venus.

Iconography.   The study of pictographic language and image systems used to represent ideas. In the development of writing, pictographic expressions usually precede more abstract hieroglyphic or alphabetic writing.

Inferior conjunction.   This occurs when a retrograde planet crosses in front of the sun on its way to becoming a morning star.

Intellectus.   See *noetic*.

Izapa.   A pre-Classic site in southern Chiapas, Mexico, near the Guatemala border. A significant ceremonial and astronomical site of the Izapan civilization that preserves some of the earliest carved portrayals of episodes from the Hero Twin myth, dated to 400 BC–50 AD. Was also involved in the formulation and adoption of the Long Count calendar.

K'awil.   A deity connected with Jupiter and concepts of transcendence and transformation.

Logograph.   An image that represents a word or a morpheme (the smallest meaningful unit of language). Logographs, or logograms, are commonly known also as "ideograms" or "hieroglyphs." Strictly speaking, however, ideograms represent ideas directly rather than words and morphemes.*

Long Count calendar.   A system of time counting developed sometime between 400 BC and 36 BC by the Maya that basically uses five place-value levels: the Kin (day), the Uinal (20 days), the Tun (360 days), the Katun (7,200 days), and the Baktun (144,000 days). A typical date in the Long Count, from Baktun to Kin, is written: 9.16.4.1.1. It is a cycles within cycles system, an expression of a cyclic time philosophy rather than a linear time philosophy.

Mayanism.   The essential core ideas or teachings of Maya religion and philosophy. A counterdefinition of Mayanism has developed on Wikipedia that uses the term to identify popular and New Age appropriations and misconceptions of Maya ideas. This is a problematic use of the term, because it contradicts the consistently proactive meanings ascribed to analogous terms, such as "Hinduism" or "Buddhism."

Meme.   An adopted unit or element of cultural ideas, symbols, or practices transmitted from one mind to another, often unconsciously, through speech, gestures, or rituals.*

Mesoamerica.   The area between Central Mexico and Central America, including Belize, Mexico, Guatemala, El Salvador, and Honduras.

Metaphoragrams.   A term coined and used by Maya scholar J. Eric S. Thompson which highlights his conviction that Maya hieroglyphic writing contained and could convey much more than phonetics or even ideographs. As the term suggests, the glyphs conveyed, via metaphor, other sets of information, similar to how contemporary Maya day-keepers utilize word puns and rhymes to access a larger set of interrelated meanings. Along these lines, Thompson also said the glyphs were *anagogical* (see entry).

Milky Way–ecliptic cross (the cross formed by the Milky Way and the ecliptic).   The two locations in the sky where the Milky Way crosses over the ecliptic. One is in Sagittarius and one is in Gemini.

Nahuatl.   The Central Mexico culture and language.

Neoplatonism.   The modern term for a school of religious and mystical philosophy, based on the teachings of Plato and early Platonists, that took shape in the third century AD, whose members included Macrobius and Plotinus. The earlier Middle Platonists, such as Numenius and Porphyry, also subscribed to Pythagorean ideas.

New Year's Day in Maya calendars.   New Year's Day is the first day of the haab. Since different cultural groups followed different haab placements, New Year's Day occurs at different times for different groups. Also, since leap year was not recognized in the Maya haab, New Year's Day precesses backward around the Gregorian calendar at the rate of one day every four years. This does not complicate the universally shared sacred count of 260 days.

Noetic, intellectus.   The word "noetic" ultimately derives from the Greek word voῦç (nous), meaning "intellect, higher mind, thought." It is associated with the direct knowing or intuition of *noesis*, involving a faculty of understanding superior to discursive, deductive reason.*

Nondual awareness.   Awareness of the interdependence of subject and object. Nondualism is a philosophy rooted in the direct experience that separateness is an illusion, and that the illusion of separateness is maintained only in more limited states of consciousness.*

North Celestial Pole.   The center of the earth's rotation projected into the northern sky. The stars appear to revolve around it. It sometimes corresponds to a star, but because the earth is slowly wobbling (see the precession of the equinoxes), it traces a circle in the northern skies very slowly over some 26,000 years.

One Hunaphu.   The father of the Hero Twins in *The Popol Vuh*.

Ontology.   The philosophical study of the nature of being, existence, or reality in general, as well as of the basic categories of being and their relations.

Pan-Mayanism.   A term used by anthropologists Kay Warren and Victor Montejo, as early as 1997, to discuss and explain unifying political and cultural movements among the indigenous Maya of Mexico and Central America.

Pedagogue.   One who is *pedantic* (see entry) in his or her style of writing or teaching. A person who evinces this style is pedagogical.

Pedantic.   Describes a teacher or scholar who is characterized by a narrow concern for book learning and formal rules.

Perennial Philosophy.   The notion of the universal recurrence of philosophical insight independent of epoch or culture, including universal truths on the nature of reality, humanity, or consciousness.* See also *Primordial Tradition*.

Performative contradiction.   A lack of fit between the content and the performance (or sense) of the speech act. For example, "all statements must be false" creates a vicious circle. As pointed out by philosopher Ken Wilber, to assert that "there are no absolutes" is also a performative contradiction, revealing the inherent absurdity of one of modern deconstructionist philosophy's most cherished premises.*

Photon Belt.   A fringe idea that developed in the 1980s involving the belief in an energetic beam of light that sweeps through the galaxy, possibly emanating from the Galactic Center, or different density sectors of the galaxy that our solar system passes through during different eras. It has become loosely attached to 2012 and ideas involving contact with beings from the Pleiades. See also *galactic synchronization*.

Popol Vuh.   A document recorded by Maya elders in the 1550s, possibly based on an older hieroglyphic book. It preserves within it a World Age doctrine, the story of the Hero Twins, as well as lineage titles and genealogies of Quiché Maya leaders. Some of the episodes preserved in *The Popol Vuh* are also found on Classic Maya vases and carved in stone at the pre-Classic site of Izapa.

Precession of the equinoxes.   The earth spins once around its axis every twenty-four hours. The earth also exhibits a very slow wobble, changing its orientation in space such that the *North Celestial Pole* (see entry) traces a circle in the northern skies. One complete wobbles takes approximately 26,000 years. Precession affects the position of the sun on the solstices and equinoxes in relation to background features such as stars, constellations, and the Milky Way. The position of the sun on, for example, the March equinox precesses slowly backward along the *ecliptic* (see entry), moving into a different constellation every 2,160 years.

Pre-Classic Period.   2500 BC to 200 AD. Its beginnings are marked by the development of the first ceramic traditions in Central and Western Mexico. Also known as the Formative Period, it is divided into three phases: the Early (2500–1200 BC), Middle (1500–600 BC), and Late (600 BC–200 AD).

Pre/trans fallacy.   According to philosopher Ken Wilber, the nonrational stages of consciousness (what Wilber calls "prerational" and "transrational" stages) can be easily confused with one another. One can reduce supposed "transrational" spiritual realization to prerational regression, or one can elevate prerational states to the transrational domain. For example, Wilber claims that Freud and Jung commit this fallacy. Freud considered mystical realizations to be a fallacy of reduction. Wilber thinks that Jung commits the converse form of the same mistake by considering prerational myths to reflect divine realizations. Likewise, prerational states may be misidentified as postrational states. Wilber characterizes himself as having fallen victim to the pre/trans fallacy in his early work.* See http://wilber.shambhala.com/html/books/cowokev1_intro.cfm.

Primordial Tradition.   A school of religious philosophy that holds its origins in the *philosophia perennis et universalis*, or Perennial Philosophy, which is in turn a development of the prisca theologia of the Middle Ages. The early exponents in the early-twentieth-century revival of this view of reality include Ananda Coomaraswamy, René Guénon, and Aldous Huxley. The Primordial Tradition seeks to establish a fundamental substratum of religious belief in all authentic religious teachings, adhering to the principle that universal truths are a cross-cultural phenomenon and transcendent of their respective Traditions, mythologies, and religious beliefs. The idea of the Primordial Tradition was well received by both practitioners and the academic community, and its development was actively endorsed by the International Conference of Religions in Chicago, 1893. The Primordial Tradition does not elevate any Tradition or religion above another, and instead upholds the truth claims of all authentic religions and spiritual movements. Adherents of the Primordial Tradition can be found in any religious system, such as Hinduism, Buddhism, Paganism, Christianity, or Islam.* The Maya and other New World indigenous civilizations have been excluded from belonging to the Primordial Tradition, a situation that is no longer tenable. See also *Perennial Philosophy*.

Quetzalcoatl.   A Nahuatl deity that is the same as the Maya Kukulcan. Also called the Plumed Serpent, this deity embodies the principle of uniting opposites and transcending duality. In some teachings, a "quetzalcoatl" is an enlightened person who has integrated the dual cosmic forces within his or her own being.

Sacred Calendar.   Although this term usually refers to the 260-day cycle by itself, it can also refer to the complete framework of time cycles used by the Maya.

Sacred cycle.   Refers to the 260-day cycle (the tzolkin).

Sacred Day of Venus.   The sacred day (including its number coefficient) that begins a Venus Round. Example: 1 Ahau is the traditional Sacred Day of Venus. Ahau, by itself, is simply the Senior Sacred Day (coefficient is required to designate the Sacred Day apart from any occurrence of Ahau).

Senior day-sign (senior year bearer).   Of the four year bearers, the most senior one initiates the 52-haab Calendar Round. The most revered day-sign; can vary from group to group.

Seven Liberal Arts.   A seven-tiered system of initiation and education that took form in the Middle Ages and has led to the modern collegiate system of grades and degrees. It was originally based on the Neoplatonic conception of seven planetary spheres of increasing or decreasing proximity to the divine empyrean.

Seven Macaw.   A bird deity in *The Popol Vuh* that exemplifies the motivations and goals of self-serving egoism, thus embodying that archetype.

Sidereal year.   The time taken by the earth to orbit the sun once with respect to the fixed stars. Hence it is also the time the sun takes to return to the same position with respect to the fixed stars after traveling once around the ecliptic (as viewed from earth).

Sinusoidal orbit of our solar system around the Galactic Center, above and below the galactic plane.   A full orbital circuit in this process is completed in roughly 250 million years. Because our solar system occasionally physically passes through the galactic midplane, this sinusoidal orbital motion is often confused with the galactic alignment, which is the apparent shifting of the sun (on the equinoxes or solstice) around the ecliptic, caused by the precession of the equinoxes, completing a full cycle every 26,000 years.

Stela, stelae.   Carved standing monuments often found at archaeological sites. Many contain tzolkin/haab and Long Count dates, or iconographic depictions.

Syncretism.   The process by which the Maya assimilated to Christian and European values. The process occurred largely in terms of surface details and formal behavior, while essential spiritual beliefs of the Maya were retained.

13-Baktun cycle.   A period of time in the Maya Long Count. It equals 1,872,000 days, or approximately 5125.36 years. It is an expression of a doctrine of World Ages and occurs in association with Creation Texts. The current 13-Baktun cycle began on August 11, 3114 BC, and ends on December 21, 2012.

Toponym.   A name or glyph used to designate a place or location—for example, a Maya city.

Traditionalist philosopher.   A philosopher who subscribes to the perspective of *the Perennial Philosophy* (see entry), which is also called Traditionalism.

Tropical year.   365.2422 days.

Tzolkin.   The sacred count of days (260-day cycle). Derived from the Quiché Maya term *chol'qij* (count of days).

Tzolkin/Haab, Tzolkin/Haab framework.   Conventional combining of tzolkin and haab calendars to designate a unique calendrical position within the 52-haab Calendar Round period. For example, 4 Ahau 3 Kankin is a tzolkin/haab date, which occurs only once every Calendar Round.

Vague solar year.   365 days, otherwise known as the haab.

Venus calendar.   The system by which morning star appearances of Venus are predicted. Consists of the nestled cycles of tzolkin, haab, and Venus.

Venus cycle.   The synodical period of Venus. Equals 583.92 days; the Maya used a 584-day approximation.

Venus emergence as morning star.   The first day on which Venus becomes visible in the eastern morning sky after inferior conjunction (passing in front of the sun). Reckoned to occur four days after perfect inferior conjunction.

Venus Round.   The period of 104 haab that synchronizes the primary cycles of the Maya Calendar Round (the tzolkin and haab) with Venus. Provides a framework by which the astronomical phenomena associated with Venus can be predicted.

Waxaklahun Ub'ah K'awil.   The Copan king who ruled between 695 AD and 738 AD. He erected the famous stelae in the Grand Plaza. Commonly used English translation of his name is 18 Rabbit.

World Age doctrine.   The belief that humanity passes through distinct chapters or phases of evolution and/or devolution. Many cultures subscribed to a World Age doctrine, which is closely connected to concepts of cyclic time.

Xbalanque.   One of the Hero Twins from *The Popol Vuh*. Refers to the day-sign Ix and the full moon.

Xibalba.   The Maya underworld. The portal or road to Xibalba is called the *xibalbe* or *xibalba be* in *The Popol Vuh*, and it corresponds to the dark rift in the Milky Way.

Year bearers.   The sequence of four day-signs on which the first day of the haab can occur. There are four because of the relationship between the 20 day-signs of the tzolkin and the 365 days of the haab. 20 divides into 365 evenly with five days left over; thus, every year the year bearer advances by five.

Zero counting.   Used by various groups to count the twenty days in the haab months from 0 to 19. The Ixil and Quiché Maya dropped zero counting at some point and began counting the haab days with 1.

Zero date, base date.   Pertaining to the Long Count, corresponding to 0.0.0.0.0. The term "base date" is also used for other types of calculation bases found in Maya inscriptions.

*Definitions and discussions marked with an asterisk were adapted from their respective Wikipedia entries.

TIMELINE OF THE 2012 STORY

August 11, 3114 BC. 13.0.0.0.0. Beginning date of the current 13-Baktun cycle of the Long Count. It is a mathematical back-calculation generated when the Long Count system was inaugurated sometime between 355 BC and the first century BC.

355 BC. Long Count inauguration date suggested by Munro Edmonson; a hypothetical calendar reconstruction.

400 BC–1 BC. Izapa is thriving and its stone carvings are made, depicting early episodes of the Hero Twin Myth.

36 BC. Earliest dated monument in the Long Count, from Chiapa de Corzo.

31 BC. Long Count monument from Tres Zapotes.

19 BC. Latest possible date for a fragmented Long Count monument from Tak'alik Ab'aj, a "sister city" to Izapa. It may date to 39 BC, making it the oldest known dated Long Count monument.

37 AD. Long Count date from El Baúl.

41 AD. Ending of Baktun 8.

83 AD and 103 AD. Early Long Count dates on Stela 5 from Tak'alik Ab'aj.

197 AD. Linda Schele's dating of the Hauberg Stela.

292 AD. Dated monument from Tikal with full Calendar Round and Long Count information. It defined, for a previous generation of scholars, the beginning of the Classic Period (300 AD to 900 AD). Today the origins of Maya civilizations have been pushed back by new archaeological findings.

435 AD. Ending of Baktun 9.

620 AD–820 AD. Many Long Count dates at Classic Maya sites. Distance Numbers are used and Era beginning and end dates are found at sites such as Quiriguá, Coba, Palenque, Copán, and Tortuguero.

612 AD. Balam Ajaw, king of Tortuguero, was born.

652, October. 13-Baktun Creation Date (3114 BC), first mentioned at Copán.

669, January. 13-Baktun end date (2012 AD) recorded at Tortuguero.

711 AD, December 3. (9.14.0.0.0). Astronomically significant Long Count date found at many sites, including Piedras Negras, Calakmul, Tortuguero, Palenque, Tikal, and Copán.

738, May 1.   Copán king 18 Rabbit is ritually decapitated. It happened at the "Black Hole."

830 AD.   Ending of Baktun 10; Classic Maya civilization begins failing.

909 AD.   Last carved Long Count monument, from Toniná: 10.4.0.0.0.

1000 AD.   The Long Count calendar tradition continues in manuscript form, with Long Count dates and distance numbers recorded in the Maya's Dresden Codex, Madrid Codex, and Paris Codex.

1100 AD–1500 AD.   Katun counting is preserved in Yucatán. A Short Count form of the Long Count (a 13-Katun *May*-cycle, or Prophecy cycle) is implemented.

1224 AD.   Baktun 11 ending, probably noted in Yucatán.

1520s–1570s.   The Conquest. Maya books are burned. Bishop Diego de Landa active in Yucatán, writes his *Relacion de los cosas de Yucatan.*

1520s–1700s.   The *Chilam Balam* prophecy books are compiled by Maya leaders in Yucatán. They contain much earlier Katun prophecies and other historical information.

1550s.   The Hero Twin Myth (*The Popol Vuh*) recorded by Quiché elders in Guatemala.

1618.   Baktun 12 ending celebrated in Yucatán.

1697.   The Itza Maya finally acquiesce to Spanish rule in Flores, Petén.

1700.   Francisco Ximénez translates *The Popol Vuh* in Guatemala.

1752.   Short Count system recalibrated in Yucatán, changing the 20-year Katun cycle to a 24-year cycle. The continuity of the Katun sequencing is affected.

1761.   Maya reform leader Jacinto Canek captured, tortured, and killed by Spanish army in Mérida, along with many of his followers.

1770s–1790s.   Spanish travelers take note of ancient ruins of Palenque.

1810s. Memory of pre-1752 placement of Short Count tradition dies with elders.

1800–1820s.   Explorers such as Count Waldeck visit Maya sites.

1839.   Catherwood and Stephens record monuments at Copán and Quiriguá containing Long Count glyphs.

1860s.   Brasseur de Bourbourg publishes *The Popol Vuh* and de Landa's *Relacion.*

1880s.   Maudslay makes high-quality photographs of Maya monuments, including Long Count inscriptions.

1880s.   Förstemann decodes the Dresden Codex in Germany.

1897.   Goodman's appendix to Maudslay published, containing free-floating charts for Long Count dates.

1905.   Joseph T. Goodman publishes "Maya Dates" in *American Anthropologist.* This is the correlation of the Maya and Gregorian calendars that would be confirmed in the 1920s.

1926–1927. Juan Martínez Hernández and J. Eric S. Thompson confirm Goodman's work, producing the original GMT (Goodman-Martínez-Thompson) correlation.

1927. Thompson publishes an article with a chart that could be extrapolated to reach an estimated cycle ending of December 23, 2012, but this never appears to have been done. The cycle ending remained unstated in the literature until Coe's 1966 book *The Maya*.

1920s–1940s. Ethnographic evidence for the survival of the 260-day tzolkin calendar in the Guatemalan highlands is documented. Invites a reassessment of the correlation by Thompson.

1946. Morley's *The Ancient Maya* is published, with incomplete Long Count tables, using the original GMT correlation.

1950. Thompson revises the original GMT by 2 days. The result brings the 13-Baktun cycle ending into alignment with December 21, 2012, although the fact has yet to be stated in the literature.

1956. The second edition of Morley's *The Ancient Maya* contains updated Long Count tables, using the revised GMT-2 correlation, but the tables are still incomplete.

1966. Michael Coe's *The Maya* is published. It is the first source to mention the 13-Baktun cycle ending of the Long Count, but the book miscalculates it as December 24, 2011 AD.

1967. William S. Burroughs mentions 2012 in a parody magazine, according to the findings of John Hoopes.

1975. The cycle ending is treated fully by Frank Waters in his *Mexico Mystique*, but he used Coe's 2011 date. McKenna mentions 2012 in *The Invisible Landscape*. Argüelles mentions 2012 in *The Transformative Vision*.

1975–1990. Argüelles develops his Maya calendar system and associates Tony Shearer's 1987 Harmonic Convergence date with a "twenty-five-year countdown" to 2012. McKenna is elaborating his Time Wave Zero model, now connected to December 21, 2012. Peter Balin mentions 2012 in his 1978 book *Flight of the Feathered Serpent;* Peter Tompkins mentions 2011 in his 1976 book *Mysteries of the Mexican Pyramids.* Barbara Tedlock mentions 2012 in her 1982 book *Time and the Highland Maya.* Argüelles's *The Mayan Factor* appears in 1987.

1988. Maya scholar Munro Edmonson writes, in his *Book of the Year*, that the solstice placement of the cycle ending in 2012 was unlikely to be a coincidence. For almost two decades after this other scholars asserted, when asked, that it must be a coincidence.

1992. John Major Jenkins publishes his book *Tzolkin*, which offered a method by which shifting seasonal quarters were tracked in the Long Count, suggesting how December 21, 2012, might have been targeted.

1992–1993.   Linda Schele's breakthrough work on hieroglyphic decipherments, Maya Creation Mythology, and astronomy.

1991–1995.   Popular books on the Mesoamerican calendar, such as *The Mayan Prophecies* and Scofield's *Day-Signs,* start appearing. Argüelles's Dreamspell system released in late 1991.

1994.   Jenkins publishes his 2012 alignment theory, connecting the era-2012 alignment of the December solstice sun and the dark rift to Maya Creation Mythology and astronomy. Research culminates in the 1998 relase of his book *Maya Cosmogenesis 2012,* offering a full reconstruction of the origins and intention of the Long Count/2012 cosmology.

1998.   Geoff Stray's Internet site Diagnosis 2012 is founded and becomes an indispensable resource for reviews and insights on all things 2012.

2000–2009.   An explosion of books, films, and websites devoted to 2012 flood the marketplace. Scholars, Maya elders, popular writers, the *New York Times,* and documentaries cover and comment on 2012.

2005.   Geoff Stray's book *Beyond 2012* is published.

2005.   Victor Montejo's *Maya Intellectual Renaissance* is published. Discussion of the indigenous "Baktunian movement."

2006.   Robert Sitler publishes "The 2012 Phenomenon," the first academic treatment of the topic.

2006, April.   The 2012 text from Tortuguero is translated and discussed, with varying opinions on its importance.

2007.   Michael Grofe completes his PhD dissertation, which argues convincingly for accurate knowledge of the rate of the precession of the equinoxes in the Dresden Codex.

2008.   Barb MacLeod offers her "3-11 Pik formula," detailing a precession-based mechanism in the Classic Period inscriptions used by Maya kings.

2009, February.   The first academic 2012 conference takes place, held at Tulane University in New Orleans.

2009, February–March.   New discoveries on dark-rift astronomy and 2012 connections at Tortuguero and Copán made by Grofe and Jenkins (see Chapter 7).

2009, November.   Sony Pictures releases mass media 2012 movie.

The 2012 story is, of course, not yet finished. As of May 31, 2009 (a 4 Ahau day), there are exactly 5 tzolkin cycles (1,300 days) remaining to December 21, 2012. We might wish to recognize the 260-day time resonance countdown of 4 Ahau dates: May 31, 2009; February 15, 2010; November 2, 2010; July 20, 2011; April 5, 2012;

December 21, 2012. Interestingly, the initiation day of contemporary day-keeper practice, 8 B'atz (8 Monkey), occurs on December 12, 2012, nine days before 13.0.0.0.0.

December 21, 2012.   The cycle-ending date of the 13-Baktun period of the Maya Long Count calendar.

December 21, 2012 AD = 13.0.0.0.0 = 4 Ahau 3 Kankin

NOTES

1. Frontispiece poem: Jenkins, John Major. *Shadow, Stone, and Green.* Denver, CO: Four Ahau Press, 2008.

INTRODUCTION: AN UNSTOPPABLE IDEA

1. Tedlock, Dennis (trans.). *The Popol Vuh: The Definitive Edition of the Mayan Book of the Dawn of Life and the Glories of Gods and Kings,* revised edition. New York: Simon & Schuster, 1996, p. 70.
2. McKenna, Terence. "The Light of the Third Millennium." Talk given in Austin, Texas, 1997. http://edj.net/mc2012/TM-Light.mp3 (at 35:10).
3. Fox news report with Dr. Michio Kaku. April 25, 2009. http://www.youtube.com/watch?v=hujQg2E_fDw. Dr. Kaku himself doesn't assert this, but the banner beneath the report does.

CHAPTER 1. RECOVERING A LOST WORLD

1. Covarrubias, Miguel. *Mexico South.* New York: Alfred A. Knopf, 1947, p. 187.
2. *Proceedings of the National Academy of Science,* March 24, 2009. www.pnas.org.
3. Weatherford, Jack. *Indian Givers.* Ballantine Books, 1989.
4. de Landa, Friar Diego. *Yucatan Before and After the Conquest,* trans. by William Gates. Baltimore: The Maya Society, 1937. Also at Sacred Texts online: http://sacred-texts.com/nam/maya/ybac/ybac59.htm.
5. Goetz, Delia, and Sylvanus Morley (English trans. after the Spanish trans. of Adrián Recinos). *The Popol Vuh: The Sacred Book of the Ancient Quiché Maya,* original trans. by Francisco Ximénez. Norman, Oklahoma: University of Oklahoma Press, 1950, p. 6.
6. Tedlock, Dennis (trans.). *The Popol Vuh,* revised edition, 1996, pp. 22–25.
7. Perera, Victor, and Robert D. Bruce. *Last Lords of Palenque.* Berkeley and Los Angeles: University of California Press, 1982; Bruce, Robert D. *Lacandon Dream Symbolism.* 2 vols. Mexico: Ediciones Euroamericanas, 1975–1979.
8. Graham, Ian. *Alfred Maudslay and the Maya, A Biography.* Norman, Okla.: University of Oklahoma Press, 2002, p. 99.
9. Fuentes, Carlos. *Myself with Others: Selected Essays.* New York: Farrar, Straus and Giroux, 1988.
10. Durán, Fray Diego. *Book of the Gods and Rites of the Ancient Calendar,* trans. by Fernando Horcasitas and Doris Heyden. Norman, Okla.: University of Oklahoma Press, 1971, p. xii.
11. Robertson, William. *The History of America,* 1777. Quoted in Tompkins, Peter, *Mysteries of the Mexican Pyramids.* New York: Harper & Row, 1976, p. 40.
12. de Pauw, Cornelius. *Recherches Philosophiques sur les Américains,* 1769. Quoted in

Tompkins, Peter, *Mysteries of the Mexican Pyramids.* New York: Harper & Row, 1976, p. 42.

13. Porterfield, Kay Marie. "Ten Lies about Indigenous Science—How to Talk Back." http://www.kporterfield.com/aicttw/articles/lies.html. See also Porterfield, Kay Marie, and Emory Dean Keoke. *The Encyclopedia of American Indian Contributions to the World: 15,000 Years of Invention and Innovation,* which details more than 450 examples of indigenous science and independent innovation from the abacus to zucchini.

14. Stephens, John Lloyd. *Incidents of Travel in Central America, Chiapas & Yucatan.* London: Century, 1988, p. 49.

15. Tompkins, Peter. *Mysteries of the Mexican Pyramids.* New York: Harper & Row, 1976, pp. 166–167.

16. Woolley, Benjamin. *The Queen's Conjurer: The Science and Magic of Dr. John Dee.*

17. Salisbury, Jr., Stephen. *The Mayas, the Sources of Their History: Dr. Le Plongeon in Yucatan, His Account of Discoveries.* Worcester: Press of Charles Hamilton, 1877, p. 65.

18. Ibid., p. 65.

19. Coe, Michael. *Breaking the Maya Code,* revised edition, 1999, p. 138; Long, Richard. "Maya and Mexican Writing." *Maya Research* 2 (1). New Orleans, 1935.

20. Coe, Michael. *Breaking the Maya Code,* revised edition, 1999, p. 138.

21. Graham, Ian. *Alfred Maudslay and the Maya, A Biography.* Norman, Oklahoma: University of Oklahoma Press, 2002, p. 102.

22. Goodman, Joseph T. *The Archaic Maya Inscriptions.* Volume 5 of Maudslay, Alfred, *Biologia Centrali-Americana,* 1897, pp. ii–iv.

23. Ibid., p. iv.

24. Ibid., p. v.

25. Coe, Michael. *Breaking the Maya Code,* revised edition, 1999, p. 140.

26. Thompson, J. Eric S. *Maya Hieroglyphic Writing: An Introduction.* Publication 589, Washington, D.C.: Carnegie Institution of Washington, 1950, p. 295. For essays exploring anagogical themes in world literature, see Strelka, Joseph P. *Anagogic Qualities of Literature.* University Park and London: The Pennsylvania State University Press, 1971.

27. Campbell, Joseph. *The Hero with a Thousand Faces,* second edition. Princeton, N.J.: Princeton University Press, 1968, p. 3.

28. Houston, Stephen. "Classic Maya Depictions of the Built Environment." *Function and Meaning in Classic Maya Architecture,* ed. Stephen Houston. Washington, D.C.: Dumbarton Oaks Research Library and Collection, 1998, p. 355; and discussion, pp. 348–363.

29. Thompson, J. Eric S. "A Correlation of the Mayan and European Calendars." Chicago: Field Museum of Natural History, Anthropological Series, 17(1):1–22, 1927, pp. 19–21. http://www.archive.org/details/correlationofmay171thom.

Chapter 2. The Long Career of the Long Count

1. Malmström, Vincent. *Cycles of the Sun, Mysteries of the Moon.* Austin, Tex.: University of Texas Press, 1997, p. 258.

2. Tedlock, Barbara. "The Road of Light: Theory and Practice of Mayan Skywatching." *The Sky in Mayan Literature,* ed. by Anthony F. Aveni. New York: Oxford University Press, 1992, pp. 18–42.

3. Wilber, Ken. *No Boundary*. Boston and London: Shambhala Publications, 1981.

4. Edmonson, Munro. *Book of the Year: Middle American Calendrical Systems*. Norman, Okla.: University of Oklahoma Press, 1988.

5. Coe, Michael. "Cycle 7 Monuments in Middle America: A Reconsideration." *American Anthropologist* 59, 1957, p. 606.

6. Guernsey, Julia. *Rituals & Power in Stone*. Austin, Tex.: University of Texas Press, 2006, p. 14.

7. Schele, Linda, Peter Mathews, and Floyd Lounsbury. "Redating the Hauberg Stela." *Texas Notes*, No. 1, 1990. http://www.utmesoamerica.org/texas_notes/TN-01.pdf.

8. Rice, Prudence M. *Maya Calendar Origins: Monuments, Mythistory, and the Materialization of Time*. Austin, Tex.: University of Texas Press, 2007.

9. Coe, Michael. *The Maya*. Great Britain: Thames & Hudson, 1966.

10. Malmström, Vincent. "Origin of the Mesoamerican 260-Day Calendar." *Science*, 181, 1973, pp. 939–941.

11. Coe, Michael. *Mexico*, third edition, revised and enlarged. London: Thames & Hudson, 1988, p. 86.

12. Schieber de Lavarreda, Christa, and Miguel Orrego Corzo. *Abaj Takalik*. Guatemala City: Proyecto Nacional Tak-alik Ab'aj, Ministerio de Cultura y Deportes, 2001, p. 37.

13. Rice, Prudence M. *Maya Calendar Origins: Monuments, Mythistory, and the Materialization of Time*. Austin, Tex.: University of Texas Press, 2007.

14. These day-sign translations come from Dennis Tedlock, *Breath on the Mirror*. San Francisco: HarperSanFrancisco, 1994, pp. 233–234.

15. Freidel, David, Linda Schele, and Joy Parker. *Maya Cosmos: Three Thousand Years on the Shaman's Path*. New York: William Morrow and Company, 1993, p. 67ff.

16. Jenkins, John Major. "The Equation of Maya Time," in *The Solstice-Galaxy Alignment in 2012*. Denver, CO: Four Ahau Press, 2005.

17. Jenkins, John Major. "Katun Beginnings Which Conjunct Seasonal Quarters." *Tzolkin*. Garberville, CA: Borderland Sciences Research Foundation, 1994, pp. 300–301.

18. Schele, Linda, and David Freidel. *Forest of Kings*. New York: William Morrow and Company, 1990, p. 158.

19. Michael Grofe, personal communication: e-mail to me March 2009.

20. Milbrath, Susan. *Star Gods of the Maya: Astronomy in Art, Folklore, and Calendars*. Austin, Tex.: University of Texas Press, 1999, p. 293.

21. Taube, Karl. "The Jade Hearth: Centrality, Rulership, and the Classic Maya Temple." *Function and Meaning in Classic Maya Architecture*, ed. by Stephen Houston. Washington, D.C.: Dumbarton Oaks Research Library and Collection, 1998, pp. 427–478.

22. Puleston, Dennis E. "An Epistemological Pathology and the Collapse, or Why the Maya Kept the Short Count." *Maya Archaeology and Ethnohistory*, ed. by Norman Hammond and Gordon R. Willey. Austin, Tex.: University of Texas Press, 1979, pp. 63–71.

23. Grofe, Michael John. *The Serpent Series: Precession in the Maya Dresden Codex*. PhD dissertation. Davis: University of California, 2007; Grofe, Michael. "Fruit from the Cacao Tree: From the Haab' to Precession." Miami: Institute of Maya Studies newsletter, vol. 38, issues 5 and 6 (May and June, 2009).

24. Carlsen, Robert S. *The War for the Heart and Soul of a Highland Maya Town*. Austin, Tex.: University of Texas Press, 1997.

25. Edmonson, Munro. *The Ancient Future of the Itza: The Book of Chilam Balam of Tizimin*. Austin, Tex.: University of Texas Press, 1982.

26. Edmonson, Munro S. "Baktun Ceremonial of 1618." *The Fourth Palenque Round Table,* 1980, vol. VI, ed. by Merle Greene Robertson and Elizabeth P. Benson. San Francisco: Pre-Columbian Art Research Institute, 1985.

27. Stray, Geoff. "An Open Letter to Robert Sitler (and ensuing correspondence)." http://www.diagnosis2012.co.uk/sit.htm. 2006.

28. The enforced English education thrust upon Hopi children by government policy is an example of this. See Frank Waters, *Book of the Hopi.*

29. Wikipedia entry, "Jacinto Canek." http://en.wikipedia.org/wiki/Jacinto_Canek.

30. Coe, Michael. *Breaking the Maya Code,* revised edition. London: Thames & Hudson, 1999, p. 275.

31. "It could also refer to the end of the millennium at Oxlan B'ak'tun." Montejo, Victor. *El Q'anil: Man of Lightning,* English trans. by Wallace Kaufman and Susan G. Rascón. Tucson: University of Arizona Press, 2001, p. 26 and pp. 97–98.

CHAPTER 3. SEDUCTIVE SPELLS

1. Srimad Tandavaraya Swami's Tamil text, 1408–1534. English trans. by Tantavaraya Cuvamikal. Series, Publication no. 1. Thanjavur, India: Kala Samrakshana Sangkam, 1995.

2. Vinson Brown's introduction to Tony Shearer's *Lord of the Dawn, Quetzalcoatl.* Healdsburg, CA: Naturegraph Publishers, 1971, p. 3.

3. Argüelles, José. *The Transformative Vision.* Boulder and London: Shambhala, 1975, p. 304. A common error in reporting the beginning date confused the calculational year "-3113" with the historical year 3114 BC.

4. McKenna, Terence. *True Hallucinations.* San Francisco: HarperSanFrancisco, 1993, p. 111.

5. McKenna, Terence. "Temporal Resonance." *ReVision: A Journal of Consciousness and Transformation,* vol. 10, no. 1, 1987, pp. 25–30; McKenna, Terence. *The Archaic Revival.* San Francisco: HarperSanFrancisco, 1991.

6. Terence McKenna in his introduction to Jenkins's *Maya Cosmogenesis 2012,* Bear & Company, 1998, p. XXVII.

7. Griffin, David R (ed.). *Physics and the Ultimate Significance of Time.* Albany, N.Y.: State University of New York Press, 1986.

8. Waters, Frank. *Mexico Mystique.* Chicago: Sage Books, 1975, p. viii.

9. Tompkins, Peter. *Mysteries of the Mexican Pyramids.* New York: Harper & Row, 1976, p. 399.

10. PAN Agent 11 on behalf of PAN Agents 22 and 185. "Mexico—Anahuac 2002." http://www.tortuga.com/foundation/teotihuacan.html.

11. South, Stephanie. *2012: Biography of a Time Traveler.* Franklin Lakes, N.J.: New Page Press, 2009, p. 159.

12. Ibid., p. 172.

13. Shearer, Tony. "Tony Shearer: The Mythmaker." August 1987. Recorded by Thomas Lofstrom / ECS. http://video.google.com/videoplay?docid=6579324553647980067.

14. Brian Swimme's introduction to *The Mayan Factor,* 1987, p. 10.

15. Ibid., p. 146.

16. See John Major Jenkins, "On 2012 & the Galactic Alignment," Bouncing Bear Films, September 2008, http://www.youtube.com/watch?v=xYbg3_GHZ5Y.

17. South, Stephanie. *2012: Biography of a Time Traveler*. Franklin Lakes, N.J.: New Page Press, 2009, p. 303; Braden, Gregg. *Fractal Time: The Secret of 2012 and a New World Age*. Hay House, 2009; de Vinente, Enrique. "El Gran Alineamiento Galáctico." *Año Cero*. Madrid: Spain, 2009, pp. 24–32. (www.akasico.com)

18. Jenkins, John Major. *Tzolkin: Visionary Perspectives and Calendar Studies*. Garberville, CA: Borderland Sciences Research Foundation, 1994, p. 151.

19. Jenkins, John Major. "A Manifesto for Clarity." For the Institute of Maya Studies. 1995. Jenkins, John Major. "A Manifesto for Clarity." Miami: Institute of Maya Studies, 1995. http://alignment2012.com/manifesto.htm.

20. Jenkins, John Major. "Following Dreamspell." November 2002. http://Alignment2012 .com/following.html.

21. *Father Sun Speaks: Cosmic Mayan Message for the 21st Century*. VHS tape. Footage of Hunbatz Men facilitating the 1995 solar initiations at Dzibilchaltún and Chichén Itzá. Produced by Baird Bryant, conceived by Patricia Quinn. http://www.portalmarket .com/humbatz.html.

22. Keen, Sam. http://www.enlightennext.org/magazine/j16/keen.asp?page=2

23. South, Stephanie. *2012: Biography of a Time Traveler*. Franklin Lakes, N.J.: New Page Press, 2009, pp. 157–158.

24. See "History of an Idea," Appendix 1 to *Maya Cosmogenesis 2012*.

25. Dozens of other factual problems are detailed in my online review essay, http://alignment2012.com/mproph.htm.

26. Cotterell, Maurice, and Adrian Gilbert. *The Mayan Prophecies*, p. 211.

27. "Terence McKenna: The Last Interview. A Conversation with Erik Davis." Resonant Media, Lux Natura, 2003.

CHAPTER 4. BREAKTHROUGHS OR BREAKDOWN?

1. Tedlock, Barbara. "Maya Calendars, Cosmology, and Astronomical Commensuration." *New Theories on the Ancient Maya*, ed. by Elin C. Danien and Robert J. Sharer, University Museum Symposium Series, vol. 3, University Museum Monograph 77. Philadelphia: The University Museum, University of Pennsylvania, 1992, p. 224.

2. de Santillana, Giorgio. *The Crime of Galileo*. Chicago: University of Chicago, 1955.

3. Kuhn, Thomas. *The Structure of Scientific Revolutions*. Chicago: University of Chicago, 1962.

4. Insightful books on the universal doctrine of sacrifice and initiatory death-rebirth are many. Stanzione, Vincent. *Rituals of Sacrifice*. Albuquerque: University of New Mexico Press, 2003; Coomaraswamy, Ananda K. "On the Loathly Bride." *Coomaraswamy 1, Selected Papers: Traditional Art and Symbolism*, ed. by Roger Lipsey. Princeton, N.J.: Princeton University Press, 1977; Campbell, Joseph. *The Hero with a Thousand Faces*. Princeton, N.J.: Princeton University Press, 1949; Eliade, Mircea. *Rites and Symbols of Initiation*, trans. by Willard Trask. London: Harvill Press, 1958; Frazer, James. *The Golden Bough*. England, 1890; Henderson, Joseph L., and Maude Oakes. *Wisdom of the Serpent: The Myths of Death, Rebirth, and Resurrection*. New York: George Braziller, 1963; Kingsley, Peter. *In the Dark Places of Wisdom*. Inverness, CA: The Golden Sufi Center, 1999.

5. Lounsbury, Floyd. "The Base of the Venus Table in the Dresden Codex, and Its Significance for the Calendar-Correlation Problem." *Calendars of Mesoamerica and*

Peru: Native American Computations of Time, ed. by Anthony Aveni and Gordon Brotherston. Oxford: B.A.R. International, Series 174, 1983, pp. 1–26; Lounsbury, Floyd. "A Derivation of the Mayan-to-Julian Calendar Correlation from the Dresden Codex Venus Chronology." *The Sky in Mayan Literature*, ed. by Anthony F. Aveni, New York: Oxford University Press, 1992, pp. 184–206.

6. Tedlock, Dennis. "Myth, Math, and the Problem of Correlation in Mayan Books." *The Sky in Mayan Literature*, ed. by Anthony F. Aveni, New York: Oxford University Press, 1992, pp. 247–273.

7. Tedlock, Barbara. *Time and the Highland Maya*. Albuquerque: University of New Mexico Press, 1982 (revised 1992), p. 1.

8. Ethnohistorical evidence for the GMT-2 correlation followed among the Aztecs (1 Serpent = August 13, 1521, Julian) is in Edmonson, Munro. *The Book of the Year*. Salt Lake City: University of Utah Press, 1988, pp. 62–63.

9. As an example, see "the final days" (lowercase) thread on the University of Texas Mesoamerica discussion group on Google: http://groups.google.com/group /utmesoamerica.

10. Jenkins, John Major. "Academic Confusion." 1992. http://www.alignment2012.com /fap9.html.

11. Jenkins, John Major. "December 21, 2012: Some Rational Deductions." The Institute of Maya Studies newsletter, ed. by James Reed. Miami: Institute of Maya Studies, March 2008. Also here: http://www.alignment2012.com/Aprilpg3.pdf and http://www .alignment2012.com/Aprilpg6.pdf.

12. Looper, Matthew. *Quiriguá: A Guide to an Ancient Maya City*. Antigua, Guatemala: Editorial Antigua, S.A., 2007, p. 183.

13. "One of the most ambitious monumental programs dedicated to the three-stone hearth occurs at the Late Pre-Classic site of Izapa." Taube, Karl. "The Jade Hearth: Centrality, Rulership, and the Classic Maya Temple." *Function and Meaning in Classic Maya Architecture*, ed. by Stephen Houston. Washington, D.C.: Dumbarton Oaks Research Library and Collection, 1998, p. 439.

14. Looper, Matthew. "Creation Mythology at Naranjo." *Texas Notes*, No. 30, 1992.

15. Taube, Karl A. "The Birth Vase: Natal Imagery in Ancient Maya Myth and Ritual." *The Vase Book: A Corpus of Rollout Photographs of Maya Vases*, vol. 4. New York: Kerr and Associates, 1994, pp. 652–685.

16. Hunt, Eva. *Transformation of the Hummingbird: Cultural Roots of a Zinacantecan Mythical Poem*. Ithaca: Cornell University Press, 1977.

17. Brotherston, Gordon. "Astronomical Norms in Mesoamerican Ritual and Time Reckoning." *Archaeoastronomy in the New World*, ed. by Anthony Aveni. New York: Cambridge University Press, 1982, p. 129.

18. Nuttall, Zelia. "The Fundamental Principles of Old and New World Civilizations: A Comparative Research Based on a Study of the Ancient Mexican Religious, Sociological and Calendrical Systems." *Archaeological and Ethnological Papers of the Peabody Museum*, vol. II. Harvard University. Salem, MA: Salem Press, 1901.

19. de Santillana, Giorgio. *Reflections on Men and Ideas*. Cambridge, Mass.: The MIT Press, 1968, p. xi.

20. de Santillana, Giorgio, and Hertha von Dechend. *Hamlet's Mill*. Boston: Godine, 1969, p. 244.

21. Feuerstein, Georg, Subhash Kak, and David Frawley. *In Search of the Cradle of Civilization*. Wheaton, IL: Quest Books, 1995.

22. Tedlock, Barbara, and Dennis Tedlock. "Where You Want to Be." Interview in *Parabola: The Magazine of Myth and Tradition*, XVIII(3), New York, 1993, pp. 43–53.

23. Newsome, Elizabeth. *Trees of Paradise and Pillars of the World*. Austin, Tex.: University of Texas Press, 2001, p. 177ff.

24. See Jenkins, *Galactic Alignment*, 2002, p. 249ff, for a detailed discussion. See also Patrick Wallace's calculations at http://Alignment2012.com/truezone.htm.

25. Lavoie, Franklin. Personal communication, e-mails January 9–10, 2007.

26. Joscelyn Godwin, endorsement statement in Jenkins, *Galactic Alignment*, 2002.

27. Giamario, Daniel. "The May 1998 Galactic Alignment: A Shamanic Look at the Turning of the Ages." *The Mountain Astrologer* 11(2). Cedar Ridge, CA. 1998, pp. 57–61.

28. Actually, the alignment zone is a bit longer, due to the 61° angle between the galactic equator and the ecliptic. I usually refer to the thirty-six-year zone 1980–2016 for the sake of simplicity. The point is that it is unrealistic to think the galactic alignment "happens" specifically and only on December 21, 2012.

29. Jenkins, John Major. *The Center of Mayan Time*. Boulder, CO: Four Ahau Press, 1995.

30. Schele, Linda, and David A. Freidel. "The Courts of Creation: Ballcourts, Ballgames, and Portals to the Maya Otherworld." *The Mesoamerican Ballgame*, ed. by Vernon L. Scarborough and David R. Wilcox. Tucson: University of Arizona Press, 1991, p. 291.

31. Ibid., p. 309.

32. This is a generalized consensus agreed upon by most scholars, although it is not the only thing the ballgame is about. See, e.g., Fash, William L., and Jeff Karl Kowalski. "Symbolism of the Ball Game at Copán: Synthesis and New Aspects." *The Sixth Palenque Round Table, 1986*, ed. by Merle Greene Robertson. Norman, Okla.: University of Oklahoma Press, 1991, pp. 59–67.

33. Hatch, Marion Popenoe. "An Hypothesis on Olmec Astronomy, with Special Reference to the La Venta Site." *Papers on Olmec and Maya Archaeology: Contributions of the University of California Archaeological Research Facility*, No. 13. Berkeley: University of California, 1971, pp. 1–64. On Tak'alik Ab'aj's precession-tracking astronomical observatory: Tarpy, Cliff. "Place of the Standing Stones." *National Geographic*, May 2004. Alignments with a dark cloud constellation (the Fox) in a Peruvian temple: Benfer, Robert, and Larry R. Adkins. "The Americas' Oldest Observatory." *Astronomy* magazine, 35, 2008, pp. 40–43.

34. On the "materialization of time," see Prudence Rice, *Maya Calendar Origins*. 2007.

35. Kelley, David. "Mesoamerican Astronomy and the Maya Calendar Correlation Problem." *Memorias del Segundo Coloquio Internacional de Mayistas 1*. Mexico: Universidad Nacional Autónoma de México. 1989, pp. 65–95.

36. On human intersubjectivity, see Barbara Tedlock. *Time and the Highland Maya*. Albuquerque: University of New Mexico Press, 1982, pp. 4–5.

37. See "Some Iconographic and Cosmological Observations on the Symbolism of the new Stela 48 from Tak'alik Ab'aj." http://www.alignment2012.com/Takalik48.html, 2008.

CHAPTER 5. THE 2012 EXPLOSION

1. Stray, Geoff. *Beyond 2012: Catastrophe or Ecstasy*. East Sussex: England, 2005, p. 14.

2. Gonzales, Patrisia, and Roberto Rodriguez. "The Mayan Worldview of the Universe." Universal Press Syndicate. *The Denver Post*, January 2, 2000.

3. Ibid.

4. Jenkins, *Maya Cosmogenesis 2012*, pp. 327–328.

5. See Jenkins-Calleman exchange from early 2006. "Carl Calleman's latest attack on the traditional Mayan Calendar end date, December 21, 2012." http://www.alignment2012.com/eldersand2012-exchange.html.

6. Original version of the Web-circulated McFadden-Barrios interview, December 2002: http://Alignment2012.com/Barrios-McFadden.html.

7. Ibid.

8. Jenkins. "Maya Cosmogenesis: Cosmic Mother Gives Birth." http://www.alignment2012.com/fap2.html, 1995.

9. Corrected McFadden-Barrios interview, on McFadden's website. Chiron Communications: http://www.chiron-communications.com/communique%207-10.html.

10. Barrios Kanek, Gerardo, and Mercedes Barrios Longfellow. *The Maya Cholqij: Gateway to Aligning with the Energies of the Earth.* Williamsburg, MA: Tz'ikin Abaj, 2004. Cited in Joseph, *Apocalypse 2012.*

11. Original version, December 2002: http://Alignment2012.com/Barrios-McFadden.html.

12. "More About Larry Joseph." http://lawrencejoseph.wetpaint.com/page/More+about+Larry+Joseph?t=anon.

13. Joseph, Lawrence. *Apocalypse 2012*, pp. 32–33.

14. Ibid., p. 40.

15. For more on Joseph's book and others, see my "Fear and Lying in 2012-Land" in *You Are Still Being Lied To*, ed. by Russ Kick. New York: The Disinformation Company, 2009, pp. 357–366. See also Geoff Stray's review of *Apocalypse 2012* at http://www.diagnosis2012.co.uk/apoc.html.

16. Quoted from Joseph's statement in *2012: Science or Superstition?*, DVD. New York: The Disinformation Company, 2009.

17. Pawlowski, A. "Apocalypse in 2012? Date Spawns Theories, Film." CNN.com/technology. January 27, 2009. http://www.cnn.com/2009/TECH/science/01/27/2012.maya.calendar.theories/index.html?iref=newssearch. My comments on this piece of journalism at: http://Alignment2012.com/CNNinterviewerPawlowski.html.

18. Joseph, Lawrence. *Apocalypse 2012*, p. 114. See also his dire scenarios on pp. 8, 10, 126, 129, and 236.

19. Sitchin's entire Earth Chronicles series includes titles such as *Stairway to Heaven* and *The End of Days*. We can observe Sitchin's adoption of 2012 in his DVD called *2012: Will the Anunnaki Return?* In it, "with a mass of evidence, [Sitchin] analyzes Mayan lore and ancient calendars, and guides the listener through biblical prophecies, to arrive at startling conclusions and precise predictions regarding the End of Days." http://www.sitchin.com.

20. Grof, Stanislav. *The Adventure of Self-Discovery.* New York: State University of New York Press, 1988, pp. 15–18.

21. Geryl, Patrick. "How to Survive 2012." http://www.howtosurvive2012.com/htm_night/home.htm.

22. The Horizon Project. http://www.thehorizonproject.com.

23. Ibid., in the profile pages.

24. http://www.youtube.com/watch?v=K7Br-mi7b20. This is the teaser trailer for the first DVD in the series, "Bracing for Tomorrow."

25. "Episodes." http://www.thehorizonproject.com/episodes.cfm

26. Ibid.

27. http://www.youtube.com/watch?v=3KCXuhFkMfA. This is a ten-minute clip from "Bracing for Tomorrow."

28. "What Is the Galactic Alignment?" http://alignment2012.com/whatisGA.htm.
29. Jenkins, John Major. *Galactic Alignment.* Rochester, VT: Inner Traditions, 2002, p. 282; Jenkins, "Six Misconceptions," http://alignment2012.com/5misconceptions .html; Bouncing Bear interview with John Major Jenkins, 2008, http://www.youtube .com/watch?v=xYbg3_GHZ5Y.
30. http://www.youtube.com/watch?v=3KCXuhFkMfA. "Bracing for Tomorrow."
31. Ibid.
32. Henbest, Nigel, and Heather Couper. *Guide to the Galaxy.* Cambridge: Cambridge University Press, 1994. See also: http://solar-center.stanford.edu/FAQ/Qsolsysspeed .html.
33. Personal communication, February 2, 2009.
34. Jenkins, John Major. "How Not to Make a 2012 Documentary." 2006. http://alignment2012.com/historychannel.html.
35. Scofield, Bruce, and Barry Orr. *How to Practice Mayan Astrology.* Rochester, VT: Bear & Company, 2007.
36. Jenkins, "Following Dreamspell." http://Alignment2012.com/following.html.
37. Peter Meyer, "Lunar Calendars and Eclipse Finder." http://www.hermetic.ch/lcef /lcef.htm.
38. Jenkins, John Major. "Izapa and the Galactic Alignment in 2012." DVD. Denver, CO: Four Ahau Press, 2004.
39. Reviewed by Geoff Stray. http://www.diagnosis2012.co.uk/idiot.html.
40. Ibid.
41. Stray, Geoff. *Beyond 2012*, Lewes, East Sussex, UK: Vital Signs Publishing, 2005, p. 9.
42. Mike Hagan's Radio Orbit: http://www.mikehagan.com/main.htm.
43. Jenkins, John Major. http://www.alignment2012.com/historychannel.html.
44. Braden, Gregg. *Fractal Time: The Secret of 2012.* Carlsbad, Calif.: Hay House, 2009.
45. Anthology. *The Mystery of 2012.* Louisville, CO: Sounds True, 2007.
46. Eisler, Riane. *The Chalice and the Blade.* San Francisco: Harper & Row, 1988.
47. "2012." Sony Pictures, official trailer page: http://www.sonypictures.com /movies/2012/.
48. Grof, Stanislav. *Adventure of Self-Discovery.* New York: State University of New York Press, 1988, pp. 3–37.

CHAPTER 6. DOUBTING SCHOLARS

1. Grofe, Michael. PhD dissertation. *The Serpent Series: Precession in the Maya Dresden Codex.* Davis, CA: University of California, 2007, p. 335.
2. Gillespie, Susan D., and Rosemary A. Joyce. "Deity Relationships in Mesoamerican Cosmology: The Case of the Maya God L." *Ancient Mesoamerica* 9, 1998, pp. 279–296; Houston, Stephen, and David Stuart. "Of Gods, Glyphs, and Kings: Divinity and Rulership Among the Classic Maya." *Antiquity* 70, 1996, pp. 289–312.
3. King, Tom. "5 Years: 2012 and the End of the World as We Know It." December 10, 2007. See discussion section and link. http://www.lawrence.com/news/2007/dec/10 /five_years/.
4. Linguistic critique of my Nahuatl knock-knock joke. E-mail of September 12, 2008.
5. John Justeson spoke informally about his statistical analysis of the likelihood of the

solstice placement of the cycle-ending date being a coincidence at the Tulane 2012 conference, February 2009. Archived online: http://Alignment2012.com/Tulane2009 .html.

6. Aveni, Anthony, and Horst Hartung. "Water, Mountain, Sky: The Evolution of Site Orientations in Southeastern Mesoamerica." *Precious Greenstone, Precious Quetzal Feather,* ed. by Eloise Quiñones Keber. Labyrinthos, 2000, pp. 55–68.

7. Barbara MacLeod, e-mail of January 26, 2008.

8. Sitler, Robert K. "The 2012 Phenomenon: New Age Appropriation of an Ancient Maya Calendar. *Nova Religio* 9 (3), 2006, p. 29.

9. Sitler, Robert. "13 Pik: Maya Perspectives." http://www.stetson.edu/~rsitler/ 13PIK/.

10. Sitler, Robert K. "The 2012 Phenomenon: New Age Appropriation of an Ancient Maya Calendar." *Nova Religio* 9 (3), 2006.

11. Stray, Geoff. http://www.diagnosis2012.co.uk/sit.htm. Aveni's date is calculated in his 2001 book *Skywatchers* (second edition of *Skywatchers of Ancient Mexico*), Appendix B, Chapter IV.

12. Jenkins, John Major. "Maya Statements and 2012." 2006. http://www.alignment2012. com/mayan2012statements.html.

13. Aztlan discussion. http://www.famsi.org/pipermail/aztlan/2006-April/001978.html.

14. The entire exchange can be read in the Aztlan archives here: http://www.famsi.org /pipermail/aztlan/2006-April/001978.html.

15. See the University of Texas Mesoamerica discussion group: http://groups.google .com/group/utmesoamerica/browse_thread/thread/2ad64b039cb60983/0396cfd4957fd 61e?pli=1

16. Houston, Stephen. "What Will Not Happen in 2012." http://decipherment.wordpress .com/2008/12/20/what-will-not-happen-in-2012/.

17. Jenkins, John Major. "In the Roots of the Milky Way Tree." *New Dawn Magazine.* No. 97. Australia, July–August 2006.

18. Houston, Stephen. "What Will Not Happen in 2012." http://decipherment.wordpress .com/2008/12/20/what-will-not-happen-in-2012/.

19. Ibid., comments section.

20. Ibid.

21. Houston, Stephen. "Classic Maya Depictions of the Built Environment." *Function and Meaning in Classic Maya Architecture,* ed. by Stephen Houston. Washington, D.C.: Dumbarton Oaks Research Library and Collection, 1998.

22. University of Texas Mesoamerica discussion group: http://groups.google.com/group/ utmesoamerica/browse_thread/thread/a636bb7dfc6d7e85/c412ee3a86e38b1a.

23. Wikipedia "Mayanism" entry, accessed March 7, 2009. http://en.wikipedia.org/wiki /Mayanism.

24. Aztlan discussion group: http://www.famsi.org/pipermail/aztlan/2008 -January/003957.html.

25. Ibid.

26. Hoopes, John. "William S. Burroughs & 2012" thread on Tribe2012: http://2012.tribe .net/thread/6b96e7c5-4ad7-4d0c-aed6-f513ecfc03bc.

27. Aztlan discussion group: http://www.famsi.org/pipermail/aztlan/2008 -January/003957.html.

28. Irvin, Jan. Interviews with John Hoopes and John Major Jenkins, podcasts #004 and #008. http://gnosticmedia.podomatic.com/.

29. Coe, Michael. *The Maya,* first edition. 1966, p. 174.

30. Ibid.

31. Anastas, Benjamin. "The Final Days." *The New York Times Sunday Magazine.* July 1, 2007. The article is preserved here: http://www.alignment2012.com/NYTimes.html.

32. Institute of Maya Studies newsletter, March 2008. Also here: http://www .alignment2012.com/Aprilpg3.pdf and http://www.alignment2012.com/Aprilpg6.pdf.

33. Strous has updated his website since our exchange transpired in 2004: http://www .astro.uu.nl/~strous/AA/en/2012.html. I have archived offline the original version, which I quoted from.

34. Jenkins exchange with Stephen Tonkin. http://alignment2012.com/tonkins-error .html.

35. Zap, Jonathan. http://alignment2012.com/zap-on-tonkins-error.html. Also on www .zaporacle.com.

36. de Santillana, Giorgio. *The Crime of Galileo.* Chicago: University of Chicago Press, 1955; de Santillana, Giorgio. "Galileo and Oppenheimer." *Reflections on Men and Ideas,* 1968, pp. 120–136.

37. "Word of Mouth." NPR radio program. December 31, 2008. http://www.nhpr.org /wordofmouth.

38. "Bad Astronomy." http://www.badastronomy.com/.

39. Nassim Haramein on the orbital motion of our solar system: http://uk.youtube.com /watch?v=ir5sQEg0rs4&feature=related.

40. Geoff Stray. http://www.diagnosis2012.co.uk/idiot.html.

41. Jenkins, John Major. Original 2000 essay reprinted in *Galactic Alignment.* Rochester, VT: Bear & Company, 2002, pp. 40–42.

42. Pointed out to me by Michael Grofe, e-mail of February 2009. Grofe, Michael. "Palenque's Temple XIX and the Creation Stories of Central Mexico: Flint, Fire, and Tlaltecuhtli." n.d.

43. Transcript of Barb MacLeod's interview for the film "Breaking the Maya Code" at: http://www.nightfirefilms.org/breakingthemayacode/interviews/ MacLeodTRANSCRIPT.pdf.

44. Bibliographical resource for Maya Studies research: http://Alignment2012.com /bibbb.htm.

45. Stuart, David, and Stephen Houston. "Classic Maya Place Names." *Studies in Pre-Columbian Art and Archaeology* #33, Washington, D.C.: Dumbarton Oaks, 1994, p. 80.

46. Jenkins, "Commentary on Stuart and Houston's Study of Mayan Place Names." 1995. http://www.alignment2012.com/fap11.html.

47. Van Stone, Mark. "It's Not the End of the World: What the Ancient Maya Tell Us About 2012." http://www.famsi.org/research/vanstone/2012/index.html, 2008.

48. Aztlan discussion group: http://www.famsi.org/pipermail/aztlan/2008 -December/005363.html.

49. Aztlan discussion group: http://www.famsi.org/pipermail/aztlan/2008 -December/005366.html.

50. Online resource for the Tulane 2012 conference of February 2009: http://alignment2012.com/Tulane2009.html.

51. David Stuart. http://www.alignment2012.com/CNNinterviewerPawlowski.html.

52. "Six Points Essential for a Fair Critique of the 2012 Topic"—a four-page document I handed out at Tulane. http://Alignment2012.com/Six-essential-points-Tulane .html.

53. Audio clips and/or the full recording of Aveni's talk will remain available for informational purposes on: http://alignment2012.com/Tulane2009.html. Aveni's quotes from various authors are transcribed directly from his reading.

54. Geoff Stray. http://www.diagnosis2012.co.uk/logo.htm.

55. Pawlowski, A. "Apocalypse in 2012? Date Spawns Theories, Film." CNN .com/technology. January 27, 2009. http://www.alignment2012.com /CNNinterviewerPawlowski.html. Compare to Joseph's comments in *Apocalypse 2012*, pp. 8, 10, 114, and 126.

56. Newsome, Elizabeth. *Trees of Paradise and Pillars of the World.* Austin, Tex.: University of Texas Press, 2001.

57. Looper, Matthew G. "Quirigua Zoomorph P: A Water Throne and Mountain of Creation." *Heart of Creation: The Mesoamerican World and the Legacy of Linda Schele*, ed. by Andrea Stone. Tuscaloosa, Ala.: University of Alabama Press, 2002, p. 199.

58. The Lacandon Maya conceive of the Milky Way's bulge in Sagittarius as the roots of a giant tree. Bruce, R. D., C. Robles U., and E. Ramos Chao. *Los Lacandones 2, Cosmovision Maya.* Publicaciones 26. Mexico City: Instituto Nacional de Antropología e Historia, Departamento de Investigaciones Antropológicas, 1971.

59. Western science and philosophy marginalize the insights of Traditionalist philosophy. See: Coomaraswamy, Ananda K. *Coomaraswamy 1, Selected Papers: Traditional Art and Symbolism*, ed. by Roger Lipsey. Princeton: Princeton University Press, 1977; Corbin, Henry. *Temple and Contemplation*, trans. by Philip Sherrard. London: KPI Ltd., 1986; Guénon, René. *Fundamental Symbols: The Universal Language of Sacred Science.* Cambridge, UK: Quinta Essentia, 1995; Nasr, Seyyed Hossein. *Knowledge and the Sacred.* Albany: State University of New York Press, 1989; *The Betrayal of Tradition*, ed. Harry Oldmeadow; *Science and the Myth of Progress*, ed. by Mehrdad M. Zarandi; Wolfgang Smith. *The Wisdom of Ancient Cosmology*; René Guénon, *The Reign of Quantity and the Signs of the Times*, trans. by Lord Northbourne. New York: Penguin Books, 1972. Good books on Gnosis and Gnosticism include *The Gnostic Religion* by Hans Jonas, *Gnosis* by Dan Merkur, and *Gnosis* by Kurt Rudolph.

60. *Publishers Weekly* on Aveni's scientism, from a review on the Amazon.com listing for Aveni's book *Behind the Crystal Ball*: "This informative but stacked-deck history of science and magic . . . presupposes a readership that embraces a scientific-materialistic worldview that sees little or no sense in the pursuit of so-called magical practices."

61. More info on the keynote address and the Sunday panel, including audio clips, is here: http://alignment2012.com/Tulane2009.html.

62. Aveni, Anthony, and Horst Hartung. "Water, Mountain, Sky: The Evolution of Site Orientations in Southeastern Mesoamerica." *Precious Greenstone, Precious Quetzal Feather*, ed. by Eloise Quiñones Keber. Labyrinthos, 2000.

63. Jenkins, John Major. "Open Letter to Mayanists and Astronomers." http://www .alignment2012.com/openletter.htm.

64. Aveni, Anthony, and Horst Hartung. "Water, Mountain, Sky: The Evolution of Site Orientations in Southeastern Mesoamerica." *Precious Greenstone, Precious Quetzal Feather*, ed. by Eloise Quiñones Keber. Labyrinthos, 2000, p. 58.

65. Field trip to Izapa in 2006 to measure the ballcourt. http://www.alignment2012.com /izapa-solstice-2006.html.

66. Lowe, Gareth, Thomas A. Lee, Jr., and Eduardo Martinez Espinoza. "Izapa: A Guide to the Ruins and Monuments." *Papers of the New World Archaeological Foundation*, No. 31. Provo, UT: Brigham Young University, 1982; Norman, V. Garth. "Izapa Sculpture, Part 1: Album." *Papers of the New World Archaeological Foundation*, No. 30. Provo, UT: Brigham Young University, 1973; Norman, V. Garth. "Izapa Sculpture, Part 2: Text." *Papers of the New World Archaeological Foundation*, No. 30. Provo, UT: Brigham Young University, 1976; Norman, V. Garth. *Astronomical Orientations of*

Izapa Sculptures. Master's thesis, Anthropology Department. Provo, UT: Brigham Young University, 1980.

67. Aveni, Anthony, and Horst Hartung. "Water, Mountain, Sky: The Evolution of Site Orientations in Southeastern Mesoamerica." *Precious Greenstone, Precious Quetzal Feather*, ed. by Eloise Quiñones Keber. Labyrinthos, 2000, p. 55.

68. Dennis Tedlock's comments can be heard during the Sunday panel. http://alignment2012.com/Tulane2009.html.

CHAPTER 7. THE GALACTIC ALIGNMENT THEORY: UPDATE

1. Looper, Matthew. "The 3-11-pih Title in Classic Maya Inscriptions." *Glyph Dwellers*, Report 15, December 2002. http://nas.ucdavis.edu/NALC/R15.pdf.

2. Grube, Nikolai, A. Lacadena, and S. Martin. "Chichén Itzá and Ek Balam: Terminal Classic Inscriptions from Yucatán." *Notebook for the XXVIIth Maya Hieroglyphic Forum at Texas*. Austin, Tex.: Maya Workshop Foundation, 2003.

3. Barb MacLeod's paper, "The 3-11 Pik Formula," was circulated at the Maya Meetings in Austin in March 2008. It is reproduced here: http://Alignment2012.com /3-11PikFormula.html.

4. Grofe, Michael J. "Calculations of the Tropical Year and Precessional Cycles: Two Bone Fragments from Tikal Burial 116," n.d., 2003.

5. Grofe, Michael J. "The Recipe for Rebirth: Cacao as Fish in the Mythology and Symbolism of the Ancient Maya." The Foundation Research Department. Foundation for the Advancement of Mesoamerican Studies, Inc., 2009, www.famsi.org/research/ grofewriting. Grofe's latest observations were made very recently, in February of 2009, and are thus as yet unpublished. His overall work integrates epigraphic decipherment and astronomy, a sensitivity that very few epigraphers have. Grofe's unpublished manuscripts include: "The Sidereal Year and Precession in the Cross Group of Palenque" and "Astronomical References in Tortuguero Monument 6."

6. Aveni's considered comments are found in the DVD film *2012: Science or Superstition?* The Disinformation Company, 2009.

7. Taube, Karl. "The Jade Hearth: Centrality, Rulership, and the Classic Maya Temple." *Function and Meaning in Classic Maya Architecture*, ed. by Stephen Houston. Washington, D.C.: Dumbarton Oaks Research Library and Collection, 1998.

8. Gronemeyer, Sven. *Tortuguero, Tabasco, Mexico: History of a Classic Maya Site as Known from Its Inscriptions*. 2004. http://www.sven-gronemeyer.de.

9. Grofe to Jenkins, personal e-mail communication. February 20, 2009.

10. See the archive of Copan Notes online: http://utmesoamerica.org/CopanNotes.php.

11. Alexander, Helen. "God K on Ceramic Vessels." Foundation for the Advancement of Mesoamerican Studies, http://www.famsi.org/research/alexander/godkceramic.pdf, p. 1.

12. Newsome, Elizabeth. *Trees of Paradise and Pillars of the World*. Austin, Tex.: University of Texas Press, 2001, p. 172.

13. Jenkins, John Major. "Evidence for a Black Hole in Maya Creation Texts." Appendix 4 of *Maya Cosmogenesis 2012*. 1998, pp. 351–356.

14. Milbrath, Susan. *Star Gods of the Maya*. Austin. Tex.: University of Texas Press, 1999, pp. 264-266.

15. Harris, John F., and Stephen K. Stearns. *Understanding Maya Inscriptions: A*

Hieroglyphic Handbook, second revised edition. Philadelphia: University of Pennsylvania Museum of Archaeology and Anthropology, 1997; Coe, Michael, and Mark Van Stone. *Reading the Maya Glyphs.* London: Thames & Hudson, 2001; Macri, Martha, and Matthew Looper. *The New Catalog of Maya Hieroglyphs.* Norman, Okla.: University of Oklahoma Press, 2003; Montgomery, John. *How to Read Maya Hieroglyphs.* New York: Hippocrene Books, Inc., 2002.

16. The possible reading of the "broken sky" toponym as jagged mountain peaks in the immediate geography was suggested by Simon Martin in "A Broken Sky: The Ancient Name of Yaxchilan as *Pa' Chan.*" *The PARI Journal,* vol. 4, no. 1, summer 2004. http://www.mesoweb.com/pari/journal/.

17. Jenkins, John Major. *Galactic Alignment.* 2002, p. 217.

Part II: 2012 and The Big Picture

1. James, William. *A Pluralistic Universe.* London: Longmans, Green, and Co., 1909, p. 292.

2. Rumi. "Sheba's Throne." *The Essential Rumi.* Trans. by Coleman Barks. San Francisco: HarperSanFrancisco, 1995, p. 190.

Chapter 8. Sacred Science and Perennial Philosophy

1. Daumal, René. *Mount Analogue,* Shambhala edition, 1992, p. 104.

2. Carlson, John B. "A Geomantic Model for the Interpretation of Mesoamerican Sites: An Essay in Cross-Cultural Comparison." *Mesoamerican Sites and World Views,* ed. by Elizabeth P. Benson. Washington, D.C.: Dumbarton Oaks. 1981, pp. 143–216.

3. Frazer, James, *The New Golden Bough.* Criterion Books, 1959, p. 223ff.

4. Huxley, Aldous. Introduction to *The Song of God, Bhagavad Gita.* Mentor paperback, 1972, p. 17.

5. Coomaraswamy, Ananda. *Guardians of the Sun-Door.* Louisville, KY: Fons Vitae, 2004, pp. viii–ix.

6. Nasr, Seyyed Hossein. Introduction to *Guardians of the Sun-Door.* Louisville, KY: Fons Vitae, 2004, p. ix.

7. Huxley, Aldous. Introduction to *The Song of God, Bhagavad Gita.* Mentor paperback, 1972, p. 12.

8. Ibid., p. 13.

9. Guénon, René. *The Reign of Quantity and the Signs of the Times,* trans. by Lord Northbourne. New York: Penguin Books, 1972; Guénon, René. *Crisis of the Modern World,* trans. by Arthur Osborne. Ghent, New York: Sophia Perennis et Universalis, 1996.

10. Zerzan, John. *Twilight of the Machines.* Port Townsend, WA: Feral House, 2008.

11. Wikman, Monika. *Pregnant Darkness: Alchemy and the Rebirth of Consciousness.* Berwick, ME: Nicolas-Hays, Inc., 2004, p. 29.

12. Oldmeadow, Harry (ed.). *The Betrayal of Tradition: Essays on the Spiritual Crisis of Modernity.* Bloomington, IN: World Wisdom, Inc., 2005.

13. Wilber, Ken. *Sex, Ecology, Spirituality,* revised edition. Boston and London: Shambhala, 2001, p. 211.

14. Ibid.

15. The relationship is a bit more nuanced than this summary allows; see Ira Progoff's *Jung, Synchronicity, and Human Destiny: Noncausal Dimensions of Human Experience.* New York: Julian Press, 1973.

16. Jung, Carl. *Synchronicity: An Acausal Connecting Principle,* trans. by R.F.C. Hull. Princeton, N.J.: Princeton University Press, 1973.

17. Wasiutynski, Jeremi. *The Solar Mystery.* Oslo: Solum Forlag, 2003, p. 15.

18. Wind, Edgar. *Pagan Mysteries in the Renaissance,* revised and enlarged edition. New York: W. W. Norton & Company, Inc., 1968.

19. Woodhouse, C. M. *Gemistos Plethon, the Last of the Hellenes.* Oxford: Clarendon Press, 1986.

20. Wasiutynski, Jeremi. *The Solar Mystery.* Oslo: Solum Forlag, 2003, p. 15.

21. Ibid.

22. Ibid., p. 16.

23. Ibid., p. 14.

24. Dewey, John. "The Need for a New Party." *John Dewey: The Later Works, 1925–1953,* vol. 6. Carbondale, IL: Southern Illinois University Press, 1989, p. 163.

CHAPTER 9. THE FULFILLMENT OF THE MAYA PROPHECY

1. Tedlock, Dennis (trans.). *The Popol Vuh,* second edition, 1996, p. 73.

2. For more on this, see Jenkins, John Major. *Unlocking the Secrets of the 2012.* 3-CD audio. Louisville, CO: Sounds True, 2007; Jenkins, John Major. "The Origins of the 2012 Revelation." *The Mystery of 2012.* Louisville, CO: Sounds True, 2007.

3. Iraq war casualties: http://icasualties.org/oif/.

4. Hanley, Charles J. "Massive New Embassy in Iraq Flaunts U.S. Power, Critics Say." Associated Press. April 15, 2006. http://www.commondreams.org/headlines06/0415-07.htm.

5. http://mediamatters.org/items/200604270005.

6. Ibid.

7. Ibid.

8. Hermann Göring's comments were made in a private conversation with prison psychologist and U.S. Army Captain Gustave M. Gilbert during the Nuremberg trials. Gilbert, G. M., *Nuremberg Diary.* New York: Farrar, Straus and Company, 1947, pp. 278–279.

9. Valenti, Jack. "Speech before the Los Angeles World Affairs Council." October 1, 1998. Posted on the *Los Angeles World Affairs Council* website.

10. Shaheen, Jack. *Reel Bad Arabs: How Hollywood Vilifies a People.* Media Education Foundation, 2007. http://www.mediaed.org/videos/MediaRaceAndRepresentation/ReelBadArabs/studyguide/ReelBadArabs.pdf.

11. Joseph Goebbels. http://thinkexist.com/quotes/joseph_goebbels/.

12. Michael Parenti, http://www.radioproject.org/transcript/1998/9839.html.

13. Keith Olbermann. http://www.msnbc.msn.com/id/3036677/#31416352.

14. Hall, Kevin G.. "Obama to propose new financial regulator, stronger Fed." http://news.yahoo.com/s/mcclatchy/20090617/pl_mcclatchy/3253921, June 16, 2009; Rachel Maddow show. http://www.msnbc.msn.com/id/26315908/ns/msnbc_tv-rachel_maddow_show/#31416637

15. Scheer, Robert. "Obama's Economic Misfits Finally Get It." June 17, 2009. http://www.truthdig.com/report/item/20090617_obamas_economic_misfits_finally_get_it/.

16. Heller, Stanley. "Worst Movie of the Year: Brzezinski and Charlie Wilson's War." December 26, 2007. http://www.counterpunch.org/heller12262007.html; "Zbigniew Brzezinski: How Jimmy Carter and I Started the Mujahideen." *Le Nouvel Observateur,* 1998. http://www.counterpunch.org/brzezinski.html.
17. Brzezinski, Zbigniew. *Between Two Ages: America's Role in the Technetronic Era.* New York: Penguin Books, 1976, p. 253.
18. The Rachel Maddow Show. "Obama Digs into the Financial World," June 17, 2009. http://www.msnbc.msn.com/id/26315908/ns/msnbc_tv-rachel_maddow_show/#31416567
19. Howard Zinn. "Changing Obama's Military Mind Set." http://www.alternet.org/politics/140035/howard_zinn:_changing_obama's_military_mindset/
20. Ibid.
21. Campbell, Joseph, and Bill Moyers. *Joseph Campbell and the Power of Myth.* New York: Mystic Fire Video, 2001.
22. Hartmann, Thom. *Unequal Protection: The Rise of Corporate Dominance and the Theft of Human Rights.* Rodale Press, 2004.
23. Noam Chomsky interview in *The Corporation,* a film by Mark Achbar, Jennifer Abbott, and Joel Bakan. http://www.thecorporation.com, 2004.
24. Thom Hartmann, *Unequal Protection* (2004), cited at http://www.commondreams.org/views03/0101-07.
25. Thom Hartmann. http://www.commondreams.org/views03/0101-07.
26. Grover Cleveland quoted in Hartmann, Thom, *Unequal Protection,* at http://www.commondreams.org/views03/0101-07.

Chapter 10. Ending the War on Us

1. Kingsley, Peter. *In the Dark Places of Wisdom.* Inverness, CA: The Golden Sufi Center, 1999, p. 5.
2. Nasr, Seyyed Hossein. *Man and Nature: The Spiritual Crisis in Modern Man.* London: Unwin Paperbacks, 1990, p. 18.
3. Ibid., pp. 18–19.
4. Pictured in Lawlor, Robert. *Voices of the First Day.* Rochester, VT: Inner Traditions International, 1991, p. 24.
5. Gimbutas, Marija. *Goddesses and Gods of Old Europe.* London: Thames & Hudson, 1981.
6. de Waal, Frans B. M. "Bonobo Sex and Society." *Scientific American.* March 1995, p. 82.
7. Ibid., pp. 82–88.
8. McLaughlin, Corinne. "2012: Socially Responsible Business and Nonadversarial Politics." *The Mystery of 2012.* Louisville, CO: Sounds True, 2007.
9. Spretnak, Charlene. *The Resurgence of the Real.* Addison-Wesley, Inc., 1997, p. 35.

Chapter 11. The Maya Renaissance

1. Montejo, Victor. "The Road to Heaven." *Indigenous Traditions and Ecology.* p. 193.
2. Harbury, Jennifer. *Bridge of Courage: Life Stories of Guatemalan Companeros & Companeras.* Monroe, Maine: Common Courage Press, 1995, 2002.

3. Waller, James. *Becoming Evil*. Oxford: Oxford University Press, 2002, pp. 198–199.

4. Victor Montejo, biography: http://nas.ucdavis.edu/site/people/faculty/documents/montejo_cv_08.pdf.

5. Montejo, Victor. *Maya Intellectual Renaissance*. Austin: University of Texas Press, 2005.

6. *The Oxford Encyclopedia of Mesoamerican Cultures*, vol. 2, ed. by Davíd Carrasco. Oxford: Oxford University Press, 2006, p. 439.

7. Ibid., p. 438.

8. Montejo, Victor. "Road to Heaven: Jakaltec Maya Beliefs, Religion, and Ecology." *Indigenous Traditions and Ecology: The Interbeing of Cosmology and Community.* Harvard: Center for the Study of World Religions, 2001, p. 175.

9. Tedlock, Dennis (trans.). *The Popol Vuh*, second edition. New York: Touchstone Books, 1996, p. 356.

10. Montejo, Victor. "Road to Heaven." *Indigenous Traditions and Ecology*, 2001, p. 181.

11. Ibid., pp. 176–177.

12. Montejo, Victor. *Maya Intellectual Renaissance*. 2005, p. 118.

13. Montejo, Victor. *El Q'anil: Man of Lightning*. Tucson: University of Arizona Press, 2001, p. 154.

14. Montejo, Victor. *Maya Intellectual Renaissance*. 2005, p. 121ff.

15. Carlsen, Robert S., and Martín Prechtel. "Weaving and Cosmos Amongst the Tzutujil Maya of Guatemala." *Res* 15, 1988, pp. 122–132; Carlsen, Robert S., and Martín Prechtel. "The Flowering of the Dead: An Interpretation of Highland Maya Culture." *Man (N.S.)* 26, 1990, pp. 23–42; Jenkins, John Major. *Mayan Sacred Science*. Boulder, CO: Four Ahau Press, 1994/2000.

16. Victor Montejo. *Maya Intellectual Renaissance: Identity, Representation and Leadership*. Austin: University of Texas Press, 2005, pp. 120–122.

17. Ibid.

18. Cook, Garrett. *Renewing the Maya World*. Austin, Tex.: University of Texas Press, 2000, p. 205.

19. Ibid., p. 208.

20. Sitler, Robert. "13 Pik: Maya Perspectives." http://www.stetson.edu/~rsitler/13PIK/.

21. Ibid. Don Alejandro Cirilo Perez Oxlaj, head of the National Mayan Council of Elders of Guatemala in his address at the inaugural of Guatemalan President Colom in January 2008.

22. Ibid. Lorenzo Kinil of Chemax (speaking in 1930) in Paul Sullivan, "Contemporary Yucatec Maya Apocalyptic Prophecy: The Ethnographic and Historical Context" (diss.), Johns Hopkins University, 1984, pp. 291–295.

23. Sitler, Robert. "13 Pik: Maya Perspectives." http://www.stetson.edu/~rsitler/13PIK/. José María Tol Chan.

24. Ibid. Mam teacher Benito Ramirez Mendoza (2006).

25. Ibid. Don Rigoberto Itzep Chanchabac (2006).

26. Online YouTube clip of Don Rigoberto Itzep Chanchabac speaking on 2012 and the Maya calendar, in three parts: http://www.youtube.com/watch?v=icFzTdrwTLE.

27. González, Gaspar Pedro. *El 13 B'aktun: La nueva era 2012*. Published privately, 2006. http://www.yaxtebooks.com/catalog/books/featured.htm.

28. González, Gaspar Pedro. *El 13 B'aktun: La nueva era 2012*. Published privately, 2006. http://www.yaxtebooks.com/catalog/books/featured.htm. Unpublished English translation provided by Robert Sitler.

29. Henry, William. *The American Rite*. www.williamhenry.net, 2009.

30. Ereira, Alan. *The Elder Brothers' Warning*. Tairona Heritage Trust, 2009.

31. McKenna, Terence. *The Archaic Revival.* San Francisco: HarperSanFrancisco, 1991.
32. McKenna's introduction to *Maya Cosmogenesis 2012*, pp. XXVIII–XXIX.

Chapter 12. Restoring the Big Picture

1. Campbell, Joseph, and Bill Moyers. *Joseph Campbell and the Power of Myth.* New York: Mystic Fire Video, 2001.
2. Sullivan, Lawrence E. "The Attributes and Power of the Shaman: A General Description of the Ecstatic Care of the Soul." *Ancient Traditions: Shamanism in Central Asia and the Americas*, ed. by Gary Seaman and Jane S. Day. 1994, p. 34.
3. Wasson, R. Gordon, Stella Kramrisch, Jonathan Ott, and Carl A. P. Ruck. *Persephone's Quest: Entheogens and the Origins of Religion.* New Haven and London: Yale University Press, 1986; Furst, Peter. *Hallucinogens and Culture.* Novato, CA: Chandler and Sharp Publishers, 1976; Hoffman, Albert, Carl A. P. Ruck, and Gordon Wasson. *The Road to Eleusis: Unveiling the Secret of the Mysteries*, 1978.
4. Ruck, Carl A. P., Blaise Daniel Staples, and Clarck Heinrich. *The Apples of Apollo: Pagan and Christian Mysteries of the Eucharist.* Carolina Academic Press, 2000.
5. Irvin, Jan, and Andrew Rutajit. *Astrotheology & Shamanism: Christianity's Pagan Roots.* Gnostic Media, 2009.
6. Kingsley, Peter. *Reality.* Inverness, CA: The Golden Sufi Center, 2003; Kingsley, Peter. *Ancient Philosophy, Mystery, and Magic: Empedocles and Pythagorean Tradition.* Oxford: Clarendon Press, 1995.
7. Klein, Anne. *Meeting the Great Bliss Queen.* Boston: Beacon Press, 1995, p. 178.
8. Jenkins, John Major. "Mayan Shamanism and 2012: A Psychedelic Cosmology." *Toward 2012: Perspectives on the New Age*, ed. by Daniel Pinchbeck and Ken Jordan. New York: Jeremy P. Tarcher/Penguin, 2008.
9. Bache, Christopher. *Dark Night, Early Dawn.* Albany, N.Y.: State University of New York Press, 2000, p. 296.
10. Campbell, Joseph. *Hero with a Thousand Faces*, second edition. Princeton, N.J.: Princeton University Press, 1968, p. 3.
11. Ramakrishna in Hixon, Lex. *Great Swan: Meetings with Ramakrishna.* Boston and London: Shambhala, 1992, p. 171.
12. See, for example, Burckhardt, Titus. *Mirror of the Intellect.* Albany, N.Y.: State University of New York Press, 1987.
13. Bache, Christopher. *Dark Night, Early Dawn.* Albany, N.Y.: State University of New York Press, 2000, p. 298.
14. Nasr, Seyyed Hossein. *The Need for a Sacred Science.* Albany, N.Y.: State University of New York Press, 1993, p. 25.
15. Sustainable living resources and books of interest include: Pritchett, Laura (ed). *Going Green: True Tales from Gleaners, Scavengers, and Dumpster Divers.* Norman, Okla.: University of Oklahoma Press, 2009; Timpson, William, et al. *147 Tips for Teaching Sustainability.* Madison, Wis.: Atwood Publishing, 2006; Bartmann, Dan, and Dan Fink. *Homebrew Wind Power.* Buckville Publications, 2009; books of www. chelseagreen.com; Friedman, Thomas. *Hot, Flat, and Crowded: Why We Need a Green Revolution.* Farrar, Straus and Giroux, 2008; Ivanko, John, and Lisa Kivirist. *Rural Renaissance: Renewing the Quest for the Good Life.* New Society Publishers, 2009; Kunstler, James. *The Long Emergency*, 2006.

Chapter 13. After the Party

1. *The Fountain.* Written and directed by Darren Aronofsky. Warner Bros., 2006.
2. Perry, John Weir. "Spiritual Emergence and Renewal." *Spiritual Emergency: When Personal Transformation Becomes a Crisis,* ed. by Stanislav Grof and Christina Grof. New York: Tarcher, 1989, p. 67.
3. Ibid.
4. Jenkins, John Major. *Sonnets from the Sands.* http://www.tryptagonals.com. Boulder, Colo.: Four Ahau Press, 2005.

SELECTED BIBLIOGRAPHY

Alexander, Helen. "God K on Ceramic Vessels." Foundation for the Advancement of Mesoamerican Studies, http://www.famsi.org/research/alexander/godkceramic.pdf.

Anastas, Benjamin. "The Final Days." *The New York Times Sunday Magazine*. July 1, 2007. The article is preserved here: http://www.alignment2012.com/NYTimes.html.

Argüelles, José. *The Transformative Vision*. Boulder and London: Shambhala, 1975.

————. *The Mayan Factor*. Santa Fe, N.M.: Bear & Company, 1987.

————. *Dreamspell* (kit/game), 1991.

Aveni, Anthony. *Skywatchers of Ancient Mexico*. Austin, Texas: University of Texas Press, 1980, revised 2000.

———— (ed.) *The Sky in Mayan Literature*. New York: Oxford University Press, 1992.

Aveni, Anthony, and Horst Hartung. "Water, Mountain, Sky: The Evolution of Site Orientations in Southeastern Mesoamerica." *Precious Greenstone, Precious Quetzal Feather*. Ed. by Eloise Quiñones Keber. Labyrinthos, 2000.

Aztlan discussion list, Foundation for the Advancement of Mesoamerican Studies: http://www.famsi.org/mailman/listinfo/aztlan.

Bache, Christopher. *Dark Night, Early Dawn*. Albany, N.Y.: State University of New York Press, 2000.

Bakan, Joel. *The Corporation: The Pathological Pursuit of Profit and Power*. New York: The Free Press, 2005.

Balin, Peter. *The Flight of the Feathered Serpent*. Venice, CA: Wisdom Garden Books, 1978.

Bartmann, Dan, and Dan Fink. *Homebrew Wind Power*. Masonville, Colo.: Buckville Publications, 2009.

Benfer, Robert, and Larry R. Adkins. "The Americas' Oldest Observatory." *Astronomy* magazine, 35, 2008.

Braden, Gregg. *Fractal Time: The Secret of 2012 and a New World Age*. Hay House, 2009.

Brotherston, Gordon. "Astronomical Norms in Mesoamerican Ritual and Time Reckoning." *Archaeoastronomy in the New World*. Ed. By Anthony Aveni. New York: Cambridge University Press, 1982.

———. *Book of the Fourth World*. Cambridge and New York: Cambridge University Press, 1992.

Bruce, Robert D. *Lacandon Dream Symbolism*. 2 vols. Mexico: Ediciones Euroamericanas, 1975–1979.

Brzezinski, Zbigniew. *Between Two Ages*. New York: Penguin Books, 1976.

Burckhardt, Titus. *Sacred Art in East and West: Principles and Methods*. Trans. by Lord Northbourne. Bedfont, Middlesex: Perennial Books, Ltd., 1967.

———. *Mirror of the Intellect*. Albany: State University of New York Press, 1987.

Calleman, Carl Johan. *The Mayan Calendar and the Transformation of Consciousness*. Rochester, VT: Bear & Company, 2004.

Campbell, Joseph. *The Hero with a Thousand Faces*, second edition. Princeton, N.J.: Princeton University Press, 1968.

———. *The Inner Reaches of Outer Space*. New York: Harper & Row, 1986.

Campbell, Joseph, and Bill Moyers. *Joseph Campbell and the Power of Myth*. New York: Mystic Fire Video, 2001.

Carlsen, Robert S. *The War for the Heart and Soul of a Highland Maya Town*. Austin, Tex.: University of Texas Press, 1997.

Carlsen, Robert S., and Martín Prechtel. "The Flowering of the Dead: An Interpretation of Highland Maya Culture." *Man (N.S.)*, 26, 1990.

Coe, Michael. "Cycle 7 Monuments in Middle America: A Reconsideration." *American Anthropologist*, 59, 1957.

———. *Mexico*. London: Thames & Hudson, 1962.

———. *The Maya*. London: Thames & Hudson, 1966.

———. *Breaking the Maya Code*. London: Thames & Hudson, 1992; revised 1999.

Coe, Michael, and Mark Van Stone. *Reading the Maya Glyphs*. London: Thames & Hudson, 2001.

Cook, Garrett. *Renewing the Maya World*. Austin, Tex.: University of Texas Press, 2000.

Coomaraswamy, Ananda K. "On the Loathly Bride." *Coomaraswamy 1, Selected Papers: Traditional Art and Symbolism*. Ed. by Roger Lipsey. Princeton, N.J.: Princeton University Press, 1977.

———. *Guardians of the Sun-Door*. Louisville, KY: Fons Vitae, 2004.

Corbin, Henry. *Spiritual Body and Celestial Earth: From Mazdean Iran to Shi'ite Iran*. Trans. by Nancy Pearson. Princeton, N.J.: Princeton University Press, 1977.

———. *Temple and Contemplation*. Trans. by Philip Sherrard. London: KPI Ltd., 1986.

Cotterell, Maurice, and Adrian Gilbert. *The Mayan Prophecies*. London: Element Books, 1995.

Covarrubias, Miguel. *Mexico South*. New York: Alfred A. Knopf, 1947.

Desmond, Lawrence Gustave, and Phyllis Mauch Messenger. *A Dream of Maya*. Albuquerque: University of New Mexico Press, 1988.

Durán, Fray Diego. *Book of the Gods and Rites and The Ancient Calendar*. Trans. by Fernando Horcasitas and Doris Heyden. Norman, Okla.: University of Oklahoma Press, 1971.

Edmonson, Munro S. *The Ancient Future of the Itza: The Book of Chilam Balam of Tizimin*. Austin: University of Texas Press, 1982.

———. "Baktun Ceremonial of 1618." *The Fourth Palenque Round Table, 1980,* Vol. VI. Ed. by Merle Greene Robertson and Elizabeth P. Benson. San Francisco: Pre-Columbian Art Research Institute, 1985.

———. *The Book of the Year: Middle American Calendrical Systems*. Norman, Okla.: University of Oklahoma Press, 1988.

Eisler, Riane. *The Chalice and the Blade*. San Francisco: Harper & Row, 1988.

Eliade, Mircea. *Rites and Symbols of Initiation*. Trans. by Willard Trask. London: Harvill Press, 1958.

Ereira, Alan. *The Elder Brothers' Warning*. Tairona Heritage Trust, 2009.

Feuerstein, Georg, Subhash Kak, and David Frawley. *In Search of the Cradle of Civilization*. Wheaton, IL: Quest Books, 1996.

The Fountain. Written and directed by Darren Aronofsky. Warner Bros., 2006.

Freidel, David, Linda Schele, and Joy Parker. *Maya Cosmos: Three Thousand Years on the Shaman's Path*. New York: William Morrow and Company, 1993.

Friedman, Thomas. *Hot, Flat, and Crowded: Why We Need a Green Revolution*. New York: Farrar, Straus and Giroux, 2008.

Furst, Peter. *Hallucinogens and Culture*. Novato, CA: Chandler and Sharp Publishers, 1976.

Giamario, Daniel. "The May 1998 Galactic Alignment: A Shamanic Look at the Turning of the Ages." *The Mountain Astrologer,* Vol. 11, No. 2, 1998.

Gimbutas, Marija, *Goddesses and Gods of Old Europe*. London: Thames & Hudson, 1981.

Goetz, Delia, and Sylvanus Morley. *The Popol Vuh: The Sacred Book of the Ancient Quiché Maya*. English trans. after the Spanish trans. of Adrián Recinos.

Original trans. by Francisco Ximénez. Norman, Okla.: University of Oklahoma Press, 1950.

González, Gaspar Pedro. *El 13 B'aktun: La nueva era 2012.* Published privately, 2006. Unpublished English translation provided by Robert Sitler.

Goodman, Joseph T. *The Archaic Maya Inscriptions.* Appendix to Alfred Maudslay's *Biologia Centrali-Americana,* 1897.

———. "Maya Dates." *American Anthropologist,* n.s., Vol. 7, 1905.

Graham, Ian. *Alfred Maudslay and the Maya: A Biography.* Norman, Okla.: University of Oklahoma Press, 2002.

Griffin, David R. (ed.). *Physics and the Ultimate Significance of Time: Bohm, Prigogine, and Process Philosophy.* Albany, N.Y.: State University of New York Press, 1986.

Grof, Stanislav. *The Adventure of Self-Discovery.* New York: State University of New York Press, 1988.

Grof, Stanislav, and Christina Grof (eds.). *Spiritual Emergency: When Personal Transformation Becomes a Crisis.* New York: Tarcher, 1989.

Grofe, Michael J. *The Serpent Series: Precession in the Maya Dresden Codex.* PhD dissertation. Davis: University of California, 2007.

———. "Fruit from the Cacao Tree: From the Haab' to Precession." Miami: Institute of Maya Studies, newsletter, Vol. 38, issues 5 and 6 (May and June 2009).

———. "The Recipe for Rebirth: Cacao as Fish in the Mythology and Symbolism of the Ancient Maya." The Foundation Research Department. Foundation for the Advancement of Mesoamerican Studies, 2009. www.famsi.org/research/grofewriting.

———. "Palenque's Temple XIX and the Creation Stories of Central Mexico: Flint, Fire, and Tlaltecuhtli," n.d.

———. "The Sidereal Year and Precession in the Cross Group of Palenque," n.d.

———. "Astronomical References in Tortuguero Monument 6," n.d.

Gronemeyer, Sven. *Tortuguero, Tabasco, Mexico: History of a Classic Maya Site as Known from Its Inscriptions.* Master's thesis. Institut für Altamerikanistik und Ethnologie. Munich: GRIN Publishing OHG, 2004. http://www.sven-gronemeyer.de.

Guénon, René. *Man and His Becoming According to the Vedanta.* Trans. by Richard C. Nicholson. New York: The Noonday Press, 1958.

———. *The Reign of Quantity and the Signs of the Times.* Trans. by Lord Northbourne. New York: Penguin Books, 1972.

————. *Fundamental Symbols: The Universal Language of Sacred Science.* Cambridge, England: Quinta Essentia, 1995.

Guernsey, Julia. *Rituals & Power in Stone.* Austin, Tex.: University of Texas Press, 2006.

Hagan, Mike. Radio Orbit Interviews. http://www.mikehagan.com/main.htm.

Hancock, Graham. *Fingerprints of the Gods.* New York: Crown Publishers, 1995.

Hancock, Graham, and Santha Faiia. *Heaven's Mirror: Quest for the Lost Civilization.* New York: Crown Publishers, 1998.

Harbury, Jennifer. *Bridge of Courage: Life Stories of Guatemalan Compañeros & Compañeras.* Monroe, Maine: Common Courage Press, 1995, 2002.

Harris, John F., and Stephen K. Stearns. *Understanding Maya Inscriptions: A Hieroglyphic Handbook,* second revised edition. Philadelphia: University of Pennsylvania Museum of Archaeology and Anthropology, 1997.

Hartmann, Thom. *Unequal Protection: The Rise of Corporate Dominance and the Theft of Human Rights.* Rodale Press, 2004.

Hatch, Marion Popenoe. "An Hypothesis on Olmec Astronomy, with Special Reference to the La Venta Site." *Papers on Olmec and Maya Archaeology: Contributions of the University of California Archaeological Research Facility,* No. 13. Berkeley, Calif.: University of California, 1971.

Henbest, Nigel, and Heather Couper. *Guide to the Galaxy.* Cambridge, England: Cambridge University Press, 1994.

Henderson, Joseph L., and Maude Oakes. *Wisdom of the Serpent: The Myths of Death, Rebirth, and Resurrection.* New York: George Braziller, 1963.

Henry, William. *The American Rite.* www.williamhenry.net, 2009.

Hoffman, Albert, Carl A.P. Ruck, and Gordon Wasson. *The Road to Eleusis: Unveiling the Secret of the Mysteries,* 1978.

Houston, Stephen. "Classic Maya Depictions of the Built Environment." *Function and Meaning in Classic Maya Architecture.* Ed. by Stephen Houston. Washington, D.C.: Dumbarton Oaks Research Library and Collection, 1998.

————. "What Will Not Happen in 2012." http://decipherment.wordpress. com/2008/12/20/what-will-not-happen-in-2012/, 2008.

Hunt, Eva. *Transformation of the Hummingbird: Cultural Roots of a Zinacantecan Mythical Poem.* Ithaca: Cornell University Press, 1977.

Huxley, Aldous. *The Perennial Philosophy.* New York: Harper & Row, 1945.

————. Introduction to *The Song of God, Bhagavad Gita.* New York: Signet, 1972.

Irvin, Jan, and Andrew Rutajit. *Astrotheology & Shamanism: Christianity's Pagan Roots*. San Diego: Gnostic Media, 2009.

Ivanko, John, and Lisa Kivirist. *Rural Renaissance: Renewing the Quest for the Good Life*. Gabriola Island, British Columbia: New Society Publishers, 2009.

Jenkins, John Major. *Journey to the Mayan Underworld*. Boulder, CO: Four Ahau Press, 1989.

———. *Tzolkin: Visionary Perspectives and Calendar Studies*. Garberville, CA: Borderland Sciences Research Foundation, 1994.

———. "The How and Why of the Mayan End-Date in 2012 A.D." *The Mountain Astrologer*, Vol. 8, No. 1, December 1994.

———. *Mayan Sacred Science*. Boulder, CO: Four Ahau Press, 1994; revised and expanded 2000.

———. "Commentary on Stuart and Houston's Study of Maya Place Names." 1995. http://www.alignment2012.com/fap11.html.

———. *Maya Cosmogenesis 2012: The True Meaning of the Maya Calendar End-Date*. Santa Fe, New Mexico: Bear & Company, 1998.

———. *Galactic Alignment*. Rochester, VT: Inner Traditions International, 2002.

———. "Izapa and the Galactic Alignment in 2012." DVD. Denver: Four Ahau Press, 2004.

———. "The Origins of the 2012 Revelation." *The Mystery of 2012*. Louisville, CO: Sounds True, 2007.

———. *Unlocking the Secrets of the 2012*. 3-CD audio. Louisville, CO: Sounds True, 2007.

———. "December 21, 2012: Some Rational Deductions." The Institute of Maya Studies newsletter, ed. James Reed. Miami: Institute of Maya Studies, March 2008.

———. "Mayan Shamanism and 2012: A Psychedelic Cosmology." *Toward 2012: Perspectives on the New Age*, eds. Daniel Pinchbeck and Ken Jordan. New York: Jeremy P. Tarcher/Penguin, 2008.

———. "Fear and Loathing in 2012-Land." *You're Still Being Lied To*, ed. Russ Kick. New York: The Disinformation Company, 2009.

———. Online resource for the Tulane 2012 conference (February 2009): http://alignment2012.com/Tulane2009.html, 2009.

Jonas, Hans. *The Gnostic Religion*. Boston: Beacon Press, 1971.

Joseph, Lawrence. *Apocalypse 2012*. New York: Morgan Road Books, 2007.

Kelley, David H. *Deciphering the Maya Script*. Austin, Tex.: University of Texas Press, 1976.

Kingsley, Peter. *Ancient Philosophy, Mystery, and Magic: Empedocles and Pythagorean Tradition*. Oxford: Clarendon Press, 1995.

———. *In the Dark Places of Wisdom*. Inverness, CA: The Golden Sufi Center, 1999.

———. *Reality*. Inverness, CA: The Golden Sufi Center. 2003.

Klein, Anne. *Meeting the Great Bliss Queen*. Boston: Beacon Press, 1995.

Kuhn, Thomas S. *The Structure of Scientific Revolutions*. Chicago: University of Chicago Press, 1962.

Kunstler, James. *The Long Emergency*. New York: Atlantic Monthly Press, 2005.

de Landa, Friar Diego. *Yucatan Before and After the Conquest*. Trans. by William Gates. Baltimore: The Maya Society, 1937. Also at Sacred Texts online: http://sacred-texts.com/nam/maya/ybac/ybac59.htm.

Lawlor, Robert. *Voices of the First Day*. Rochester, VT: Inner Traditions International, 1991.

Lilly, John C. *The Center of the Cyclone: An Autobiography of Inner Space*. New York: Bantam Books, 1972.

Looper, Matthew G.. "Creation Mythology at Naranjo." *Texas Notes*, No. 30, 1992.

———. "The 3-11-pih Title in Classic Maya Inscriptions." *Glyph Dwellers*, Report 15, December 2002. http://nas.ucdavis.edu/NALC/R15.pdf.

———. "Quiriguá Zoomorph P: A Water Throne and Mountain of Creation." *Heart of Creation: The Mesoamerican World and the Legacy of Linda Schele*, ed. Andrea Stone. Tuscaloosa and London: University of Alabama Press, 2002.

———. *Lightning Warrior*. Austin, Tex.: University of Texas Press, 2003.

———. *Quiriguá: A Guide to an Ancient Maya City*. Antigua, Guatemala: Editorial Antigua, S.A., 2007.

Lowe, Gareth W., Thomas A. Lee, Jr., and Eduardo Martinez Espinoza. *Izapa: An Introduction to the Ruins and Monuments*. Papers of the New World Archaeological Foundation, No. 31. Provo, UT: Brigham Young University, 1982.

MacLeod, Barb. "The 3-11 Pik Formula." Circulated at the Maya Meetings in Austin in March 2008. Reproduced here: http://Alignment2012.com/3-11PikFormula.html.

Macri, Martha, and Matthew Looper. *The New Catalog of Maya Hieroglyphs*. Norman, Okla.: University of Oklahoma Press, 2003.

Malmström, Vincent. *Cycles of the Sun, Mysteries of the Moon.* Austin, Tex.: University of Texas Press, 1997.

Martin, Simon, and Nikolai Grube. *Chronicles of the Maya Kings and Queens.* London: Thames & Hudson, 2000.

Maudslay, Alfred P. *Biologia Centrali-Americana.* Appendix by J. T. Goodman. Ed. by F. DuCane Godman and Osbert Salvin. *Archaeology,* Vols. 55–59. London: R. H. Porter and Dulau, 1889–1902.

McKenna, Terence. *The Archaic Revival.* San Francisco: HarperSanFrancisco, 1991.

———. *True Hallucinations.* San Francisco: HarperSanFrancisco, 1993.

———. "The Light of the Third Millennium." Talk given in Austin, Texas, 1997. http://edj.net/mc2012/TM-Light.mp3.

McKenna, Terence K., and Dennis J. McKenna. *The Invisible Landscape: Mind, Hallucinogens, and the I Ching.* New York: Seabury Press, 1975.

McLaughlin, Corinne. "2012: Socially Responsible Business and Nonadversarial Politics." *The Mystery of 2012.* Louisville, CO: Sounds True, 2007.

Meeus, Jean. *Mathematical Astronomy Morsels.* Richmond, VA: Willmann-Bell, 1997.

Men, Hunbatz. *Secrets of Mayan Science and Religion.* Santa Fe, N.M.: Bear & Company, 1990.

Milbrath, Susan. *Star Gods of the Maya: Astronomy in Art, Folklore, and Calendars.* Austin, Tex.: University of Texas Press, 1999.

Montejo, Victor. "The Road to Heaven: Jakaltec Maya Beliefs, Religion, and Ecology." *Indigenous Traditions and Ecology: The Interbeing of Cosmology and Community.* Harvard: Center for the Study of World Religions, 2001.

———. *El Q'anil: Man of Lightning.* English trans. by Wallace Kaufman and Susan G. Rascón. Tucson: University of Arizona Press, 2001.

———. *Maya Intellectual Renaissance.* Austin, Tex.: University of Texas Press, 2005.

Montgomery, John. *How to Read Maya Hieroglyphs.* New York: Hippocrene Books, 2002.

Morley, Sylvanus. *The Ancient Maya.* Stanford, CA: Stanford University Press, 1946.

Nasr, Seyyed Hossein. *Knowledge and the Sacred.* Albany, N.Y.: State University of New York Press, 1989.

———. *Man and Nature: The Spiritual Crisis in Modern Man.* London: Unwin Paperbacks, 1990.

———. *The Need for a Sacred Science.* Albany, N.Y.: State University of New York Press, 1993.

Newsome, Elizabeth. *Trees of Paradise and Pillars of the World*. Austin, Tex.: University of Texas Press, 2001.

Norman, V. Garth. *Izapa Sculpture, Part 1: Album*. Papers of the New World Archaeological Foundation, No. 30. Provo, UT: Brigham Young University, 1973.

———. *Izapa Sculpture, Part 2: Text*. Papers of the New World Archaeological Foundation, No. 30. Provo, UT: Brigham Young University, 1976.

Nuttall, Zelia. "The Fundamental Principles of Old and New World Civilizations: A Comparative Research Based on a Study of the Ancient Mexican Religious, Sociological and Calendrical Systems." *Archaeological and Ethnological Papers of the Peabody Museum, Vol. II*. Harvard University. Salem, MA: Salem Press, 1901.

Oldmeadow, Harry (ed.). *The Betrayal of Tradition: Essays on the Spiritual Crisis of Modernity*. Bloomington, IN: World Wisdom, 2005.

Pawlowski, A. "Apocalypse in 2012? Date Spawns Theories, Film." CNN.com/technology. January 27, 2009. http://www.alignment2012.com/CNNinterviewerPawlowski.html.

Perera, Victor, and Robert D. Bruce. *Last Lords of Palenque*. Berkeley and Los Angeles: University of California Press, 1982.

Perry, John Weir. "Spiritual Emergence and Renewal." *Spiritual Emergency: When Personal Transformation Becomes a Crisis*. Ed. by Stanislav Grof and Christina Grof. New York: Tarcher, 1989.

Pinchbeck, Daniel. *2012: The Return of Quetzalcoatl*. New York: Tarcher, 2006.

Popenoe Hatch, Marion. "An Hypothesis on Olmec Astronomy, with Special Reference to the La Venta Site." In *Papers on Olmec and Maya Archaeology*, No. 13. Berkeley: University of California, 1971.

Porterfield, Kay Marie, and Emory Dean Keoke. *The Encyclopedia of American Indian Contributions to the World: 15,000 Years of Invention and Innovation*. New York: Facts on File, 2002.

Pritchett, Laura (ed). *Going Green: True Tales from Gleaners, Scavengers, and Dumpster Divers*. Norman, Okla.: University of Oklahoma Press, 2009.

Rice, Prudence M. *Maya Calendar Origins: Monuments, Mythistory, and the Materialization of Time*. Austin, Tex.: University of Texas Press, 2007.

Robicsek, Francis. *Copán: Home of the Mayan Gods*. New York: Museum of the American Indian, Heye Foundation, 1972.

Ruck, Carl A.P., Blaise Daniel Staples, and Clarck Heinrich. *The Apples of Apollo: Pagan and Christian Mysteries of the Eucharist*. Carolina Academic Press, 2000.

Rudolph, Kurt. *Gnosis: The Nature and History of Gnosticism.* San Francisco: HarperSanFrancisco, 1987.

Sahagún, Bernardino de. *Florentine codex, General History of the Things of New Spain, Book 7.* Trans. by Arthur J. O. Anderson and Charles E. Dibble. Santa Fe, New Mexico: School of American Research, Archaeological Institute of America, 1953.

Salisbury, Jr., Stephen. *The Mayas, the Sources of Their History: Dr. Le Plongeon in Yucatan, His Account of Discoveries.* Worcester, MA: Press of Charles Hamilton, 1877.

Santillana, Giorgio de. *The Crime of Galileo.* Chicago: University of Chicago Press, 1955.

————. *Reflections on Men and Ideas.* Cambridge and London: Massachusetts Institute of Technology Press, 1968.

Santillana, Giorgio de, and Hertha von Dechend. *Hamlet's Mill: An Essay on Myth and the Frame of Time.* Boston: Gambit, 1969.

Schaef, Anne Wilson. *When Society Becomes an Addict.* San Francisco, HarperOne, 1988.

Schele, Linda, and David A. Freidel. *Forest of Kings.* New York: William Morrow and Company, 1990.

————. "The Courts of Creation: Ballcourts, Ballgames, and Portals to the Maya Otherworld." *The Mesoamerican Ballgame.* Edited by Vernon L. Scarborough and David R. Wilcox. Tucson: University of Arizona Press, 1991.

Schele, Linda, Peter Mathews, and Floyd Lounsbury. "Redating the Hauberg Stela." *Texas Notes*, No. 1, 1990. http://www.utmesoamerica.org/texas_notes/TN-01.pdf.

Schieber de Lavarreda, Christa, and Miguel Orrego Corzo. *Abaj Takalik.* Guatemala City: Proyecto Nacional Tak'alik Ab'aj, Ministerio de Cultura y Deportes, 2001.

Scofield, Bruce. *Day-Signs.* Amherst, MA: One Reed Publications, 1991.

Scofield, Bruce, and Barry Orr. *How to Practice Mayan Astrology.* Rochester, VT: Bear & Company, 2007.

Shaheen, Dr. Jack. *Reel Bad Arabs: How Hollywood Vilifies a People.* www.reelbadarabs.com, 2007.

Shearer, Tony. *Lord of the Dawn, Quetzalcoatl.* Healdsburg, CA: Naturegraph Publishers, 1971.

————. *Beneath the Moon and Under the Sun.* Albuquerque, N.M.: Sun Books, 1975.

———. "Tony Shearer: The Mythmaker." Recorded by Thomas Lofstrom / ECS, August 1987. http://video.google.com/videoplay?docid=6579324553647980067.

Sitler, Robert K. "The 2012 Phenomenon: New Age Appropriation of an Ancient Maya Calendar." *Nova Religio* 9 (3), 2006.

———. "13 Pik: Maya Perspectives." http://www.stetson.edu/~rsitler/13PIK/.

Smith, Huston. *Forgotten Truth: The Primordial Tradition*. New York: Harper & Row, 1976.

Smith, Wolfgang. *The Wisdom of Ancient Cosmology*. Oakton, VA: Foundation for Traditional Studies, 2003.

South. Stephanie. *2012: Biography of a Time Traveler*. Franklin Lakes, N.J.: New Page Press, 2009.

Stanzione, Vincent. *Rituals of Sacrifice*. Albuquerque: University of New Mexico Press, 2003.

Stephens, John Lloyd. *Incidents of Travel in Central America, Chiapas & Yucatan*. London: Century, 1988.

Stray, Geoff. *Beyond 2012: Catastrophe or Ecstasy*. East Sussex, England: Vital Signs Publishing, 2005.

———. *2012 in Your Pocket*. Glastonbury, UK: Straydog Books, 2008.

Stuart, David. *The Inscriptions from Temple XIX at Palenque*. San Francisco: The Pre-Columbian Art Research Center, 2005.

Stuart, David, and Stephen Houston. "Classic Maya Place Names." *Studies in Pre-Columbian Art and Archaeology,* no. 33. Washington, D.C.: Dumbarton Oaks, 1994.

Sullivan, Lawrence E. "The Attributes and Power of the Shaman: A General Description of the Ecstatic Care of the Soul." *Ancient Traditions: Shamanism in Central Asia and the Americas*. Ed. by Gary Seaman and Jane S. Day. Niwot, CO: The University Press of Colorado, 1994.

Sutton, Ann, and Myron Sutton. *Among the Maya Ruins*. Rand McNally & Co., 1967.

Tarpy, Cliff. "Place of the Standing Stones." *National Geographic,* May 2004.

Taube, Karl. "The Jade Hearth: Centrality, Rulership, and the Classic Maya Temple." *Function and Meaning in Classic Maya Architecture*. Ed. by Stephen Houston. Washington, D.C.: Dumbarton Oaks Research Library and Collection, 1998.

Tedlock, Barbara. *Time and the Highland Maya,* Albuquerque: University of New Mexico Press, 1982, revised 1992.

———. "The Road of Light: Theory and Practice of Mayan Skywatching." *The Sky in Mayan Literature*. Ed. by Anthony F. Aveni. New York: Oxford University Press, 1992.

Tedlock, Barbara, and Dennis Tedlock. "Where You Want to Be." Interview in *Parabola: The Magazine of Myth and Tradition*, XVIII (3), New York, 1993.

Tedlock, Dennis. *The Popol Vuh: The Definitive Edition of the Mayan Book of the Dawn of Life and the Glories of Gods and Kings*. New York: Simon and Schuster, 1985; revised and expanded edition, 1996.

———. "Myth, Math, and the Problem of Correlation in Mayan Books." *The Sky in Mayan Literature*. Ed. by Anthony F. Aveni. New York: Oxford University Press, 1992.

———. *Breath on the Mirror: Mythic Voices & Visions of the Living Maya*. San Francisco: HarperSanFrancisco, 1994.

Thompson, J. Eric S. "A *Correlation* of the Mayan and European Calendars." *Chicago: Field Museum* of Natural History, Anthropological Series, 17(1):1–22, 1927. http://www.archive.org/details/correlationofmay171thom.

———. *Maya Hieroglyphic Writing: An Introduction*. Publication 589, Washington, D.C.: Carnegie Institution of Washington, 1950.

Timpson, William, et al. *147 Tips for Teaching Sustainability*. Madison, WI: Atwood Publishing, 2006.

Tompkins, Peter. *Mysteries of the Mexican Pyramids*. New York: Harper & Row, 1976.

2012. Directed by Roland Emmerich. Sony Pictures, 2009. Official trailer page: http://www.sonypictures.com/movies/2012/.

2012: Science or Superstition? Written and directed by Gary Baddeley. New York: The Disinformation Company, 2009.

University of Texas, Mesoamerica discussion group: http://groups.google.com/group/utmesoamerica/.

Waal, Frans B. M. de. "Bonobo Sex and Society." *Scientific American*, March 1995.

Waller, James. *Becoming Evil*. Oxford, England: Oxford University Press, 2002.

Wasiutynski, Jeremi. *The Solar Mystery: An Inquiry into the Temporal and Eternal Background of the Rise and Fall of Modern Civilization*. Oslo: Solum Forlag, 2003.

Wasson, R. Gordon, Stella Kramrisch, Jonathan Ott, and Carl A. P. Ruck. *Persephone's Quest: Entheogens and the Origins of Religion*. New Haven, Conn., and London: Yale University Press, 1986.

Waters, Frank. *Mexico Mystique: The Coming Sixth World of Consciousness*. Chicago: Sage Books, 1975.

———. *Mountain Dialogues*. Athens, Ohio and Chicago: Sage/Swallow Books, 1981.

Watts, Alan. *The Supreme Identity: An Essay on Oriental Metaphysic and the Christian Religion*. New York: Pantheon Books, 1950.

Wikman, Monika. *Pregnant Darkness: Alchemy and the Rebirth of Consciousness*. Berwick, ME: Nicolas-Hays, 2004.

Wilber, Ken. *Sex, Ecology, Spirituality*. Revised edition. Boston and London: Shambhala Publications, 2001.

———. *No Boundary*. Boston and London: Shambhala Publications, 1981.

Wind, Edgar. *Pagan Mysteries in the Renaissance*. Revised and enlarged edition. New York: W. W. Norton & Company, 1968.

Zarandi, Mehrdad M. (ed.) *Science and the Myth of Progress*. Bloomington, IN: World Wisdom, 2003.

Zerzan, John. *Twilight of the Machines*. Port Townsend, WA: Feral House, 2008.

Index

ACKNOWLEDGMENTS

My heartfelt thanks go to Mitch Horowitz and Gabrielle Moss at Tarcher, for embracing the need for this book, working hard on a turbocharged schedule, and for helping fine-tune the clear expression of my ideas. Thanks also to Brianna Yamashita for helping to lasso important publicity opportunities and events. Books don't manifest themselves without the help of designers, editors, proofreaders, and innumerable others. My gratitude is extended to everyone involved. Thanks are due to Jim Reed for help with graphics; to Michael Grofe, Larraine Tennison, and Robert Palmer for reading and commenting on various sections of the evolving book; and to Robert Sitler for graciously giving permission to reproduce the Maya comments on 2012 he collected on his field trips. The multidimensional help and humor from my friend Curt Joy are always appreciated. Thank you to Barb MacLeod for permission to use her Cycle 7 drawing; to Francis Robicsek; to Jacquelyn Sundstrand in the Special Collections Department of the University of Nevada, Reno; to Coleman Barks for the excerpt from Rumi's "Sheba' s Throne"; and to Stan Grof for kind words and support. Geoff Stray's eagle-eye analyses of so many 2012 manifestations have been incredibly helpful—one could not ask for a better colleague. My sincere love and gratitude goes to my extended family and especially to my wife, Ellen, for patiently enduring the time-consuming creative demands of this book and the many ongoing challenges of my career. Finally, I offer my deep respect and humble thanks to the ancient Maya nik wak'inel (those who "gazed into the center"), and to the modem Maya leaders and spiritual guides who preserve and practice the essential teachings.

ABOUT THE AUTHOR

John Major Jenkins is a pioneer of the modern 2012 movement. The author of nine previous books on the subject, he has worked to clarify misconceptions and is credited with showing how a rare "galactic alignment" underlies the 2012 cycle-ending date, and is a concept deeply embedded within Maya traditions. As a visiting scholar, Jenkins has taught classes at the Institute of Maya Studies in Miami, the Esalen Institute, Naropa University in Boulder, Colorado, and many other venues both nationally and abroad. He is the director of The Center for 2012 Studies and moderates the Update2012.com social networking information portal. He lives in Colorado.